Inventing the Way of the Samurai

Inventing the Way of the Samurai examines the development of the 'way of the samurai'—*bushidō*—which is popularly viewed as a defining element of the Japanese national character and even the 'soul of Japan'. Rather than a continuation of ancient traditions, however, *bushidō* developed from a search for identity during Japan's modernization in the late nineteenth century. The former samurai class were widely viewed as a relic of a bygone age in the 1880s, and the first significant discussions of *bushidō* at the end of the decade were strongly influenced by contemporary European ideals of gentlemen and chivalry. At the same time, Japanese thinkers increasingly looked to their own traditions in search of sources of national identity, and this process accelerated as national confidence grew with military victories over China and Russia.

Inventing the Way of the Samurai considers the people, events, and writings that drove the rapid growth of *bushidō*, which came to emphasize martial virtues and absolute loyalty to the emperor. In the early twentieth century, *bushidō* became a core subject in civilian and military education, and was a key ideological pillar supporting the imperial state until its collapse in 1945. The close identification of *bushidō* with Japanese militarism meant that it was rejected immediately after the war, but different interpretations of *bushidō* were soon revived by both Japanese and foreign commentators seeking to explain Japan's past, present, and future. This volume further explores the factors behind the resurgence of *bushidō*, which has proven resilient through 130 years of dramatic social, political, and cultural change.

Oleg Benesch is Anniversary Research Lecturer in History, specializing in the history of early modern and modern Japan. Before arriving at the University of York, Dr Benesch was Past & Present Fellow at the Institute of Historical Research at the University of London. He has spent almost six years living and researching in Japan, including two years each at Hitotsubashi University and Reitaku University in Tokyo. Dr Benesch's publications and teaching interests cover a variety of fields, including Japanese intellectual, religious, and social history, Chinese intellectual history, as well as the transnational history of modern East Asia. He has presented his research findings at academic conferences and invited lectures throughout East Asia, Europe, North America, and Australia.

Inventing the Way of the Samurai

Nationalism, Internationalism, and Bushidō in Modern Japan

OLEG BENESCH

OXFORD
UNIVERSITY PRESS

OXFORD
UNIVERSITY PRESS

Great Clarendon Street, Oxford, OX2 6DP,
United Kingdom

Oxford University Press is a department of the University of Oxford.
It furthers the University's objective of excellence in research, scholarship,
and education by publishing worldwide. Oxford is a registered trade mark of
Oxford University Press in the UK and in certain other countries

First published 2014
First published in paperback 2016

Published in the United States of America by Oxford University Press
198 Madison Avenue, New York, NY 10016, United States of America

British Library Cataloguing in Publication Data
Data available

Library of Congress Cataloging in Publication Data
Data available

ISBN 978–0–19–870662–5 (Hbk.)
ISBN 978–0–19–875425–1 (Pbk.)

Acknowledgements

From first becoming interested in *bushidō* almost twelve years ago, my research has been made possible by the very generous support I received from many great people and institutions in Japan, North America, and Europe. In Japan, I extend my thanks to Itō Shuntarō for initially encouraging me to pursue my interest in *bushidō*. I am extremely grateful to Yoshida Yutaka for invaluable advice and guidance on conducting historical research in Tokyo, and for providing me with the opportunity to do so. Lee Yeounsuk kindly helped me find my feet and engage with other researchers in the field. I thank Toshitada Kitsukawa for introducing me to new sources and approaches in Japanese historiography. During my years in Japan, I benefited from the support of Hitotsubashi University, Reitaku University, and Kanagawa University, as well as the Ministry of Culture, Sports, Science, and Technology (MEXT). Guo Qiang, Ahmet Gülmez, Hattori Eiji, Miyata Chigusa, Tan Rutaitip, and Sakaki Hatsumi have been great and supportive friends since our time at Reitaku, and discussions with Biankah Bailey, Colin Barey, Trevor Kew, and Brett Robson are always thought-provoking.

This project began in earnest during my doctoral study, and I am especially indebted to the faculty, staff, and students at the University of British Columbia who offered me constant support, guidance, and insight during my time there. I owe special thanks to my doctoral supervisors, Nam-lin Hur and Peter Nosco, whose astute guidance is largely responsible for any contributions this study may make to the field, and whose excellent practical advice and support during and after the PhD made my research possible. William Wray introduced me to a variety of methods and resources for historical research. I want to thank Tim Brook, Thomas Conlan, David Edgington, and Karl Friday for their incisive questions and extensive advice on my PhD thesis, which proved invaluable in my subsequent research work. I would also like to thank Denis Gainty for his detailed and helpful suggestions that have contributed directly to this book. In this regard, I am indebted to Dennis Frost and the Dissertation Reviews team for providing a tremendous service to new academics. I am grateful for the friendship and engaging discussions I had at UBC with Maiko Behr, Nathen Clerici, Chris Craig, Gideon Fujiwara, Asato Ikeda, Tomoko Kitagawa, Jasmina Miodragovic, Jeff Newmark, Eiji Okawa, Minami Orihara, Frank Rausch, Guy Shababo, Hidemi Shiga, Robban Toleno, Kaori Yoshida, and Dafna Zur.

In the UK, I am indebted to the Past & Present Society for their generous support during a year as Past & Present Fellow at the Institute of Historical Research, University of London. Miles Taylor very kindly provided support and advice as I settled into a new research environment, and James Lees helped ensure that my transition to the IHR was a smooth one. Stephen Dodd welcomed me to the research community at the School of Oriental and African Studies, and our conversations gave me new insights on *bushidō*. Naoko Shimazu has graciously introduced me to many other historians and scholars of Japan in the UK and abroad, and has been a wonderful source of information and engaging discussions. During my visits to Cambridge, Barak Kushner has been a most gracious host, supporting me with advice and conversations that have led to many new departures in my research. Discussions with Richard Bowring made me consider different angles on samurai thought, and his ideas have helped me refine my own.

As the manuscript began to come together, I received much kind support and advice from Alexandra Walsham and Matthew Hilton, the editors of the Past & Present Book Series. At Oxford University Press, Stephanie Ireland and Cathryn Steele have been a pleasure to work with as they shepherded the project along. I also owe a debt of gratitude to the four anonymous readers for the press, whose detailed comments challenged me to improve the manuscript in several significant ways. Ran Zwigenberg and Nathan Hopson kindly read the final chapter and provided invaluable feedback. I extend my sincere thanks to all those who have contributed to this project along the way, and regret that I was not able to incorporate all of their suggestions. The responsibility for any shortcomings this book may have is, of course, entirely my own.

I am grateful for the support of an Anniversary Research Lectureship at the University of York, which has allowed me the time to complete and thoroughly revise the text. This process has been greatly assisted by the congenial and welcoming environment created by my colleagues in the Department of History, and I greatly appreciate their continued indulgence of my many questions, research and otherwise.

Finally, I am most indebted to my family. Helena Simmonds has not only graciously put up with my fascination with *bushidō*, but provided indispensable practical help by proofreading countless drafts. Renate, Walter, and Ilya Benesch have been tremendous sources of moral and practical support through years of education and research.

In this book, all Japanese, Chinese, and Korean names appear with the family name first, except for those individuals who publish primarily in European languages. Diacritical marks are used for Japanese terms to reflect original usage. Words that have become common in English, including many Japanese place names, are rendered without diacritics.

Contents

Introduction

The history of chivalry in Europe has shown that temporal separation need not dull the longing for a past ideal, and the romanticization of chivalric codes did not decline as the centuries passed between medieval knighthood and its supposed ideological heritage. The popular appeal of knightly tales in the early seventeenth century inspired Cervantes to satirize it in *Don Quixote*, while Mark Twain mocked similar nineteenth-century currents in the United States in *A Yankee in King Arthur's Court* (1889). The continued influence of the chivalric ideal in Europe can be seen in institutions such as the Most Excellent Order of the British Empire (established 1917), Ordine al Merito della Repubblica Italiana (1951), and Ordre national du Mérite (1963). The traditional awarding of knighthoods to honour outstanding individuals reflects the popular view of chivalry as an ethic of exemplary behaviour, even if its specific prescriptions were not always clear or widely practised.

Discourse on the heritage of knighthood has not been limited to the West, however, and the concept most frequently compared with European chivalry can be found in Japan. From the last decade of the nineteenth century onwards, the origins and character of *bushidō* (the 'way of the samurai') have been subjects of debate among scholars, politicians, writers, and the general public in Japan and abroad.[1] *Bushidō* has been posited as the very 'soul' of the Japanese people, the 'animating spirit' and 'motor force' of the country long after the samurai class ceased to exist.[2] In its popular interpretation, the tenets ascribed to *bushidō* include courage, benevolence, politeness, selflessness, sincerity, honour, loyalty, self-control, and a strong sense of justice—virtues also found in texts romanticizing the European chivalric ideal. This similarity is not coincidental, as the first significant discussions of modern *bushidō* were directly inspired by English discourse on the roots of the gentleman in medieval knighthood. One of the greatest revivals of idealized knightly virtues in the modern world occurred in eighteenth- and nineteenth-century England, where reinterpretations of chivalry influenced education, architecture, literature, and art, as well as providing a rapidly industrializing society with moral

---

[1] Although the term '*bushidō*' (武士道) is frequently translated as 'the way of the warrior', or 'the way of the samurai', this translation becomes problematic when discussing the history of the subject, as it is only one of many terms found in Japanese texts dealing with the issue. For the sake of eliminating as much ambiguity as possible, this study will rely on Romanization of the original Japanese terms to the extent that it is practical to do so.

[2] Nitobe Inazo (1939), *Bushido: The Soul of Japan* (Tokyo: Kenkyusha), p. 98.

guidelines supposedly rooted in ancient and noble tradition.[3] Conversely, the presence of so many familiar elements beneath an intriguing 'Oriental' veneer greatly aided a tremendous surge in Western interest in *bushidō* that occurred in the early twentieth century.

Today, *bushidō* frequently appears in popular Japanese culture, and is also invoked by politicians, business people, athletes, and other public figures. *Bushidō* has been suggested as the key factor behind Japanese economic success in the 1980s, as well as more recent achievements in international baseball and football (soccer) competitions. Commentators have credited *bushidō* with the composed public response to the 2011 Tohoku earthquake, tsunami, and subsequent nuclear crisis, while referring to workers at the damaged Fukushima power plant as 'nuclear samurai'. In the past decade, some Japanese politicians have sought to reintroduce the '*bushidō* spirit' into the Fundamental Education Law to address a perceived malaise among the nation's youth attributed to a lack of moral education. Promoters of *bushidō* in the political sphere have been joined by senior military figures who use *bushidō* in their arguments for a more assertive foreign policy including overseas engagements, including overseas engagements. Given the role of *bushidō* as a prominent ideological support for Japanese militarism in Asia and the Pacific before 1945, this connection has similarly problematic connotations as statements by Western leaders invoking Crusader imagery with regard to military action in the Arab world.

In spite of the enduring popularity of *bushidō* in such diverse fields, the most influential work on the subject continues to be Nitobe Inazō's (1862–1933) enigmatic *Bushido: the Soul of Japan* (1899), which often serves as a 'textbook-like standard'.[4] The resilience and unrivalled popularity of *Bushido: the Soul of Japan* are peculiar aspects of *bushidō* discourse, as it is only one of thousands of books and articles on the subject. The reasons behind the wealth of commentaries on *bushidō* in modern Japan reflect the great diversity of interpretations of the subject. The popular view holds that *bushidō* began to develop as a martial ethic in the late twelfth century, but that samurai were too preoccupied with warfare and practical matters to formally codify *bushidō* before the late sixteenth century. According to this account, aspects of *bushidō* evolved as the role of the samurai in Japanese society changed before being effectively eliminated by successive government reforms in the early Meiji period (1868–1912). It is commonly suggested that Nitobe Inazō formulated and popularized an idealized version of this martial ethic, which was appropriated and adapted by the Meiji, Taishō (1912–26), and early Shōwa (1926–89) governments as a ruling ideology that redirected loyalty from feudal lords to the emperor. The simplistic account of the development of *bushidō* is problematic, however, and relies on pre-war theories that conflated diverse historical

---

[3] See Girouard, Mark (1981), *The Return to Camelot: Chivalry and the English Gentleman* (Yale University Press); Alexander, Michael (2007), *Medievalism: The Middle Ages in Modern England* (New Haven: Yale University Press).
[4] Takahashi Tomio (1991), *Bushi no kokoro, Nihon no kokoro 2* (Tokyo: Kondō shuppansha), pp. 426–7.

periods and ideologies to provide legitimacy for the modern imperial state and nation.

In the early twentieth century, *bushidō* became a subject in both civilian and military education, from ethics instruction to history lessons. The *bushidō* found in the first new textbooks after the Russo-Japanese War of 1904–5 was not exclusively chauvinistic, but evolved in this direction until a militaristic, emperor-focused interpretation of *bushidō* became a significant component of the ideological structures of the Japanese empire in the 'dark valley' of the 1930s and 1940s. During this period, an 'imperial' interpretation of *bushidō* became an important propaganda tool used to encourage and justify actions that led to the tragedies of the war in East Asia and the Pacific. Simultaneously, it was used by the Allies to objectify and dehumanize Japanese people as *bushidō*-driven automatons. The integration of *bushidō* ideology into the Japanese education system for almost forty years ensured that the concept retained a presence in the postwar era, albeit in different forms.

After 1945, many scholars dismissed what they regarded as corrupting modern developments in *bushidō* and turned to re-examining the historical samurai to draw conclusions regarding 'traditional' Japanese culture and behavioural patterns. In the past four decades, *bushidō* has been a common theme in popular and academic works seeking to explain a wide variety of phenomena, and students of Japanese history, culture, and language inevitably find themselves confronted with discussions of *bushidō*. The term is also used in the titles and marketing materials of films, books, comics, video games, and martial arts competitions in Japan and around the world. Instructors of Japanese-related subjects are often uncertain as to how to respond to questions regarding *bushidō*, or are frustrated by students' expectations that they address the subject in depth. Norio Ota has discussed the great popularity of *bushidō* among students in the many countries where he has taught the Japanese language, and instead calls for the 're-discovery of the non-bushido tradition in Japan'. In Ota's view, which is shared by many educators, *bushidō* overshadows non-martial elements of Japanese culture and society, as well as putting undue pressure on Japanese to identify with an ambiguous martial ideology.[5] Shigeno Saburō expresses a similar view in *Against Bushido* (*Han bushidō ron*) (2014), criticizing the tremendous popularity of what he considers an anachronistic ideology with no relevance to modern democratic society.[6]

For Japanese and foreign students of Japan, the inevitable encounter with *bushidō* raises problems due to the vast amount of material on the subject, which makes it difficult to obtain an accurate overview. On the other hand, there are few scholarly treatments of *bushidō*, especially in English. *Bushidō* was ignored by many scholars after 1945, until its popular revival in the 1970s and 1980s as people sought cultural factors to explain Japan's economic success. Many historians during this time

---

[5] Ota, Norio, 'Re-discovery of the Non-Bushido Tradition in Japan', paper presented on 3 Oct. 2010 at the 23rd Annual Conference of the Canadian Association for Japanese Studies, held at the University of British Columbia.

[6] Shigeno Saburō (2014), *Han bushidō ron* (Tokyo: Bungeisha).

dismissed *bushidō* as an anachronism and its popularity as a passing phenomenon, a situation similar to that which occurred in 1912 when renowned Japanologist Basil Hall Chamberlain (1850–1935) attacked *bushidō* as a modern invention with no basis in earlier history.[7] Chamberlain recalled that *bushidō* was virtually unknown little more than a decade earlier, and criticized it accordingly. Today, a great number of popular works are opposed by a handful of critical texts, and Nitobe's well-known and widely available work is often the first port of call for those seeking an introduction to *bushidō*. In spite of its influence and status as a classic text, however, *Bushido: the Soul of Japan* is of limited use for understanding the samurai or pre-Meiji history or thought. Instead, Nitobe's work and the reactions to it are far better suited as aids to understanding the dynamics of modern Japanese intellectual and social history, especially in the context of the search for identity in the newly international age in which he lived. Similarly, the revival of Nitobe's view of *bushidō* in the late twentieth century reveals a great deal about the political, social, and economic conditions from the 1980s to the present.

As Chamberlain's writings indicate, the study of *bushidō* is complicated by issues of terminology, specifically the confusion between the historical and historiographical use of the term '*bushidō*' itself. An obscure literary term before the 1890s, '*bushidō*' has become a broad descriptive word for Japanese samurai thought and behaviour.[8] This is problematic in translations of historical documents into modern Japanese and other languages, which frequently render diverse terms such as *budō* (the martial way), *shidō* (the way of the samurai/gentleman), *hōkōnin no michi* (the way of the retainer), *otoko no michi* (the way of masculinity), *heidō* (the way of the soldier), and many others uniformly as *bushidō*, giving the impression that a homogenous and widely accepted tradition existed, when this is not supported by the evidence. A related source of confusion is the historiographic use of '*bushidō*', which can similarly imply the existence of a unified samurai ethical tradition. Ultimately, the most effective method of minimizing the confusion between historiographical and historical uses of '*bushidō*' is the use of historical terms specific to the relevant periods and locations, or, if the argument and evidence should warrant, neutral descriptors such as 'samurai ethics'. This is the approach taken in this study, which uses the term '*bushidō*' to refer to the ideology of the same name that developed from mid-Meiji onwards. In this context, the concepts '*bushidō*' and 'modern *bushidō*' are used synonymously, with the latter preferred in cases where confusion might otherwise arise.

COMPARATIVE CONTEXTS

The lack of examination of modern *bushidō* can be attributed to several factors. The sudden popular revival of *bushidō* in the 1980s made some scholars reluctant

---

[7] Chamberlain, Basil Hall (1912), *The Invention of a New Religion* (London: Rationalist Press).

[8] For a more detailed overview of the etymology and development of the term '*bushidō*', including its first appearance in the seventeenth century and its absence from Edo-period popular culture, see Benesch, Oleg (2011), *Bushido: The Creation of a Martial Ethic in Late Meiji Japan* (PhD dissertation at the University of British Columbia), pp. 5–14.

to address what appeared to be a passing phenomenon with little or no historical basis. Another factor was the difficulty of obtaining a broader historical perspective on the 1980s, as scholars working in the last two decades of the twentieth century were also 'living' this history. These factors were compounded by the lack of examination of pre-war *bushidō* discourse, which has resulted in uncertainty regarding the nature and origins of the concept, making it difficult to approach and contextualize. The major gaps in the study of *bushidō* complicate not only our understanding of modern discourses on the subject, but can also influence research into earlier Japanese history. This study builds on and reassesses the existing scholarship as it examines the development of modern *bushidō*. The approach taken is generally chronological, while also referring to the broader significance of texts and historical events where this is warranted. By examining the historical processes that contributed to the development of modern *bushidō*, this study revisits several fundamental issues that have not been adequately resolved, in order to explain the continued popularity of the concept.

The notion that *bushidō* is a modern invention has been put forth by a number of scholars over the past century, but this view has failed to make a sufficient impact on popular discourse. Both popular culture and many scholarly works continue to treat *bushidō* as a traditional ethic originally codified and/or practised by samurai. This is partially due to the nature of works critical of the historical pedigree of *bushidō*, which tend to either dismiss the concept as a modern invention or criticize the historical accuracy of specific interpretations, especially Nitobe's *Bushido: The Soul of Japan*. While essentially correct, these critical approaches often lack persuasiveness as they do not provide a sufficiently detailed or convincing alternative narrative for the development of modern *bushidō*. Due to the sheer number and variety of *bushidō* theories, critiques of specific interpretations tend to leave unaffected *bushidō* discourse as a whole. Similarly, it is not possible to prove that a samurai ethic did not exist through a positivistic approach to pre-Meiji Japanese history. Historians of medieval and early modern Japan have not found any widely accepted ethical systems that could be convincingly portrayed as the origins of modern *bushidō*, but this does not preclude the discovery of such an ethic in the future, however unlikely this may be. For this reason, the classification of *bushidō* as a modern invention requires a detailed examination of its development.

In addition to providing a narrative of the development of *bushidō* as a modern invention, this study considers a number of related issues. First, if *bushidō* is a modern invention, who invented it? As this study shows, *bushidō* was not invented by either nationalistic traditionalists or Nitobe Inazō, but originated in a confluence of intellectual and social trends around the overseas journeys of journalist and politician Ozaki Yukio (1858–1954) in the late 1880s. Ozaki's comments on *bushidō* as a potential counterpart to English chivalry and the English 'gentlemanship' that he idealized inspired a discourse on *bushidō* among some of the most progressive and internationally experienced Japanese thinkers in the early 1890s. So successful was this development that, by the end of the decade, English observers of Japan unfavourably compared the 'degeneration' of European chivalry with the 'unbroken' heritage of the samurai spirit. The high profile of English ideals in

Meiji Japan is reflected in the history of the word 'gentlemanship', in regular use in English from the sixteenth to the early twentieth century.[9] 'Gentlemanship' largely disappeared from the English language after this time, replaced by the related terms 'gentlemanhood' and 'gentlemanliness'; however, it survives in Japanese as '*jentorumanshippu*', reflecting usage when the concept of the 'English gentleman' was first introduced to Japan.

Second, is *bushidō* uniquely Japanese? In spite of its source of inspiration, Meiji *bushidō* was certainly not a mere copy of foreign ideals. On the other hand, the widespread view that *bushidō* is a singular national ethic that somehow explains the Japanese 'character', is also problematic. While certainly unique in its specific combination of cultural and social influences, the invention of *bushidō* follows patterns found in other societies dealing with issues of tradition, modernity, progress, and national identity as part of the process of modernization in the late nineteenth and early twentieth centuries. Eric Hobsbawm has referred to the period 1870–1914 as one of 'mass production of tradition' in Europe, and similar processes followed in many other parts of the world, albeit with varying delays.[10] Accordingly, scholarship on the invention of tradition, which has already been applied to other aspects of modern Japan, is relevant to the study of *bushidō*.[11] Research on the invention and development of the *bushidō* tradition should further include comparative elements, as the earliest *bushidō* theorists were strongly influenced by and sometimes explicitly followed contemporary developments in the West. In contrast, foreign commentators, most prominently in China and the West, were also enamoured with the developing *bushidō* discourse and hoped to (re)import aspects of it in order to improve their own societies.

A third question arises from the staying power of *bushidō*. How did it become widely accepted as a traditional ethic, and how was it revived repeatedly after falling out of fashion when other ideological constructs were not? While taking a comparative approach, this study also examines those aspects of the invention of *bushidō* that were unique to Japan, and which have contributed significantly to its continued popularity. Many characteristics of *bushidō* are indeed found in comparable ideologies in other societies that often served as models for *bushidō* theorists, but the development of *bushidō* depended on the unique combination of social, political, and intellectual currents within Japan's specific historical experience. The reasons behind the great popularity of *bushidō* today can be found in the earliest Meiji discourse on the subject: *bushidō* was initially developed by a progressive, internationalist group of individuals whose ideals resonated more with postwar Japanese thought than with many of their contemporaries. The popular *bushidō* of today shares many characteristics with the *bushidō* theories of the 1890s, which

---

[9] Bradley, Henry (1901), *A New English Dictionary on Historical Principles: Founded Mainly on the Materials Collected by the Philological Society*, vols. 4, F and G (Oxford: Clarendon Press), p. 120.

[10] Hobsbawm, Eric J. (1983), 'Mass-Producing Traditions: Europe 1870–1914', in Eric J. Hobsbawm and Terence Ranger, *The Invention of Tradition* (Cambridge: Cambridge University Press), pp. 263–307.

[11] See the essays in Vlastos, Stephen (ed.) (1998), *Mirror of Modernity: Invented Traditions in Modern Japan* (Berkeley: University of California Press).

established the concept in Japan and gave it the historical legitimacy and flexibility that enabled it to survive the turbulent twentieth century. *Bushidō* is unusual in its resilience in contrast with the majority of nationalistic concepts appropriated for ideological service by the militaristic state in the years before 1945 and rejected along with it immediately after. These others have not recovered and today are found primarily in rightist discourse.

Stephen Vlastos has provided a model for the examination of modern invented traditions, arguing that 'establishing their invention is only the first step. The significant findings will be historical and contextual. How, by whom, and to what social and political effect are certain practices and ideas formulated, institutionalized, and propagated as *tradition*?'[12] These latter issues are significant, as they determine whether an invented narrative becomes accepted and assumes the role of tradition. In this context, the more varied and complex the answers to Vlastos' questions, the greater the resilience of the invented tradition in question. Focusing especially on the period from the late eighteenth century to the present, Eric Hobsbawm sees invented traditions as belonging to three overlapping types:

> a) those establishing or symbolizing social cohesion or the membership of groups, real or artificial communities, b) those establishing or legitimizing institutions, status, or relations of authority, and c) those whose main purpose was socialization, the inculcation of beliefs, value systems, and conventions of behaviour.[13]

These categories are useful for examining *bushidō*, as it served all three functions at various times. *Bushidō* was first debated around 1890 as a Hobsbawm type c) invented tradition, and was popularized as a type a) after 1895. In the early twentieth century, *bushidō* became an ideological tool of type b) used by the Japanese government, while maintaining characteristics of a) and c). After 1945, *bushidō* returned as an invented tradition of type a), although there have been concerted efforts to re-establish it as a type c) in the past decade. This broad applicability of *bushidō*, which is a function of the fluid nature of its content, has been a primary factor behind its resilience.

Responding to the work of Vlastos and others, Dipesh Chakrabarty discusses some of the issues that have been raised by Hobsbawm's analytical model, pointing out that while especially effective 'as a tool for unmasking "ideology", in particular the ideologies of the nation-state and capitalism', problems arise when the ideology thus exposed is viewed as a vacuum to be filled by historical 'reality'.[14] This can be seen in a few of the critical works on *bushidō* that began to appear in the early twentieth century. Okakura Kakuzō (Tenshin, 1862–1913), for example, rejected *bushidō* and sought to replace it with a peaceful 'teaism', while Hagiwara Sakutarō (1886–1942) similarly argued for the primacy of pacifistic aesthetic traditions in

---

[12] Vlastos, Stephen (1998), 'Tradition: Past/Present Culture and Modern Japanese History', in Stephen Vlastos (ed.), *Mirror of Modernity: Invented Traditions in Modern Japan* (Berkeley: University of California Press), p. 5.

[13] Hobsbawm, Eric J., 'Mass-Producing Traditions', p. 9.

[14] Chakrabarty, Dipesh (1998), 'Afterword: Revisiting the Tradition/Modernity Binary', in Stephen Vlastos (ed.), *Mirror of Modernity: Invented Traditions in Modern Japan* (Berkeley: University of California Press), p. 287.

Japan. Okakura, Hagiwara, and a minority of other dissenting voices dismissed *bushidō* as a modern invention and attempted to replace it with their own 'real' traditions, but these were merely cases of substituting one invented tradition with another.[15] For critics of *bushidō*—including many people in Japan—it is important to understand and expose its processes of invention as a way of countering the *bushidō* stereotype of Japanese having an inherently martial character, a view that many find inaccurate and frustrating. Recent studies have supported the contention that arguments pertaining to the nature of a 'national character' of any group are problematic, even more so if these are based on specific agendas rather than 'disinterested' research and observation.[16]

The use of concepts such as 'invented tradition' and 'ideology' is complicated by issues of definition. John Gerring has identified dozens of different definitions for the latter concept alone.[17] This study does not seek to engage comprehensively with the debates on these concepts, but the ways in which they are understood here should be discussed briefly. The often ambiguous and evolving nature of modern *bushidō* prevents the concept from fitting neatly into any established categories. Here, *bushidō* is treated primarily as an invented tradition and ideology, with the understanding that these concepts are distinct but can overlap significantly. Not all invented traditions are ideologies, and certainly not all ideologies are invented traditions. In its most common usage, however, as a traditional samurai ethic and/or defining trait of the Japanese 'national character', *bushidō* is best treated as an invented tradition, with the specific context and content of this usage determining its ideological character.

One criticism of the exegetical model of the invention of tradition has been that as human constructs, traditions are constantly changing and evolving, making it difficult to argue for their specific invention. This may disqualify some traditions from examination using this conceptual framework, but as a tradition with a clearly definable period of invention at the end of the nineteenth century, *bushidō* meets a narrower definition of invented tradition. From the late 1880s onward, *bushidō* has been continually reinvented in different ways, often by the same individuals. Sometimes these have been cases of almost pure invention with no connection to earlier history aside from the term '*bushidō*', while in other cases specific historical sources and terminology have been used in attempts to reanimate what were believed to be historical traditions. Ultimately, however, all modern *bushidō* theories are later constructs with no direct continuity from pre-Meiji history, while it is precisely the claims to such continuity that make *bushidō* an invented *tradition*.

Much of the legitimacy of *bushidō* has come from its alleged historical roots as a traditional ethic, even if these were not supported by the evidence. With its status

---

[15] Bialock, David T. (2000), 'Nation and Epic: *The Tale of the Heike* as a Modern Classic', in Haruo Shirane (ed.), *Inventing the Classics: Modernity, National Identity, and Japanese Literature* (Stanford: Stanford University Press), p. 162.

[16] McCrae, R. R. 'Cross-Cultural Research on the Five-Factor Model of Personality (Version 2)', *Online Readings in Psychology and Culture* (Unit 6, Chapter 1/V2) June, 2009.

[17] Gerring, John (2001), *Social Science Methodology: A Criterial Framework* (Cambridge, MA: Cambridge University Press), pp. 71–86.

as an invented tradition firmly in mind, this study also treats *bushidō* as one of many ideologies in modern Japan. Some of these ideologies were invented traditions, most were admittedly modern, and many were imports from the West. Social Darwinism, for example, was an ideological construct that took its legitimacy from supposedly scientific ideas of progress rather than tradition, and became influential throughout East Asia. In comparing *bushidō* with other ideologies of modern Japan, it can be useful to focus on their commonalities, and the characteristic of being an invented tradition may not always be the most relevant aspect of *bushidō* in this context.

In treating *bushidō* as an ideology, this study uses 'ideology' in a similar way to Malcolm Hamilton's definition of the concept:

> An ideology is a system of collectively held normative and reputedly factual ideas and beliefs and attitudes advocating a particular pattern of social relationships and arrangements, and/or aimed at justifying a particular pattern of conduct, which its proponents seek to promote, realise, pursue or maintain.[18]

In her work on modern Japanese ideologies, Carol Gluck sees ideology as an 'essential social element…All societies produce ideologies which in turn help to reproduce the social order. [this definition avoids] the common, but restrictive, equation of ideology with a systematic and manipulative political program'. This latter distinction is significant with regard to *bushidō* ideology, as the emphasis on its use in military education and propaganda, especially in early Shōwa, can obscure the diversity of the discourse. According to Gluck, at no point in modern Japan was there a monolithic ideology or ideology production process.[19] Even a seemingly cohesive ideology such as *bushidō* was the result of complex interactions between many different individuals and groups with widely varying motivations, who were subjected to a plethora of social and cultural factors.

The broad consensus established around the turn of the twentieth century on the existence of a *bushidō* tradition masked the diversity of the underlying discourses. While *bushidō* began its modern life as a native Japanese equivalent of European chivalry and 'gentlemanship', it soon came to be interpreted as a 'way of the samurai', drawing upon the former martial class, and subsequently as a more esoteric 'way of the warrior' rooted in mythohistory and related to the nation's divine and unique spirit. The existence of these various *bushidōs*, which overlapped, combined, and competed for popular acceptance, was crucial to the long-term survival of the ideology over the course of more than a century of upheaval and change. Once invented and disseminated in its myriad forms, the *bushidō* tradition was selectively altered and redefined to suit the needs of its interpreters, Japanese and foreign, without losing its apparent historical legitimacy. Conversely, *bushidō* experienced its greatest crises when too successfully tied to a specific person, period, or ideology that was subsequently discredited or otherwise fell out of

[18] Hamilton, Malcolm B., 'The Elements of the Concept of Ideology', *Political Studies* 35:1 (March 1987), p. 38.
[19] Gluck, Carol (1985), *Japan's Modern Myths* (Princeton: Princeton University Press), pp. 6–7.

favour. Ultimately, *bushidō* was able to weather these storms due to the inherent diversity from its organic development in Meiji, which allowed it to rebound relatively quickly even as its ideological partners were relegated to history.

Inevitable changes in intellectual, social, and political conditions mean that even the most resilient ideologies do not retain an unwaveringly high profile in a single field over decades. At times of great upheaval, especially, ideologies become linked with one another or with certain concepts, and subsequently decline together. *Bushidō* has endured because its flexibility has allowed it to move between different genres and spheres of discourse, rising and falling at various times. Accordingly, this volume traces the evolution of *bushidō* through a variety of intellectual, popular, political, educational, and other discourses to provide a continuous narrative of its development, rather than examining its trajectory in any one area in which its influence may have waxed and waned.

OVERVIEW

As Eric Hobsbawm has argued, the invention of tradition should be expected to 'occur more frequently when a rapid transformation of society weakens or destroys the social patterns for which "old" traditions had been designed'.[20] In this context, Chapter 1 examines a form of nostalgic *bushidō* discourse that arose in the turbulent environment of the 1850s and 1860s, marked by the involvement of prominent activist figures such as Yoshida Shōin (1830–59) and Yokoi Shōnan (1809–69). A number of late Edo period (*c*.1603–1868) thinkers received considerable exposure in modern *bushidō* discourse, especially after 1900, and their close temporal proximity to modern theorists means that they have often been considered as bridges between Edo and Meiji *bushidō*. The content of *bushidō* in the last fifteen years of the Edo period ('Bakumatsu') was specific to the period and to certain groups active at the time, however, and its influence on modern Meiji *bushidō* is in need of review.

Chapter 1 discusses the formative influences on Bakumatsu *bushidō*, in the absence of an established and continuing tradition of samurai ethics for thinkers to draw upon. Bakumatsu commentators were largely critical of their own time and instead looked to a romanticized distant past before the alleged decline of the samurai. These nostalgic—or, strictly speaking, antiquarian—views of the samurai followed a pattern that had been repeated for several centuries. As Fred Davis argues, 'Whatever in our present situation evokes it, nostalgia *uses the past*—falsely, accurately, or...in specially reconstructed ways—but it is not a product thereof'.[21] Tales of samurai in the Edo period tended to be idealized accounts of medieval warriors that emphasized combat, bravery, and glory—martial elements that were deemed to be in short supply during the era of peace under Tokugawa family rule

---

[20] Hobsbawm, Eric J., 'Introduction: Inventing Traditions', in Eric J. Hobsbawm and Terence Ranger, *The Invention of Tradition* (Cambridge: Cambridge University Press), p. 4.
[21] Davis, Fred (1979), *Yearning for Yesterday: A Sociology of Nostalgia* (The Free Press), pp. 10–11.

(*c*.1600–1868). In contrast, discussions of ethics and contemporary issues tended to be phrased in Confucian terms and their applicability was not typically limited to the samurai.

Just as arguments linking the few Bakumatsu writers on *bushidō* to earlier discourse are often problematic, the first chapter also reconsiders the impact Bakumatsu discourse had on Meiji developments. This latter influence, although significant, occurred after *bushidō* discourse had already become established after the Sino-Japanese War of 1894–5, and Edo *bushidō* theorists did not have a direct connection to or formative influence on the first modern exponents of the subject. This situation was directly related to popular perceptions of the samurai in early Meiji, when the former class distinctions were abolished and many samurai fell into poverty as they struggled to adapt to the rapidly changing social order. A number of rebellions in the 1870s contributed to negative views of the samurai, and the idea that a samurai-based ethic should serve as a model for the whole nation had little popular appeal through the 1880s.

Chapter 2 is concerned with the origins of modern *bushidō* in the period from the late 1880s to the beginning of a popular '*bushidō* boom' after 1895. Specifically, it examines the writings of Ozaki Yukio and the handful of commentators on his *bushidō* theories active before the Sino-Japanese War. Their works drove the development of later *bushidō* discourse, and were in turn strongly influenced by three broad trends in Japanese thought at the time. The first of these was the maturation of Japan's relationship with the West, a process marked by a more nuanced re-evaluation of the idealistic adoration or rejection that defined attitudes towards the West held by many Japanese thinkers in early Meiji. The second factor was a change in Japan's views of China, which became increasingly negative in the years leading up to the Sino-Japanese War. The third factor that influenced the first generation of modern *bushidō* theorists was an increased interest in their nation's culture. Whereas Japanese in the 1880s would still claim to be embarrassed by traditional aspects of their culture in front of foreigners, by the early 1890s interest and pride in their own heritage was growing rapidly. The interplay between these three trends was evolving and influenced individual *bushidō* theorists to varying degrees, but the trends were important to all of them.

In addition to these broader trends, the presence of a foreign 'other' or 'others' was an essential element in the development of modern *bushidō* discourse, and the first formulators of *bushidō* were equally or more influenced by current events beyond Japan's borders than they were by the historical samurai class. In this vein, the rehabilitation of the samurai image in the context of *bushidō* was inspired by contemporary European discourse on chivalry and 'gentlemanship', which served to legitimize the search for comparable sources of morality in the historical Japanese equivalent of knighthood. This development had a reciprocal influence on trends in historiography that sought to redefine the Japanese past in terms of European models, with concepts such as 'feudalism' and 'medieval' gaining broad acceptance. Within a decade, Westerners and Japanese would come to see Japanese society as the heir of medieval knighthood and as a potential model for other nations to channel the strength of their own feudal past.

Chapter 3 examines the '*bushidō* boom' that began soon after the Sino-Japanese War, and traces its development through the Russo-Japanese War of 1904–1905. Buoyed by the success of the earlier conflict, much Japanese thought became increasingly nationalistic, and it was natural that a 'native' ethic such as *bushidō* would gain broad currency during this period. Whereas earlier *bushidō* theories tended to be more 'internationalist' than nationalistic, the character of discourse changed considerably after 1895. The newly confident and often chauvinistic *bushidō* that marked the *bushidō* boom of late Meiji built on the earlier foundations but quickly superseded them. This change in tone even led early *bushidō* theorist Uemura Masahisa (1858–1925) to criticize the appropriation of the concept by nationalistic and militaristic elements in 1898.

Uemura's frustration at the 'misuse' of *bushidō* reveals one of the greatest strengths of the ethic: resilience. The legitimacy bestowed on the concept by its alleged relationship with the historical samurai, combined with a lack of concrete historical roots that could be used to define or refute it, meant that *bushidō* was an ideal vehicle for nationalist sentiments of the type that came to the fore around 1900. As a concept with national relevancy, *bushidō* was implicitly used in the process of integrating Japan's many strong regional identities into a unified whole. Important branches of the military and government were dominated by people from certain regions until well into the twentieth century, resulting in considerable dissatisfaction among those without these connections. Emphasizing local samurai heroes, incidents, and ideals was a method of boosting regional pride, while at the same time integrating these local manifestations of *bushidō* into broader discourse helped promote acceptance of a greater national identity.

Bushidō combined easily with other concepts such as *Yamato damashii* (the national 'Yamato spirit' supposedly originating in Japan's ancient kingdom of that name) and *kokutai* (national polity) to form nationalistic and militaristic ideologies. This volume examines the roles of the 1898 journal *Bushidō*, Nitobe Inazō, and the philosopher Inoue Tetsujirō (1855–1944) in the spread and development of *bushidō*. Nitobe's significance to Meiji *bushidō* theory was not nearly as great as his current reputation would indicate, but he was also involved in the discourse from a considerably earlier time than is generally assumed. In contrast, Inoue Tetsujirō was the undoubted primate of *bushidō* from 1901 until 1945, and was instrumental in developing the government-sanctioned and emperor-focused 'imperial' *bushidō* that became a highly influential ideology from the Russo-Japanese War onwards.

It was only during the second half of the *bushidō* boom, from 1905 until 1914, that *bushidō* became a widely popular subject in Japan and abroad. Chapter 4 examines how imperial *bushidō* ideology became firmly established, and how this and other *bushidō* interpretations spread throughout literature, academia, sport, religion, and other spheres of public life. Through government support and legitimization by Inoue and other official figures, *bushidō* came to play a central role in military and civilian education, especially with the growth of spiritual education programmes used to indoctrinate troops with the desired virtues of loyalty and self-sacrifice. Imperial *bushidō* also played a key role in the national ethics education programme known as 'National Morality', outlined by Inoue in a series of articles and books beginning in 1908. At the same time, the popularity and unquestioned patriotic credentials of *bushidō* led to its frequent mention by writers of literature and popular fiction, while academics wrote many volumes on the subject. Members of religious orders and promoters of various types of sport, native and foreign, called upon *bushidō* to popularize their causes and give them the patriotic legitimacy deemed so important at the time. Foreign interpreters of Japan also showed great interest in *bushidō*, further raising its profile. By the end of the Meiji period, Japanese public life was saturated with *bushidō*, and there were few Japanese or foreigners interested in Japan who had not heard of it and some of its tenets.

Trends at the time of the Meiji emperor's (1852–1912) death indicated that *bushidō* would continue to expand its reach, but this was not to be the case. Chapter 5 discusses the sudden decline of *bushidō* around 1914, which was closely tied to the end of Meiji period and the dramatic suicide of General Nogi Maresuke (1849–1912). After examining the influences that led to this change in *bushidō*'s fortunes, this chapter discusses the state of *bushidō* discourse in the Taishō period before its popular revival in early Shōwa. Analysis of *bushidō*'s role in the 1910s and 1920s reveals that the strengths and resilience that characterized modern *bushidō* from its origins in late Meiji made a resurrection of the concept not only possible, but highly likely. While *bushidō* lost its popular appeal soon after Meiji, it had become established in the education system and retained its presence and legitimacy as a historical ethic in the minds of most Japanese.

In the 1930s, this high degree of recognition allowed *bushidō* to become a key component of the legitimizing ideology of the imperial state, and the *bushidō* of this period fulfilled many of the criteria used by Marxist scholars of functional ideology as a 'systematic and manipulative political program'.[22] Chapter 6 examines the practical application of *bushidō* in the military and in general education texts such as the notorious *Principles of the National Polity* (*Kokutai no hongi*) and other materials used for 'spiritual education'. The lines between civilian and military life became increasingly blurred as the 1930s progressed, with the country sinking deeper into conflict with China while preparing for an expanded total war. When this came in the early 1940s, *bushidō* had a major influence on the wartime behaviour of Japanese troops and their adversaries, whereby the illusion of the importance of *bushidō* ideology could be more devastating than the acts it inspired. This was manifested in Japanese troops' legitimate attempts to surrender, which were often treated with suspicion by Allied forces and dealt with using lethal force.

While *bushidō* was a key component of the ideological militarization of society in early Shōwa, it also reached new levels of dissemination in popular culture during this same period. The large-scale promotion and dominance of imperial *bushidō* often obscures the continuing diversity of discourse, however, and a number of significant critics of the state-sponsored interpretation emerged from all sides of the political spectrum. This chapter examines a number of the challenges faced by

---

[22] Gluck, Carol, *Japan's Modern Myths*, p. 7.

imperial *bushidō*, including issues resulting from its problematic historiography and the fantastical elements introduced to *bushidō* by the official emperor-centred ideology. Conversely, a number of rightists criticized *bushidō* for not inculcating sufficient imperial loyalty, while others invoked it to justify violent attacks on the government in the name of the emperor. The great breadth of these discourses added to the cumulative exposure to *bushidō* among the population, and contributed significantly to its perceived legitimacy and acceptance.

Chapter 7 broadly examines the trajectory of *bushidō* discourse in the postwar period, when the concept went through further cycles of popularization and decline. After 1945, most people strongly rejected imperial *bushidō* along with other wartime ideologies, and *bushidō* as a whole was largely ignored in the immediate postwar. Due to the diversity of Shōwa discourse, however, *bushidō* soon began to be revived, largely shorn of militarism and other problematic elements. Many scholars who had written on the subject before 1945 were able to revise their theories for the new order, although some continued to promote imperial *bushidō* largely unchanged. Academic historians were among the most engaged participants in postwar *bushidō* discourse, with many motivated to respond to the popular perception that *bushidō* had been corrupted in early Shōwa. The dominant approach was to seek 'real' *bushidō* in sources relating to the premodern samurai, often with little consideration for modern influences. This development was reflected in popular developments when *bushidō* began to attract broader interest again in the 1960s, with these interpretations also focusing on the period before Meiji and ignoring modern trends.

The late 1960s saw a minor revival of a more nationalistic *bushidō*, with novelist and playwright Mishima Yukio (1925–70) its most representative and popular figure. This revival was fairly short-lived, however, as Mishima's dramatic suicide by *seppuku* in 1970 had a similarly shocking effect on mainstream society as General Nogi's death almost sixty years before. This incident conveyed the image of *bushidō* as an anachronistic and potentially extreme ideology, and it remained largely the domain of historians and cultural theorists. From the 1980s, *bushidō* experienced another, more lasting popular revival, this time centred on the theories of Nitobe Inazō. The pacifism, internationalism, and morality inherent in Nitobe's work resonates with segments of contemporary society, although more nationalistic *bushidō* interpretations are also finding favour among conservatives and figures close to the military. Chapter 7 considers this most recent and ongoing resurgence of *bushidō*. Contemporary *bushidō* is deeply indebted to previously neglected prewar writings, as commentators on both sides of the political spectrum have turned to Meiji and early Shōwa *bushidō* texts and ideas to promote their postwar agendas.

1

Before *Bushidō*: Considering Samurai Thought and Identity

SAMURAI IN HISTORICAL CONTEXT

The development of *bushidō* was an essentially modern phenomenon, with core symbols borrowed from the historical samurai. Modern theorists often carefully selected aspects of earlier history, philosophy, and legend to support their specific *bushidō* interpretations. This process of appropriation tended to ignore or distort the historical contexts of the texts and tales used as evidence, and the effects of this are still evident. While the samurai were a useful quarry for modern *bushidō* theorists to mine, their historical reality could also be problematic for *bushidō* discourse. In the Meiji period (1868–1912), negative popular views regarding the condition of the *shizoku*—former samurai—made the wide dissemination of a warrior-based ethic unlikely, and the inspiration for *bushidō* ultimately came from elsewhere. These complications also meant that it took more than a decade from the publication of the first significant texts promoting *bushidō* in the late 1880s to the concept becoming a household word in the early twentieth century.

When *bushidō* discourse did develop, many of its proponents unconsciously followed certain patterns common to earlier texts regarding the samurai. The most striking similarity was a pronounced nostalgia for a vanished martial ideal that the writers had not personally experienced, but were convinced had existed in the past. In this sense, although there is no compelling evidence for the existence of a meaningful or widely accepted samurai ethic before Meiji, there were a few widespread assumptions that inspired texts which modern theorists later included in various *bushidō* canons. The selective nostalgia that Meiji promoters of *bushidō* felt for an earlier time was shared by many thinkers in the Edo period (*c.* 1603–1868), including those promoting Confucian ideas, the study of National Learning, as well as other schools of thought.

With regard to the later development of *bushidō*, the most significant nostalgia was that directed towards Japan's medieval period (*c.* late twelfth to late sixteenth centuries), which Edo commentators viewed as an age when warriors were still able to apply their martial skills and demonstrate their practical value on the battlefield. These idealized interpretations did not necessarily correspond to any historical reality, but they set a pattern for popular representations of medieval warriors that continues today. As Cameron Hurst and Karl Friday point out, most interpretations of *bushidō* in the twentieth century were not grounded in the historiography of medieval Japan.[1] Elsewhere, Friday criticizes the retrospective idealization of the samurai, arguing that there was no significant ritual in early medieval warfare, let alone an accepted ethical system, while Hurst discusses the lack of martial codes in Japan before the seventeenth century.[2] Thomas Conlan emphasizes the pragmatic transactional basis of loyalty in fourteenth-century Japan, and his arguments can be seen partly as a response to *bushidō*-influenced popular conceptions of Japanese warriors.[3] Current historians of medieval Japan do not consider *bushidō* a useful exegetical tool, and it is rarely found in their scholarship. The term '*bushidō*' has not been found in any medieval texts, and the consensus among historians is that no comparable concepts existed at the time under any other name.

Writers interested in the history and thought of the Edo period are more commonly drawn to *bushidō* and the texts usually cited as important sources are almost all products of this time, even if many of these were largely unknown before the modern period. The early eighteenth-century *Hagakure*, for example, which glorifies the warriors of an earlier age, was only published in the twentieth century. The idealization of the medieval battlefield was also reflected in narrative accounts of historical conflicts popularized in theatre and print. The Edo period is certainly the most significant source of historical materials used by modern *bushidō* theorists, but reading these sources can be problematic. Much of what is popularly considered to be the *bushidō* canon, including the works of Yamaga Sokō (1622–85), Nakae Tōju (1608–48), Yamamoto Tsunetomo (1659–1719), and Daidōji Yūzan (1639–1730), was carefully selected, compiled, and interpreted in the early twentieth century for political and practical expediencies rather than in the spirit of 'disinterested' scholarship. There is a strong, if often unconscious tendency for writers on *bushidō* to examine earlier samurai thought and behaviour through interpretive lenses ground primarily in Meiji.

The nostalgia felt by samurai in the Edo period also depended on another notion—that of belonging to an exclusive class, with some recent scholars arguing that the awareness of being *bushi*—translated as 'warrior' or 'samurai'—was what distinguished *bushi* from the rest of society.[4] The nature of this awareness, however, varied considerably in different times and regions, especially towards the end of the Edo period. Another common theme found in documents relating to the samurai was the notion of 'the two ways of letteredness and martiality' (*bunbu ryōdō*), with almost all commentators agreeing that a balance between martial and civil virtues was essential. This ideal was important enough to be given priority in

[1] Hurst III, G. Cameron, 'Death, Honor, and Loyalty: The Bushidō Ideal', *Philosophy East and West* 40:4 (Oct. 1990), pp. 511–27; Friday, Karl F., 'Bushidō or Bull? A Medieval Historian's Perspective on the Imperial Army and the Japanese Warrior Tradition', *The History Teacher* 27:3 (May 1994), pp. 339–49.

[2] Friday, Karl F. (2004), *Samurai, Warfare, and the State in Early Medieval Japan* (New York: Routledge), pp. 135–63; Hurst III, G. Cameron (1997), 'The Warrior as Ideal for a New Age', in Jeffrey P. Mass (ed.), *The Origins of Japan's Medieval World* (Stanford: Stanford University Press), p. 210.

[3] Conlan, Thomas (2003), *State of War: The Violent Order of Fourteenth-Century Japan* (Ann Arbor: University of Michigan Press).

[4] Kanno Kakumyō (2004), *Bushidō no gyakushū* (Tokyo: Kōdansha gendai shinsho), p. 225.

the shogunate's official *Regulations for the Military Houses*. In spite of widespread agreement on the importance of balancing martiality and letteredness, however, the meaning of these two concepts was not always clear, nor was this binary only invoked by samurai. Similarly, with certain significant exceptions, the Confucian ideals and arguments that comprise the bulk of ethical texts from the Edo period were not always limited to a specific class, or even Japan. In a farewell letter written before participating in the famous Akō Incident, Ōtaka Gengo (1672–1703) justified his actions by stating that the ancient way of the warrior of China and Japan did not allow vendettas to remain unfulfilled.[5] Conversely, the few texts that did address the samurai exclusively tended to restrict the applicability of their message to certain domains or even families. The *Hagakure*, which came to be described as the 'bible of *bushidō*' in the twentieth century, explicitly limited its scope to the Nabeshima domain of Kyūshū and portrayed samurai of other areas, especially the Kamigata region of Kyoto and Osaka, as degenerate city-dwellers.[6] As Yamamoto Hirofumi has argued, there were no written works which large numbers of samurai could have used to understand the 'way of the warrior'.[7]

Pre-Meiji texts had little influence on the early development of modern *bushidō*, and came to be selectively invoked for legitimization only after the outlines of discourse had already been established. Nonetheless, their suitability for this purpose reveals a certain samurai-specific significance. This was one important criterion by which Edo documents were selected for modern *bushidō* canons, although other factors often weighed more heavily in the minds of editors. The retrospective uniform labelling of very diverse philosophies as '*bushidō*' has given the idea of a historical samurai ethic broad currency, and the great influence certain historical texts and incidents have on modern *bushidō* discourse means that they should not simply be dismissed. Furthermore, the gap between the abolition of the samurai and the beginning of *bushidō* discourse in Meiji was less than two decades, meaning that most of the early theorists had either been or at least had direct experience of actual samurai.

The portrayal of *bushidō* as a national character in modern Japan had precedents among Edo-period writers who differentiated themselves from an external 'other'. Luke Roberts uses the terms 'nation' and 'national' to refer to Japan after 1868, while describing certain aspects of early modern culture as 'protonational'.[8] This study follows this convention, as the 'national' idea of a unique Japanese character was an important theme in many 'prenational' *bushi* writings. Protonational theories concerning Japan's martial nature, as opposed to the excessive—and

---

[5] Smith II, Henry D., 'The Capacity of Chūshingura', *Monumenta Nipponica* 58:1 (Spring 2003), p. 15.
[6] Maruyama Masao (1974), *Studies in the Intellectual History of Tokugawa Japan* (Princeton: Princeton University Press), p. 332; Roberts, Luke S. (2012), *Performing the Great Peace: Political Space and Open Secrets in Tokugawa Japan* (Honolulu: University of Hawai'i Press), p. 47.
[7] Yamamoto Hirofumi (2006), *Nihonjin no kokoro: bushidō nyūmon* (Tokyo: Chūkei shuppan), p. 19.
[8] Roberts, Luke S., *Performing the Great Peace: Political Space and Open Secrets in Tokugawa Japan*, pp. 8–10.

'weak'—civility of the Chinese 'other', were often discussed by warriors who saw their class as the designated embodiment of this character, even if they did not agree on their role in this context, nor on the degree of success with which they were fulfilling it. The relationship between civil and martial virtues was one of the most ancient and divisive issues in *bushi* thought, affecting protonational and national discourses on Japanese identity well into the modern period.

Within Japan, the Tokugawa shogunate (*c.*1603–1868) used legislation to separate warriors from the other classes, resulting in the development of certain forms of class consciousness. Furthermore, the paradoxical situation of the samurai in the Edo period—as a warrior class in a period of peace—was a considerable impetus for arguments justifying their exalted position in the social order. Before the early seventeenth century, opportunities for the practical application of martial skills made abstract theories regarding warriorhood seem unnecessary, and few texts from this time were deemed useful by modern *bushidō* theorists. Another factor that made early texts less relevant to *bushidō* was the absence of a defined warrior class beyond a certain elite before the Azuchi-Momoyama period (*c.*1568–1600), and the distinction between warrior and civilian among lower-ranking or part-time fighters was not always clear.[9] Douglas Howland argues that only at the end of the sixteenth century did the concept of *mibun* (social status) became important in Japan as a representation of 'a conservative wish to reduce social fluidity and to fix social status'.[10] During the fixing of the social classes in the late sixteenth and early seventeenth centuries, the *bushi* were losing the practical distinction of being active warriors, as there was little or no opportunity for applying the martial skills that theoretically justified samurai domination of the political sphere.

During the Edo period, changing economic conditions meant that class distinctions were often at odds with social status, and scholars are fundamentally reconsidering the applicability of the concepts of 'class' and 'status' in this context. The situation was further complicated by regional differences, as certain groups were considered samurai in some domains but not in others.[11] This partially accounts for the great discrepancies in the percentage of the population that was considered to be samurai in different domains. Sekiyama Naotarō's analysis of the period 1870–73 concludes that the percentage of samurai in various domains ranged from under four per cent to more than twenty-seven per cent, with a national average of 6.40 per cent.[12] In spite of the ostensibly rigid divide between samurai and commoners, economic necessity resulted in a certain degree of fluidity, especially in the lower orders. Albert Craig points out that even reducing terms in official

[9] Gomi Fumihiko has discussed the variety of warriors in late Heian and Kamakura, and the difficulties in differentiating between groups of warriors, pirates, and bandits. Gomi Fumihiko (1997), *Sasshō to shinkō: bushi wo saguru* (Tokyo: Kakugawa sensho), pp. 140, 256.

[10] Howland, Douglas R., 'Samurai Status, Class, and Bureaucracy: A Historiographical Essay', *The Journal of Asian Studies* 60:2 (May 2001), p. 355.

[11] Howland, Douglas R., 'Samurai Status, Class, and Bureaucracy', pp. 361–62, 374.

[12] Sekiyama Naotarō (1958), *Kinsei Nihon no jinkō kōzō: Tokugawa jidai no jinkō chōsa to jinkō jōtai ni kansuru kenkyū* (Tokyo: Yoshikawa kōbunkan), pp. 307–14.

posts could not accommodate the many samurai in need of work, and that '[B]y as early as 1705 almost a quarter of the vassals of the shogun were jobless. The best qualified were taken for posts appropriate to their rank, and the rest—including the young, the old, the sick, and the incompetent—were left idle'.[13] As the period went on, samurai found their social status increasingly challenged by economically powerful commoners, some of whom purchased or received samurai privileges such as the right to wear swords. For example, the representatives of the Kaitokudō merchant academy in Osaka were granted permission to wear swords when meeting with government officials.[14] Luke Roberts discusses situations where villagers assumed the mantle of samurai within the limits of village society, although they would give up this pretense if visited by officials from outside the community.[15]

Some samurai sought to legitimize their privileged social standing and a number of texts later incorporated into modern *bushidō* canons were products of this Edo period dynamic. Furthermore, of the few documents concerning pre-Tokugawa events taken up into modern *bushidō* discourse, the majority were written or heavily edited after the 1650s. Recent scholars largely dismiss the idealized accounts of medieval warriors as later products reflecting seventeenth-century concerns rather than actual battlefield conduct. Even Inoue Tetsujirō, who traced the history of the 'unique Japanese *bushidō* spirit' to the mythical Plain of High Heaven, admitted that *bushidō* had not been codified before the late seventeenth century, when the samurai had sufficient respite from warfare to pursue literary activities.[16] With regard to warrior ethics, the importance of the earlier period lies primarily in providing Edo thinkers with a historical space and reference points that, in an idealized form, could be summoned to lend legitimacy to the domination of the political order by the samurai.

This romanticization of earlier history is evident in the enigmatic *Hagakure* of Yamamoto Tsunetomo, which was compiled in the early eighteenth century and structured around a series of anecdotes involving the ancestral lords of the Nabeshima domain. The *Hagakure*'s famous opening line equating the way of the samurai with finding death set the tone for behavioural guidelines modelled on an idealized view of the battlefield. According to Yamamoto, the martial nature and readiness to serve gave *bushi* the right to have power of life and death over non-samurai, who were innately inferior.[17] The institution of rudeness-killing (*burei-uchi*) did permit samurai to kill commoners for perceived slights, but the obvious social disorder that this practice was likely to cause meant that it was rarely

---

[13] Craig, Albert (1961), *Choshu in the Meiji Restoration* (Cambridge: Harvard University Press), p. 13.

[14] Najita, Tetsuo (1987), *Visions of Virtue in Tokugawa Japan: The Kaitokudō Merchant Academy of Ōsaka* (Chicago: University of Chicago Press), p. 74.

[15] Roberts, Luke S., *Performing the Great Peace*, pp. 34–35.

[16] Inoue Tetsujirō (1901), *Bushidō* (Tokyo: Heiji zasshi sha), p. 41.

[17] This view can also be found in the seventeenth-century *Kōyōgunkan*, which stated that it was not possible for commoners to be like *bushi*. Sagara Tōru, ed. (1968), *Kōyōgunkan, Gorinsho, Hagakure-shū (Nihon no shisō 9)* (Chikuma shobō), p. 83.

applied.[18] This can be seen in an 1824 incident described by Roberts, in which a samurai wife killed an inferior in her house and claimed that he had been rude. The investigating officials did not dispute this, but still punished her and all members of the household for creating a situation in which a potential troublemaker was present in the private area of the home.[19] There was no love lost on the other side of the class divide either, and the disdain most commoners had for the samurai has been described as 'legendary'.[20] Andō Shōeki (1703–62), for example, derided the samurai as parasites on society, while the National Learning scholar Kamo no Mabuchi (1697–1769) put forth the oft-cited social criticism that the more people one killed, the higher one's rank, inferring that the shogun was the biggest murderer in the land.[21] By the mid-nineteenth century, however, increasing social mobility had blurred some distinctions among warriors and between warriors and commoners, and even many influential *bushi* questioned the innate supremacy of their class.

Along with the *Hagakure*, perhaps the most influential Edo period texts cited in modern *bushidō* discourse were the writings of the strategist Yamaga Sokō, who justified the exalted status of the samurai as follows:

> The tasks of a samurai are to reflect on his person, to find a lord and do his best in service, to interact with his companions in a trustworthy and warm manner, and to be mindful of his position while making duty his focus. In addition, he will not be able to prevent involvement in parent-child, sibling, and spousal relationships. Without these, there could be no proper human morality among all the other people under Heaven, but the tasks of farmers, artisans, and merchants do not allow free time, so they are not always able to follow them and fulfill the Way. A samurai puts aside the tasks of the farmers, artisans and merchants, and the Way is his exclusive duty. In addition, if ever a person who is improper with regard to human morality appears among the three common classes, the samurai quickly punishes them, thus ensuring correct Heavenly morality on Earth. It should not be that a samurai knows the virtues of letteredness and martiality, but does not use them. Therefore, formally a samurai will prepare for use of swords, lances, bows, and horses, while inwardly he will endeavor in the ways of lord-vassal, friend-friend, parent-child, brother-brother, and husband-wife relations. In his mind he has the way of letteredness, while outwardly he is martially prepared. The three common classes make him their teacher and honour him, and in accordance with his teachings they come to know what is essential and what is insignificant...
>
> Therefore, it can be said that the essence of the samurai is in understanding his task and function.[22]

[18] Ikegami, Eiko (1995), *The Taming of the Samurai: Honorific Individualism and the Making of Modern Japan* (Cambridge, MA: Harvard University Press), pp. 244–45.

[19] Roberts, Luke S., *Performing the Great Peace*, p. 31.

[20] Pincus, Leslie (1996), *Authenticating Culture in Japan: Kuki Shūzō and the Rise of National Aesthetics* (Berkeley: University of California Press), pp. 130–32.

[21] Holmes, Colin and A. H. Ion, 'Bushido and the Samurai' *Modern Asian Studies* 14:2 (1980), p. 310; Kanno Kakumyō, *Bushidō no gyakushū*, pp. 39–40.

[22] Yamaga Sokō (1970), *Yamaga Sokō (Nihon shisō taikei 32)* (Tokyo: Iwanami shoten), pp. 32–33. Translation adapted from: Benesch, Oleg (2011), 'Samurai Thought', in James Heisig et al. (ed.), *Japanese Philosophy: A Sourcebook* (Honolulu: University of Hawaii Press), p. 1109.

Yamaga reasoned that one of the major differences between samurai and common-ers was that the former had more time to focus on the nature of ethical behaviour and could therefore serve as moral guides for the rest of society, a role similar to idealized Confucian gentlemen. Yamaga's proposal was compromised by factors such as unemployment and low stipends, which rendered many *bushi* unable to make an idealistic 'Way' their 'exclusive duty,' and Yamaga spent much of his own life in search of a patron. In addition, the specific content of the 'Way' he outlined was not sufficiently clear or widely accepted so as to serve as a useful moral guide.[23] Furthermore, Yamaga's preferred term '*shidō*' lacks the overt martiality of '*bushidō*', instead invoking images of Confucian gentlemen-scholars. As Howland argues, although Confucian models were applied by Yamaga, Ogyū Sorai (1666–1728), and others to provide a theoretical justification for samurai rule, the parallels drawn between samurai and Chinese gentlemen-scholars were not entirely satisfactory, as contemporary Japanese scholars and foreign observers realized full well.[24]

Both the *Hagakure* and Yamaga's writings were incorporated into the mod-ern *bushidō* canon, but neither of these texts was especially influential before the twentieth century. Due also to its controversial and potentially subversive content, the *Hagakure* was only circulated within Nabeshima domain in manuscript form and not published until after the Russo-Japanese War. Yamaga's works were bet-ter known, but were not very influential during or immediately after his lifetime. Slanderous claims regarding Yamaga's association with the loyal retainers of Akō (discussed later on) as well as Yamaga's own exile to that domain, contributed to the closure of his school in the eighteenth century. His teachings were only kept alive in several *tozama* domains—'outer' houses that declared loyalty to the Tokugawa only belatedly—where they would be revived in the late Tokugawa period through the efforts of Yoshida Shōin and other activists.[25] The same was true of another text often cited by modern *bushidō* theorists, Daidōji Yūzan's *Primer on the Martial Way*, compiled in the early eighteenth century and first published in 1834.[26]

Regional and temporal variations in the warrior class over the Edo period, which tended heavily towards bureaucratization for those samurai fortunate enough to be employed, resulted in a perceived need for definition and legitimization of the role of the *bushi* in an age of peace. Towards the end of the period, especially, samurai felt considerable pressure to identify characteristics that made them different from and superior to the other classes. The sense that their position was under threat contributed to the vitriol directed towards commoners in the writings of some samurai, but, especially towards the end of the Edo period, both samurai and non-samurai increasingly rejected the notion that there were fundamental differ-ences between the classes. Depending on the specific region and period, the strati-fications within the *bushi* and commoner ranks created situations in which the

---

[23] Takayanagi Mitsutoshi (1960), *Bushidō: Nihon bunka kenkyū 8* (Tokyo: Shinchōsha), pp. 3–7.

[24] Howland, Douglas R. 'Samurai Status, Class, and Bureaucracy', p. 356.

[25] Tucker, John Allen, 'Tokugawa Intellectual History and Prewar Ideology', *Sino-Japanese Studies* 14 (2002), pp. 40–41; Uenaka Shuzo, 'Last Testament in Exile: Yamaga Sokō's *Haisho Zampitsu*', pp. 127–28.

[26] Kōsaka Jirō (1987), *Genroku bushigaku: 'Budō shoshinshū' wo yomu* (Tokyo: Chūōkōron), p. 15.

differences within classes were often greater than between them. Henry D. Smith relies on the stratification within the ranks to explain a discrepancy in accounts of the 1703 Akō Incident, which famously involved forty-seven masterless samurai, only forty-six of whom surrendered to the authorities and were condemned to *seppuku* in the aftermath. According to Smith, the forty-seventh and lowest-ranked samurai, Terasaka Kichiemon (1665–1747) was dismissed by the group immediately following the event as they did not want his status as a foot soldier (*ashigaru*) to reflect on the rest of them and cause difficulties or embarrassment. The government responded by simply striking his name from the list of accused.[27]

The ostensibly elevated status of *bushi* in the Tokugawa social order, and their awareness of the same, were the most meaningful theoretical factors connecting the majority of *bushi*. Their status was primarily a political and professional distinction, and the very diverse religious, behavioural, and ethical views of the samurai were more likely to be determined by influences other than their profession. This diversity makes it possible to select certain examples of warrior writings and behaviour to argue for almost any interpretation of the 'nature' of *bushi*, and such discussions tend to be a reflection of the times and situation of their authors rather than an accurate depiction of any greater 'way of the samurai'. Samurai were naturally aware of their special social status, but this consciousness of belonging to an elite varied greatly depending on time, location, and the specific situation of the individual *bushi*, especially if they were economically inferior to some commoners. For many samurai, the differences within their class seemed greater than those between the classes, and class consciousness did not serve as the basis for a widely accepted ethic, nor was it easily integrated into nationalistic modern *bushidō* ideologies that could serve a supposedly classless society.

THE AKŌ VENDETTA IN SAMURAI CONSCIOUSNESS AND HISTORICAL CONTEXT

While it is difficult to find common points of reference that could be used for a broad comparison of warrior thought before 1868, the Akō Incident of 1703 is one event that often serves as a fulcrum for attempts to excavate a Japanese warrior ethic. This event is frequently mentioned in discussions of samurai ethics and behaviour, and has influenced modern *bushidō* discourse from at least 1901, when Inoue Tetsujirō described the loyal retainers of Akō as the manifestation of *bushidō*.[28] The Akō Incident became one of the most popular sources for samurai narratives by the mid-eighteenth century and from Meiji onward was incorporated into *bushidō*-related reassessments that posited it as the key event in Japanese warrior history.

The number of individuals directly involved in the incident itself was relatively small, especially when compared with some of the rebellions and uprisings that

---

[27] Smith II, Henry D., 'The Trouble with Terasaka', *Japan Review* 16 (2004), pp. 5, 38–41.
[28] Inoue Tetsujirō, *Bushidō*, p. 51.

occurred during the Edo period, but its symbolic importance far outweighed its immediate political impact. Many scholars examined the possible motivations and ethics of the incident and earlier thinkers were reconsidered in its light. Yamaga Sokō, for example, was later credited with influencing the actions of the Akō samurai, a historically questionable claim that nevertheless contributed to him being revered as the 'sage of *bushidō*' by modern writers. The lack of reliable information regarding the events that transpired complicates attempts to situate the Akō affair in the historical framework of samurai thought and behaviour. The popularity of subsequent dramatizations of the incident has served to further obfuscate the motives and roles of the central actors, and certain misconceptions continue to dominate discourse even after historians have demonstrated their inherent problems.

According to the generally accepted outline of the incident, the lord of Akō domain, Asano Naganori (1667–1701), was in charge of ceremonies receiving emissaries from the imperial court to Edo castle. In the course of these events, he drew his sword and lightly wounded Kira Yoshinaka (1641–1703), the shogunate's chief protocol officer. Asano was arrested for the capital crime of drawing his sword in the castle and condemned to *seppuku* the same day. His domain was confiscated by the shogunate and his retainers were dispersed and became masterless samurai. Twenty-two months later, a group of forty-seven of these retainers under the leadership of Ōishi Yoshio (1659–1703) attacked Kira's residence in Edo and beheaded him. They took Kira's head to Asano's grave at Sengakuji, from where forty-six of the samurai notified the shogunate and calmly awaited arrest. After six weeks of deliberation by the government, the samurai were sentenced to death by *seppuku*, thereby concluding the incident.

The paucity of historical evidence has led later commentators to speculate on many possible explanations for the original feud between Asano and Kira, from romantic competition to commercial rivalries to psychological issues. There is similar disagreement with regard to the later attack on Kira's mansion, although there is considerably more evidence regarding this event. The modern popular view of this incident is that the Akō samurai were motivated by vengeance for the death of Asano, in line with their 'samurai duty'. Taken in the broader context of the Edo period, the Akō Incident is an anomaly, representing possibly the *only* case of a lord being avenged by his retainers. Of the 118 separate revenge killings recorded during this time, 115 were carried out by family members avenging a slain father, brother, mother, or uncle. Two of the three remaining incidents were perpetrated by non-samurai, leaving the Akō vendetta as a unique case of retainers carrying out a revenge killing during the Edo period.[29] These figures also reflect the character of the Tokugawa system, which permitted revenge only in cases where the killing of an older direct relation—usually a father—had gone unpunished.[30]

Government and society could be understanding when the situation involved the death of a family member, but ties to a lord or higher-ranking samurai were not

---

[29] Kokushi daijiten henshū iinkai, ed. (1983), *Kokushi dai jiten* (Vol. 3) (Tokyo: Yoshikawa kobunkan), pp. 348–53.
[30] Ikegami Eiko, *The Taming of the Samurai*, p. 247.

considered sufficient grounds for exacting lethal vengeance. Smith indicates that there may be a case for familial ties or sexual relationships between Asano and certain of his samurai, which would give the vendetta a more mundane yet plausible background within the historical context.[31] Had he been alive at the time, Yamaga Sokō could have agreed with this hypothesis, as he had criticized the extreme displays of loyalty known as *junshi*—suicide following the death of one's lord—as an unfortunate consequence of sexual relations between samurai.[32] The Akō affair was also problematic because, even if lord-vassal vendettas had been accepted practice, this incident did not fit the definition. As a number of observers pointed out after the attack, Kira did not kill Asano, but was merely the plaintiff in a case in which the shogunate condemned Asano to death.

Rather than an exemplary manifestation of representative samurai behaviour, the uniqueness of the Akō Incident is a primary reason that it continues to attract a great deal of interest. Theorists have outlined a wide variety of possible motivations for Ōishi and his compatriots, indicating dissatisfaction with the simplistic view of the incident as a pure vendetta. The execution of Asano and confiscation of his domain cost the former Akō retainers their livelihood and positions, and years after the incident, the Confucian scholar Satō Naokata (1650–1719) accused them of acting not from any higher ideals, but simply to regain their former status and income.[33] Some commentators have also attributed economic motives to the Akō samurai, arguing that they had hoped to distinguish themselves in front of potential new employers through the successful prosecution of the vendetta. This argument is supported by the lack of evidence of preparation for death on the part of the avengers. According to Smith, although subsequent accounts of the incident state that the forty-seven considered *seppuku*, no provision seems to have been made for the period following the attack, and there was some considerable disagreement between the members of the band regarding the proper course of action after the completion of their mission.[34]

The motivations of the Akō retainers will probably remain subjects of debate, and the discord amongst the forty-seven indicates that each had his own reasons for participating in the action. Smith, relying on Miyazawa Seiichi and Taniguchi Shinko, presents compelling evidence that some of the Akō samurai were influenced by romanticized accounts such as the medieval *Taiheiki* (*Record of Great Peace*), and may have sought to emulate the great deeds found in Japanese and Chinese historical narratives.[35] Given the anomalous character of the Akō affair and the uncertainty surrounding its details, its primary significance in the context of *bushidō* and samurai ethics lies less in the incident itself, but rather in the responses to it.

---

[31] Smith II, Henry D., 'The Capacity of Chūshingura', p. 12.
[32] Ikegami Eiko, *The Taming of the Samurai*, p. 310.
[33] Satō Naokata (1974), 'Satō Naokata 47 nin no hikki', in Ishii Shirō (ed.), *Kinsei buke shisō (Nihon shisō taikei 27)*, (Tokyo: Iwanami shoten), p. 379.
[34] Smith II, Henry D., 'The Trouble with Terasaka', pp. 41–43.
[35] Smith II, Henry D., 'The Capacity of Chūshingura', pp. 13–15.

Partially due to the shogunal prohibition on the publication of works concerning the Akō Incident, which was in force until the 1850s, many of the contemporary sources that discussed the incident were in the form of manuscripts circulated among Confucian scholars. As a result, the surviving commentaries have been criticized as being 'Confucian thinking about samurai' rather than representing actual samurai thought.[36] As early as the 1730s, Goi Ranshū (1695–1762), himself a teacher of Zhu Xi's Neo-Confucianism, attacked other Confucian critics of the Akō samurai, arguing that Confucian scholars could never comprehend the ways of thinking that motivated warriors.[37] This charge failed to account for the writings of the Akō samurai themselves, however, as Smith points out: 'virtually no precedent existed for avenging the death of one's lord—a fact of which certain of the Akō [samurai] were acutely aware, leading them to seek justification instead in Chinese Confucian texts'.[38] Confucian ethics were introduced into the incident by the Akō samurai themselves, and criticisms by Confucian scholars cannot be simply dismissed as coming from a value system different from and foreign to that in which the Akō samurai acted.

Even among Confucian commentators there was great diversity of opinion concerning the incident. Goi's direct target was Dazai Shundai (1680–1747), who took the Akō samurai to task on the fundamental issue of the legitimacy of their vendetta. Dazai reasoned that there were no grounds for attacking Kira, as he had not killed their lord or even condemned him to death. Instead, the shogunate should have been their actual target, and it was merely cowardice that drove them to go after the much easier target of Kira.[39] Dazai argued that, rather than sneaking around and biding their time, the Akō samurai should have made a heroic final stand at their former lord's castle, in which case their numbers would surely have been far greater.[40] Dazai's former teacher Ogyū Sorai (1666–1728) took a more pragmatic stance, criticizing the Akō samurai's violent act as counterproductive and disruptive to the social order. Instead, Ogyū argued, they should have worked within the law to regain their confiscated domain in the name of Asano's son, rather than compounding their lord's initial crime through further, more serious transgressions.[41]

On another side of the argument were a large number of Confucian scholars who supported the actions of the Akō samurai. Goi lauded the samurai for their selflessness and single-minded devotion to duty, dismissing as 'foolish' the notion that they should have perished at Akō castle. Arguing that Ōishi did not expect to live, Goi speculated that, in the unlikely event of receiving a shogunal pardon,

---

[36] Smith II, Henry D., 'The Capacity of Chūshingura', p. 4 n. 7.

[37] Goi Ranshū (1974), 'Baku Dazai Jun Akō 46 shi ron', in Ishii Shirō (ed.), *Kinsei buke shisō (Nihon shisō taikei 27)* (Tokyo: Iwanami shoten), p. 421.

[38] Smith II, Henry D., 'The Capacity of Chūshingura', p. 6.

[39] Dazai Shundai (1974), 'Akō 46 shi ron', in Ishii Shirō (ed.), *Kinsei buke shisō (Nihon shisō taikei 27)*, (Tokyo: Iwanami shoten), p. 407.

[40] Dazai Shundai, pp. 407, 408.

[41] Ogyū Sorai (1974), '47 shi ron', in Ishii Shirō (ed.), *Kinsei buke shisō (Nihon shisō taikei 27)*, Tokyo: Iwanami shoten), p. 400.

Ōishi would surely have returned to Sengakuji and committed *seppuku* at his lord's grave.[42] The head of the shogunal Shōhei School, Hayashi Hōkō (1644–1732), was another scholar who supported the Akō samurai. Hayashi saw them as tragic figures who were doomed by their circumstances, and relied on Chinese Confucian texts to argue that revenge was their inescapable duty. Hayashi also conceded that the shogunate—his employer—was correct in executing them for their transgressions against the law, arguing that the actions of both sides were in accordance with rightness and duty.[43] Muro Kyūsō (1658–1734) took a similar view, relying on the examples of the legendary Chinese figures Bo Yi and Shu Qi to portray Ōishi and his followers as tragic heroes and the shogunate as acting in accordance with the law.[44] The surviving documents reveal deep divisions among Confucian scholars in their evaluations of the Akō Incident, and a variety of Chinese precedents were invoked to bolster their arguments.

The charge that Confucian criticism of the Akō samurai was not relevant typically assumes the existence of a separate, widely accepted ethical norm that was more suitable for judging samurai behaviour. Modern promoters of *bushidō* often contend that the vendetta was in keeping with samurai ethics at the time, but there are few surviving non-Confucian commentaries. This is due partially to the government ban on publications about the incident, although the number of Confucian commentaries reveals its limitations. A more fundamental factor was that there was no widely accepted 'way of the samurai' that could plausibly serve as an alternative evaluative framework. To be sure, even Confucian scholars mentioned 'unique' aspects of Japan's martial character in their discussions of the vendetta, and Goi supported the Akō samurai's action on these grounds. Dazai Shundai also referred to the influence of native characteristics, claiming that when Japanese samurai saw their lord killed, they would go crazy and try to do right through killing. According to Dazai, virtuous people who saw this would think it a useless death, but that this 'way' existed nonetheless on the basis of the traditions of the land and house.[45] Dazai disagreed with Goi on this point, however, and criticized the Akō samurai using both Confucian and 'Japanese' arguments, stating that their actions were what Mencius called 'righteousness that is not righteousness'.[46]

One of the few assessments of the Akō vendetta made primarily in the context of samurai ethics can be found in the *Hagakure*. Like Dazai, Yamamoto Tsunetomo condemned the Akō samurai on the basis of what he considered appropriate warrior behaviour, although his reasoning and conclusions were considerably different. According to Yamamoto, the Akō samurai should have attacked Kira's residence immediately on hearing the news of Asano's death, for even though this futile effort would have resulted in their certain death and failure to kill Kira, their

[42] Goi Ranshū, 'Baku Dazai Jun Akō 46 shi ron', p. 421–22.

[43] Hayashi Hōkō (1974), 'Fukushū ron' in Ishii Shirō (ed.), *Kinsei buke shisō (Nihon shisō taikei 27)* (Tokyo: Iwanami shoten), p. 374.

[44] Muro Kyūsō (1974), 'Akō gijin roku', in Ishii Shirō (ed.), *Kinsei buke shisō (Nihon shisō taikei 27)*, Tokyo: Iwanami shoten), pp. 272–73.

[45] Goi Ranshū, 'Baku Dazai Jun Akō 46 shi ron', p. 407.

[46] Goi Ranshū, pp. 407, 408.

honour would have been intact and this would have eliminated the danger of Kira dying of other causes before they could act. Yamamoto also argued that they compounded this grievous mistake by waiting for the authorities, rather than committing *seppuku* immediately on arrival at Sengakuji.[47]

The Akō Incident presented the government with an unprecedented situation and many different approaches to the matter were considered. Regardless of their motivations, the Akō samurai had committed serious offences, not least of which was the murder of a high official. At the same time, they had not rebelled directly against the shogunate, had notified the officials, and waited peacefully at Sengakuji to be arrested after the incident. In consideration of this, the forty-six samurai who surrendered on the morning after the attack were sentenced to death by *seppuku* rather than a less honourable common execution. The complexity of the government's deliberations concerning the appropriate charges and punishments was reflected in the diversity of subsequent debates on the incident, even if the participants relied primarily on Confucian morality. Ultimately, the few surviving texts from the time that judge the Akō samurai on the basis of 'samurai ethics' were generally more critical of the vendetta than modern promoters of *bushidō* have been, and neither the Akō Incident nor the myriad reactions to it provide compelling evidence for the existence of a broadly accepted warrior ethic.

BALANCING LETTEREDNESS AND MARTIALITY

The diversity of Japanese warriors in different regions, historical periods, and ranks is reflected in their writings, but there are certain concepts found in many texts by and for warriors that have been presented as evidence for the existence of a samurai ethic. Attitudes towards loyalty and death have frequently been mentioned in this context, but there was no general agreement on the content or importance of these ideals. Unilateral loyalty to superiors was highly unusual on medieval battlefields, and the reality of the Tokugawa peace made pronouncements extolling the virtues of self-sacrifice seem anachronistic and potentially subversive. Olivier Ansart examines the concept of *chū*—usually translated as 'loyalty'—in the seventeenth and eighteenth centuries, demonstrating the lack of any consensus regarding its meaning or requirements among samurai in the Edo period.[48] In addition to the disagreements between written sources, the reality of 'samurai' practices was often obfuscated by misleading idealizations, both contemporary and retrospective.

One concept that can be found in texts from almost all periods of Japanese history, and is useful for understanding the diversity and shifts in thought, is the binary of *bun* and *bu*, meaning 'civil' or 'letteredness' (*bun*) and 'military' or 'martiality' (*bu*). From the time of its introduction from China, where it is known as *wen-wu*, the nature of the relationship between *bun* and *bu* was an important theoretical

---

[47] Yamamoto Tsunetomo (1978), *Hagakure zenshū* (Gogatsu shobō), p. 36.
[48] Ansart, Olivier, 'Loyalty in Seventeenth and Eighteenth Century Samurai Discourse', *Japanese Studies* 27:2 (Sept. 2007), pp. 139–54.

consideration for civilian and military officials. Its influence remained strong long after the samurai had been abolished, with the official Imperial Japanese Army organ *Kaikōsha kiji* referring to it as the 'most important concept for the modern age' in 1927.[49] The pervasiveness of *bun-bu* theories makes the binary a useful tool for the comparative examination of other concepts posited as characteristic of samurai thought.

References to *bun* and *bu* appear in the very earliest Japanese histories, including the *Nihon shoki* (*Records of Japan*) of 720.[50] At this early stage, the concept was understood in much the same manner as in contemporary Tang China, and several court posts made use of the term. *Bun* and *bu* were considered to be the two pillars of successful government, and letteredness was given distinct priority over martiality as it had been in China. With the rise of provincial warrior power and the formation of the first shogunate in the late twelfth century, the importance of military competence increased. In the Kamakura period (1185–1333), *bun* and *bu* were widely understood to be the domains of courtiers and warriors, respectively, and few individuals were acknowledged to have fulfilled both roles. The locus of power gradually shifted towards warrior government, and by the fourteenth century the notion of warrior rule was widely accepted, with the tasks of civil and military administration the responsibility of a single group.[51] Cameron Hurst analyzes fourteenth-century texts, especially warrior house codes, indicating that writers regarded *bu* as self-evident, and therefore focused their attentions on *bun* in order to develop the civil skills and cultural knowledge required to run a government.[52] In the turmoil of the late fifteenth and sixteenth centuries, it was necessary for warriors to rule and defend their domains against constant threats, and the skilled application of both *bun* and *bu* was considered indispensible for survival. As a result, the unity of *bun* and *bu*, often compared with the 'two wings of a bird' or 'two wheels of a cart' in contemporary documents, was one of the most widely repeated themes in the warrior house codes of the period.

Bun-bu thought continued into the Edo period, becoming an important theme in the Tokugawa *Buke shohatto* (*Regulations for the Military Houses*) of 1615, as well as in successive reissues. Sporadic conflicts and rebellions continued well into the seventeenth century, but the warrior class began to shift away from the battlefield towards a more peaceful existence, influencing theories of *bun* and *bu*. The *bun-bu* binary is found in a great number of samurai writings from the Edo period, which tended to describe the two as inseparable, but gave primacy to martiality over letteredness. The increasing dissemination of Confucian ideas and sophistication of Japanese philosophers, combined with the growth of native schools of thought, also took *bun-bu* philosophy in new directions.

Bun-bu thought in mid-Edo differed from earlier discourse in two important aspects: proto-nationalism; and a shift from the practical to the metaphysical.

---

[49] Okada Meitarō, 'Bushidō rinri no shiteki kenkyū (part 2)' *Kaikōsha kiji* 641 (1927), p. 23.
[50] Shiraki Yutaka, 'Bunbu kakusho', *Jissen joshi daigaku kiyō* 7 (March 1962), pp. 89–91.
[51] Hurst III, G. Cameron, 'The Warrior as Ideal for a New Age', p. 226.
[52] Hurst III, G. Cameron, 'The Warrior as Ideal for a New Age' pp. 215–20.

Japan's military leadership structure prompted many thinkers to identify *bun* and *bu* with China and Japan, respectively, and some argued that Japan's emphasis on martiality arose from the nature of the country. Writing in the early eighteenth century, Daidōji Yūzan held that 'The virtues of this land are different from others, and even the lowest farmers, townsmen, and craftsmen will be prepared and carry a rusty short sword. This is the custom of the martial land of Japan'.[53] Some Japanese thinkers sought religious support for their views, tracing Japan's martial nature back to the country's founding myths. One oft-repeated explanation contended that the Japanese had been divinely endowed with a unique martial spirit by the very creation of the archipelago as drops falling from the tip of a heavenly jeweled spear thrust into the primordial sea by the deities Izanagi and Izanami.[54]

A second characteristic of Edo *bun-bu* thought that set it apart from earlier Japanese interpretations was its increased use as a political or philosophical binary rather than referring to practical civil and martial virtues. According to Nakae Tōju (1608–1648), 'the common explanations of *bun* and *bu* show a great lack of knowledge. To common people, writing songs, composing poetry, mastering literature, having a gentle disposition, and becoming refined are considered to be *bun*. It is said that learning and knowing mounted archery, military drill, and strategy, and having a stern and fierce disposition are *bu*'. Nakae considered this an artificial and incorrect approach, as 'Originally, *bun* and *bu* were a single virtue, and not a thing that could be separated'. Nakae saw the 'intuition of human nature' as a 'single virtue that can be distinguished into *bun* and *bu*', just as 'all of creation is one force' that could be distinguished between *yin* and *yang*. 'Just as *yin* is the root of *yang*, and *yang* is the root of *yin*, *bun* is the root of *bu*, and *bu* is the root of *bun*... *Bun* is correctly practising the way of filial piety, brotherliness, loyalty, and trustworthiness. *Bu* is striving to eliminate things that obstruct filial piety, brotherliness, loyalty, and trustworthiness'.[55]

Even thinkers who accepted the notion of Japan as the divine martial country warned against the excessive practice of martial arts, which were growing rapidly in popularity. As Nakae's student Kumazawa Banzan (1619–91), who also defined Japan as the 'country of *bu*', wrote in the peaceful late seventeenth century, 'if one greatly values bows, arrows, and guns, it is like making death ten times as important as life'. According to Kumazawa, 'Warriors who are blind to *bun* and without the reason of the teaching of the Way [Confucianism] will have minds that merely lean towards martiality and consider it to be most important'. Furthermore, 'calling a person who knows civil arts and military arts a master of "the two ways of *bun* and *bu*" is not unusual. However, this should be called "knowing the two arts of *bun* and *bu*." If one only studies arts without wisdom, benevolence, and

---

[53] Daidōji Yūzan (1942), 'Budō shoshinshū', in Saeki Ariyoshi et al. (ed.), *Bushidō zensho* 2 (Tokyo: Jidaisha), p. 306.

[54] Benesch, Oleg, 'National Consciousness and the Evolution of the Civil/Martial Binary in East Asia', *Taiwan Journal of East Asian Studies* 8:1:15 (June 2011), pp. 129–71.

[55] Nakae Tōju, 'Bunbu mondō', in Saeki Ariyoshi et al. (eds.), *Bushidō zensho* 2 (Tokyo: Jidaisha) (1942), pp. 246–47.

courage, it can scarcely be called knowing the "two ways".'[56] Kumazawa distinguished between *bun* and *bu* as 'ways' rather than as mere 'arts', reasoning that, if a person served his lord with unfailing devotion and did great work while forgetting himself and his home, he could be an example of both *bun* and *bu* even if he were illiterate and unlearned.[57] The lack of applications for practical military techniques in the Edo period, juxtaposed with the continued awareness of samurai as a warrior class, contributed to increased philosophical abstraction of the *bun-bu* binary.

Those samurai directly involved in the practice of martial arts also emphasized the importance of both *bun* and *bu*, although their approach tended to be more practical than philosophical. The swordsman and Shintō scholar Izawa Nagahide (Banryū; 1668–1730), for example, stressed the importance of training in various martial arts, but qualified this by stating that:

> It is generally thought that we are military men and should therefore only study *bu*, but without learning *bun* it is impossible to know the true meaning of *bu*...In order to learn *bun-bu* one must first study literature and realize the way of loyalty and filial piety, and only afterwards study military techniques.[58]

In contrast with Izawa's estimation of literature, Yamamoto Tsunetomo gave martiality primacy over letteredness, recommending that written documents be immediately burned and destroyed after use, for reading was the task of courtiers, whereas warriors had to focus on their martial role.[59] There was broad agreement on the importance of both *bun* and *bu* throughout the Edo period, although there was considerable debate regarding the gap between the practical and theoretical levels of discourse. The majority of commentators called for a balance between martiality and letteredness, but differences in interpretation typically led to accusations that one aspect or the other was being neglected or excessively favoured, as could already be seen in early writings such as those of Nakae Tōju.

Significantly, social criticism typically referred to an earlier time—in either China or Japan—when an ideal balance of martiality and letteredness had supposedly regulated society. This view held that samurai had declined and degraded over the centuries, although the ancient ideal from which they had fallen varied greatly depending on the individual commentator. Izawa Nagahide, for example, cited the 'Song scholars' as having 'said of *bun-bu* that one should "first master letteredness, then acquire martiality, and all affairs will be settled through the way of *bun* and *bu*"'.[60] In contrast, nativistic thinkers who advocated martiality tended to invoke Japan's mythical past as the true source of the country's character. In spite of the diversity of these arguments

[56] Kumazawa Banzan (1942), 'Shūgi washo (shōroku)', in Saeki Ariyoshi et al. (eds.), *Bushidō zensho 4* (Tokyo: Jidaisha), pp. 121–22.

[57] Kumazawa Banzan, 121–22.

[58] Izawa Nagahide (Banryū) (1942), 'Bushi kun', in Saeki Ariyoshi et al. (eds.), *Bushidō zensho 4*, (Tokyo: Jidaisha), pp. 255–56.

[59] Saiki Kazuma et al. (eds.) (1974), *Mikawa monogatari, hagakure (Nihon shisō taikei 26)* (Iwanami shoten), p. 239 (Book 1–60).

[60] Izawa Nagahide, 'Bushi kun', pp. 255–56.

and conclusions, there was a common theme of nostalgia in almost all types of discourse regarding the samurai. Nostalgic trends increased as the Edo period drew to a close and the condition of the samurai—and the country as a whole—grew ever more uncertain.

By the middle of the nineteenth century, the Tokugawa shogunate's policies limiting Japan's contact with other countries were showing signs of weakness and unenforceability. As unauthorized landings by foreign ships increased, prescriptions relating to *bun-bu* appeared in the writings of thinkers from all major schools, and a renewed focus on martial virtues reflected the widespread belief that the samurai had become incapable of meeting foreign threats. Saitō Setsudō (1797–1865) and other Orthodox Zhu Xi Confucian scholars called on the government's *Regulations for the Military Houses* and repeated earlier arguments regarding the essential unity of *bun* and *bu*, while criticizing the large gap that had arisen between the theoretical and practical approaches to the binary. According to Saitō:

> The way of *bun-bu* is two things that become one. It is one thing that becomes two. With *bu* one should administer the virtue of *bun*, while with *bun* one should also perform valorous martial acts. To be swept up by the *bun* of the men of letters means not knowing the *bun* of the warp and woof of heaven. To lean towards the *bu* of the men of martiality means not knowing the divine *bu* that does not kill.[61]

Meanwhile, more nationalistic Confucian and nativist groups became increasingly vocal and influential. Nakamura Mototsune (1778–1851), like other nationalistic Confucians, recognized the importance of both *bun* and *bu*, but more closely identified the two concepts with China and Japan respectively. According to Nakamura's 1848 *On Militarism*, 'Our country is the land of martiality. The Western lands [China] are the land of letteredness. For the land of letteredness to value *bun* and the land of martiality to value *bu* is an ancient pattern'. In ancient Japan, Nakamura argued, 'rebellions did not occur and external enemies did not enter. The higher were safe and the lower were at peace'. How did the government rule in this period before Confucianism or Buddhism had entered Japan, Nakamura asked rhetorically. 'Rule was purely with *bu*. The *bu* of our country is the natural way of our country'.[62] Expanding on this subject, Nakamura argued that 'Ours is the martial country. We have *bushidō*. Not relying on Confucianism or using Buddhism is the natural way of our country. The land of *bun* values filial piety, while the land of *bu* values loyalty'.[63] Nakamura's nostalgic nationalism echoed the views of many of his contemporaries, while he criticized earlier Tokugawa scholars for having been overly critical of martiality: '[Ogyū] Sorai said that *bushidō* was a wicked learning created in the Warring States period. [Yamazaki] Ansai said that

---

[61] Saitō Setsudō (1942), 'Shidō yōron', in Saeki Ariyoshi et al. (eds.), *Bushidō zenshō* 6 (Tokyo: Jidaisha), p. 316.
[62] Nakamura Mototsune (1942), 'Shōbu ron', in Saeki Ariyoshi et al. (eds.), *Bushidō zenshō* 6 (Tokyo: Jidaisha), p. 320.
[63] Nakamura Mototsune, pp. 329–30.

our country is heretical. These are the words of jaundiced Confucians who do not know *bushidō*.'[64]

Nostalgic and nationalistic criticism was most evident in the writings of the Mito school, which advocated 'reverence for the emperor and resistance against foreign barbarians' (*sonnō jōi*). Tokugawa Nariaki (1800–1860), the head of Mito domain, argued in 1833 that *bun* and *bu* were both essential, and studying only the (Chinese) way of letteredness would 'lead to the greatest possible confusion'. Believing that the samurai had become overly pacified, he exhorted them to practise martial arts in accordance with the 'great way of the country of the gods'.[65] According to Nariaki, 'even a single samurai on his own must be prepared like a samurai. However, in the Great Peace [of the Tokugawa period], samurai no longer practise the martial way, they eat as much as they can, wear warm clothes, and until today live comfortable and peaceful lives, forgetting what they have received from their superiors'.[66]

Some members of the National Learning movement took a similar approach, as can be seen in the writings of Tomobayashi Mitsuhira (1813–64): 'In the Western lands [China] letteredness is primary and martiality subordinate. In the imperial country [Japan] martiality is primary to letteredness. This is because the national polity [*kokutai*] of the imperial country is not the same as foreign countries.' Tomobayashi argued that 'In the Western lands *bun* and *bu* are different. Their civil officials do not deal with military affairs, and their military officials do not deal with civil matters. In ancient times in our imperial country, *bun* and *bu* were one, and civil officials dealt with military matters while military men learned letters'.[67] Samurai from many different schools and backgrounds were united in their belief that the current state of *bun-bu* was deeply flawed, and they called for a reintroduction of 'true' martiality and letteredness, with special emphasis on the former, 'native', virtue. News of the Opium War and the perceived threat of foreign invasions resulted in a greater emphasis on martiality from the 1840s onward, and much of later *bun-bu* discourse should be understood in the context of the rising proto-nationalism tied to burgeoning nativist movements such as National Learning and the Mito school.

Criticism of the state of *bun* and *bu* at the end of the Edo period was widespread, and satirists risked official ire by mocking official attempts to enforce a balance of letters and martiality among the samurai, inferring that 'there was no one among the retainers of the shogun who was interested in engaging in either intellectual or physical training'.[68] Perhaps the best overview of the disparate discourses can be found in Yokoi Shōnan's *Three Discourses on Governing the Country*. According to Yokoi, everyone agreed that '*bun* and *bu* are the key to the way of

---

[64] Nakamura Mototsune, pp. 329–30.

[65] Tokugawa Nariaki (1942), 'Kokushi hen', in Saeki Ariyoshi et al. (eds.), *Bushidō zensho 7* (Tokyo: Jidaisha), pp. 23–24.

[66] Tokugawa Nariaki, p. 39.

[67] Tomobayashi Mitsuhira (1942), 'Omoide gusa', in Saeki Ariyoshi et al. (eds.), *Bushidō zensho 7* (Tokyo: Jidaisha), pp. 209–210.

[68] Burns, Susan L. (2003), *Before the Nation: Kokugaku and the Imagining of Community in Early Modern Japan* (Durham, NC: Duke University Press), p. 28.

ruling the country, which is the profession of the samurai'. However, the proponents of *bun* relied solely on Chinese classics and tended to 'enter into a flow of empty reasoning about broad subjects, and in extreme cases they merely memorize texts'. In comparison, advocates of *bu* spend their time practising martial arts or engaged in superficial banter. 'As a result, scholars look at fighters carelessness and roughness, and despise their lack of usefulness, while fighters mock the scholars haughtiness and effeminate manner, as well as their inability to endure anything. The two groups cannot be reconciled'.[69]

Yokoi believed that these difficulties arose from a failure to understand the origins of *bun* and *bu*. When the concepts originated in China in the age of the legendary Emperor Shun, there was no literature nor were there military techniques. Instead, *bun-bu* referred to virtues of the emperor. The association with military techniques was a result of the Japanese medieval period, when warlords introduced and taught martial skills. After the end of the Sengoku ('warring states') period (*c.* late fifteenth to late sixteenth centuries), argued Yokoi, cultural pursuits neglected during the centuries of turmoil were revived, and many people studied literature, causing the 'way of the samurai' (*shidō*) of the Edo period to be excessively focused on civil matters. This led to a weakening of the warrior class from its earlier heyday, as 'originally, *bu* was the principal content of *shidō*. Therefore, if one knows what a *bushi* is, he cannot fail to understand *bushidō*'.[70] While the majority of samurai had become overly bookish and weak, Yokoi charged that another group of warriors calling themselves 'men of *bu*' taught military techniques without any knowledge of letteredness.[71] As a result of this division between *bun* and *bu*, Yokoi argued, the samurai class had reached a deplorable state where they were generally inferior to farmers in physical strength and endurance.[72]

As one of the most common and enduring themes in samurai writings, the *bun-bu* binary is a useful point of reference for understanding the diverse character of *bushi* ethics. While there was a broad consensus on the importance of maintaining a balance between letteredness and martiality, there were considerable differences between interpretations. The concepts could be understood practically, as they often were in earlier history, but also as abstract philosophical concepts, and even as the basis for proto-nationalistic arguments, with this latter interpretation making *bun-bu* relevant to more than a single class. Even if thinkers agreed on the importance of the 'two ways of *bun-bu*', their specific interpretations of those concepts could make their arguments completely opposed to one another. In spite of its pervasiveness in samurai thought, the absence of an accepted interpretation of *bun-bu* reflects the problems inherent in attempts to identify a meaningful and coherent samurai ethic.

---

[69] Yokoi Shōnan (1971), 'Kokuze sanron', in *Watanabe Kazan, Takano Chōei, Sakuma Shōzan, Yokoi Shōnan, Hashimoto Sanai (Nihon shisō taikei 55)* (Tokyo: Iwanami shoten), p. 458.
[70] Yokoi Shōnan, pp. 456, 461.   [71] Yokoi Shōnan, p. 460.
[72] Yokoi Shōnan, pp. 463–64.

THE CRISIS OF THE SAMURAI AND THE
LIMITS OF NOSTALGIA

Nostalgia for an idealized past was one of the most consistent influences on the self-perception of Japanese *bushi* for much of their existence, and provided a reference point for social criticism. Idealization of earlier periods is often associated with conservative elements in many societies, with military organizations and social groups responsible for the conduct of war tending toward conservativism insofar as maintaining the prevailing order ensures their positions of power. Furthermore, for fighters engaged in the turmoil of the battlefield, there is a tendency to imagine that the conduct of war was somehow more ethical and ordered in earlier times, as Karl Friday observes.[73] Michael Adams discusses this phenomenon with regard to the Second World War, the memory of which was sanitized by Americans despairing at the more publicized problems with the conflict in Vietnam.[74]

In the case of Japan, the *bushi* were among the most active promoters of nostalgic narratives romanticizing and reinventing the past. This causes difficulties for historians of Japan, as the most popular and influential accounts of medieval warfare were composed long after the events they described, and primarily tended to reflect the conditions, concerns, and desires of their authors. In this way, famous accounts of twelfth-century wars and rebellions were products of the thirteenth and fourteenth centuries, war tales describing fourteenth- and fifteenth century campaigns were largely composed in the late fifteenth and early sixteenth centuries, and many narratives concerning the unification wars of the late sixteenth century were the result of seventeenth-century nostalgia and revision. In the eighteenth century, Yamamoto Tsunetomo and Daidōji Yūzan espoused controversial martial ideals defined by an idealized view of the age of warfare, which had largely ended almost a century earlier. Yamamoto's *Hagakure*, as well as many other premodern and early modern texts on warrior ethics, should be seen as social criticism seeking legitimacy in romanticized history, rather than as expressions of widely held views.

As Japan came under ever-greater threats from abroad during the nineteenth century, the warrior class—whose status was legitimized by their responsibility for ruling and defending the country—turned increasingly to an idealized past for guidance. This shift reflected broader nativistic intellectual currents that had been gaining in strength throughout the Edo period, but the unique status of the martial elite gave their responses the greatest urgency. Sonoda Hidehiro describes the period from 1840 to 1880 as one of 'decline of the warrior class', and feelings of powerlessness, anger, and frustration led many samurai to seek active roles in the defense and reformation of the country, intensifying discourse on the need for martial virtues.[75] Arguments concerning intangible changes such as a loss of

---

[73] Friday, Karl F. (2004), *Samurai, Warfare, and the State in Early Medieval Japan* (New York: Routledge), pp. 135–63.

[74] Adams, Michael C. C. (1994), *The Best War Ever: America and World War II* (Baltimore: Johns Hopkins University Press).

[75] Sonoda Hidehiro, 'The Decline of the Japanese Warrior Class, 1840–1880', *Japan Review* 1 (1990), pp. 73–111.

spirit or general degeneration among the samurai were some of the most common themes in late Tokugawa writings, attesting to a widespread feeling that the samurai had declined from an earlier ideal.

One of the most prominent examples of nostalgic activism was Chōshū samurai Yoshida Shōin, who was later lionized later as the teacher of many leading figures in the new government. Yoshida's execution by the shogunate in the course of the Ansei Purge of 1858–59 gave him the status of a martyr for the emperor and country, and he became a powerful symbol in the modern period. Yoshida's view of the samurai echoed that of many other thinkers of his day: they had degenerated over the course of the Tokugawa peace due to the separation of *bun* and *bu,* and had to be 'remilitarized' if they were to save Japan. In a commentary on Mencius, Yoshida discussed the necessity of samurai to be willing to die for their fathers, lords, domains, and especially their country, with later scholars in the imperial period focusing on this last aspect of Yoshida's thought. Yoshida argued that strengthening the spirit and the inculcation of martial virtues would solve any problems, including hunger, cold, and other tangible concerns.[76] According to Yoshida, the use of *bu* was more appropriate to an age of crisis and conflict, as Japan was experiencing in the years following Commodore Perry's arrival in 1853. Yoshida criticized prevailing attitudes towards military service, emphasizing *bu* as an all-encompassing concept of proper attitudes and behaviour that contained both *bun* and *bu,* loyalty and filial piety, as well as Confucianism and all other teachings.[77]

Yokoi Shōnan's views in the early 1850s were similar to Yoshida's in their nostalgia and uncompromising anti-foreignism, but by the 1860s he had grave doubts regarding the recovery of the glorious samurai past. According to Yokoi, major reforms were necessary for the sake of the country, and he outlined his proposals concerning currency policies, military defenses, agriculture, trade, and other issues. With regard to the samurai, Yokoi was not convinced that there was a place for all *bushi* in the reformed military he proposed, and their numbers had become a burden on the state. Yokoi argued that samurai should contribute to society by pursuing other professions, such as silkworm raising, fishing, metalworking, and sericulture.[78] Although he described the majority of samurai as 'arrogant soldiers' who could not currently compete with the West, Yokoi also hoped that it would be possible to recover the lost martial spirit.[79] His progressive policy suggestions were received favourably by the government, which gave him influential positions, but his willingness to adapt also led to Yokoi's assassination by imperial loyalist extremists.

In spite of Yokoi's advocacy for the warrior class and his romanticized view of their distant past, he foresaw an existential crisis if the *bushi* could not prove

---

[76] Hirose Yutaka (ed.) (1943), *Kō-Mō yowa* (Tokyo: Iwanami shoten), pp. 23, 193, 336, 36.

[77] Yoshida Shōin (1940), *Yoshida Shōin zenshū Volume 4* (Tokyo: Iwanami shoten), pp. 222, 215, 266.

[78] Yokoi Shōnan, 'Kokuze sanron', pp. 443–44.

[79] Minamoto Ryōen, 'Yokoi Shōnan ni okeru jōi ron kara kaikoku ron he no tenkai', *Ajia bunka kenkyū* 26 (March 2000), p. 221.

their usefulness relative to the other classes. These fears were realized in early Meiji, when nostalgia was no longer sufficient to stop the successive reforms that eliminated samurai privileges. Instead, samurai resistance to these changes further eroded what little nostalgic goodwill there may have been among the former commoner classes, many of whom were glad to be free of their traditional overlords. Meiji reforms were resented in many sections of society, with the commoner classes having to make personal sacrifices necessitated by the new school system and conscription orders, as well as by increased interference from the centre.[80] This was exacerbated by the rapidity of reform, with prescriptions against Buddhism, the introduction of the Western calendar, and changes to administrative structures contributing to the discontent. In addition, while the Meiji system ostensibly removed much of the institutional inequality of the Tokugawa social structure, real social mobility was still limited, fostering resentment among those who had hoped for rapid improvement.

In comparison, the upper classes, including many former samurai, were not affected by the loss of youth labour resulting from educational demands, and were able to obtain exemptions from conscription through the payment of 270 Yen, a not insignificant sum at the time.[81] As Hirota Teruyuki points out, the *bushi* class were not widely considered to be more suitable for military service, and the relatively high proportion of former samurai in the officer ranks was due primarily to the fact that they had suddenly been made redundant and were in need of income.[82] In accordance with government preference for commoner conscripts, the burden of military service fell most heavily on the urban and rural poor, leading to widespread draft avoidance and even the publication of manuals detailing techniques for failing army physicals.[83]

The government's policies affected the samurai in different ways, with many *daimyō* and other high-ranking figures eagerly becoming part of the new nobility, thereby raising their social status and eliminating their often considerable debts. This move angered many samurai from the lower ranks, as it shattered the traditional structures upon which they depended.[84] The role of the samurai in the modern state was widely debated, with arguments concerning the nature of their influence continuing into the present day. On the one hand, the *shizoku*—former samurai—were considered to be a potentially valuable resource. They were seen as

[80] Luke Roberts argues that many of the commoner protests against changes in the 1870s were rooted in resistance to increased interference by the state, which eliminated much of the former space for local maneuvering and control (Roberts, Luke S., *Performing the Great Peace: Political Space and Open Secrets in Tokugawa Japan*, p. 194).

[81] Harada Keiichi (2001), *Kokumingun no shinwa: heishi ni naru to iu koto* (Tokyo: Yoshikawa kobunkan), p. 52.

[82] Hirota Teruyuki (1997), *Rikugun shōkō no kyōiku shakaishi: risshin shusse to tennōsei* (Tokyo: Seori shobō), p. 150.

[83] Coox, Alvin D. (1975), 'Chrysanthemum and Star: Army and Society in Modern Japan', in David MacIsaac (ed.), *The Military and Society: The Proceedings of the Fifth Military History Symposium* (Washington, DC: Office of Air Force History) pp. 39–42.

[84] Yates, Charles L. (1995), *Saigō Takamori: The Man behind the Myth* (New York: Kegan Paul International), p. 141.

natural leaders who often had higher levels of education than the other classes, and it was hoped that their skills could be applied to the demands of the modernization process. Some historians and cultural theorists have credited the samurai as the key factor behind Japan's rapid development after 1868, while attributing China and Korea's failure to modernize as quickly to the lack of a samurai equivalent in those countries. On the other hand, the continued existence of the samurai also posed considerable problems, as their stipends placed a tremendous burden on the state, while the lack of practical skills among many samurai left them ill-equipped to find new roles in the modern world. These issues inspired proposals for drastic solutions, and a proposed invasion of Korea would have removed unwanted samurai from the country. This idea was ultimately rejected due to apprehension regarding the potential reactions of the Western powers, but it reflected the serious concern that the government felt with regard to samurai issues.

There was fundamental agreement on all sides that the samurai could not simply continue as they had before. Those who saw the samurai as a liability desired the complete abolition of their special privileges and stipends, while those who focused on the potential benefits that the *shizoku* could bring to the nation as a whole hoped that samurai virtues could be applied to new tasks. At the same time, even supporters of the *shizoku* believed that they had degenerated from an earlier ideal and would have to be reformed, a nostalgic view consistent with much of earlier discourse. Significantly, this nostalgia was for a romanticized distant past, not for the immediate past of late Tokugawa, memories of which were still vivid and could not serve effectively as an idealized model.

As many samurai feared, the abolition of the Tokugawa domain system was followed by the gradual elimination of samurai stipends and special status in a series of reforms in early Meiji, with the resulting discontent a significant factor in a number of disturbances that shook Japan in the 1870s. The largest uprising occurred in 1877, when thousands of former samurai gathered in Satsuma and instigated a rebellion that the new government could only put down with great loss of life. The Restoration hero Saigō Takamori became the popular figurehead of this uprising, although he seems to have accepted this role only reluctantly.[85] In spite of the diverse social backgrounds and motivations of participants in early Meiji disturbances, the view that the Satsuma Rebellion was the culmination of a series of samurai uprisings signaling the end of the class was—and is—highly influential on popular views of the samurai.

The violence of the Satsuma Rebellion seemed to dramatically illustrate the gap between popular society and the former samurai who had been left behind, and the conflict is often portrayed as a civil war between the commoners who made up the bulk of the modern army and their 'traditional oppressors, the *samurai*'.[86] This

---

[85] As Charles Yates has argued, concern for the future of the samurai class was but one motivation of the rebels, especially Saigō (Yates, Charles L. (1998) 'Saigō Takamori in the Emergence of Meiji Japan', in Peter Kornicki (ed.), *Meiji Japan: Political, Economic and Social History 1868–1912* (New York: Routledge), pp. 190–97).

[86] Calman, Donald (1992), *The Nature and Origins of Japanese Imperialism: A Reinterpretation of the Great Crisis of 1873* (London: Routledge), pp. 141–43.

class-based interpretation was also influential at the time, as popular sentiments towards the *shizoku* in early Meiji were mixed and often hostile. Based on his experiences in Japan in the early 1870s, William Elliot Griffis wrote of the recent past that '... the majority [of samurai] spent their life in eating, smoking, and lounging in brothels and teahouses, or led a wild life of crime in one of the great cities. When too deeply in debt, or having committed a crime, they left their homes and the service of their masters, and roamed at large'.[87] Griffis' description of the samurai as violent loafers and a burden on society may have overstated the situation, but it reflected widely-held negative views of the samurai in Japan at the time. Persistent, if unfounded, rumors that peasant lands would be confiscated and redistributed to newly disenfranchised samurai increased popular resentment and unrest.[88]

Attitudes towards the samurai in early and mid-Meiji are reflected in a variety of sources, from satirical poetry to essays on social issues. Contemporary newspapers reveal the tension between *shizoku* and the rest of society in both coverage of current events and editorial commentaries mocking their troubles.[89] Criticism of the *shizoku* in the media provoked defensive responses, as in a letter to the editor of the *Yomiuri shinbun* published on August 28, 1875, and signed by a 'Mr. Kadowaki, a *shizoku* in Yotsuya.' Kadowaki lamented the fact that the newspapers were constantly attacking the former samurai by focusing on their supposed laziness and ineptitude for business. This was an exaggeration, he claimed, stating that while many *bushi* may have done little but sit around waiting for their stipends in the past, things had changed. In addition, Kadowaki argued that perhaps one in ten *shizoku* might insist on their *bushi* status and fail in their ventures due to a sense of entitlement, but it was unfair for the popular media to paint all former samurai with the same brush.[90] Kadowaki's protestations notwithstanding, the phrase 'samurai business practice' (*bushi/shizoku no shōhō*) became a metaphor for failed entrepreneurship early in the Meiji period, and stories of *shizoku* incompetence in business abounded.[91]

Resentment of the samurai, especially the ruling clique dominated by the former domains of Satsuma and Chōshū, was complemented by calls for sympathy for the many destitute *shizoku* who struggled to adapt to the new order, with solicitations for compassion and support appealing to the 'past accomplishments' of the samurai and their ancestors on behalf of the country.[92] Some *shizoku* continued to complain of unfair treatment after the Satsuma Rebellion—such as a group of about 350 who gathered at the prefectural offices in Hyōgo to demand the resumption of their stipend payments—but by the second decade of Meiji it was clear that their material benefits and status had been irretrievably lost.[93]

---

[87] Griffis, William Elliot (1887), *The Mikado's Empire* (New York: Harper), p. 278.

[88] Hane, Mikiso (2003), *Peasants, Rebels, Women, and Outcastes: The Underside of Modern Japan* (Rowman & Littlefield), p. 16.

[89] *Yomiuri shinbun*, 5 April 1876, p. 3.   [90] *Yomiuri shinbun*, 28 August 1875, p. 2.

[91] For an example of this usage, see: *Yomiuri shinbun*, 8 Nov. 1877, p. 2.

[92] For example: Ikushima Hajime (1882), *Seidan tōron hyakudai* (Tokyo: Matsui Chūbei), pp. 88–89; Fukuhara Kenshichi (1881), *Nihon keizai risshihen* (Osaka), pp. 17–20.

[93] *Yomiuri shinbun*, 22 Dec. 1878, p. 2.

The residual frustration among some former samurai was apparent in a depressing police report concerning an inebriated down-and-out Tokyo *shizoku* who smashed a fence and assaulted his drinking companions, while shouting insults at commoners and insisting that he was a 'former *bushi*'.[94] *Schadenfreude* frequently won out over sympathy, however, and early Meiji was marked by a proliferation of satirical poems on the subject of the decline of the samurai, portraying them tilling fields or losing their sexual prowess on account of not having any more idle time to devote to honing their renowned skills.[95] The traditional saying that 'flowers are cherry blossoms and men are *bushi*' was considered anachronistic, and some commentators described the *shizoku* not as cherry blossoms, but rather as hanging wisteria blossoms blowing in the wind.[96]

Anti-samurai resentment lingered well into the 1880s, as reflected in a two-part editorial on the subject of *bushidō* published in 1885:

> before Genroku [1688-1704]...*bushi* suppressed letteredness and created a special spirit called *bushidō*, whereby the *bushi* had an arrogant attitude like a unique race among the four classes and stood atop society....there was even the bizarre and abnormal situation in which *bushi* would see townsmen and farmers and cut them down like worthless dirt....due to living in the midst of the last two hundred years of the Great Peace, *bushi*, townsmen, and farmers became magnanimous and indifferent to things and affairs....as a result [after Genroku] *bushi* allowed true *bushidō* to decay and exist only in name, while Chinese studies, poetry, and letteredness surpassed martiality in the trends of the time...for the first time in Japan, the *bushi* were faced with poverty and took up the abacus to compete with townsmen and farmers for profits or to take bribes and mix public and private matters.[97]
> ...when trying to understand the mentality known as *bushidō*, this *bushidō* mentality was extreme displays of false bravado and sophistry towards townsmen and farmers, while at the same time the interactions between *bushi* were filled with great respect and care to avoid causing others to lose face...[98]

The *bushidō* described here did not excite any nostalgia, and was merely seen as a stage of development of the human character in Japan, and not a very admirable one at that. The author argued that the Japanese character had to change for the country to succeed, and did not look to the nation's past for guidance for the future.

The view that a martial phase was a part of civilizational development was echoed by the journalist Tokutomi Sohō (1863–1957) in his 1886 *The Future Japan*. According to Tokutomi, Meiji Japan had put the military stage of its social evolution behind it, and was heading towards an industrial and democratic future.[99] Tokutomi compared the soldiers of the modern imperial army with the samurai, pointing out

---

[94] *Yomiuri shinbun*, 23 April 1879, p. 2.

[95] Brink, Dean Anthony, 'At Wit's End: Satirical Verse Contra Formative Ideologies in Bakumatsu and Meiji Japan', *Early Modern Japan* (Spring 2001), pp. 26–27.

[96] *Yomiuri shinbun*, 23 March 1883. *Yomiuri shinbun*, 24 April 1879.

[97] *Yomiuri shinbun*, 9 Dec. 1885, p. 1.   [98] *Yomiuri shinbun*, 13 Dec. 1885, p. 1.

[99] Tokutomi Iichirō (Sohō) (1989), *The Future Japan* (Edmonton: University of Alberta Press), p. xxxiii.

that both groups were required to practice military skills, and had their movements restricted by their superiors. In addition, both samurai and modern soldiers lived off of the common people, without producing anything of their own. The crucial difference, according to Tokutomi, was that the modern military existed to serve the people, while in the past the people had existed to serve the samurai. The result was a terribly unjust society in which wealth was concentrated with the samurai, especially those in the cities, even though these did no labour that might merit their extravagant lifestyles.[100] For Tokutomi, the samurai and the social structure they had dominated were relics of the past that were relevant to the modern age only as symbols of an earlier developmental stage of Japan's inevitable progress to a brilliant future.

The following year, politician and scholar Katō Hiroyuki (1836–1916) gave a lecture to the Great Japan Education Association discussing the state of ethics instruction in Meiji.[101] Katō was the pre-eminent Social Darwinist of the time, and his thought was primarily based on European sources, especially during the 1880s.[102] In this lecture, Katō outlined the state of ethics before 1868, when:

> the upper levels of Japanese society relied on Mencius' Confucianism, while the lower levels relied on Shakyamuni's Buddhism as their moral teachings. Especially among the higher classes, there was also a type of thing called *bushidō* that reinforced moral-ity. However, after the Restoration, society shifted entirely towards Westernization.[103]

According to Katō, Confucianism had lost its influential position immediately after the Restoration, as the teachings of Mencius went 'against the civilizational ideas of present Japan'. The abolition of the domain system caused the *shizoku* to fall into poverty, and Confucianism disappeared together with *bushidō*. Katō mentioned recent efforts to revive Confucianism, but gave no indication of simi-lar activities concerning *bushidō*, which did not warrant further discussion.[104] For Katō, as for Tokutomi, the samurai class was a relic of the past. In an 1889 essay concerning the role of force in government and society, Katō described the samurai right to use force against commoners as a negative example of private control of the means of violence, arguing that these should be left up to the control of the state.[105]

By the late 1880s the popular image of the *shizoku* was not one of admiration, and there was little yearning for the Tokugawa past in this regard. As Carol Gluck argues, although the notion of 'Edo-as-tradition' became popular in the 1890s, it 'began its Meiji career as the bygone old order, which excited little favourable comment or nostalgia except perhaps among former shogunal retainers and other chronological exiles...'[106] The samurai spirit seemed anachronistic at best, and the

[100] Tokutomi Sohō, pp. 134–38.

[101] Katō Hiroyuki (1887), *Tokuiku hōan* (Tokyo: Tōkyō yūeisha).

[102] Davis, Winston (1996), *The Moral and Political Naturalism of Baron Kato Hiroyuki* (Berkeley: Institute for East Asian Studies), p. vii.

[103] Katō Hiroyuki, *Tokuiku hōan*, pp. 1–2.   [104] Katō Hiroyuki, pp. 2–3.

[105] Katō Hiroyuki, 'Wanryoku ha toku ni kokka no shuken ni takusubeshi', *Tensoku* 1:9 (1889), pp. 212–17.

[106] Gluck, Carol (1998), 'The Invention of Edo', in Stephen Vlastos (ed.), *Mirror of Modernity: Invented Traditions in Modern Japan* (Berkeley: University of California Press), pp. 267–69.

notion that a 'way of the samurai' could benefit the new Japan as a national ethic met with bemusement. On the other hand, the passing of time and concerns with other issues caused outright hostility to the *shizoku* to wane, and their popular image began to soften into a mixture of irrelevance and anachronism by the last decade of the nineteenth century.

2

First Explanations of *Bushidō* in the Meiji Era

EVOLVING VIEWS OF CHINA, THE WEST, AND JAPAN

After the Meiji Restoration of 1868, Japan introduced sweeping reforms to its bureaucratic, military, and educational structures. This process involved importing and adapting foreign systems of government and organization with the aid of European and American advisors. These changes were reflected in the Westernization of many aspects of society, including diet, dress, and behaviour, a process that occurred most rapidly among the upper classes in major urban centres. Western styles and accoutrements became fashionable, and the pro-Western Meiji Six Society (Meirokusha) became a symbol of the drive towards 'civilization and enlightenment' (*bunmei kaika*). Knowledge of foreign languages and foreign experience were seen as pathways to success, and translated texts such as Samuel Smiles' *Self-Help* became tremendously popular.[1]

In spite of the great changes, tangible improvements in the social conditions of many Japanese were slow to come, and much of the initial optimism that had greeted the new government had dissipated by the 1880s. Policies such as mass conscription and the creation of modern schools were widely resented in the countryside, where they placed new burdens on the people. This disappointment with the Meiji establishment also brought resentment towards the West, as many of the institutional changes were Western in origin and were discussed using foreign terms and concepts. As a result, while the Western-style institutions continued to expand and evolve, they became less explicitly foreign, with foreign content in Japanese textbooks gradually replaced by native ideas. The Meiji primary school system used a succession of Western models, with imported content, before returning to more traditional Confucian ideals around 1882.[2] While the early textbooks focused on historical figures such as George Washington and Benjamin Franklin, revisions of school texts following the promulgation of the Imperial Rescript on Education

---

[1] For a discussion of the influence of these texts, see Kinmonth, Earl H. (1981), *The Self-Made Man in Meiji Japanese Thought: From Samurai to Salary Man* (Berkeley: University of California Press).

[2] Westney, D. Eleanor (1987), *Imitation and Innovation: The Transfer of Western Organizational Patterns to Meiji Japan* (Cambridge, MA: Harvard University Press), p. 14; Araki Ryūtarō (1986), 'Nihon ni okeru Yōmeigaku no keifu', in Ōkada Takehiko (ed.), *Yōmeigaku no sekai* (Tokyo: Meitoku shuppan), p. 412.

in 1890 eliminated most references to foreigners by 1900.[3] Not only was the formal content of the new textbooks different, but also the messages they contained. The early texts focused on freedom and progressive values, contradicting the authoritarian tone of imperial rescripts.[4] Textbook writers increasingly drew on careful selections from the *Taiheiki* and other older military narratives that 'emphasized such virtues as self-sacrifice and loyalty', especially towards the emperor, and these works represented a significant portion of the educational literary canon by the 1890s.[5]

Even Japanese with strong Western connections began to argue for a renewed emphasis on Eastern values. Nishi Amane (1829–97), a founding member of the Meiji Six Society who had studied in Holland, was a well-known translator credited with the creation of many new terms for foreign concepts, such as the word '*tetsugaku*' as a translation of 'philosophy'. By the 1880s, however, Nishi was arguing for the implementation of a Confucian-style education system as necessary for the good of the nation.[6] Nishimura Shigeki (1828–1902), who wrote widely on Japanese morality, was another member of the Meiji Six Society and notable promoter of Confucian values. Katō Hiroyuki commented on the strength of this Confucian revival in 1887, observing that the *Analects* and 'pure Chinaism' were being taught to many of the upper classes.[7] Arguably, Confucianism became more widely diffused during the mid-Meiji period than ever before in Japanese history, as its concepts and terminology were important tools for uniting the new state and for standardizing language.[8] Widespread unease towards excessive 'Western' individualism resulted in an increased emphasis on Eastern virtues, primarily Confucianism, although this was a 'modern hybrid' rather than a faithful continuation of any previous traditions.[9] During the decade between 1887 and 1896, reactions to earlier Westernizing trends became stronger, resulting in the growth of nationalistic thought that incorporated Shinto and Confucian ideals, and was manifested on an institutional level by the Imperial Rescript on Education.[10]

This 'return' to Confucianism would prove short-lived, however, due to its persistent connection with the unpopular *ancien régime* of the Tokugawa, as well as the readily observable decline of the Qing dynasty.[11] Confucian values did not

---

[3] Kaigo Tokiomi (ed.) (1969), *Kindai Nihon kyōkasho sōsetsu kaisetsu hen* (Tokyo: Kōdansha), p. 113.

[4] Kaigo Tokiomi, pp. 108–09.

[5] Shirane Haruo (2000), 'Curriculum and Competing Canons', in Haruo Shirane (ed.), *Inventing the Classics: Modernity, National Identity, and Japanese Literature* (Stanford: Stanford University Press), p. 240.

[6] Minami Hiroshi (2006), *Nihonjin ron: Meiji kara kyō made* (Tokyo: Iwanami gendai bunko), p. 28.

[7] Katō Hiroyuki (1887), *Tokuiku hōan* (Tokyo: Tōkyō yūeisha), p. 3.

[8] Kurozumi Makoto, 'Kangaku: Writing and Institutional Authority', *Journal of Japanese Studies* 20:2 (summer 1994), p. 216.

[9] Swale, Alistair (2003), 'Tokutomi Sohō and the Problem of the Nation-State in an Imperialist World', in Dick Stegewerns (ed.), *Nationalism and Internationalism in Imperial Japan: Autonomy, Asian Brotherhood, or World Citizenship?* (New York: RoutledgeCurzon), p. 9.

[10] Kurozumi Makoto, 'Kangaku: Writing and Institutional Authority', pp. 216–17.

[11] For a discussion of the former, see: Eizenhofer-Halim, Hannelore (2001), *Nishimura Shigeki (1828–1902) und seine Konzeption einer 'neuen' Moral im Japan der Meiji-Zeit* (Neuried: Ars Una), p. 217.

disappear, but the deterioration of Japan's relationship with China in the early 1890s over issues of control in Korea, combined with the obvious weakness of China in relation to the West, strongly affected Japanese nationalism and attitudes towards the continent. Furthermore, Japan's association with Asia was often seen as a handicap in efforts at treaty revision and in gaining acceptance from Western powers.[12] Japanese travellers in the West were frustrated by being mistaken for Chinese, and felt that the 'backward' state of their Asian neighbours reflected poorly on Japan. The famous 1885 editorial 'On Escaping from Asia' ('Datsu A ron')—typically seen as educator Fukuzawa Yukichi's (1834–1901) response to the failure of a reformist *coup-d'etat* in Korea—was an early expression of this view.[13]

By the 1890s, even those who had earlier advocated wholesale adoption of Western systems, culture, and language began to distance themselves from this approach, as reflected in the author and publisher Tokutomi Sohō's shift from French-influenced popular rights activist to ultra-nationalist after the Sino-Japanese War (1894–95). Disillusionment arising from Western attitudes towards Japan tempered admiring views of the West, but firsthand experience with foreign 'others' also led many Japanese to an increased awareness of their own culture.[14] Carol Gluck discusses the creation of Edo as a historic space in mid-Meiji, pointing out that there was considerable interest in the subject from the 1890s onward.[15] Nostalgia for the period before 1868 was driven by dissatisfaction with the present and uncertainty regarding the future, and further fuelled by a sense of loss of identity, as native social structure, traditions, and religions were thought to be under threat of displacement by Western elements. Interest in the idealized past resulted in a surge in the popularity of Edo-period works such as the heroic epics *A Treasury of Loyal Retainers* and *Nansō satomi hakkenden* in the 1880s.[16] Fukuzawa Yukichi recalled the Akō Incident as a favourite topic of debate and discussion for him and his peers, attesting to the popularity of these narratives even among 'Westernized' Japanese.[17] These tales were sensationalized accounts of Japanese warriors set in a distant past, far removed from the image of the *shizoku* at the time. In this sense, renewed interest in the early nineteenth-century comedic novel *On Shank's Mare*, which mocked haughty samurai and celebrated the craftiness and wit of commoners, reflected popular views of the *shizoku*.[18] For the samurai, as for other aspects of Tokugawa Japan, a certain amount of time had to elapse before a credible process

---

[12] Pyle, Kenneth B. (1969), *The New Generation in Meiji Japan: Problems of Cultural Identity, 1885–1895* (Stanford: Stanford University Press), pp. 156–57.

[13] Pyle, Kenneth B., p. 149.

[14] Minami Hiroshi, *Nihonjin ron: Meiji kara kyō made*, p. 15.

[15] Gluck, Carol (1998), 'The Invention of Edo', in Stephen Vlastos (ed.), *Mirror of Modernity: Invented Traditions in Modern Japan* (Berkeley: University of California Press), pp. 264, 267.

[16] Shirane Haruo, 'Curriculum and Competing Canons', p. 245.

[17] Fukuzawa Yukichi: Kiyooka Eichi (trans.) (1966), *The Autobiography of Yukichi Fukuzawa* (New York: Columbia University Press), p. 78.

[18] Kornicki, Peter F., 'The Survival of Tokugawa Fiction in The Meiji Period', *Harvard Journal of Asiatic Studies* 41:2 (Dec. 1981), p. 472.

of nostalgic idealization could occur, and this was prolonged by the continued presence of the *shizoku* in society.

By 1890, most Japanese no longer had meaningful personal experience of the Edo period beyond perhaps childhood memories which might have evoked nostalgic feelings, further removing obstacles to a positive popular reassessment of the samurai. Among former commoners, resentment towards the *shizoku* was no longer as widespread, as the tangible privileges associated with this status had largely been eliminated, and the majority of former samurai had blended into the larger society. The rehabilitation of Saigō Takamori by the emperor in February 1889 further reduced the residual stigma, as did official activities commemorating Yoshida Shōin in the late 1880s. Yoshida was inducted into Yasukuni Shrine in 1888 and awarded the Senior Fourth Rank in 1889, followed by a flurry of hagiographies, statue-building, and other commemorative events.[19] Several of Yoshida's former students held positions at the highest levels of government, further enhancing his perceived influence. The fading of negative memories of the Tokugawa period among the general population did not mean that the subsequent exaltation of an idealized samurai image was a forgone conclusion, however; its rehabilitation in the context of *bushidō* depended on a number of interrelated factors influenced more by geopolitical developments and foreign ideas than changes in domestic social attitudes.

THE *BUSHIDŌ* OF OZAKI YUKIO

Changing attitudes towards the samurai in mid-Meiji were both reflected in and influenced by the writings of Ozaki Yukio. Born into a minor samurai family in what is now Kanagawa prefecture, Ozaki was by his own account a weak and sickly child. In 1871, Ozaki followed his father to Takasaki prefecture, where he had taken up a post in the prefectural office. His father's duties included torturing suspected criminals and he took Ozaki along to observe this activity, as well as beheadings and *seppuku*. Ozaki surmised that his father was attempting to strengthen him and cure him of cowardice by exposing him to as much death and suffering as possible, but these measures made Ozaki even more timid and repulsed by bloodshed, earning him harsh scoldings.[20]

At sixteen, Ozaki left his parents and headed to Tokyo in search of an education, briefly attending Fukuzawa Yukichi's Keiō Gijuku before dropping out in 1876 to study science and mathematics elsewhere, albeit with limited success. Even after Ozaki left Keiō, Fukuzawa held him in high esteem, and they continued to maintain a close relationship. Ozaki later admitted not having been sufficiently appreciative of Fukuzawa's support and advice, and regretted his rebellious actions against his mentor. Once, when Ozaki submitted an essay to Fukuzawa for

---

[19] Yoshida Shōin (1940), *Yoshida Shōin zenshū Volume 1* (Tokyo: Iwanami shoten), pp. 47–48.

[20] Ozaki Yukio: Hara Fujiko (trans.) (2001), *The Autobiography of Ozaki Yukio: The Struggle for Constitutional Government in Japan* (Princeton, NJ: Princeton University Press), pp. 3–14.

consideration, the latter reprimanded him for his verbose writing style. Fukuzawa glanced through the paper sceptically while picking at his nose hair, and asked Ozaki who his intended audience was. Ozaki replied that he desired that the intelligentsia of this world read his writing, to which Fukuzawa responded with 'You fool! You have to write for monkeys! That's what I do'.[21] Readers of Ozaki's work may question the impact of Fukuzawa's advice, but Ozaki's writing career took off soon after, and in 1877 Fukuzawa's introduction was instrumental in his being appointed editor-in-chief of the *Niigata shinbun*.

During his time in Niigata, Ozaki gained prominence through the publication of an extended editorial series, *On Militarism* (*Shōbu ron*), based on a lecture he had given to a group of naval officers in Tokyo in 1879. In *Shōbu ron*, Ozaki examined the traditional civil-martial binary of *bun-bu*, arguing that Japan had become weak through excessive emphasis on civil virtues from the seventeenth century onward, when the lack of practical applications for martial skills caused them to be degraded.[22] In the centuries before 1600, Japan had gone too far in the other direction, as an overemphasis on martial virtues led to domestic warfare and the invasion of Korea, while the warlord Toyotomi Hideyoshi's (1536–98) excessive focus on *bu* caused the downfall of his family.[23] Ozaki also made unchecked martiality responsible for Europe's Dark Ages, as well as the Satsuma Rebellion of 1877.[24] On the other hand, Ozaki portrayed the demise of the Hanseatic League as a consequence of neglecting martial affairs. Unlike Japan, Ozaki wrote, the countries of the West had found a balance between civil and martial virtues, with England the best example of this. England's naval domination of its European rivals allowed it to take over Dutch and French trade, driving them out of India and seizing Spanish possessions in the Americas. Ozaki lauded English women for being attracted to naval officers and his audience would certainly have shared his hope that Japanese women would follow the English model in this respect.[25] Reiterating this view in his later autobiography, Ozaki wrote: 'The English nature is also seen in the way in which the women view the opposite sex. They seem to find robust, well-built men the most handsome—in sharp contrast to Japanese women, who see handsomeness in pale and sickly actor types'.[26]

Ozaki blamed the degeneration of martiality for defeats inflicted by Western ships at Kagoshima and Shimonoseki, and he described Japan's attempts to compete with the powers as analogous to a sheep charging into an ambush of tigers. Ozaki derided attempts to conduct international relations with virtue and benevolence as the 'empty words of Confucians', and considered it far more important to strengthen the country.[27] While advocating greater military spending, Ozaki did not feel that merely purchasing weapons or increasing troop numbers would

---

[21] Ishida Hideto, 'Fukuzawa Yukichi to Ozaki Yukio', *Jikyoku* 144 (Jan. 1949), pp. 27–28; Ozaki Yukio, *The Autobiography of Ozaki Yukio: The Struggle for Constitutional Government in Japan*, p. 35.

[22] Ozaki Yukio, *Shōbu ron*, p. 39.   [23] Ozaki Yukio, *Shōbu ron*, pp. 94–95.

[24] Ozaki Yukio, *Shōbu ron*, p. 23.   [25] Ozaki Yukio, *Shōbu ron*, pp. 99–102.

[26] Ozaki Yukio, *The Autobiography of Ozaki Yukio: The Struggle for Constitutional Government in Japan*, p. 108.

[27] Ozaki Yukio, *Shōbu ron*, pp. 59–60.

be effective, as weaklings and cowards could not be transformed into effective soldiers. Instead, martial virtues had to be promoted in primary schools in order to form the martial character of the people at a young age. Teaching materials should instill bravery and courage, such as the Ming epics *Tales of the Water Margin* and *Three Kingdoms*, as well as the *Nansō satomi hakkenden*, while physical exercise and military drill should be introduced into schools as they were in the West.[28] These measures were essential for promoting the six martial virtues outlined by Ozaki: frankness, bold thriftiness, courage, quick-mindedness, generosity, and liveliness.[29] Ozaki's omission of loyalty and self-sacrifice is noteworthy in light of later *bushidō* discourse, and this list reflected broader contemporary trends towards self-improvement and personal advancement.

Ozaki revealed many of his own personal concerns and desires in *Shōbu ron*, suggesting that martiality could be promoted in society by reducing the level of policing in Japan, especially the harsh measures directed towards people involved in politics, a field that interested him greatly. Similarly, Ozaki's recommendation that a lower number of highly skilled troops would result in a more effective military reflected his own desire to escape military service. Shortly after presenting the *Shōbu ron* lecture, Ozaki was forced to undertake an exam for military duty himself. Although Ozaki was only 157 cm tall and weighed roughly 45 kg, the examining officer passed him as a top-grade recruit out of spite after Ozaki provoked his ire. Ozaki claimed to have earned the officer's enmity by resisting his attempts to inspect Ozaki's teeth with his unwashed hand immediately after physically inspecting the genitalia of the previous recruit. As a result, Ozaki was forced to borrow 300 yen from friends in order to buy his way out of military service.[30] Insisting on the importance of a strong military, Ozaki claimed that his desire to avoid service was due to his frailty, which prevented him from contributing much to Japan's defence.

Ozaki's treatment of contemporary China in *Shōbu ron* foreshadowed aspects of his later *bushidō* theories, as well as popular discourse on the subject. While recommending Ming epic novels as tools for instilling a martial spirit, Ozaki dismissed the Qing dynasty as weak and effeminate largely due to the long periods of peace that had followed.[31] Ozaki levelled this same criticism at Japan, although he argued that the 'civil weakness' had originated in China before being imported by Japanese Confucians. A few years later, in 1884, Ozaki experienced China directly when work as a reporter for the *Hōchi shinbun* took him to Shanghai for two months to cover a military conflict between France and the Qing.[32] Ozaki returned to Japan even more convinced of the inferiority of China and Korea relative to Japan and the West, and his attitude towards the continent

---

[28] Ozaki Yukio, *Shōbu ron*, pp. 74–77.   [29] Ozaki Yukio, *Shōbu ron*, p. 37.
[30] Ozaki Yukio, *The Autobiography of Ozaki Yukio: The Struggle for Constitutional Government in Japan*, pp. 56–57.
[31] Ozaki Yukio, *Shōbu ron*, pp. 99–100.
[32] Ozaki Yukio (1955), 'Yū Shin ki (Records of a Journey to Qing)', *Ozaki Gakudō zenshū* 4 (Tokyo: Kōronsha), pp. 239–300.

was similar to Fukuzawa's 'On Escaping from Asia', which was published soon after Ozaki's return to Japan.[33] Back home, Ozaki wrote a series of polemical articles attacking China and Korea in 1884 and 1885, influenced also by the failure of progressive reformers in both countries.[34] Ozaki's disparaging views of China were enhanced by a unique dynamic that influenced many Meiji travellers to the continent. Matsuzawa Hiroaki points out that, from the 1860s onward, well-off Japanese experienced China from a similar point of view as Westerners, since they would often journey on Western ships, stay in foreign legations in Hong Kong and Shanghai, and read European newspapers regarding political events.[35] As Ozaki observed, having Western suits made for a reasonable price in Shanghai was seen as one of the greatest perks for Japanese visitors.[36]

The *Shōbu ron* editorials became very popular and were republished in book form in 1880, 1887, and 1893. This prominence helped Ozaki obtain a government position in Tokyo in 1882 in the office of Ōkuma Shigenobu (1838–1922), whose Constitutional Reform Party (Rikken Kaishintō) Ozaki joined. Although he was soon out of work again as the result of a government reshuffle, Ozaki had embarked on a parallel career as a politician, which would eventually supersede his journalistic exploits. The association with Ōkuma led to problems as well as opportunities in 1887, when Ozaki and several others were banished from Tokyo for three years as a response to party activities against the handling of treaty reform. Deciding to make the most of the situation, Ozaki left Japan to spend time in America and Europe, sending travel reports and other dispatches back to the *Chōya shinbun*, an influential newspaper close to the Constitutional Reform Party.[37] Ozaki would later rise to high office in Japan as a government minister, party head, and mayor of Tokyo, but his activities before 1895 are most significant in the context of *bushidō*.

Ozaki's journey to Shanghai in 1884 convinced him that Japan was superior to its continental neighbours and had to take an active role in East Asian affairs; he also came to believe that it was not sufficient for Japan to merely adopt European culture and systems. His travels to America and Europe in 1888–90 reinforced Ozaki's belief that modern institutions were necessary, but, like the various nations of Europe, Japan had its own structures, cultures, writings, customs, and climate, all of which defined and protected the nation.[38] In his articles on *bushidō*, Ozaki attempted to create—or, according to his later writings, revive—a Japanese institution that corresponded to what he saw as the key to the success of British

[33] Ozaki Yukio, *The Autobiography of Ozaki Yukio*, pp. 80–81.

[34] Ozaki Yukio (1955), 'Tai Shin tai Kan ronsaku', *Ozaki Gakudō zenshū* 2 (Tokyo: Kōronsha), pp. 78–187.

[35] Matsuzawa argues that this situation shaped Japan's policy and general views towards China at least until 1945. Matsuzawa Hiroaki (1993), *Kindai Nihon no keisei to seiyō keiken* (Tokyo: Iwanami shoten), pp. 167–170.

[36] Ozaki Yukio, *The Autobiography of Ozaki Yukio*, pp. 77–80.

[37] Nakahara Nobuo, 'Ozaki Yukio ni okeru nashonarizumu: Meiji 21-23 nen *Ōbei manyūki wo chūshin ni*', *Rekishigaku kenkyū* 265 (June 1962), p. 45.

[38] Ozaki Yukio (1955), 'Ōbei man'yū ki', *Ozaki Gakudō zenshū* 3 (Tokyo: Kōronsha), pp. 512–13.

merchants and diplomats on the international stage: the English notion of gentlemanship. The high status of the English in the contemporary world view was heavily reinforced by their portrayal in idealistic texts such as Samuel Smiles' *Self-Help*, the 1871 translation of which was one of the most influential and popular books in Meiji Japan.[39] Originally published in 1859 to great acclaim, *Self-Help* posited the English gentleman as the embodiment of moral rectitude, with the final chapter, 'Character—the True Gentleman', defining him as 'one whose nature has been fashioned after the highest models'.[40]

While impressed with American technology, Ozaki did not much care for the culture he found there. He described the Americans as unrefined, and was most disappointed in the rudeness and disorder he observed during a visit to congressional debates in Washington DC. On arriving in England from New York, however, Ozaki claimed to have been immediately impressed by English society. The technological advancement and quality of life in London lagged behind that of the United States, Ozaki wrote, but the character of the English was unparalleled in the world. He had formed this conviction in Japan through avid reading of idealistic texts such as John Edgar's *The Boyhood of Great Men* (1854) and Francis Hitchman's 1879 biography of Benjamin Disraeli; and Ozaki found England to be awash with noble talk of gentlemanly ideals.[41] As Philip Mason wrote late in the last century, ' "Gentleman" is not a fashionable word today. Indeed, it can hardly be used without apology and is sometimes used with a sneer. Yet for most of the 19th century and until the Second World War, it provided the English with a second religion, one less demanding than Christianity'.[42] One of the most significant aspects of Victorian discourse on gentlemanship was the widespread notion that its roots could be traced directly back to medieval chivalry, reinforced in the popular mind by the novels of Sir Walter Scott and works such as Kenelm Henry Digby's *The Broad-Stone of Honour, or Rules for the Gentlemen of England* (1822). Commenting on the 1850s, Mark Girouard observes, 'knights in armour were now as likely to suggest moral struggles as military battles, and to symbolise modern gentlemen as depict mediaeval heroes. Chivalric metaphors came naturally to the lips of any educated man or woman. Chivalry was working loose from the Middle Ages'.[43]

The 'rediscovery' of the medieval English past had far-reaching consequences, with Scott's novels inspiring a culture of 'chivalric gentlemanship' in the American

---

[39] Kinmonth, Earl H. *The Self-Made Man in Meiji Japanese Thought: From Samurai to Salary Man.* pp. 10–11.

[40] Smiles, Samuel (1866), *Self-help: with Illustrations of Character and Conduct* (Boston: Ticknor and Fields), p. 412.

[41] Edgar, John G. (1854), *The Boyhood of Great Men: Intended as an Example to Youth* (New York: Harper & Brothers); Hitchman, Francis (1879), *The public life of the Right Honourable the Earl of Beaconsfield* (London: Chapman & Hall); mentioned in Ozaki Yukio (1955), *Ozaki Gakudō zenshū* 1 (Tokyo: Kōronsha), pp. 556, 713.

[42] Mason, Philip (1982), *The English Gentleman: The Rise and Fall of an Ideal* (London: Andre Deutsch), p. 12.

[43] Girouard, Mark (1981), *The Return to Camelot: Chivalry and the English Gentleman* (New Haven, CT: Yale University Press), p. 146.

South, while in Germany even nationalistic anti-liberal traditionalists such as Paul de Lagarde looked to the English ruling class as a behavioural model for a new nobility.[44] This influence was also felt in Japan, and Ozaki was one of many people around the world who had formed an idealistic opinion of English gentlemen through extensive reading of Victorian texts. Ozaki tended to interpret his personal experiences in the West in this context, and his appraisal of England was overwhelmingly positive. One frequently recounted incident occurred when Ozaki decided to take a boat out on the Thames, settling on a fare with the owner of one vessel. Before he could board, however, the captain of another boat came up and tried to take Ozaki to his own craft, angering the first boatman. This led to a heated argument over Ozaki's custom, and the two boatmen finally resorted to settling the matter with fisticuffs. When both were ready, they squared up and swung at one another until the first boatman landed a blow on the nose of the second, knocking him down in what Ozaki described as a rain of blood. To Ozaki's amazement, the first boatman then helped his fallen adversary to his feet, and the two squared up a second time. The result was the same, with the second boatman going down in a bloody heap yet again. This process was repeated until the second boatman finally declined the offer of another round, whereupon his adversary helped him to the edge of the water so he could rinse the blood off of his face and clothes. Having looked after his defeated rival, the first captain returned to Ozaki, apologized for the delay, and they boarded the boat without further ado.[45]

Ozaki considered this incident to be most significant, as it encapsulated his understanding of English gentlemen. Ozaki was impressed that these were not mere ruffians, but dignified riverboat owners who risked their health and safety for their honour over the matter of Ozaki's fare. The fare itself was an insignificant sum, Ozaki surmised, and in Japan people would have quietly accepted such a trivial offence. Ozaki took the English readiness to fight to be a mark of gentlemanly vigour and recalled seeing a great many fights during his time in London, reflecting the popularity of pugilism as a hallmark of the English ideal of the gentleman sportsman.[46] What most impressed Ozaki, however, was the spirit of fair play that he saw in the fight, with the first boatman repeatedly helping his opponent up after knocking him down. Ozaki claimed to have witnessed many fights in Japan, where a downed combatant was likely to be beaten even more thoroughly than before, and certainly not given the chance to get back up and fight again. Ozaki's accounts convey the impression that almost everything he saw in England confirmed the high opinion of English gentlemen and gentlemanship he had encountered in Victorian moral tomes, and interpreted his experiences to strengthen those convictions.

---

[44] Stern, Fritz (1974), *The Politics of Cultural Despair: A Study in the Rise of the Germanic Ideology* (Berkeley: University of California Press), pp. 59–61.

[45] Ozaki frequently retold this story, varying the details over the years. One version had the boatmen fencing with oars. For two versions, see Ozaki Yukio (1913), *Seiji kyōiku ron* (Tokyo: Tōkadō), pp. 212–13 and Ozaki Yukio, *The Autobiography of Ozaki Yukio: The Struggle for Constitutional Government in Japan*, pp. 107–08.

[46] Mason, Philip, *The English Gentleman: The Rise and Fall of an Ideal*, pp. 81–105.

In September 1888, Ozaki sent a dispatch titled '*Shinshi* (Gentleman)' to the *Chōya shinbun*. This article explained the virtues of English gentlemen to a Japanese audience, while at the same time criticizing the shortcomings Ozaki perceived among many of his countrymen who had taken to referring to themselves as *shinshi*. According to Ozaki, although the term 'gentleman' was often translated as *shinshi*, this did not capture the full meaning of the English original. In Japan, a *shinshi* was generally viewed as someone with a great deal of money and a luxurious lifestyle including requisite accoutrements such as gold watches, top hats, black carriages, and pastimes such as buying *geisha* and participating in card games. Unfortunately, Ozaki continued, these qualities differed greatly from those of an English gentleman, and the terms were not equivalent. Whereas Japanese *shinshi* 'spread immorality', 'took bribes', and were grovellers and snivellers who distinguished themselves through immoral behaviour, the English gentleman was responsible for 'upholding morality and refining society' in that country, and any gentleman who committed but one mean offence in word or deed would no longer be known by that title. Ozaki lamented that, as there was no other term for 'gentleman' in Japanese, he was forced to use *shinshi* in his article, but made it clear that he was referring to English gentlemen when he did so.[47]

Ozaki wrote that an Englishman became known as a gentleman on the basis of his deeds and actions, with material wealth irrelevant in this regard. If a man's heart and intentions were good, he would be known as a gentleman even if he were poor. Conversely, some English aristocrats were disparaged as 'not being gentlemen' in spite of their nobility and vast material wealth. As traits of English gentlemen, Ozaki listed characteristics such as 'never forgetting higher ideals, valuing honour and rightness, and acting for the good of the country while forgetting private interests. One must be courageous but not violent, gentle but not weak…and all actions must be based on utmost trustworthiness'.[48] To Ozaki, the word 'gentleman' signified the pinnacle of grace and refinement, and to be called a 'true gentleman' by one's peers was the 'greatest goal of an Englishman'.

According to Ozaki and many Victorians, gentlemen were unique to England and did not exist in other European nations. Although the French had adopted the term '*gentilhomme*', Ozaki wrote, there were no gentleman in that nation. Ozaki cited the letters of Thomas Arnold (1795–1842), the former head of Rugby school, whose 1827 journey to France led him to a damning verdict: 'The thing that surprises me most about France is the complete lack of gentlemen. There is not one person who has the education and attitude of a true gentleman. Even if there are some people who appear to be gentlemen, these are just outward appearances and decorations'.[49] This heavily edited passage revealed Ozaki's bias towards the

---

[47] Ozaki Yukio, 'Ōbei man'yū ki', p. 744.   [48] Ozaki Yukio, 'Ōbei man'yū ki', p. 745.
[49] Ozaki Yukio, 'Ōbei man'yū ki', p. 746. The text here is my translation of Ozaki's Japanese. The original passage translated by Ozaki is from a letter sent by Arnold from Joigny, France, on 6 April 1827: 'Again I have been struck with the total absence of all gentlemen, and of all persons of the education and feelings of gentlemen. I am afraid that the bulk of the people are sadly ignorant and unprincipled, and then liberty and equality are but evils'. (Stanley, Arthur Penrhyn (1845), *The Life and Correspondence: Thomas Arnold, D. D., Late Head-Master of Rugby School, and Regius Professor of Modern History in the University of Oxford in Two Volumes*, Volume II (London: B. Fellowes of Ludgate

English in citing a personal letter written over sixty years earlier as evidence that England had a monopoly on gentlemanship in Europe.[50] While Englishmen holding Arnold's views certainly existed in late Victorian times, the opinions expressed in the letter were more representative of the 1820s, when memories of the French Revolution and Napoleonic wars were still fresh. Given Ozaki's breadth of learning and personal experience, it is likely that his reliance on antiquated texts was calculated to bolster his existing arguments and not borne out of ignorance of contemporary discourse.

Echoing the views of many Victorian idealists, Ozaki sought the roots of English gentlemanship in the feudal tradition and medieval knighthood, although the ethic had evolved since. This connection was important to Ozaki, for it provided the basis of his developing *bushidō* theory. While agreeing with Dr Arnold that gentlemen were an English phenomenon that could not be found in other nations, Ozaki believed that Japan had a corresponding concept in '*bushi*', which was superior to '*shinshi*' as a translation of 'gentleman'. Similar to English gentlemen, Japanese *bushi* had their roots in a feudal age. Like gentlemen, *bushi* valued honour, did not commit mean or crude acts, did not bow to the strong or torment the weak, and were ashamed to sit idle and lose their dignity and prestige, to name a few of the similarities that Ozaki considered too numerous to count. Unfortunately, he continued, *bushidō* declined after the warrior class disappeared and the Japanese people had become shameless and frivolous. Unlike the English, Ozaki wrote, the Japanese were too 'excitable' and did not realize the importance of the qualities that made up *bushidō*, causing the ethic to be boycotted. The result of this was a decline in propriety, shame, courage, and rightness, while superficiality, toadying, coarse speech, and selfishness had increased.[51] In light of his earlier *Shōbu ron*, Ozaki saw this moral degeneration as a process that had occurred over the course of several centuries, and was not merely a recent development.

Ozaki cited the bestselling moralistic tome *John Halifax, Gentleman* as demonstrating the irrelevance of wealth to gentlemanship in England. In Japan, *shinshi* were defined exclusively by their wealth and manner, regardless of their mean intentions, but the 'major reason that the English are respected throughout the world is not their wealth, but their gentlemanly qualities', which were also qualities representative of Japanese *bushi*. Ozaki warned that if the Japanese continued to ignore the greater good and boycott *bushidō*, even if many people became wealthy, the nation would not be able to escape the 'fate of the Jews and Chinese' and would not be respected by the rest of the world.[52] Ozaki's anti-Semitic statement reflected views prevalent in Europe at the time, just as his views towards China, while influenced by his experiences as a privileged foreign traveller in Shanghai, were representative of broader trends and attitudes in Japan.

Street), p. 368). Ozaki altered the passage to remove Arnold's criticism of liberty and equality, values that Ozaki fought for in Japan.

[50] Elsewhere, Ozaki describes negative attitudes towards Germans, writing that the English call them 'the Chinese of Europe' (Ozaki Yukio, 'Ōbei man'yū ki', p. 725).

[51] Ozaki Yukio, 'Ōbei man'yū ki', p. 747.   [52] Ozaki Yukio, 'Ōbei man'yū ki', p. 747.

In March 1891, having returned to Japan the previous year, Ozaki wrote a second article on *bushidō*, similar to the first in its essential arguments, but with a significantly different tone. In the first article, Ozaki lamented the decline of *bushi* virtues in Japan and the state into which *bushidō* had fallen in comparison with the English 'feudal' legacy. The 1891 article also praised the virtues of English gentlemanship, but the air of almost resigned complaint gave way to an exhortation to recover samurai virtues and aggressively compete on the international stage. Specifically, Ozaki saw *bushidō* as the key to success for Japanese businessmen and traders:

> in England they are called gentleman, here they are called *bushi*. Although the terms are different, they are ultimately the same. What makes English merchants without equal under heaven is that most of them have the preparation of gentlemen, and are not cowardly or unskilled. The merchants of other countries are dazzled by insignificant interests, and easily divide their virtues, but the English merchants do not, they are completely trustworthy and even if they die they will not break their word. For this reason, all people under heaven desire to deal with them. The success of English trading is primarily due to the high degree of trust in their merchants. This high degree of trust is because they are rich in the qualities of honesty and chivalry, is this not called the English quality of gentlemanship? Is this not called the quality of *bushi* of our country? Therefore, it can be said that those who do not know *bushidō* will not be great merchants, and in other words, if the level of *bushidō* falls then business can certainly not burn brightly.[53]

If Japan desired to become a 'civilizational heaven' and trade with other nations, Ozaki argued, it should not neglect *bushidō* for even a single day. Without the 'beautiful characteristic nature' of the *bushi*, it would be impossible to carry out great projects or reap great benefits, as those who conducted business in a secret and underhanded way would only be minor figures in the world markets. According to Ozaki, dealing in mean and contemptible ways in the modern business world was analogous to desiring to cross a river but smashing one's boat.[54]

Ozaki's approach had become more prescriptive, and he argued that just as 'gentlemanly' and 'ungentlemanly' were two powerful words that decided the failure or success of a person in England, the term *bushi* should have a similar force in Japan. As the old proverb stated, 'flowers are cherry blossoms, and men are *bushi*'. Japanese merchants could only succeed in business and trade if they were as trusted as English merchants, and this had to be achieved by being strictly faithful, honouring agreements, and avoiding coarse and vulgar speech, all of which were tenets of Ozaki's *bushidō*. Successful business houses had always had a virtuous spirit that helped the weak and challenged the strong, Ozaki continued, and none succeeded by being servile. If Japan's merchants did not respect and follow *bushidō*, they would surely fail among the 'roaring tigers and phoenixes' of the contemporary business world.[55]

[53] Ozaki Yukio (1955), *Ozaki Gakudō zenshū* 3 (Tokyo: Kōronsha), p. 229.
[54] Ozaki Yukio (1893), *Naichi gaikō* (Tokyo: Hakubundō), p. 30.
[55] Ozaki Yukio (1955), *Ozaki Gakudō zenshū* 3 (Tokyo: Kōronsha), pp. 230–31.

The *bushidō* outlined by Ozaki in these articles was the most influential commentary on the subject before the Sino-Japanese War, and *bushidō* discourse before 1895 developed primarily in response to Ozaki's arguments. In addition to initiating discourse, several characteristics of Ozaki's *bushidō* stand out in comparison with the more nationalistic mainstream *bushidō* interpretations of the early twentieth century. Ozaki wrote on *bushidō* while travelling in the West, and his experiences motivated him to find a native Japanese equivalent for English gentlemanship, just as Nitobe Inazō would seek a counterpart for Christian morality a decade later. The portrayal of Japan in Ozaki's two articles changed significantly, with the first more critical than the second. In comparison, the views of England expressed in his Meiji writings were largely positive, diminishing their popular appeal in the long term. Ozaki was also defensive about his opinions regarding the West, deriding other Japanese he met abroad as 'ignorant youth and stubborn geezers who don't know the language. They'd be better off spending time in [the Tokyo booksellers' district] Kanda and reading books about the West'.[56] While maintaining that English gentlemanship was superior to most other ethical systems, by 1891 Ozaki argued with certainty that *bushidō* could fulfill a similar role in Japan.

Ozaki's experiences in England convinced him of the validity of an ethical system ostensibly based on medieval knighthood, and inspired him to explore the possibility of a samurai-based ethic. The prominent discourse on chivalric gentlemanship in the world's greatest empire of the day legitimized the spiritual rehabilitation of the samurai as national ideal. Ozaki's first steps in this direction in 1888 were somewhat hesitant, but by 1891 he argued forcefully for the dissemination of *bushidō* in Japan, encouraged by changing popular views towards the samurai in the interim. Developments in Ozaki's personal situation during this time also influenced his confidence in both himself and his country, as he went from being a lonely exile in London to an ambitious member of parliament in the heady days of the first Imperial Diet, which convened in 1890.

Although Ozaki did not claim that Japan had reached the same 'civilizational' level as England, by 1890 he was considerably more confident when comparing Japan with the West. In 1888, Ozaki described Western civilization as so valuable that it might be worth paying the price of Japan's independence in order to obtain it, but from 1890 he began to argue for the superiority of aspects of Japanese civilization.[57] Relying on differences he perceived in both physiological and cultural traits between Japanese and Westerners, Ozaki commented on his experiences in Western clothing stores. Trousers and shirts were always cut too generously, Ozaki wrote, but hats in Western shops were always too tight, reflecting the relatively large size of Japanese heads. Ozaki attributed this difference to the Japanese emphasis on the spirit versus the Western focus on the physical body.[58] Elsewhere, Ozaki categorized the West as being driven by 'animalistic' progress as opposed to

---

[56] Ozaki Yukio, 'Ōbei man'yū ki', p. 581.   [57] Ozaki Yukio, 'Ōbei man'yū ki', p. 569.
[58] Ozaki Yukio (1955), *Ozaki Gakudō zenshū* 3 (Tokyo: Kōronsha), pp. 171–74.

Japan's desire for 'spiritual' advancement.[59] In spite of his adulation for England, Ozaki was disparaging of many other Western nations, a more nuanced approach that reflected broader trends in Japanese intellectual circles as debates on treaty revision and mixed residence raged in the early 1890s.

The elitism of Ozaki's *bushidō* is noteworthy, especially in the context of later developments, and he argued that the label '*bushi*' should be restricted to individuals who had earned this distinction through their deeds. Like gentlemanship, *bushidō* was not accessible to all people, and those who understood and practised it would be called on to guide those who did not. Ozaki advocated a fundamentally meritocratic approach, but his arguments with regard to the structure of society echoed earlier writers such as Daidōji Yūzan, Yamamoto Tsunetomo, and especially Yamaga Sokō in the sense that *bushi* had a monopoly on proper behaviour, whatever this might be, and must therefore guide the other classes. In contrast, the official Meiji narrative was that previous class distinctions had been formally eliminated and that all men had become soldiers. This ostensible equality was an important part of the ideals of the Imperial Japanese Army, and was seemingly vindicated by the modern forces' suppression of the 1877 Satsuma Rebellion, while a core tenet of later mainstream *bushidō* thought was that the warrior ethic had entered into all Japanese after 1868. In this sense, the influence of idealized English views of social class and gentlemanship meant that Ozaki's insistence on meritocracy was at odds with the *bushi*-dominated society that existed before, while the elitism of his *bushidō* differed from the ostensibly classless character of later ideology.

Ozaki's *bushidō* was further set apart from prior and subsequent interpretations of warrior ethics by his failure to discuss martial matters and the concept of loyalty, focusing instead on business, a profession for which most earlier *bushi* had nothing but contempt. Ozaki's promotion of *bushidō* while disregarding military issues did not resonate with most readers in the early twentieth century, and his similarly vague position on loyalty differed from the views of later writers. On the other hand, Ozaki's *bushidō* was consistent with his arguments in *Shōbu ron*, which did not discuss loyalty as a martial virtue, and considered *bu* primarily in the context of assertiveness, independence, and ambition. Ozaki did not specifically address loyalty in his writings on martial ethics, nor did he discuss the role of the emperor in this context, either as a target for loyalty or otherwise.

Ozaki's most significant statements on loyalty and *bushidō* were his assertions that *bushi* should be 'strictly faithful', yet also 'challenge the strong' and avoid 'servility'. In this case, the virtue of faithfulness referred primarily to business partners, not superiors or feudal lords. The idea that one should challenge the strong and avoid servility conflicted with many other interpretations of loyalty, especially the absolute loyalty towards emperor and nation demanded by later *bushidō* interpretations. It reflected Ozaki's personal convictions, however, and his later opposition to the Pacific War with the United States (1941–45) resulted in his brief imprisonment. Ozaki's recommendation to challenge the strong, as well as his

---

[59] Ozaki Yukio, *Ozaki Gakudō zenshū* 3, pp. 190–93.

admiration for fair play, anticipated Nitobe Inazo's similarly Victorian statements a decade later:

> Fair play in fight! What fertile germs of morality lie in this primitive sense of savagery and childhood. Is it not the root of all military and civic virtues? We smile (as if we had outgrown it!) at the boyish desire of the small Britisher, Tom Brown, 'to leave behind him the name of a fellow who never bullied a little boy or turned his back on a big one'. And yet, who does not know that this desire is the cornerstone on which moral structures of mighty dimensions can be reared?[60]

Although *bushidō* would develop in different directions in the twentieth century, Ozaki's articles instigated modern discourse on the subject. His early writings were noted by other theorists, and an article in the journal *Bushidō* in 1898 introduced his work to the next generation of *bushidō* scholars. The specific conditions under which Ozaki was inspired to write on *bushidō* are significant, as his studies and travels directly challenged him to reassess Japan's culture. The relationship between Ozaki's *bushidō* theories and the social and cultural conditions in which he lived reflected the complex developments in Japanese national consciousness around 1890, and foreshadowed many of the issues that Nitobe Inazō and other internationalist *bushidō* theorists would wrestle with a decade later.

FUKUZAWA YUKICHI'S VIEW OF MARTIAL HONOUR

Ozaki's *bushidō* theories successfully captured the zeitgeist and responses were not long in coming. In late 1891, his former mentor Fukuzawa wrote *Yasegaman no setsu* (*On Dignified and Unyielding Resilience*), criticizing the 1868 surrender of Edo Castle to imperial loyalist armies by the shogunal commander Katsu Kaishū (1823–99). Fukuzawa shared Ozaki's concern for the nation and agreed that *bushidō* had an important role to play in Japan, but the focus of his concern differed considerably. Whereas Ozaki discussed *bushidō* in the context of the future of Japanese mercantilism, Fukuzawa claimed to be concerned with national security and the influence of Japan's cultural reputation on its foreign relations. *Yasegaman no setsu* ostensibly dealt with a domestic controversy, but was also concerned with Japan's changing position relative to Asia and the West.

Fukuzawa's views on nationalism and warrior ethics as outlined in *Yasegaman no setsu* were most relevant to *bushidō*, but his personal conflicts and the public debates on treaty revision were also important catalysts for this text.[61] In 1860, 26-year-old Fukuzawa met Katsu Kaishū on the ship *Kanrin Maru* as they travelled to America with the first Japanese mission to cross the Pacific. Both men were supporters of the Tokugawa regime throughout the 1860s, although only Katsu held important official positions. Aside from traditional allegiance, their reasons for supporting the

⁶⁰ Nitobe Inazo (1939), *Bushido: The Soul of Japan* (Tokyo: Kenkyusha).
⁶¹ Iida Kanae, '*Yasegaman no setsu* to *Hikawa seiwa*: Katsu Kaishū to Fukuzawa Yukichi no aida', *Mita gakkai zasshi* 90:1 (April 1990), pp. 1–18. Cited inSteele, M. William, '*Yasegaman no setsu*: On Fighting to the Bitter End', *Asian Cultural Studies Special Issue* (2002), pp. 139–40.

Tokugawa during the turbulent end of the regime were quite different, if similarly pragmatic, with Fukuzawa fearing the establishment of a xenophobic—specifically, anti-Western—government should the imperial loyalists emerge victorious.[62] Fukuzawa was convinced of the importance of Western science, technology, and institutions to Japan's future, and was concerned by the anti-foreign rhetoric of the imperial loyalist movement. Katsu sought to prevent upheaval and bloodshed which could weaken the nation even further relative to the Western powers, and supported the Tokugawa as long as reform of the existing system seemed possible. When the imperial loyalist armies approached Edo, Katsu negotiated a surrender to Saigō Takamori rather than risking a military confrontation that, regardless of the outcome, would place Japan at the mercy of foreign powers. This pragmatic decision earned Katsu the eternal enmity of Fukuzawa, who claimed that the surrender of Edo had practically and spiritually sold out the nation.

Yasegaman no setsu was concerned with the nature of nationalism and the formation of modern nation-states. Fukuzawa did not see any natural necessity for nations to form, but observed that once such a community was created, its citizens would do their utmost to promote its interests and disregard those of other states. Patriotism and loyalty to the ruler would be acclaimed as the highest virtues, and, even if a nation had many regions with distinct characteristics and interests, these must realize their unity and act together to face foreign threats.[63] Fukuzawa believed that these patriotic feelings manifested themselves in the ethic of *yasegaman*, which William Steele translates as 'fighting to the bitter end'.[64] The term '*yasegaman*' also has connotations that go beyond dogged determination, and implies maintaining a patient dignity in the face of insurmountable odds or certain defeat. Fukuzawa saw Belgium and Holland as prime examples of *yasegaman*, which drove them to preserve the honour and glory of their independence, without which they would certainly have been swallowed up by their larger neighbours through conquest or voluntary amalgamation.[65] In this case, *yasegaman* referred not only to military resistance against France and Germany, but also to the pride with which these nations insisted on their cultural and linguistic independence during times of peace.

Fukuzawa saw evidence for *yasegaman* in many different societies, but especially his own, referring to the 'great ethic of *yasegaman* intrinsic to us Japanese'.[66] Furthermore, *yasegaman* was the same as the warrior spirit that was the 'basis of the nation', and *bushidō* demanded fighting on even when expecting failure.[67] According to Fukuzawa, the warrior spirit in Japan was realized in the *bushi* of the Mikawa region, and the success of the Tokugawa family was due entirely to

[62]   Steele, M. William, '*Yasegaman no setsu:* On Fighting to the Bitter End', p. 139.

[63]   Fukuzawa Yukichi (2004), *Meiji jūnen teichū kōron, yasegaman no setsu* (Tokyo: Kōdansha gakujutsu bunko), pp. 50–51.

[64]   Steele, M. William, '*Yasegaman no setsu:* On Fighting to the Bitter End', p. 139.

[65]   Fukuzawa Yukichi, *Meiji jūnen teichū kōron, Yasegaman no setsu*, p. 53.

[66]   Fukuzawa Yukichi, *Meiji jūnen teichū kōron, Yasegaman no setsu*, p. 61.

[67]   Fukuzawa Yukichi, *Meiji jūnen teichū kōron, Yasegaman no setsu*, pp. 61, 63. Fukuzawa uses a number of terms synonymously with *bushidō* in this text, including *bushi no ikiji, shiki, shifū, shijin no fū*, and *bushi no kifū*.

the willingness of these warriors to fight to the death on their behalf, regardless of the odds against them.[68] Fukuzawa described the warrior spirit as having been forged during the Sengoku period (*c.* late fifteen to late sixteenth centuries), and continually refined and strengthened during the rest of the 'feudal' age as small warrior houses fought for their independent existence among the overwhelmingly large domains.

In contrast to this ancient ideal, Fukuzawa nostalgically lamented that the 'important great ethic' of *yasegaman* had been damaged by certain Tokugawa retainers who decided to surrender and sue for peace during the restoration wars twenty years earlier, thereby critically injuring the warrior spirit that had been cultivated over many 'hundreds and thousands' of years.[69] Fukuzawa criticized the early stage at which Katsu surrendered, when the government forces had lost but one battle and still held Edo Castle. As a comparison, Fukuzawa described the actions of naval commander Enomoto Takeaki (1836–1908), who held out at the Goryōkaku fort in Hokkaido for several more months before surrendering from a truly hopeless position. Although he still rebuked Enomoto for not perishing alongside his men, Fukuzawa commended him for acting in accordance with *bushidō* by holding out for as long as he did.[70] In contrast, Katsu's cowardly and short-sighted actions had irreparably damaged the warrior spirit and the nation as a whole. The surrender of Edo was beneficial to Japan's economy in the short term, argued Fukuzawa, but the long-term damage it caused to the warrior spirit and *yasegaman* was a national tragedy, and Katsu should have spent the rest of his days in repentance and disgrace for failing in his duty to *bushidō*.[71]

Fukuzawa explained *yasegaman* as an essential attribute for the successful negotiation of international relations even in times of peace, without which the Great Japanese Empire would not be able to secure its continued independence in the civilized world.[72] Katsu's actions severely threatened this independence, as foreigners observing the events of 1868 were stunned by the ease with which a seemingly powerful 270-year old government crumbled when challenged by the forces of only two or three large domains. Fukuzawa feared that the lack of warrior spirit displayed by Katsu would become apparent if Japan was challenged by foreign powers, which were more likely to take an aggressive stance after observing the ease with which the shogunate was overthrown.[73] Fukuzawa considered the future of the warrior spirit to be critically important to Japan's development over the next century, and claimed to have written *Yasegaman no setsu* to call attention to this crisis, rather than to settle old scores with Katsu or Enomoto.[74]

Fukuzawa's views regarding the supposed Meiji degeneration of the warrior spirit—and the importance of its regeneration to Japan's future success—echoed Ozaki's *bushidō*, although there were also significant differences between the two. Whereas Ozaki largely neglected to mention martial affairs in his *bushidō* theories,

---

[68] Fukuzawa Yukichi, *Meiji jūnen teichū kōron, Yasegaman no setsu*, p. 54.
[69] Fukuzawa Yukichi, p. 55.   [70] Fukuzawa Yukichi, pp. 63–65.
[71] Fukuzawa Yukichi, pp. 55–56.   [72] Fukuzawa Yukichi, p. 54.
[73] Fukuzawa Yukichi, pp. 56, 58. [74] Fukuzawa Yukichi, pp. 68–69.

military action was an important theme in Fukuzawa's work. On the other hand, the two agreed that the strength of spirit and individualism they found so admirable in the West also existed in Japan, but had recently been weakened. Self-reliance and independence were the foundations of a 'civilizational spirit' that Fukuzawa desired to find in contemporary society, and both men agreed that these qualities were most pronounced in the former *bushi* class. For this reason, Fukuzawa viewed the redirection of loyalty from domainal lords to the nation as a positive development, as the spirit of the warrior class had to be cultivated and promoted as much as possible, rather than being destroyed or lost.[75]

As Fukuzawa's comments on independence and self-reliance indicate, the loyalty he advocated towards the nation was not the unconditional obedience to the emperor prescribed by many later promoters of *bushidō*. Fukuzawa saw patriotism as a positive force, but he was also a staunch defender of the peoples' rights to dissent and protest. In his *Commentary on the National Problems of 1877 (Meiji jūnen teichū kōron)*, dated 1877 but published together with *Yasegaman no setsu* in 1901, Fukuzawa criticized the attacks on Saigō Takamori that filled the newspapers at the time. Fukuzawa argued that the end of the Satsuma Rebellion marked the elimination of the right to protest in Japan, and that 'higher principles' (*taigi meibun*) had come to mean nothing more than blindly following the government.[76] Although Fukuzawa addressed the subject of loyalty in greater depth than Ozaki, his views reflected contemporary Western ideas regarding patriotism, not absolute and unquestioning devotion to emperor and state.

Fukuzawa's warrior ethics were rooted in his complex relationship with the samurai class into which he was born. Following the official abolition of the Tokugawa class distinctions in early Meiji, Fukuzawa surrendered his own low-ranking *shizoku* status and became a commoner in a show of solidarity. Around this time, Fukuzawa criticized the affectations of the samurai, especially their fondness for swords in an age when they had no practical application.[77] Sixteen years later, the jurist Ienaga Toyokichi (1862–1936) wrote of Fukuzawa striking 'a heavy blow at the arrogance and extreme love of military glory of the Samurai class, with whom to die for the cause of his sovereign, whatever that cause might be, was the highest act of patriotism'. According to Ienaga, Fukuzawa struck this blow by arguing that 'Death is a democrat, and that the Samurai who died fighting for his country, and the servant who was slain while caught stealing from his master, were alike dead and useless'.[78]

On the other hand, Fukuzawa was famously proud of his renounced samurai heritage and greatly disliked being mistaken for a commoner.[79] In spite of his

[75] Inoue Isao (2004), 'Tokugawa no ishin: sono kōdō to rinri', in Inoue Isao (ed.), *Kaikoku to bakumatsu no dōran (Nihon no jidai shi* 20) (Tokyo: Furukawa Kōbunkan), p. 263.

[76] There is doubt regarding the exact date of this text as it remained unpublished, and the primary evidence for it having been written in 1877 is Fukuzawa's own claim. Koyasu Nobukuni (2003), *Nihon kindai shisō hihan: ikkokuchi no seiritsu* (Tokyo: Iwanami gendai bunko), pp. 307, 308.

[77] Fukuzawa Yukichi; Dilwoth, David A., Hurst III, G. Cameron (trans.) (2009), *An Outline of a Theory of Civilization* (New York: Columbia University Press), p. 38.

[78] Iyenaga Toyokichi (1891), *The Constitutional Development of Japan 1863–1881* (Dodo Press).

[79] Fukuzawa Yukichi, *The Autobiography of Yukichi Fukuzawa*, p. 392f.

earlier criticisms, Fukuzawa had a fascination with swords and swordplay that was recounted by several sources. The Unitarian missionary Arthur May Knapp (1841–1921) described a demonstration of swordsmanship by Fukuzawa during a visit at the latter's home: 'A mere touch of the hilt of the old sword had transformed the leading educator of the realm into the fierce samurai, ready on the instant with either weapon or life to devote himself to his country's weal'. Writing in 1898, Knapp described Fukuzawa as exemplifying the samurai spirit, which the American portrayed as superior to rapidly fading European chivalry.[80] Fukuzawa's eclectic samurai ideal incorporated individualism, self-reliance, and independence, echoing Ozaki's *bushidō* and setting it apart from pre-Meiji writings on warrior ethics, as well as from the majority of *bushidō* theories that would appear in the following decades.

Fukuzawa and Ozaki largely agreed in their views on loyalty and the continued importance of warrior ethics, but they differed with regard to the elitism of their *bushidō*. Ozaki's *bushidō* was comparable to English gentlemanship in the sense that it was a virtue to which one aspired but could only be realized by a minority. In contrast, Fukuzawa was more strongly influenced by American egalitarianism, leading him to publicly reject class distinctions such as had existed under the Tokugawa.[81] This differentiated Fukuzawa's *bushidō* from both Ozaki's interpretation and most Edo writings on the role of samurai. The classless and nationalistic view of *bushidō* became a dominant theme in later mainstream *bushidō* theory, which superimposed the warrior mentality on to all Japanese.

The influence of geopolitical developments on *Yasegaman no setsu* is evident in Fukuzawa's concern for Japan's security in the face of foreign threats. As the most prominent Meiji internationalist, Fukuzawa's earlier writings foreshadowed the trend towards a reassessment of Japan's status relative to the West, which became especially pronounced during the treaty negotiations around 1890. From the 1870s onward, Fukuzawa argued for the realization of 'independent self-respect' in Japan, and frequently criticized Westerners' belief in their own superiority.[82] Accordingly, *Yasegaman no setsu* portrayed the Western powers primarily as a foreign threat that could take advantage of a Japan weakened by the compromising of its warrior spirit.

Fukuzawa's widely publicized writings on Japan's relationship with China and the West reflected—and helped to create—the nationalistically confident spirit of late Meiji. In contrast, his theories of warrior ethics as discussed in *Yasegaman no setsu* had their greatest impact in Japan shortly before his death. Several copies of *Yasegaman no setsu* were supposedly printed in 1891 and distributed to Katsu, Enomoto, and others along with a note affirming Fukuzawa's intent to publish the work at some point in the future, but this did not occur until a month before

---

[80] Knapp, Arthur May (1898), *Feudal and Modern Japan* (London: Duckworth), pp. 40–73.
[81] Iida Kanae, 'Fukuzawa Yukichi to bushidō: Katsu Kaishū, Uchimura Kanzō oyobi Nitobe Inazō to no kanren ni oite', *Mita gakkai zasshi* 83:1 (April 1990), p. 17.
[82] Minami Hiroshi, *Nihonjin ron: Meiji kara kyō made*, pp. 18–19.

Fukuzawa's death in early 1901.[83] The decade that elapsed between the writing and publication of *Yasegaman no setsu* makes it a useful gauge for changes in Meiji *bushidō*. While the majority of early texts on *bushidō* were largely neglected by the beginning of the twentieth century, Fukuzawa's prominence meant that *Yasegaman no setsu* was widely read on publication in 1901, and critiques by Inoue Tetsujirō, Uchimura Kanzō (1861–1930), Tokutomi Sohō, and other prominent commentators on *bushidō* illustrated the evolution of *bushidō* over the 1890s.

UEMURA MASAHISA AND EARLY CONNECTIONS BETWEEN *BUSHIDŌ* AND CHRISTIANITY

Like Ozaki and Fukuzawa, Protestant minister Uemura Masahisa (1858–1925) contributed to *bushidō* discourse on either side of the Sino-Japanese War, although he engaged with it more actively after the war. His first discussions of *bushidō* in 1894 addressed issues raised by Ozaki and, as Uemura commented on other manifestations of *bushidō* throughout the Meiji period, his work is a useful barometer for changes in discourse. Like earlier writers, Uemura was motivated to write on *bushidō* by concerns beyond Japan, and was influenced by similar contemporary currents reassessing Japan's relationship with China and the West. Uemura's Christian faith enhanced his focus on Japan's interactions with the West, foreshadowing the great interest in *bushidō* displayed by other prominent Japanese Christians, including Nitobe Inazō and Uchimura Kanzō. Following a foreign faith necessarily gave Japanese Christians a more personal 'international' perspective, especially in a difficult period of rising nationalism. The Tokugawa ban on Christianity was a recent memory and anti-Christian sentiments continued to be widespread. The tension between Uemura's patriotism and adherence to a foreign faith is clear in his writings, and *bushidō* provided a possibility for uniting these two aspects of Japanese-Christian identity.

Uemura was born in Edo in 1858, the eldest son of a mid-ranking samurai, and the family was soon caught up in the chaos of the Meiji Restoration. Falling into poverty, Uemura's father moved the family to Yokohama in 1868 in search of better opportunities, although these were slow to come.[84] One advantage that

---

83   Inoue Isao, 'Tokugawa no ishin: sono kōdō to rinri', p. 262. Katsu and Enomoto, whose exploits featured prominently in the *Yasegaman no setsu*, sent letters acknowledging that they had received the work and, according to Inoue Isao, Ishikawa Kanmei (1859–1943), the editor of the *Jiji shinpō*, published these responses together with the *Yasegaman no setsu* through Fukuzawa's newspaper in 1892 (Iida Kanae, 'Fukuzawa Yukichi to bushidō: Katsu Kaishū, Uchimura Kanzō oyobi Nitobe Inazō to no kanren ni oite', p. 23). This earlier publication, which is subject to debate, would have been fairly limited in scope, since commentaries on the text did not appear until after 1901, when they ignited a heated debate in academic circles. The limited distribution of the text before 1901 reflects Fukuzawa's concerns that both the *Yasegaman no setsu* and the related *Meiji jūnen teichū kōron* were inflammatory and should not be published until his death. Koyasu Nobukuni maintains that Fukuzawa did not publish the works before 1901 (Koyasu Nobukuni, *Nihon kindai shisō hihan: ikkokuchi no seiritsu*, pp. 307, 322).
84   Aoyoshi Katsuhisa (1941), *Dr. Masahisa Uemura: A Christian Leader* (Tokyo: Maruzen & Co.), p. 17.

Yokohama did provide was close proximity to the foreign community and Uemura was able to study at the Brown English School under the direction of Presbyterian Rev. James Ballagh. Uemura was baptized in 1873 and ordained five years later after finishing his studies at Tokyo Itchi Shin Gakkō.[85] After setting up Shitaya Itchi church in 1880 and serving as pastor for three years, in 1885 Uemura formed the Ichibanchō church, precursor to the Fujimichō church where he would serve as pastor until his death.[86] In 1888, Uemura set off on a journey to the West, reportedly turning down scholarships to Columbia and Princeton universities in order to deepen his study through travel and informal study in London.[87] Like Ozaki and Fukuzawa before him, the direct experience of the West gained by Uemura on this sojourn influenced his *bushidō* theories and broader thought.

Strong convictions and an independent spirit defined Uemura's political and religious activities, as both Japanese and foreign contemporaries recounted. Uemura had reservations about the activities and attitudes of many of the foreign missionaries in Japan, concerns he shared with Uchimura Kanzō and many other Japanese Christians, and the organizations he established were not afraid to challenge their foreign counterparts. At the same time, Uemura's staunch patriotism did not prevent him from challenging nationalistic developments, and he was willing to speak out when others would not. In 1890, Uemura became one of the few vocal supporters of Uchimura Kanzō in the so-called 'lèse majesté incident,' in which Uchimura was deemed to have failed to bow sufficiently before the copy of the Imperial Rescript on Education displayed at the First Higher School. Most Japanese Christians either kept silent or expressed favourable views towards the promulgation of the rescript, and when Uchimura himself conceded in what had by that point become a national debate, Uemura condemned him for this change of position.[88] Uemura's bold essay equating the government's policy on the rescript with idol worship provoked the banning of his *Fukuin shūhō* (*Evangelical Weekly*) newspaper, which he relaunched the following year as the *Fukuin shinpō* (*New Evangelical Report*).[89]

Uchimura's failure to bow turned widespread apprehension regarding Christianity into outright hostility. In the increasingly nationalistic climate of mid-Meiji, the patriotic credentials of followers of 'alien' faiths, including Buddhism but especially Christianity, were under constant suspicion and frequent attack. Buddhism was recovering from early Meiji policies promoting a new form of state Shinto at its expense, a process that involved the confiscation of Buddhist property and

---

[85] Amemiya Eiichi (2007), *Wakaki Uemura Masahisa* (Tokyo: Shinkyō shuppan sha), pp. 170, 202.

[86] Amemiya Eiichi, pp. 333–34.

[87] Prang, Margaret (1997), *A Heart at Leisure from Itself: Caroline MacDonald of Japan* (Vancouver: UBC Press), p. 54.

[88] Irokawa Daikichi: Marius Jansen (trans.) (1988), *The Culture of the Meiji Period* (Princeton, NJ: Princeton University Press), p. 251; Davis, Winston, 'The Civil Theology of Inoue Tetsujirō', *Japanese Journal of Religious Studies* 3:1 (March 1976), p. 11.

[89] Morioka Iwao and Kasahara Yoshimitsu (1974), *Kirisuto kyō no sensō sekinin* (Tokyo: Kyobunkan), pp. 120–21; Ohnuki-Tierney, Emiko (2002), *Kamikaze, Cherry Blossoms, and Nationalisms: The Militarization of Aesthetics in Japanese History* (Chicago: University of Chicago Press), p. 93.

destruction of many temples. Buddhists' desire to demonstrate their patriotism further threatened the position of Christianity in mid-Meiji, as many Buddhist groups devoted more energy to denouncing Christianity than to presenting arguments regarding the contributions of their own faith to the national project.[90] On the whole, Christian responses to these challenges avoided confrontation, but Uemura went on the offensive. Claiming to speak as a citizen of a modern nation, rather than as a Christian, Uemura argued that worship of the rescript violated the separation between religion and politics characteristic of constitutional government, and did not befit Japan's aspirations to be a modern state.[91]

Uemura contended that Christians were actually more patriotic than the self-professed 'ultra-nationalists', as their love for the nation was 'true Christian love' that would bring the nation on to the correct path. In contrast, the ultra-nationalists were taking the nation in the wrong direction, and their 'patriotism with a dull and stupid heart is like striving to destroy the country'.[92] While the ultra-nationalists saw the emperor and nation as the supreme objects of patriotic sentiment, Uemura viewed the nation as an ordered unit in a greater world order, which was in turn part of the highest order, that of the kingdom of God.[93] Love for his nation was an important part of Uemura's theological framework, but he felt compelled to reject certain elements of contemporary nationalistic ideology, including the notion of a divine emperor and the worship of imperial rescripts.

Japanese Christians in Meiji were forced to find ways of reconciling loyalty to their specific nation and their universal religion. Patriotic feelings came to the fore with the outbreak of the Sino-Japanese War in 1894, and support for military action was as strong in the Christian communities as in the rest of the populace. The mood of the time was reflected in events surrounding the Japan Peace Society, which ceased publication of its journal *Heiwa* (*Peace*) and was disbanded by Japanese Quakers in support of the war.[94] Uemura spoke for many of his Christian compatriots:

> ...the Sino-Japanese incident...will become the point of Japan's arrival on the world stage. From the development of business and industry to the spread of missionary work in Asia, this war will truly be the curtain-raiser on this role of the Japanese people. When thinking of this, Japanese Christians must experience extreme passion and intense desire and pray to God that this incident will increase the honour of the Japanese Empire, create a great record for the future, and even help open the edge of world civilization.[95]

The positive reactions to the conflict made it clear that their 'foreign' faith did not necessarily preclude Japanese Christians from being fervent patriots, although

---

[90] Thelle, Notto R. (1987), *Buddhism and Christianity in Japan* (Honolulu: University of Hawaii Press), pp. 153–54.
[91] Ashina Sadamichi, 'Uemura Masahisa no Nihonron (1): kindai Nihon to kirisutokyō', *Ajia/Kirisutokyō/tagensei* 6 (March 2008), p. 17.
[92] Ashina Sadamichi, pp. 15–16.   [93] Ashina Sadamichi, pp. 3–4.
[94] Sumiya Mikio (1983), *Nihon Purotesutanto shi ron* (Tokyo: Shinkyō shuppansha), p. 104.
[95] Ashina Sadamichi, 'Uemura Masahisa no Nihonron (1): kindai Nihon to kirisutokyō', p. 7.

many who had written of the coming conflict in glowing terms were disillusioned by the reality of the war and turned to more pacifistic teachings after its conclusion.[96]

Uemura expressed his strong feelings for his country shortly before the war in two articles on *bushidō* published in March and June 1894. Uemura's *bushidō* attempted to reconcile native values with foreign ones, in this case the 'warrior spirit' and Christianity. Echoing Ozaki and Fukuzawa, Uemura claimed to have been motivated to write on *bushidō* by the perceived decay in morality and vitality that had taken place during the first twenty-five years of Meiji: 'current society is anesthetized and lifeless as never before. Without turning to Christianity we will not be able to revive this country. At the same time, we must look to our past'.[97] Uemura identified the major roots of this societal degradation as Westernization undercutting Japanese traditions and ethics, while modernization exacerbated this by promoting materialism and increasing feelings of inequality among the people.[98] Like many of his contemporaries, Uemura felt that a moral vacuum had developed during Meiji and had become one of the most pressing issues facing the country.

In establishing points of reference between Japan and Europe, Uemura was especially interested in European and Japanese medieval periods. Like Ozaki Yukio, Uemura sought the foundations for Western economic and military primacy in feudal knighthood, pointing out that medieval Europe was partitioned and dominated by warlike barbarian Teutonic tribes following the successive collapses of the Roman and Holy Roman Empires:

> in feudal society another unique type of spirit was born. Fearing God and respecting man, revering the old and cherishing the young, earnestly striving for justice, this spirit did not shrink from flood or fire. Readily exposing false accusations and crushing arrogance, helping the weak and facing the strong, in turn being composed and silently praying for the emperor, offering one's life for God or the church with purpose and dedication, and especially showing loving respect to women, all of these were viewed as being sacred. Historians have given this a name and call it chivalry. In short, this is what is known as warriors grasping a sword with the right hand and holding the Holy Scriptures in the left.[99]

According to Uemura, this spirit of chivalry, this 'love of freedom and reverence for independence... formed and nurtured in the dense Teutonic forests... received the Christian baptism and came to take on a completely new appearance...'. This warrior spirit continued to reside in Europe's holy places and was key to the success of modern Western nations.[100]

[96] Howes, John F. (2005), *Japan's Modern Prophet: Uchimura Kanzo 1861–1930* (Vancouver: UBC Press), pp. 127–30.

[97] Uemura Masahisa (1966), 'Kirisutoyō to bushidō', *Bushidō* 1:2 (March 1898), 13–22; also in *Uemura Masahisa chosakushū* 1 (Tokyo: Shinkyō shuppansha), p. 396.

[98] Ashina Sadamichi, 'Uemura Masahisa no Nihonron (1): kindai Nihon to kirisutokyō', pp. 7–8.

[99] Uemura Masahisa, 'Kirisutokyō to bushidō', pp. 391–92.

[100] Uemura Masahisa, p. 392.

In comparison, Uemura argued that Japan had from ancient times been known as a martial land, and that 'the thing known as *bushidō* is that which has come to take the most distinguished and beautiful form of the spirit that worships martiality'.[101] In Uemura's view, *bushidō* reached the pinnacle of its development under the Tokugawa, when 'the vitality of society was in the *bushi*, and the vitality of the *bushi* was in *bushidō*, while those areas of society that had *bushidō* had the truest character and were the best regulated'.[102] However, when feudal society collapsed, the Buddhism and Confucianism that supported *bushidō* collapsed with it, and when the samurai put away their swords and bows, they also put away *bushidō*, this 'beautiful flower of the human mind' nurtured by the Japanese for hundreds of years.[103] Uemura called on his countrymen to not stand idly by as their spiritual inheritance from the warrior class disintegrated or, even worse, was intentionally expunged from society. '*Bushidō*', he argued, 'is truly like a type of religion, and society was able to maintain its life through it... Society must revive the old *bushidō*. Or rather, what I desire is a *bushidō* that has received the baptism'.[104] Uemura argued that Japan could not succeed without relying on both Christianity and its own historical past in order to fill the void left by the 'collapse' of Buddhism and Confucianism.

Less than two months before the outbreak of the Sino-Japanese War, Uemura published another article on *bushidō*, in which he voiced common concerns regarding the perceived degeneration of contemporary society:

> Japan's unique martial character is something that its citizens should be proud of. How our ancestors trained and worked to create the style of this martial character! Even if it can be said that the temperament of the *bushi* had more than a few strange elements, it must also be said that it contained the light and salt of Great Japan. With every passing day we become more vulgar and soft, are led by the followers of the religion of learning how to profit, and the principles of the people are eating and drinking. In this, our country, we must understand the great urgency of preserving the fading light of our ancestors that is *bushidō*, and conserving its essence. This is the way of patriotism, and the duty of descendants to their distant ancestors.[105]

Scholars had forgotten that the preservation of the warrior essence was critical for the future of the nation, Uemura warned, and this was a most pressing political issue. The world had changed, he wrote, and simply revering *bushidō* in the old way was no longer feasible, necessitating other methods of preserving the warrior spirit.

Here, Uemura rhetorically addressed Ozaki's arguments: 'Could trade be the thing that preserves *bushidō*? No. It is like trying to draw breath in a vacuum'. Furthermore, 'Today's education is useless. It merely fosters men with clever technical abilities. Politics are useless. National affairs should be done in the school of the way of the samurai (*shidō*)'.[106] Meiji political and social structures had diminished

---

[101] Uemura Masahisa, p. 393.   [102] Uemura Masahisa, p. 394.
[103] Uemura Masahisa, p. 394.   [104] Uemura Masahisa, pp. 394–95.
[105] Uemura Masahisa (1966), 'Nani wo motte bushidō no sui wo hozon sen to suru ka', *Uemura Masahisa chosakushū* 1 (Tokyo: Shinkyō shuppansha), p. 397.
[106] Uemura Masahisa, 'Nani wo motte bushidō no sui wo hozon sen to suru ka', p. 398.

the value placed on righteous spirits, Uemura contended, and despaired when comparing the 'factory-like private schools' with the *shijuku* schools of earlier times. The modern schools were responsible for the decline of the ethic of 'sacrificing oneself for the common good...specifically required to swiftly and victoriously smash the materialistic spirit with a spirit of responsibility, duty, loyalty, and furious righteousness'. According to Uemura, the great task of solving these issues had fallen exclusively to Japanese Christians, who should '...frequently theorize on the relationship between *bushidō* and Christianity...'[107]

Both Uemura and Ozaki agreed that the foundations of contemporary Western power were to be found in medieval knighthood, and proposed a new ethic that resurrected traditional ideals and combined them with supposedly proven elements from Western history. Whereas Ozaki focused on secular elements of English chivalry and gentlemanship that could benefit Japanese businessmen, Uemura dismissed the notion that *bushidō* was related to mercantilism. Instead, he stressed Christian influences as he simultaneously proposed the national conversion of Japan to Christianity. Uemura saw the emphasis on trade in Ozaki's *bushidō* as a part of the 'materialistic spirit' that had taken over Japan during Meiji, and also criticized the burgeoning political arena in which Ozaki was rapidly becoming an important figure.

Uemura was willing and, through his newspapers, able to address issues of popular interest. His advocacy for Christianity would always place him outside mainstream *bushidō* discourse, but his commentaries and criticism reflected the development of *bushidō* thought during the late Meiji and Taishō periods. A series of articles published by Uemura in March 1898 addressed the growing post-war interest in *bushidō*. The first of these articles, which sought *bushidō* in Paul's letter to the Corinthians, criticized contemporary discourse: 'The Japanese have a habit of taking pride in calling on the ambiguous Yamato spirit and claiming that they have a sole monopoly on *bushidō*. This is nothing but a biased view. *Bushidō* can definitely not be said to be unique to our country'. Uemura listed Turkey, Rome, Greece, England, and Tartary as examples of other nations that possessed *bushidō*, and attacked the increasing involvement of ultra-nationalists in *bushidō* discourse following the victory over China.[108] These chauvinistic movements distressed Uemura by rejecting the Western ideals that not only inspired and legitimized his *bushidō*, but also provided the all-important link with Christianity.

The Christian character of Uemura's *bushidō* theories set them apart from those of Ozaki and Fukuzawa, but their aims and motivations were consistent with this early discourse. All three writers reassessed Japan's relationship with the West in their search for a modern native ethic, while simultaneously considering the existence of a *bushidō* equivalent in the West to be an important legitimating factor. The Sino-Japanese War changed this dynamic by sweeping aside earlier insecurities and concerns, and the *bushidō* discourse that came after this watershed was generally more nationalistic, diminishing the direct influence of the earlier texts

---

[107] Uemura Masahisa, p. 398.   [108] Uemura Masahisa, pp. 399–403.

on popular perceptions of the subject. Accordingly, Uemura's *bushidō* theories were read primarily by Japanese Christians, and it has been argued that Uemura directly inspired Nitobe Inazō's writings, although conclusive evidence for this is still outstanding.[109] In addition to being an early promoter and popularizer of *bushidō*, Uemura monitored developing discourse, and was one of a small number of informed critical voices willing and able to oppose the chauvinistic currents in mainstream *bushidō* discourse in the late 1890s and beyond.

SUZUKI CHIKARA: *BUSHIDŌ*, MILITARISM, AND THE RISE OF CULTURAL NATIONALISM

A very different response to Ozaki Yukio's *bushidō* is found in the writings of Suzuki Chikara (Tengan; 1867–1926), who sought to reposition Japan in the world order. Suzuki's emphasis on the national spirit echoed contemporary comparisons of Western and Japanese culture by Miyake Setsurei (1860–1945) and others, but differed in seeking this spirit in the pre-Meiji samurai.[110] In contrast to Ozaki, Suzuki emphasized the martial characteristics of the *bushi* in his 1893 *Kokumin no shin seishin* (*The True Spirit of the Nation*), and further argued that the *bushi* virtues of diligence, economy, loyalty, and honour were essential in the global struggle for survival and supremacy. Suzuki supported the Sino-Japanese War, as Ozaki, Fukuzawa, and Uemura had done, but went further by invoking the warrior spirit to promote militaristic expansionism in East Asia. Suzuki was primarily concerned with Japan's status relative to the rest of the world, and in many ways, his theories were forerunners of the militaristic *bushidō* interpretations of the early twentieth century.

Suzuki was born in 1867 in Fukushima and his background provides some insight into his motivations for writing *Kokumin no shin seishin* at the age of twenty-six. Younger than Ozaki, Fukuzawa, and Uemura, Suzuki did not have any meaningful memory of the reality of life in the samurai-controlled Edo period, although he shared a strong dislike for the Satsuma- and Chōshū-dominated government. This bias was enhanced by his origins in the Tokugawa loyalist domain of Aizu, which saw some of the fiercest fighting during the civil war of 1868 and was the scene of the famous suicides of the White Tigers of Aizu (*byakkotai*).[111] Suzuki developed an idealistic nostalgia for the Tokugawa age and the *bushi* who dominated it, and saw himself primarily as a Fukushima *shizoku* even after moving to Tokyo at the age of fourteen.[112] In 1886, Suzuki translated the German educator

[109] Chien Shiaw-hua, 'Xi lun zhicun zhengjiu zhi jidujiao yu wushidao guanxi', *Dong hua renwen xuebao* 8 (Jan. 2006), pp. 147–72.

[110] Miyake Setsurei's 'Shin-zen-bi Nihonjin' and *Gi-aku-shū Nihonjin* were both published in 1891 (see Minami Hiroshi, *Nihonjin ron: Meiji kara kyō made*, pp. 43–44).

[111] Minami Hiroshi (1996), 'Kaisetsu', *Sōsho Nihonjin ron 2: Kokumin no shin seishin* (Tokyo: Ozorasha), p. 3. For a discussion of the *byakkotai* incident, seeRankin, Andrew (2011), *Seppuku: A History of Samurai Suicide* (Tokyo: Kodansha International), pp. 184–94.

[112] Shimonaka Kunihiko (1979), *Nihon jinmei dai jiten* 3 (Tokyo: Heibonsha), pp. 482–83.

Clemens Klöpper's *Repetitorium der Geschichte der Paetagogik*, an expansive history of educational systems around the world, attesting to his understanding of the German language and awareness of conditions outside Japan.[113]

Following a brief stay at a preparatory school in Tokyo, Suzuki abandoned his studies in order to travel to the Asian continent. After falling ill in China, Suzuki travelled to Nagasaki to convalesce, during which time he wrote an overview of the city that emphasized its close historical and economic ties with China.[114] Suzuki developed a fondness for Nagasaki, later spending a great deal of time there and meeting dignitaries such as Sun Yat-sen (1866–1925) when they passed through the city. Having recovered, Suzuki returned to Tokyo and in 1890 began publishing *Active Youth* (*Katsu seinen*), a magazine extolling the virtues of the Japanese spirit.[115] Suzuki further refined his emphasis on the Japanese spirit in his *The Locus of Strength* (1892), which began to develop many of the themes found in *Kokumin no shin seishin*, including the investigation of Japan's ancient militarism.[116] In 1893, Suzuki became editor-in-chief of Akiyama Teisuke's (1868–1950) *Niroku shinpō* newspaper, which had close ties with powerful nationalist organizations, including the Gen'yōsha (Dark Ocean Society) and later the Kokuryūkai (Amur River Society).[117] These connections gave *Niroku shinpō* exclusive access to various groups of Japanese adventurers active on the Asian continent, and regularly reported on their activities and the situation in China and Korea.

One of these organizations, a loose collection of young adventurers and 'journalists' centred on the Ōsaki Law Office in Pusan, became very important for both the newspaper and Suzuki personally, and his involvement with their activities reflected the ideals promoted in his writings. This group of '*Chōsen rōnin*' ('masterless samurai in Korea') was dominated by *shizoku* in their twenties, who felt locked out of education and career paths due to their birth in domains outside the influential imperial loyalist group. Like many other members of the 'second generation of Meiji', these individuals were disillusioned by the meagre opportunities available to them, but had grown up with the bounties of modernization and firmly believed in Japan's national strength.[118] This drove many young men to seek their fortunes abroad in the spirit of the *Niroku shinpō's* creed: 'Japan should rule all of Asia, the European powers all of Europe and Africa, the USA all of the Americas, and the South Pacific could be divided between them all'.[119]

---

[113] Klöpper, Clemens: Suzuki Chikara (trans.) (1889), *Kyōiku tetsugaku shi* (Tokyo: Hakubundō). This is a combined publication of two volumes that were published separately in November 1886 and March 1889, respectively.

[114] Suzuki Chikara (1890), *Nagasaki miyage: shin shin* (Nagasaki). The publication of this text was apparently partially funded by the China Japan Trade Commission (Shina Nihon bōeki shōkai), and the last ten pages of the work consist of an advertising supplement from this organization.

[115] Suzuki Chikara (1891), *Katsu seinen* (Tokyo: Hakubundō).

[116] Suzuki Chikara (1892), *Masurao no honryō—ichimei tōzai risshihen* (Tokyo: Gakuenkai), pp. 56–63.

[117] Minami Hiroshi, 'Kaisetsu', p. 4.

[118] Kang Ching-Il, 'Tenyūkyō to 'Chōsen mondai': 'Chōsen rōnin' no tōgaku nōmin sensō he no taiō to kanren shite,' *Shigaku Zasshi* 97:8 (1988), pp. 1339, 1341–42.

[119] Kang Ching-Il, p. 1341.

As Sino-Japanese relations deteriorated over the 'Korea problem' in 1893–94, the Ōsaki Law Office group hatched a plan to join with the Tonghak peasant rebellion sweeping across the Korean countryside and drive out the Qing forces stationed in the country. The group desired a temporary alliance with the Tonghak to pursue their common aim of overthrowing the anti-Japanese government, after which they hoped to outmanoeuvre the Tonghak leaders and create a new Japanese-Korean government.[120] In order to realize their aims, Ōsaki Masayoshi (1865–?), an adventurer who headed the group's law office headquarters, travelled to Tokyo to request funding from the sympathetic *Niroku shinpō*. Here, he convinced Suzuki to use his connections with Matono Hansuke (1858–1917) and Tōyama Mitsuru (1855–1944) of the Gen'yōsha to arrange funding as well as additional manpower, and even persuaded Suzuki to accompany him back to Korea to join his cause. Travelling to Pusan via Osaka and Fukuoka, Suzuki and Ōsaki received considerable funds from sympathizers, but were only able to collect three more men due to close monitoring of Gen'yōsha activities by the secret police.[121]

After regrouping in Pusan, the group of fourteen adventurers, who now called themselves the Ten'yūkyō (Order of Divine Chivalry), set out to make contact with the Tonghak and carry out a military strike on a Qing base in the north of the country. The Ten'yūkyō tried unsuccessfully to purchase weapons around Pusan before raiding a Japanese-owned mine and making off with ten pounds of dynamite and several guns. The Japanese legation in Pusan subsequently designated the Ten'yūkyō as bandits, but took no significant action to apprehend them. The group's grand plans ultimately came to naught and they split up at the outbreak of the Sino-Japanese War, with Suzuki falling ill and returning to Japan via Seoul.[122] The Ten'yūkyō were involved in a number of sensationalized incidents exclusively reported by the *Niroku shinpō* in Tokyo—then billed as the 'mouthpiece of the Ten'yūkyō'. These gripping reports from the field led to a considerable increase in the paper's circulation, and the success of this business model led the *Niroku shinpō* to later repeat it by sending reporters to accompany Japanese troops suppressing the Boxer Rebellion.[123] On the whole, the Ten'yūkyō's adventure was an outlet for frustrated young *shizoku* who felt disenfranchised and disillusioned in their own country, yet were confident of Japan's strength and saw its rightful position as the leader of East Asia.

Suzuki's personal background and experiences on the continent, combined with his ideas regarding the Japanese spirit and the strength of the nation, made him quickly consent to joining the Ten'yūkyō. Following a European-influenced education, Suzuki became disillusioned with the West and turned towards Eastern values. While respecting China's cultural and historical accomplishments, Suzuki was critical of contemporary developments and concluded that both Western and Chinese thought were alien to Japan. Instead, Japan had to focus on its own 'true

---

[120] Kang Ching-Il, pp. 1336–38.   [121] Kang Ching-Il, p. 1329.
[122] Kang Ching-Il, p. 1335.
[123] Kang Ching-Il, pp. 1323–24. Chae Soo Do, 'Kokuryūkai no seiritsu: genyōsha to tairiku rōnin no katsudō wo chūshin ni', *Hōgaku shinpō* 109:1/2 (2002), p. 172.

spirit of the nation' and promote 'national spirit-ism' (*kokkon shugi*), concepts manifested in the former *bushi* class and their '*bushidō* learning', which should serve as the model for the nation.

Kokumin no shin seishin was a reaction to broader trends, but its rejection of foreign models and ideas also went further than earlier discourse. Suzuki acknowledged that a number of nationalists, including Tani Tateki (1837–1911), Miura Gorō (1847–1926), Takahashi Kenzō (1855–98), Kuga Katsunan (1857–1907), and Sugiura Shigetake (1855–1924), had grasped the concept of 'national purity' in their examinations of the 'true spirit' of Japan. Suzuki also mentioned Ozaki Yukio and Inoue Tetsujirō as men who had travelled widely and understood the importance of the state. Ultimately, he dismissed all of these thinkers as being too Westernized and following foreign models even in their nationalism, when the current state of the world made it essential for Japan to promote its own 'true national spirit.' Just as the Confucian scholars of a previous age 'drank Chinese learning into their brains', Meiji Japanese were becoming overly enamoured with Western thought. While this had brought superficial technical advancement, Suzuki claimed, the stagnation of the Japanese spirit in recent decades had resulted in a split personality that could only be overcome by a return to native virtues.[124]

Suzuki was not alone in his criticism of foreign influences and the degeneration of modern society, but he took Meiji nationalistic thought in a new direction by seeking the 'true national spirit' of Japan in the former *bushi*. While Ozaki, Fukuzawa, and Uemura discussed samurai virtues in parallel with Western ideals, Suzuki contended that Japanese ethics were far superior to those of other nations. Long ago, he argued, the warrior class had formed the 'marrow of society' and were the arbiters of morality. Farmers and townsmen provided the means of production, while the *bushi* instilled virtues of loyalty and duty and provided a model to guide the behaviour of the entire nation.[125] During this time, *bushi* were compelled to follow unswervingly the 'teaching of *bushidō*', and risked banishment or having to commit *seppuku* if they acted irresponsibly or lost face for themselves or their lords. Like Ozaki, Suzuki saw the decline of the samurai occurring from the early seventeenth century onward, and described the spirit of the Tokugawa *bushi* as 'completely rotten and corrupted'.[126]

The *bushi* then became the new middle class of Meiji, Suzuki wrote, and their conduct and morality were entirely untested. Under this system, if a man's ability in even one area was slightly above average, he could join the 'forest of officials', as the demand for Western things created a situation in which translators and interpreters of minor talent earned far more than their meagre abilities justified. Suzuki, whose access to the Meiji system was complicated by his place of birth, charged that even minimal knowledge of Western literature could lead to high salaries in government and industry, resulting in an elite class of 'crowned monkeys' who had taken over the salaries of the *bushi* but lost their spirit.[127] The solution he proposed

---

[124] Suzuki Chikara (1893), *Kokumin no shin seishin* (Tokyo: Hakubuntō), pp. 1–4; Minami Hiroshi, *Nihonjin ron: Meiji kara kyō made*, p. 45.
[125] Suzuki Chikara, *Kokumin no shin seishin*, p. 8.   [126] Suzuki Chikara, p. 27.
[127] Suzuki Chikara, p. 10–12.

to these problems was to help people understand morality by eliminating two 'evil thoughts', namely 'the subservient spirit of worshipping the foreign and forgetting the native' and 'the delusion of worshipping logic and reason'.[128]

To eliminate the first of these two 'evil thoughts', Suzuki insisted that Japanese must rid themselves of the belief that they could not challenge the West. Awe of Western power and institutions had resulted in many negative changes during the Meiji period, with the Western-style parliamentary system an 'assault on the emperor's power' and a disguised attempt to make Christianity the state religion.[129] Suzuki considered Western weapons to be vital to Japan, but described military uniforms and other imported accoutrements as 'meaningless' and detrimental to society.[130] Similarly, Suzuki advocated restricting the use of Western languages as much as possible, with important texts being translated by a few specialists and read in Japanese, while the creation of new terms using Chinese characters would 'complete' the language. This would have the added benefit of eliminating the need for foreign instructors who were liable to mislead the people. Suzuki considered the effectiveness of this policy to have been proven by the Chinese commander Zeng Guofan (1811–72), who led the suppression of the Taiping rebellion three decades earlier. Zeng realized the importance of Western weaponry, importing modern arms and implementing European drilling methods at the military academies he built, but wisely rejected Western instructors, instead relying on Chinese to research and teach the subjects themselves. In this way, Suzuki continued, 'although Chinese are today derided for being stubborn barbarians, they have admirably maintained their own culture and heritage'.[131]

Suzuki admonished his countrymen to not forget the 'native' virtues of loyalty, filial piety, thrift, and diligence, which were the 'soul and nature of Japan' and the 'absolute standard for ethics that leads to happiness and beauty'.[132] The Westernized educational policies of the Meiji government threatened to 'create foreigners in Japan' and should be replaced by 'national spirit education'. All foreign teachings should be secondary to the study of national literature and language, which would reverse the degenerative process by which Japanese were 'forgetting *budō* and becoming lewd believers in Christianity'. Suzuki charged teachers with failing in their task by not discussing right and wrong or superior and inferior, but merely counting scores on tests; he called on them to encourage 'pure spirits and emphasize decorum' while ensuring that students learn the virtues of purity and rightness.[133] There had never been another country that valued its warriors as much as Japan had, Suzuki claimed, and this spirit had to be recovered and implemented in the education system.[134]

Arguing that Japan's martial culture was superior to those of other nations, Suzuki advocated the spread of Japanese language and culture to other countries, by force if necessary. He found historical precedents for military intervention overseas

[128] Suzuki Chikara, p. 44.
[130] Suzuki Chikara, p. 146.
[132] Suzuki Chikara, pp. 61, 63, 64.
[134] Suzuki Chikara, p. 94.

[129] Suzuki Chikara, pp. 95–98, 124.
[131] Suzuki Chikara, pp. 135–37.
[133] Suzuki Chikara, pp. 134–38.

in the Sengoku period, pointing out that the Japanese had been known as *wakō* pirates who terrorized the coasts of China and Taiwan. This 'natural spirit', Suzuki claimed, should be revived to drive Japan's advance into these regions with equal aggressiveness as the Western powers. In contrast, Suzuki referred to the negotiating approach to treaty reform taken by the statesman Inoue Kaoru (1836–1915) as 'mental illness', since diplomacy could only be used for peace. Instead, he argued that Japan should expand its national rights not only through trade and navigation, but take up arms to spread its language and culture throughout the world.[135]

Several discoursal trends intersected in *Kokumin no shin seishin*. Suzuki's international experience and awareness were similar to those of other early *bushidō* theorists, but his criticism of foreign thought separated him from those seeking native equivalents to Western ethical concepts. Suzuki insisted on Japanese cultural superiority, rather than mere equality, and Minami Hiroshi argues that Suzuki's firm belief in the exceptional nature of the Japanese spirit made him the first thinker in the developing nationalistic discourse commonly referred to as 'Japaneseness theory' (*Nihonjin ron*) to anchor his cultural theory in the samurai.[136] Like Fukuzawa, Suzuki preferred his own concept to the label '*bushidō*', but the ideas he developed as 'the true spirit of the nation' were the most complete early outline of what would come to be understood as *bushidō* after the Sino-Japanese War. In addition, the connections that Suzuki drew between *bushidō*, cultural nationalism, imperialism, and militarism would have very real effects on Japan and the rest of East Asia. As for Suzuki himself, he returned to publishing, founding influential nationalistic papers such as the *Kyūshū hi no de shinbun* and *Tōyō hi no de shinbun*, while his prominence and connections helped him get elected to the lower house of the Imperial Diet.[137] In addition to his official political roles, Suzuki was able to influence Japanese decision-making through his connections with the Gen'yōsha and the Kokuryūkai (Amur River Society), which he helped found in 1901.

THE FOUNDATIONS OF MODERN *BUSHIDŌ*

As discussions of *bushidō* began to appear in academic works, historians also turned to the subject. In a series of articles published in the *Journal for the Promotion of Historical Studies* in 1893, Tokyo Imperial University history professor Shigeno Yasutsugu (1827–1910) sought the origins of the martial spirit in Japan's earliest recorded history, arguing that even though the term '*bushidō*' did not exist, the ancient Mononobe family were the prototype of Japan's warriors.[138] Shigeno juxtaposed the concept of *bushidō* with the rule of law, defining it as a political term referring to rule by martial force.[139] Shigeno's historiographical use of

---

[135] Suzuki Chikara, pp. 81–94.
[136] Minami Hiroshi, *Nihonjin ron: Meiji kara kyō made*, p. 45.
[137] Minami Hiroshi, 'Kaisetsu', p. 4.
[138] Shigeno Yasutsugu, 'Bushidō ha Ōtomo-Mononobe futauji no okiri hōritsu seiji ha Fujiwara uji ni naru', *Shigaku fukyū zasshi* 8 (1 April 1893), p. 7.
[139] Shigeno Yasutsugu, p. 10.

bushidō demonstrated that the concept was beginning to acquire legitimacy even among scholars of history, although their examinations of *bushidō* in subsequent decades were often intended to justify its application in modern Japan. The two approaches of conducting historical research (Shigeno) and creating a prescriptive ethic (Ozaki) were often conflated, as could be seen in an 1891 article on *bushidō* by historian and later Gakushūin University professor Matsumoto Aijū (18??– 1935), who attempted to treat *bushidō* historically while relating it to the present. Matsumoto defined *bushidō* as the manifestation of Japan's martial essence, tracing its history to Amaterasu and the Age of the Gods. Matsumoto referred to *bushidō* as a historical relic that could not be applied directly to modern society, but speculated that it might be able to contribute a few unspecified elements to compensate for the lack of ethics in some corners of society beyond the reach of the modern legal system.[140]

The handful of editorials and articles published on *bushidō* in the early 1890s reflect the gradual growth of discourse, and *bushidō* was still far from being popularly accepted. An 1891 editorial described *bushidō* as a thing of the past:

> ... in this nation from ancient times, in the time of the Tokugawa the ethical mind of the samurai and common people was dominated by Confucianism, Buddhism, and so-called *bushidō*. The great spread of false theories should be eliminated, for the results of superstitions and misunderstandings are far-reaching and cause countless errors to occur... When the old order was reformed by the Restoration, the roots of morality (incomplete as they were) were also swept away, Confucianism became servile and was driven out, while Buddhism lost its strength when it lost its vermilion seal. Western ethics came to dominate books and courses. Even the progress of Christianity is not very rapid. Because society does not have any strength to sanction, moral customs are largely deteriorating to an extreme point, and making money becomes the sole goal of human life.[141]

The editorial argued that Japan had to construct a new morality carefully, considering the strengths and weaknesses of foreign systems before introducing them to Japan, while the complete adoption of foreign traits or total rejection of native elements would be mistaken approaches. *Bushidō* was dismissed as an obsolete relic, although preceding the term with the qualifier 'so-called' (*iwayuru*) reveals that *bushidō* was receiving some mention.[142] The lead article in the 3 July 1892 edition of the *Yomiuri shinbun* was similarly dismissive of the relevance of *bushidō*, stating that while the 'feudal age' had *bushidō* loyalty, the present day was defined by freedom and popular rights and abuse of the lower classes was no longer widespread.[143]

In addition to the creeping legitimization of samurai-based ideologies, the term '*bushidō*' also began to become established around this time. The word was largely unknown before the late 1880s, and only used sporadically by a small number of authors in the following decade. The increasing appearance of the term throughout

---

[140] Matsumoto Aijū, 'Bushidō', *Tōyō tetsugaku* 4:2 (15 April 1897), pp. 90–94.

[141] *Yomiuri shinbun*, 22 July 1891, p. 2.

[142] See, for example, Yoshikawa Akimasa's article published in response to the Imperial Rescript on Education; cited in Fuji Naotomo (1956), *Nihon no bushidō* (Osaka: Sōgensha), p. 153.

[143] *Yomiuri shinbun*, 3 July 1892.

the 1890s was also related to the linguistic evolution of the words *budō* and *shidō*, as popular interest in the martial arts increased. As martial arts were standardized and codified, the character *dō* (way) came to replace the earlier *jutsu* (skills), while '*budō*' narrowed in meaning until, by the 1890s, it referred almost exclusively to martial arts.[144] Nitobe Inazō alluded to this shift in meaning in lectures held in the early 1930s:

> Some thirty years ago, when I first wrote an essay on the moral code of the Japanese and called it 'Bushido', there was raised a question both in Japan and among some scholars abroad as to the legitimacy of such a term. They had heard of *Shido* or *Budo* but never of 'Bushido'...Since it was made a class morality of the knights, samurai, it laid particular stress on honor; and because it was primarily meant for observance by that class, we may call it Bushido, the Way of the Fighting Knights.[145]

By the time Nitobe's *Bushido: The Soul of Japan* was published in 1900, it would have seemed anachronistic to discuss samurai ethics using the term *budō*. Instead, writers on the samurai in the 1890s appropriated '*bushidō*', which was essentially synonymous with *budō* in the few instances in which it had been used before Meiji.

The developmental trajectory of *shidō*, another term used synonymously with *bushidō* at various times, is less clear. Although still used by writers such as Uemura Masahisa and Suzuki Chikara in the early 1890s, *shidō* fell into disuse and essentially disappeared by the end of Meiji as *bushidō* gained in prominence. When the third reprint of Suzuki's *The Locus of Strength* appeared in 1900, his new preface highlighted *bushidō* as the 'unique locus of the Yamato race', whereas the term had not appeared in the original 1892 edition.[146] In the 1850s, Yokoi Shōnan had still argued that a remartialized *shidō* was the solution to Japan's problems, drawing a connection between *shidō* and the oft-maligned 'soft' warriors of the Tokugawa age. This identification of *shidō* with Edo samurai-bureaucrats contributed to its reduced popularity after 1868, as did its implicit connection with Confucianism. Unlike *bushidō*, *shidō* was originally a Chinese term, and was not immune to the increasingly negative views of China. Popular desire for native concepts and terms responded to *bushidō*, which stepped into the breach from the margins of Tokugawa discourse.

The negative popular attitudes toward the former samurai in the 1880s made it unlikely that the catalyst for *bushidō* would come from within, at least at this time. Instead, Meiji *bushidō* was inspired—and simultaneously legitimized—by romanticized European ideals of chivalry and gentlemanship that impressed Japanese travellers and students of European history and culture. While these reactions may seem naïve in retrospect, they reflected influential currents in many Western societies at the time, especially in the elite circles that well-off Japanese travellers tended to encounter abroad. Their impact was enhanced by a desire among many

---

[144] Inoue Shun (1998), 'The Invention of the Martial Arts: Kanō Jigorō and Kōdōkan Judo', in Stephen Vlastos (ed.), *Mirror of Modernity: Invented Traditions in Modern Japan*, (Berkeley: University of California Press), p. 163.

[145] Nitobe Inazō (1936), *Lectures on Japan* (Tokyo: Kenkyusha), pp. 124–25.

[146] Suzuki Chikara, *Masurao no honryō—ichimei tōzai risshihen* (1900), p. 2.

Westerners to convey a positive and superior image of their culture to foreign visitors, which often resulted in excessively romantic and idealized portrayals. The use of European chivalry as a model for *bushidō* would later have a significant impact on views of Japan in other countries, as Westerners responded favourably to familiar ideals in an exotic new form.

The theorists directly inspired by Ozaki, including Fukuzawa Yukichi, Uemura Masahisa, and Suzuki Chikara, belonged to different generations and had different social and religious backgrounds, but were all born as samurai before 1868, sensitizing them to issues concerning the class. This personal samurai heritage further provided an impetus to extol the virtues of the class, as many Edo-period samurai had done. Even Fukuzawa, who demonstrably renounced his samurai status, maintained a distinct pride in his background. In addition to their shared heritage, all four of these *bushidō* theorists were acutely aware of Japan's evolving place in an international world and spent considerable time abroad, exposing them to idealized discourses on chivalry popular in the West. The existence of a moral ideal based on medieval warriors in Europe, and the role this martial spirit was popularly thought to have played in the global dominance of modern Western empires, legitimized the use of the samurai as a basis for a new ethical system that might have a comparable strengthening effect in Japan. Direct experience of foreign societies strongly coloured early views on *bushidō*, and set a precedent for the *bushidō* theorists that followed.

Ozaki Yukio and the first generation of *bushidō* theorists initiated trends that would dominate later discourse, although their writings on the subject would be largely ignored or even rejected in the twentieth century. Their ideas regarding internationalism contributed to their becoming controversial figures, with Ozaki, Fukuzawa, and Uemura considered especially problematic by chauvinistic nationalists who were drawn to *bushidō* after 1895. Conversely, these three disapproved of new mainstream developments, and did not contribute significantly to later *bushidō* discourse. Although many of their ideas were dismissed soon after the Sino-Japanese War, they imbued *bushidō* with a diversity and flexibility that was essential to its subsequent popularity, as well as its revival in the late twentieth century. In contrast, as an aggressive nationalist and prominent member of influential rightist organizations, Suzuki Chikara's ideas on *bushidō* foreshadowed some of the more extreme interpretations that came to dominate discourse in the 1930s and early 1940s.

3

The Early *Bushidō* Boom, 1894–1905

A MODERN WAR

During the long decade spanning the Sino-Japanese (1894–95) and Russo-Japanese Wars (1904–05), Japan underwent some of the greatest transformations in its modern history. Japan entered the conflict with Qing China as an underdog in the eyes of many observers but, following an intervention in the Boxer Rebellion and victory over Russia, emerged in 1905 as a global power and model for much of the non-Western world. These military engagements affected almost all aspects of Japanese society, from culture to institutions to national confidence. As the size and profile of the imperial army and navy grew with each success, their influence on civilian society increased. The military was the vehicle by which modernization reached rural citizens, and many Western imports, including clothing, foodstuffs, and physical training methods, were introduced to the populace through military organizations. By 1905, the military had also taken its first steps towards the ideological indoctrination of troops, a strategy that would be formally codified soon after the Russo-Japanese War and subsequently extended to the rest of society. This gradual process of national militarization strongly affected the development of *bushidō*, which served to legitimize and promote theories regarding Japan's martial character both at home and abroad. While the first naval victories against China were widely credited to Japan's superior implementation of modern (Western) drill and weaponry, the defeat of Russia was believed to have demonstrated the importance of 'spirit' over materiél, with *bushidō* and 'human bullets' responsible for Japan's military success.

The writings of *bushidō* theorists reflected changes in national consciousness and confidence in Japan in the early 1890s. The promulgation of the Meiji Constitution in 1889 saw one of the major goals of political reformers achieved, in spite of the inherently conservative character of the resulting governmental structure. The new government faced considerable internal pressures, and the handling of Japan's diplomacy was an issue of great importance. Tensions with China over influence in Korea had been building since the 1870s, and the Japanese government viewed any foreign influence in the peninsula as a direct threat to Japan's security. Japanese support for reformist movements further complicated relations, as Korea followed Chinese advice and played foreign powers off against one another in a bid to maintain as much independence as possible. This delicate strategy was relatively effective until 1894, when the Tonghak peasant rebellion threatened the Korean government sufficiently for it to request Chinese assistance, which was duly provided in the form of troops. The Qing notified Japan of this action in advance, as mandated by the 1885 Treaty of Tianjin, and Japan also sent a small detachment to Korea to protect Japanese citizens residing there.

The peasant rebellion was largely suppressed by the middle of 1894, but domestic political pressures prevented the Japanese government from withdrawing its troops as demanded by China. Neither side was willing to make concessions regarding their Korean interests, and the situation escalated as Japan insisted on reforms that would strengthen the Korean government and weaken Chinese influence. Following a first engagement between Chinese and Japanese troops near Pungdo on 25 July 1894, Japan secured a series of victories, the most famous of which was the taking of the supposedly impregnable fortress at Port Arthur by General Nogi Maresuke's troops in late November. Most of the hostilities were concluded before the end of the year, although the remainder of the Chinese fleet at Weihaiwei did not surrender until the following spring. By this time, a great victory parade had already been held in Tokyo, and the war had been hailed as a succession of heroic victories by the Japanese press. According to the terms of the peace, China surrendered its interests in Korea, and ceded to Japan Taiwan and the Liaodong Peninsula, although the latter was soon returned to China under pressure from Russia, France, and Germany. This Tripartite Intervention provoked great anger in Japan, as it seemed to demonstrate that victory over China had not significantly changed Japan's status vis-à-vis the Western powers.

The outraged response to the heavy-handed Tripartite Intervention reflected an important shift in Japan's relationship with the West. Resentment towards the unequal treaties quickly gathered momentum as Japan implemented reforms such as the creation of a constitutional government, which progressed the country further along the ambiguous road to 'civilization' dictated by Western powers as the path to eventual treaty revision. The requirements for 'civilized' status remained unspecified, but by the early 1890s many Japanese believed that the minimum criteria had been fulfilled, and were accordingly frustrated with the protracted negotiations with Western diplomats. The conclusion of the Anglo-Japanese Treaty of Commerce and Navigation in the summer of 1894 finally placed Japan on a more equal footing and freed the government from concern regarding British intervention in case of war with China, which duly followed within the month.[1]

The events and debates of the 1890s were reciprocally influenced by an increased interest in 'native' aspects of Japanese culture, a trend that accelerated after success in the first 'national' war. As Carol Gluck describes it, the long process of treaty revision had helped 'to spread the gospel of national pride beyond the confines of political activity into the wider world of elite public opinion'.[2] At the same time, attitudes towards the dominant foreign 'others' continued to change with the defeat of China and the attainment of greater diplomatic equality with the West. The war boosted martial characteristics in the ongoing search for national identity, contributing to positive reassessments of the samurai in the context of *bushidō*. In

---

[1] Mitani Hiroshi (2011), 'Foreword', in Makito Saya: David Noble (trans.), *The Sino-Japanese War and the Birth of Japanese Nationalism* (Tokyo: International House of Japan), p. xiv.

[2] Gluck, Carol (1985), *Japan's Modern Myths* (Princeton, NJ: Princeton University Press), p. 114.

this sense, the growth in popularity of *bushidō* after the war was driven by many of the same factors that prompted the *bushidō* theories of the early 1890s, although they shifted in relative importance as *bushidō* began to spread from a limited elite into wider society.

RE-EVALUATING FOREIGN 'OTHERS'

The 'resurrection' of Confucian ideals had largely dissipated by the 1890s, leaving a few lasting edifices such as the Imperial Rescript on Education, and the popular image of China in Japan shifted from that of a cultural centre to a defeated adversary and/or a backward society that could benefit from Japanese guidance in order to become 'civilized'.[3] The negative views of the contemporary Qing made reliance on Confucian models of statecraft and rulership problematic for Japanese leaders, while the association of Confucianism with the discredited Tokugawa regime made it difficult to invoke traditional interpretations.[4] This was especially true of the Zhu Xi school, which had served as the Confucian orthodoxy before 1868, and Japanese thinkers sought out native traditions as possible alternatives. The centuries of Confucian education and study in Japan made the separation of 'foreign' and 'native' difficult, however, just as the attempted removal of Buddhist elements from Shinto had proven to be.

The unease with traditional Confucian teachings was partially resolved by changing the terminology used for certain concepts and focusing on other teachings, such as those of Wang Yangming, whose thought (*Yōmeigaku*) became more popular in Meiji Japan than ever before.[5] As a potential East Asian and Confucian alternative to Western thought untainted by association with the Tokugawa regime, *Yōmeigaku* was severed from its continental roots, either by disavowing its importance in China or by reinterpreting it using Japanese terminology. Many of the *bushidō* theories that emerged during late Meiji were influenced by this nativization of Wang's teachings, partially crediting them with Japan's rapid progress. These ideas found great favour among Chinese and Korean activists in Japan, prompting them to disseminate *bushidō* in their own countries, and popularizing Wang Yangming studies on the continent.[6]

The early 1890s also saw an increasing tendency to reconsider the West—the foreign 'other' by which 'civilizational progress' was to be measured. Disillusionment

[3] Zachman, Urs Matthias (2009), *China and Japan in the Late Meiji Period: China Policy and the Japanese Discourse on National Identity, 1852–1904* (London: Routledge), pp. 2–3.

[4] Tanaka, Stefan (1993), *Japan's Orient: Rendering Pasts into History* (Berkeley: University of California Press), pp. 131–32; Eizenhofer-Halim, Hannelore (2001), *Nishimura Shigeki (1828–1902) und seine Konzeption einer "neuen" Moral im Japan der Meiji-Zeit* (Neuried: Ars Una), p. 217.

[5] Ogyū Shigehiro (1995), 'Bakumatsu – Meiji no Yōmeigaku to Min Qin shisō shi', in Minamoto Ryōen (ed.), *Nihon bunka kōryū shi sōsho 3: shisō* (Taishūkan shoten), p. 429; Ogyū Shigehiro and Barry Steben, 'The Construction of "Modern Yōmeigaku" in Meiji Japan and its Impact in China', *East Asian History* 20 (Dec. 2000), pp. 95–96.

[6] See also: Benesch, Oleg, 'Wang Yangming and Bushidō: Japanese Nativization and its Influences in Modern China', *Journal of Chinese Philosophy* 36:3 (Fall 2009), 39–454.

with the West gathered momentum in the 1880s, and influential texts such as Nakae Chōmin's (1847–1901) *Discourse of Three Drunkards on Government* (1887) lowered the Occident from its pedestal as a realized civilizational ideal to the status of 'a fellow competitor on this rocky path toward progress'.[7] The journal *Nihonjin* (*The Japanese*), founded in 1888 by Shiga Shigetaka (1863–1927), collected articles that attempted to objectively re-evaluate Japan's relationship with the West, while recognizing the importance of imported science and technology. *Nihonjin* represented a new departure as its articles did not generally frame discussions in terms of superiority or inferiority, whereas writings in this context in the 1880s tended to focus on points of perceived Japanese inferiority.[8] Fukuzawa Yukichi's former student Takahashi Yoshio (1862–1937), for example, had argued that the Japanese 'race' was inferior to Europeans, and proposed 'improvement' through intermarriage to transmit 'superior foreign traits' such as physical height, weight, and cranial capacity.[9] In 1889 Inoue Tetsujirō voiced similar concerns in opposing treaty reforms that would allow mixed residence, fearing that Japanese would be disadvantaged in direct competition with foreigners living in their midst.[10] The mixed-residence debate also entered *bushidō* discourse, and an 1894 treatise on *Educational Evils of the Times* called for the increased martialization of the education system, while describing children of mixed Anglo-Japanese heritage as more interested in money, less literate, and more likely to use weapons in a fight than their purely Japanese peers.[11]

The successful conclusion of the Sino-Japanese War discredited theories of Japanese inferiority and was the catalyst for a decade-long 'golden age of Japaneseness theory'.[12] Movements towards cultural independence from—and greater equality with—the West received support from the Darwinistic social theories popular throughout much of the world in the late nineteenth century and beyond. The surge in patriotism following the war influenced activities such as the 1897 founding of the nationalistic Great Japan Society (Dai Nihon kyōkai) around Inoue Tetsujirō and Takayama Chogyū (1871–1902). While the cultural chauvinism of writers such as Ozaki, Fukuzawa, and Nitobe had typically been directed towards other Asian peoples and motivated by finding common ground between Japan and the West, after 1895 theories positing the West as inferior to Japan began to enter the popular consciousness. Minami Hiroshi places the origin of 'Japanese superiority theory' in the interval between the Sino-Japanese and Russo-Japanese Wars, a period described by Sakaue Yasuhiro as marked by a societal 'impregnation with *bushidō*'.[13]

The interest in Japanese culture and identity after 1895 also had demographic backgrounds. By this point, most Japanese were too young to have any meaningful

---

[7] Tanaka, Stefan, *Japan's Orient: Rendering Pasts into History*, p. 47.
[8] Minami Hiroshi (2006), *Nihonjin ron: Meiji kara kyō made* (Tokyo: Iwanami gendai bunko), pp. 36–40.
[9] Minami Hiroshi, *Nihonjin ron: Meiji kara kyō made*, p. 31.
[10] Gluck, Carol, *Japan's Modern Myths*, p. 136.
[11] Kosuge Ren (1894), *Kyōiku jihei* (Denpō Mura), pp. 61–68.
[12] Funabiki Takeo (2003), *Nihonjin ron saikō* (Tokyo: NHK Publishing), p. 45.
[13] Minami Hiroshi, pp. 50–51;Sakaue Yasuhiro (2001), *Nippon yakyū no keifu gaku* (Tokyo: Seikyusha), p. 96.

memories of the Tokugawa period, when the country was still divided into hundreds of smaller domains with much stronger regional ties, and only a very small elite identified with the national state before 1868.[14] Much of the research on Japanese cultural theory was done by a generation that had grown up in Meiji and was reaching intellectual maturity in the 1890s, when sufficient time had passed to positively revisit not only the Tokugawa, but samurai in general. More than a decade had elapsed since the Satsuma Rebellion, and destitute samurai were also a distant memory. This also meant that 'blockheaded samurai', which had been a staple of much humour in Japan, ceased to be an effective vehicle for comedy by the late nineteenth century.[15] William Elliot Griffis slightly revised his earlier criticism of the samurai in 1894, writing that:

> to a conscientious Samurai there is nothing in this world better than obedience, in the ideal of a true man... History reveals a state of society in which cool determination, desperate courage and fearlessness of death in the face of duty were quite unique, and which must have had their base in some powerful though abnormal code of ethics.[16]

Griffis maintained his view of the samurai as a thing of the past, but also described them as having both positive and negative attributes, opening the door for a new assessment of their role.

Popular and historiographical trends contributed to the revision of the recent past in late Meiji, when disaffection with modern society led to nostalgic idealization of Edo as a historical space in which to find 'national' traditions.[17] At the same time, Western-trained historians, both Japanese and foreign, increasingly imposed European historical models on to Japan's past, and a European 'medieval' periodization was applied to pre-modern Japan. As Thomas Keirstead has argued, this historiographical practice was not purely in the interest of scholarship, but was intended to demonstrate that Japan was 'of the few races to have been blessed with a feudal history'. The translation of the term 'medieval' as '*chūsei*' became firmly established soon after Nishi Amane suggested it in the 1890s.[18] The Europeanization of Japan's past aligned with Social Darwinist aims of demonstrating that Japan was following a similar trajectory of development as the 'most civilized' Western powers, and a medieval phase came to be viewed as a necessary stage through which to progress. Writing in 1890, Nitobe Inazō reconsidered Japan's past in 'feudal' terms:

---

[14] Vlastos, Stephen (1998), 'Tradition: Past/Present Culture and Modern Japanese History', in Stephen Vlastos (ed.), *Mirror of Modernity: Invented Traditions in Modern Japan* (Berkeley: University of California Press), pp. 10–11. Saya Makito argues that the Sino-Japanese War marked the point at which nationalism arrived in Japan (Saya Makito: David Noble (trans.) (2011), *The Sino-Japanese War and the Birth of Japanese Nationalism* (Tokyo: International House of Japan).

[15] Kushner, Barak (2006), *The Thought War: Japanese Imperial Propaganda* (Honolulu: University of Hawaii Press), p. 88.

[16] Griffis, William Elliot (1895), *Religions of Japan* (New York: Charles Scribner's Sons), p. 147.

[17] Gluck, Carol (1998), 'The Invention of Edo', in Stephen Vlastos (ed.), *Mirror of Modernity: Invented Traditions in Modern Japan* (Berkeley: University of California Press), pp. 266–67.

[18] Keirstead, Thomas, 'Inventing Medieval Japan: The History and Politics of National Identity', *The Medieval History Journal* 1:47 (1998), 47–71.

Into the old, time-worn wine-skin of feudal bondage, isolated repose and military lethargy, was suddenly poured the wine of individual liberty, international commerce and industrial activity; who can wonder if the wine-skin bursts? We will briefly glance at its rents.

Feudalism, if it failed as a political system, has nevertheless, as a social one, ever developed many and noble moral qualities. Unlike the present individualistic organization of society, where the daily relation of man with man is debited and credited with cash, feudalism bound men by personal ties to their fellows; hence personal loyalty, strong sense of honor, proud contempt of money, chivalrous admiration of valour and stoicism, military decision of character and heroic abnegation of self, were some of the traits which Feudalism nurtured.[19]

In addition to the appropriation of feudalist historiography, the further equation of European knights with samurai—as in the writings of Ozaki and Uemura—was an important component of fitting Japanese history into a Eurocentric international standard model of civilizational development and progress.

Along with the 'Westernization' of Japan's earlier history, the 'Orientalization' of the rest of Asia by Japanese historians and cultural theorists allowed the nation to remove itself from the perceived backwardness of the continent. The theoretical removal of Japan from Asia bolstered attempts to deal with the West on level terms, a project which required a unique national history and culture.[20] This ambitious undertaking resulted in significant ideological competition, and late Meiji was 'filled with empty words such as Yamato spirit, *bushidō*, and Japanese spirit'.[21] Efforts to provide content and context for these 'empty words' increased greatly after 1895, with *bushidō* one of main beneficiaries of this decentralized process of ideological production. The diversity of ideologies was determined by the situation that, in Carol Gluck's words, 'there was no single group with official, or even unofficial, status as mythmakers to the Meiji state'.[22] *Bushidō* was one of many ideological streams, and most writers on *bushidō* and other Meiji ideologies were not exclusively dedicated to any single one, but rather tended to comment on and be influenced by a variety of different trends that arose and faded over time.

THE BEGINNING OF THE *BUSHIDŌ* BOOM

After 1895, *bushidō* spread into a variety of fields, including discussions regarding social issues, culture, identity, sport, and the military, while also entering foreign writings on Japan. Concern regarding the perceived degradation of society was a significant issue from earlier discourse, and a number of thinkers looked to *bushidō* as a potential weapon for combating the evils of materialism that allegedly accompanied modernization and were undermining the nation. At the same time, victory

[19] Nitobe Inazo (1890), *The Intercourse between the United States and Japan: A Historical Sketch* (Baltimore: Johns Hopkins University Press), p. 152.
[20] Tanaka, Stefan, *Japan's Orient: Rendering Pasts into History*, pp. 19, 47.
[21] Minami Hiroshi, *Nihonjin ron: Meiji kara kyō made*, p. 79.
[22] Gluck, Carol, *Japan's Modern Myths*, p. 9.

in the Sino-Japanese War brought the concept into closer connection with the military and national strength. Contemporary accounts of the war tended to focus on Japan's military modernization, but a search for cultural reasons for Japan's success soon followed, with the 'samurai spirit' held up as the most likely candidate. In this context, foreign commentators at the time considered the possible historical influence of the samurai's spiritual heritage on the modern military, while Japanese thinkers looked to the future and contemplated how *bushidō* could best be utilized to further strengthen the nation.

The economic boost from the war contributed to the sense that a new scourge of materialism was eroding social cohesion, and it was hoped that the 'samurai virtue' of frugality could counter this development. Ueda Bin gave voice to the widespread sentiment that modernization was accompanied by a problematic shift from 'spiritual civilization' to 'material civilization'.[23] On the other hand, as Elise Tipton points out, this use of *bushidō* ignored 'Japan's own tradition of ostentatious consumption among both samurai and [commoners]'.[24] Some theorists blamed the West for the evils of modernization, but writers on *bushidō* in 1895 saw the West as a source of both problems and solutions. In his '*Bushidō* versus Hedonism,' philosopher Ōnishi Hajime (1864–1900) argued that materialism and the pursuit of pleasure had greatly improved standards of living in the West, but the constant striving for ever-higher levels of pleasure also contributed to inequality in society and caused suffering to people at the bottom. Ōnishi felt that the West also offered up solutions to these problems, such as Thomas Carlyle's focus on hard work. In Japan, Ōnishi argued, '*bushidō* must be made the national religion' as the frugal discipline and work ethic of the samurai could benefit all of society.[25] In a lecture later the same year, Ōnishi compared *bushidō* with Stoic philosophy, a theme that would be picked up by many other thinkers. According to Ōnishi, both Stoics and *bushi* were unmoved in the face of death and, although the samurai were no more, the entire country must become a martial state.[26] The educator Yuhara Motoichi (1863–1901) also promoted *bushidō* as a force for social good, lamenting that 'when one mentions *bushidō*, most people just think of rough and uncouth behaviour'. Instead, Yuhara argued, *bushidō* could serve as a basis for a system of social welfare and economic progress as it proscribed the accumulation of wealth for its own sake, but did not object to making money in the name of a greater good.[27]

---

[23] Hishikawa Yoshio, 'Meiji sanjū nendai no bunmeiron: bunmei hihyō no seiritsu to tenkai 1', *Hokkaidō Gakuen Daigaku jinbun ronshū* 6 (31 March 1996), p. 4.

[24] Tipton, Elise K. (2002), *Modern Japan: A Social and Political History* (London: Routledge), p. 84.

[25] Ōnishi Hajime, 'Bushidō tai kairakushugi', *Rikugō zasshi* 171 (March 1895). Also found in: Ōnishi Hajime (1904), 'Bushidō tai kairakushugi', *Ōnishi hakushi zenshū* (6) (Tokyo: Keiseisha), pp. 268–73.

[26] Ōnishi Hajime, 'Stoa no seishin to bushi no kifū to wo hikaku shite waga kokumin no kishitsu ni ronjioyobu', *Shūkyō* 49 (November 1895). Also found in: (1904), 'Stoa no seishin to bushi no kifū to wo hikaku shite waga kokumin no kishitsu ni ronjioyobu', *Ōnishi hakushi zenshū* (6) (Tokyo: Keiseisha), pp. 599–615.

[27] Yuhara Motoichi, 'Bushidō no shumi 1', *Ryūnankai zasshi* 37:4-8 (7 June 1895); Yuhara Motoichi, 'Bushidō no shumi 2', *Ryūnankai zasshi* 38:4-8 (30 June 1895).

In this sense, Yuhara's view reflected the argument popular among business leaders that industrial activity was ultimately for the benefit of the nation.

Bushidō discourse was still in an early stage of development in 1895, and did not feature prominently in contemporary discussions of the Sino-Japanese War. Reports emphasized Japanese bravery and commitment to the cause, comparing these favourably with the Qing 'mercenaries' who were reluctant to risk their lives. The juxtaposition of past and present was a prominent theme, and Japanese troops were portrayed as an efficient 'modern' and truly 'national' army. The distinction between 'civilized' Japan and 'barbarian' China, as Fukuzawa Yukichi described it, was also predicated on identifying the Qing with the past, which Japan demonstrably threw off in the course of the war.[28] As Inoue Jukichi wrote in his beautifully illustrated account of the war, Korea 'offered gratuitous insult to Japan by an open declaration of its contempt for a nation which was casting off its national institutions for those of the Occident'.[29] This rejection of the (Asian) past also rendered any invocation of the samurai anachronistic, and few commentators credited Japan's success to a 'samurai spirit'.

It was only after the war, when both Japanese and foreign observers began to contextualize the conflict within Japan's broader development, that attention shifted from technological and tactical factors to the potential influence of cultural characteristics on Japan's success. Criticism of Chinese 'disorganization' had been prevalent during the war, but was generally used to highlight Japan's modern efficiency rather than any unique national character. By 1896, however, the Tripartite Intervention and reports of Japanese atrocities after the fall of Port Arthur had caused considerable disillusionment with aspects of modern (Western) warfare and diplomacy. These factors, combined with Japan's heightened geopolitical stature, prompted both Japanese and foreign thinkers to revisit the war from a culturalist perspective. Nitobe Inazō examined the currents of the time in an 1896 article defending Japan's 'recent chauvinism':

> No wonder that reaction has lately been started against undue respect for European civilization... Unhappy the nation, which succumbs without a groan,—with neither power nor will to assert its claims. Are our groans,—the wail of remorse, the cry of chagrin—louder and sharper than those of other peoples? We cannot deny that we are a sensitive people. We have been so trained. Sensitiveness is a trait of *samuraism*, of *bushidō*...A sensitive nation can never bear to have itself placed in an inferior position. It will rather drown itself in the billows it raises than be silently swallowed up in a current, however stronger than itself.[30]

While Nitobe focused on Japan's sensitivity in responding to foreign pressures, journalist and educator Takenobu Yūtarō (1863–1930) focused on loyalty and honour as the most important characteristics of the samurai, arguing that '*Bushido*

---

[28] Saya Makito, *The Sino-Japanese War and the Birth of Japanese Nationalism*, pp. 39–42.

[29] Inoue Jukichi (1895), *A Concise History of the War between Japan and China* (Tokyo: Y. Okura), p. 2.

[30] Nitobe Inazō, 'Our Recent Chauvinism', *The Far East: An English Edition of Kokumin-no-tomo* 2:7 (Feb. 1896), pp. 17–24.

attained, as indeed almost everything else, the highest development under the discreet rule of the Tokugawa'.[31]

The same year, Zenone Volpicelli (1856–?) credited not only Japan's reaction but its 'unexpected successes' in the Sino-Japanese War to the samurai spirit.

'[T]he many centuries of insular isolation and the feudal system had trained the mass of the Japanese people to sentiments of loyalty, of unswerving devotion to their chieftains, and developed a spirit of heroic fortitude and love of war. The last quarter of a century had initiated the higher classes to all the science and progress of the West. When, therefore, Japan resolved to put forth her strength in a foreign war, she found herself possessed with an army composed of soldiers who were ready to advance joyfully to death at the bidding of the emperor and for the glory of their country.[32]

According to Volpicelli's account, the Japanese 'Officers and men behaved with steady valour, and there were some instances of heroism which proved that the foreign-looking uniform had not changed the spirit of the old samurai'.[33] Arthur May Knapp echoed this laudatory assessment in his historical overview *Feudal and Modern Japan*, praising the samurai spirit that had developed in the 'feudal' age before entering all Japanese in the Meiji period. Knapp argued that the widespread view that 'Japanese chivalry was but another name for the spirit of turbulence, swagger, and murder' was a misconception based on earlier foreign experiences in Japan. The negative image of the samurai was unwarranted, Knapp wrote, and 'the name of samurai is in Japan to-day the untarnished name, to its people the synonym of the same lofty virtues and heroic devotion which we associate with the truest knight of Mediaeval Romance'. Furthermore, not only was the 'name untarnished, but also knightly virtue itself has escaped the degeneration which it has suffered in Europe, and has remained to this day a stainless glory'. The European 'age of chivalry was of the briefest, its flowering lasting only two centuries while the knightly past of Japan is coterminous with the history of the Empire'.[34] Knapp repeated the increasingly popular view that the samurai spirit had entered all Japanese after the Restoration, stating that Fukuzawa Yukichi best exemplified the samurai spirit by selflessly rejecting his own samurai rank and serving the public good.

Positive appraisals of the samurai appeared with increasing regularity in both Japanese and English-language publications, contributing to the gradual acceptance of '*bushidō*' as a standard term. Many writers used *bushidō* interchangeably with *Yamato damashii* and other concepts, as did Captain S. Sakurai in *Old and New Japan: Samurais and their Descendants* (1897). Sakurai wrote that swords and

[31] Takenobu Yūtarō. 'Bushidō' *Taiyō*. 2:16 (5 Aug. 1896) 39–40; Takenobu Yūtarō. 'The Bushido or 'Ways of Samurai'' *Taiyō*. 2:16 (5 Aug. 1896) 34–38; Takenobu Yūtarō. 'Bushidō' *Taiyō*. 2:17 (20 Aug. 1896) 35–37; Takenobu Yūtarō. 'The Bushido or 'Ways of Samurai (Continued)'' *Taiyō*. 2:17 (20 Aug. 1896) 30–34. Cited in Clement, Ernest W., 'Instructions of a Mito Prince to His Retainers', *Transactions of the Asiatic Society of Japan* 26 (Dec. 1898), pp. 149–53.

[32] Volpicelli, Zenone (1896), *The China-Japan War. Compiled from Japanese, Chinese and foreign sources* (London: Sampson Low), p. 4.

[33] Volpicelli, Zenone, p. 112.

[34] Knapp, Arthur May, *Feudal and Modern Japan* (1896), pp. 49–51, 65.

seppuku had been abolished along with the 'feudal' system, 'But Yamato-Damashii, the Samurais spirit, still remains intact in the heart of those occupying the middle class. It is handed down from father to son, by a national will, as it were, and is valued more than anything else'.[35] By 1899, *bushidō* was sufficiently established in elite discourse that the Chinese reformer Liang Qichao (1873–1929), who spent considerable time in Japanese exile, described it as the 'soul of Japan' and credited it with Japan's modern success. In his 'What of the Spirit of China?' Liang exhorted his countrymen to discover and adopt a similar national spirit that would enable them to reform and strengthen the country.[36]

A COLLECTION OF WRITINGS ON *BUSHIDŌ*

The pace of development of *bushidō* changed in early 1898 with the publication of the ambitious journal *Bushidō* by the Great Japan Martial Arts Lecture Society (Dai Nihon bujutsu kōshū kai). The society was formed in April 1895, the month the peace treaty between Japan and China was signed at Shimonoseki, although little information survives regarding its origins.[37] The stated goals of the journal, which brought together various strands of *bushidō* research, reveal some of the significant ideological motivations driving *bushidō* discourse, while the breadth of interpretations and backgrounds of its contributors demonstrate the lack of consensus regarding the content of *bushidō* at the time. The prominence of the contributors and the number of advertisers indicates at least a moderate circulation of the journal, helping to establish *bushidō* as a legitimate subject of research in the following years.

The founding goal of the Great Japan Martial Arts Lecture Society was 'to practise the unique martial arts of our Japanese empire', and to hold semi-annual tournaments 'in order to give vitality to the martial arts of the great Japanese empire'.[38] The society's constitution called for branches to be established in all Japanese prefectures, and twenty-nine instructors from various schools of swordmanship were listed as members in the founding documents. In spite of these lofty aspirations, the society entered a very crowded field as one of many organizations founded in the late 1890s to promote 'traditional' martial arts in Japan. The most important of these, the Great Japan Martial Virtue Society (Dai Nihon butoku kai), was also founded in 1895, and quickly expanded to all parts of Japan. This organization drew members away from smaller groups such as the Great Japan Martial Arts

---

[35] Sakurai, S. (1897), *Old and new Japan: Samurais and their descendants* (San Francisco: Chrysanthemum Press), p. 8.

[36] Liang Qichao (1904), 'Zhongguohun anzaihu', *Yinbing shi wenji lei* 2 (Shimokobe Hangorō). For a discussion of this text and Liang's other attempts to introduce *bushidō* to China, see Chen Jidong, 'Discovering Bushidō in China: Endeavours of Liang Qichao', *Taiwan Journal of East Asian Studies* 7:2 (Dec. 2010), pp. 219–54.

[37] Nakamura Tamio (ed.) (1985), *Shiryō kindai kendō shi* (Tokyo: Shimadzu shobō), p. 31.

[38] Nakamura Tamio, *Shiryō kindai kendō shi*, pp. 32–34.

Lecture Society, which was dissolved only a few years after the publication of the *Bushidō* journal.[39]

Many of the competing martial arts organizations in Japan around the turn of the century had nationalistic and militaristic leanings, and Mizuho Tarō's editorials confirm that *Bushidō* was no exception. Mizuho's stated motivation was concern regarding the Western powers, and he saw the 'resurrection' of *bushidō* as vital to resisting and competing with their imperialistic activities. In his introductory essay to the first issue, Mizuho explained the resurgence of *bushidō* in the current situation: 'the jewelled sword should be taken from its scabbard. Look at Egypt, India, Vietnam, China, Korea, and even the South Sea Islands. All have been violently attacked and taken over by the blue-eyed, red-haired Europeans'. According to Mizuho, although Europeans first came speaking of humanitarianism, freedom, and equality, and requested diplomatic relations on this basis, as soon as the gates of a country were opened, they revealed their true intentions. A fierce struggle for existence would ensue, in the course of which Europeans would conquer the country. Their economic policies were only designed to benefit themselves, and instead of following heavenly principles they were robbers and brigands who abused their strength with animalistic actions.[40]

While all the smaller countries were conquered, Mizuho asked rhetorically, who would be able to resist subjugation in this animalistic world and reverse the beastification of humanity? 'Not India, not China, not Korea... Our Great Japanese Empire, as the protective wonder-working shrine of the Orient, as the protective deity that creates harmony between heaven and humanity, has this great responsibility. If *bushidō* is the great spirit and model of all humanity', Japan would be able to fulfill its duty in the Orient and align affairs with the Way of Heaven.[41] Mizuho gave *bushidō* global import and related it to the 'Way of heaven', simultaneously arguing that the key to realizing *bushidō* lay in the practice of martial arts, as '*bushidō* occurs through the cultivation of the more than seventy schools of swordsmanship and over twenty schools of *jūjutsu*'.[42] Here, Mizuho combined the aspirations of a 'global' *bushidō* with the practical goals of promoting martial arts as outlined in the society's charter.

Each issue of the journal *Bushidō* was divided into four sections, beginning with an introduction by Mizuho Tarō. The second section, entitled 'Hekireki kan' ('Views of Thunder'), included articles and poems from famous contributors. The third section, 'Fūu kan' ('Views of the Wind and Rain'), was comprised of articles on swordsmanship and other martial arts, while the final section, 'Manzō kan' ('Views of Ten Thousand Images'), included poetry, brief articles on history, stories, and other miscellaneous texts composed by members of the Great Japan Martial Arts Lecture Society. The February issue, which was the first and most impressive, ran to fifty-two pages and contained eleven

---

[39] Nakamura Tamio (ed.) (1994), *Kendō jiten: gijutsu to bunka no rekishi* (Tokyo: Shimadzu shobō), p. 316.
[40] Mizuho Tarō, 'Hatsujin no koe', *Bushidō* 1:1 (Feb. 1898), p. 1.
[41] Mizuho Tarō, 'Hatsujin no koe', pp. 4–5.　　　[42] Mizuho Tarō, 'Hatsujin no koe', p. 4.

articles and poems from prominent contributors, including a brief article by Ozaki Yukio on 'Commerce and *Bushidō*'.[43] The March issue contained fifty-six pages and eight articles by prominent contributors, including a lengthy reprint of Uemura Masahisa's 'Christianity and *Bushidō*'.[44] By the April issue, the number of prominent contributors had shrunk to three, and the number of pages to forty-six. The fourth and final existing issue included only a single lead article and a brief poem in the section reserved for prominent contributors, for a total of forty-two pages. Having reissued the best-known articles on *bushidō*, and solicited contributions from a number of prominent individuals, the project largely exhausted existing material on *bushidō* and apparently lost the means to procure new submissions. In contrast, the number of articles on martial arts remained steady throughout all four issues, reflecting the continually growing interest in this subject.

A tremendous array of prominent Meiji intellectuals and public figures contributed to the project in some way, be it with a piece of calligraphy or a brief note encouraging its success. The social, religious, and political backgrounds of the authors gathered in the journal reflected shifts in *bushidō* discourse and broader society. While *bushidō* theorists before 1894 were almost exclusively of samurai stock, including Ozaki, Fukuzawa, Suzuki, and Uemura, *Bushidō* contained a number of articles by men who were not descendents of samurai, including Nakamura Yūjirō (1852–1928), Fukuchi Gen'ichirō (1841–1906), Kanō Jigorō (1860–1938), Kiyoura Keigo (1850–1942), Saitō Shūichirō (1855–1910), and Ōi Kentarō (1843–1922). Most of these men—the vast majority of writers on *bushidō* were men—reached adulthood around the time of the Restoration, but by the late 1890s they were willing to overlook the problems of the old class structure and support a national ideology based on the former samurai. This attitude was vital to the broad dissemination of *bushidō* in modern Japan, where well over ninety per cent of the population was descended from classes that had generally resented the samurai. The majority of contributors to *Bushidō* were *shizoku*, but it was the acceptance of the ethic by men of 'common' stock that made it possible for Kobayashi Ichirō (1876–1944) to claim in 1902 that 'to insult *bushidō* is to insult all Japanese', and for many others to later argue that '*bushidō* did not die with the samurai... it entered all Japanese and is especially pronounced in the soldier spirit'.[45] Breaking down residual class consciousness in Japan after 1868 was a gradual process, with the conscripted military arguably the greatest force for promoting feelings of social equality.[46] The circumstance that much of this social levelling process occurred in a military environment also encouraged identification with a martial ethic nominally associated with the former samurai elite.

---

[43] Ozaki Yukio, 'Shōgyō to bushidō', *Bushidō* 1:1 (Feb. 1898), pp. 10–11.
[44] Uemura Masahisa, 'Kirisutoyō to bushidō', *Bushidō* 1:2 (March 1898), pp. 13–22.
[45] Kobayashi Ichirō, 'Bushidō no hihan (I)', *Tetsugaku zasshi* 17:187 (10 Sept. 1902), p. 73; for example, Hashimoto Minoru (1943), *Bushidō shiyō* (Tokyo: Dainihon kyōka tosho), p. 22.
[46] Yoshida Yutaka (2002), *Nihon no guntai: heishi tachi no kindai shi* (Tokyo: Iwanami shinsho 816), p. 70.

The political backgrounds of the contributors to *Bushidō* were equally diverse, although many were closely affiliated with the government and military, including Katsu Kaishū; Itō Sukeyuki (1843–1914), commander-in-chief of the Japanese combined fleet during the Sino-Japanese War; Shinagawa Yajirō (1843–1900), a student of Yoshida Shōin, hero of the Bōshin War, and interior minister in the Matsukata cabinet; Kawamura Kageaki (1850–1926), a career soldier who rose to high rank during the Satsuma Rebellion and received a baronetcy for his service in the Sino-Japanese War; and Takeda Hidenobu (1853–1902), a major general who distinguished himself in the Sino-Japanese War. With the exception of Katsu, all these military men came from the imperial loyalist domains of Satsuma, Chōshū, and Tosa.

These establishment figures were joined in the pages of the journal by Ozaki Yukio, who was banished from Tokyo for alleged anti-government activities; Nakae Chōmin, a popular rights theorist and founder of the Jiyūtō; Fukuchi Gen'ichirō, who was arrested and had his newspaper shut down for criticism of the Meiji government; Ebara Soroku (1842–1922), a politician and educator active in party politics; Kataoka Kenkichi (1843–1903), a politician and leader of the freedom and popular rights movement imprisoned for over two years for not leaving Tokyo along with Ozaki; and Ōi Kentarō, another politician and leader of the freedom and popular rights movement who was imprisoned for four years following the Osaka Incident of 1885. The involvement of this latter group in party politics, and their often antagonistic relationship with the state, show that *bushidō* was not the sole preserve of government ideologists, to the extent that the aforementioned establishment figures could be described as such.

Contributors to *Bushidō* also had diverse religious affiliations. In addition to Uemura Masahisa, at least three other Christians were involved, including Ebara Soroku, Kataoka Kenkichi, and Ōi Kentarō. Christians represented a disproportionately large number of commentators on *bushidō* from an early stage, due to their more direct and personal international experience and accordingly greater interest in their own culture. In their attempts to identify a national character, Christians were also less likely to rely on religious foundations such as Shinto or the various schools of Buddhism. For them, *bushidō* presented a possibility to define a national ethic that was easily combined with the Christian faith, as it was supposedly based on historical rather than religious ideals.

The contributor who most embodied the ultra-nationalistic interpretation of *bushidō* was Fukuba Bisei (1831–1907), a former samurai whose study of National Learning and Yamaga Sokō's strategies led him to embrace the ideals of 'revere the emperor and expel the barbarian'. Fukuba served as an educator in the palace before being dismissed for his strong objections to the introduction of foreign thought. The diversity of articles in *Bushidō* reflected that of the contributors, many of whom had little or no awareness of the concept before being approached for a contribution. Many contributions were mere congratulatory notes or poems commemorating the publication of the journal, indicating that these were directly or indirectly solicited by the publishers. Writing in the first issue of *Bushidō*,

Fukuchi Gen'ichirō admitted his uncertainty: 'although I do not know if what I acknowledge as *bushidō* is the same as that which [the publishers] do, I like the title *"Bushidō"*...'[47]

Kataoka Kenkichi, who had spent two years studying in London, sought *bushidō* in feudalism, Christianity, and Confucianism, with the Chinese classics and the Bible as its texts. According to Kataoka, 400,000 *bushi* ruled and strengthened the country in the Edo period, but in the future, Japan's Christian population must increase tenfold so that 400,000 Christians could take the role of the former warrior class and lead the country.[48] Liberal journalist and anarchist Kutsumi Sokuchū (Kesson, 1860–1925) wrote that it was no longer necessary to carry swords three *shaku* in length, but the current situation demanded mental swords five *shaku* in length in order to safeguard independence, self-realization, honesty, and humanism. Kutsumi warned against thinking in terms of past or present, East or West, and argued that all people must become one. After the Restoration, Kutsumi claimed, Japanese thought only of technology, forgetting that the purpose of education was to develop human beings, as the German philosophers and educators Johann Friedrich Herbart (1776–1841) and Johann Karl Friedrich Rosenkranz (1805–79) had taught. Inspired by German models, Kutsumi advocated military drill, exercise, and martial arts in schools, and while the old ways could not really be applied to the present day, some elements of *bushidō* might be useful in modern education.[49]

Ebara Soroku and Watanabe Noboru's contributions were more idealistic and hinted at the view of *bushidō* that would become established in military education in the early twentieth century. Ebara defined *bushidō* as 'an activity of life and death—living when you should live and dying when you should die', and compared warriors with falling cherry blossoms.[50] Watanabe tied *bushidō* to the Yamato spirit, virtues of filial piety, loyalty, duty, and bravery, further stating that its roots could be found in the very founding of the country.[51] At the opposite end of the spectrum, Ōi Kentarō expressed a critical view reminiscent of popular opinion in the 1880s, attacking *bushidō* as a product of the feudal age that was no longer relevant in a time of civilization.[52] According to Ōi, the deficiencies of *bushidō* included its emphasis on social stratification, individual action, and rejection of foreign influences, all of which were contrary to the ideals of a modern society and meant that there were no discernible benefits to be gained by reintroducing *bushidō*.[53]

---

[47] Fukuchi Gen'ichirō, 'Bushidō', *Bushidō* 1:1 (Feb. 1898), pp. 8–9.

[48] Kataoka Kenkichi, 'Hōken bushi to Kirisuto shinsha (Feudal Warriors and Christian Believers)', *Bushidō* 1:2 (March 1898), p. 6.

[49] Kutsumi Sokuchū, 'Kyōiku to bushidō (Education and *Bushidō*)', *Bushidō* 1:4 (May 1898), pp. 6–8.

[50] Ebara Soroku, 'Shukushi', *Bushidō* 1:1 (Feb. 1898), p. 9.

[51] Watanabe Noboru, 'Bushidō', *Bushidō* 1:2 (March 1898), p. 6.

[52] For a discussion of Ōi's views and his opposition to samurai and *shizoku* elites, see Jansen, Marius, 'Ōi Kentarō: Radicalism and Chauvinism', *The Far Eastern Quarterly* 11:3 (May 1952), pp. 305–16.

[53] Ōi Kentarō, 'Bushidō ni tsuite (About *Bushidō*)', *Bushidō* 1:3 (April 1898), pp. 7–8.

The journal *Bushidō* foreshadowed several key developments in the future of *bushidō* discourse, perhaps the most significant of which was specifically linking the concept to the modern Japanese military, which it did in two different ways. First, military men were selected to contribute, although they generally only provided brief words of congratulations or a poem, rather than detailed discussions. Furthermore, the March issue of the journal was dedicated to Field Marshall Yamagata Aritomo (1838–1922), whose person was synonymous with the army, and his portrait adorned the journal's inside cover. Second, Mizuho Tarō explicitly discussed the important connection between *bushidō* and the military, rhetorically asking 'who, if not the soldiers, is upholding and preserving *bushidō* today?'.[54] According to Mizuho, only soldiers could grasp the important concepts of life and death, and should therefore lead politicians, scholars, religious men, and craftsmen, just as the country was led by the *bushi* in ancient times. Mizuho's interpretation of *bushidō* was strikingly similar to the militaristic interpretations that evolved in the last decade of Meiji and came to dominate official discourse on the subject until 1945.

The year after the publication of the *Bushidō* journal, Mikami Reiji (Kaiundō, dates unknown) also explicitly drew a connection between *bushidō* and the military in his *Japan Bushidō Theory*. With a portrait of the swordsman Yamaoka Tesshū on its cover, Mikami's book was an eclectic assembly of influences also found in earlier works on *bushidō*. Like Ozaki Yukio, Mikami criticized the materialism of contemporary Japanese society, especially self-professed 'gentlemen'.[55] Instead, *Japan Bushidō Theory*, which emphasized the position of the emperor as the 'focus of *bushidō*', relied heavily on traditional religious and philosophical ideas, including Buddhism, Confucianism, Shinto, and Shingaku (the 'Heart and Mind School' founded in the eighteenth century).[56] Echoing the anti-foreign sentiments of Mizuho Tarō or Suzuki Chikara, Mikami argued that international laws and diplomacy only existed to benefit Christian nations. Westerners called themselves civilized and spoke of equality and compassion, but were actually morally impoverished and ignored their own rules in taking advantage of weaker nations.[57] Like the *Bushidō* journal, Mikami's work was ignored by most subsequent commentators on *bushidō*, but was a further sign that *bushidō* discourse was about to reach critical mass.

NITOBE INAZŌ AND THE INTERNATIONALIZATION OF *BUSHIDŌ*

The placement of Nitobe Inazō's theories in the development of modern *bushidō* is complicated by his geographical separation from the metropolitan centres in which

---

[54] Mizuho Tarō, 'Bushidō wo goji kankō suru mono ha dare zo (Who upholds and preserves *bushidō*?)', *Bushidō* 1:3 (April 1898), pp. 2–3.
[55] Mikami Reiji (1899), *Nihon bushidō* (Tokyo: Kokubunsha), pp. 2–4.
[56] Mikami Reiji, pp. 11, 233.   [57] Mikami Reiji, pp. 195–96, 198.

early discourse occurred. Nitobe was either abroad or in Hokkaido when the first works on *bushidō* appeared before the Sino-Japanese War, and was in the United States during the publication of both the *Bushidō* journal and Mikami's *Japan Bushidō Theory*. Commentators on *bushidō* posit Nitobe variously as the founder and exponent of modern *bushidō*, or the head of a 'Christian *bushidō*' distinct from mainstream 'nationalistic *bushidō*', but his impact was more ambiguous.[58] In contrast to his current image, Nitobe was not central to *bushidō* discourse in pre-war Japan, and only attained his status as a most influential writer on *bushidō* in the 1980s. On the other hand, Nitobe's life and work are useful barometers of the development of Meiji *bushidō*, and are essential for understanding foreign views of *bushidō* as well as post-war trends in Japanese discourse.

Nitobe was born in 1862 to a wealthy family in Nambu domain, near present-day Morioka. The major turning point in his life came at the age of fifteen when he went to Hokkaido to study at the Sapporo Agricultural College, an elite institution founded to facilitate the development of Hokkaido. The college employed American instructors, led by William S. Clark (1826–86), and classes were conducted in English using imported teaching materials. In this environment, Nitobe, Uchimura Kanzō, and other classmates converted to Christianity, forming what is known as the Sapporo Band. After graduation, Nitobe left Japan, and spent the period 1884–91 studying economics in the United States and Germany before returning to Sapporo to take up a teaching post. The heavy workload and harsh environment conspired to ruin Nitobe's health, and he left Japan in 1897 to convalesce in Monterey, California. Nitobe stayed in the United States for almost three years, during which time he wrote *Bushido: The Soul of Japan*. First published in Philadelphia in 1900, editions in the original English were also released in Japan the same year, and when Japanese victories in the Russo-Japanese War sparked a global surge of interest in Japanese culture and history five years later, Nitobe's book became a worldwide bestseller.

By 1900, the 38-year-old Nitobe had spent ten years abroad in the West and another thirteen in the isolated enclave that was the Sapporo Agricultural College. He was more comfortable in English than Japanese, especially with regard to written language, and lamented how little education he had received regarding Japanese history, but these uncertainties did not prevent Nitobe from holding forth as an authority on Japan in front of foreign audiences.[59] Readers of *Bushido: The Soul of Japan* are often struck by the many references to historical events and individuals from Western traditions, especially when compared with the relative paucity of Japanese sources in the book. Many foreign readers assume that as a Japanese, Nitobe's understanding of his own country must have been greater than his

---

[58] Kanno Kakumyō (2004), *Bushidō no gyakushū* (Tokyo: Kōdansha gendai shinsho), pp. 260–61. Another example of this approach can be found in Unoda Shōya (1997), 'Bushidō ron no seiritsu: seiyō to tōyō no aida', *Edo no shisō 7 (shisō shi no 19 seiki)* (Tokyo: Perikan sha).

[59] Ōta Yūzō (1986), *Taiheiyō no hashi toshite no Nitobe Inazō* (Tokyo: Misuzu shobō), pp. 29–32. Also see Ishii Shirō. 'Basil Hall Chamberlain and Inazo Nitobe: a Confrontation over Bushido', *University of Tokyo Journal of Law and Politics* 3 (2006), pp. 1–26.

knowledge of the West, but his reliance on foreign sources reflected his unique upbringing and education. In contrast, Nitobe's observations on Western culture were highly regarded by scholars in Japan and in the West, revealing this as his area of greater expertise.

Despite writing almost a decade and a major international conflict later than Ozaki Yukio and Uemura Masahisa, Nitobe's motivations in outlining his *bushidō* theories were closer to those of earlier thinkers than those of his contemporaries. Ozaki and Uemura were addressing a Japanese audience and Nitobe a foreign one, but they had a common goal of establishing a native Japanese ethical system that was comparable to Western thought and relatively independent of traditional Chinese influences. In contrast, writers on *bushidō* in 1900 generally accepted it as an ancient and unique Japanese ethic that was still relevant in the current day and age, and *bushidō* research focused on examining its character and historical roots, albeit in line with modern agendas.

Nitobe's lack of awareness regarding previous usage of the term '*bushidō*', and his overestimation of his own impact on discourse, reflect his detachment from the activities of Japanese intellectuals. Nitobe believed that he had selected a previously unknown term to label his ethic, stating that 'I named it "Bushido" or "the Way of the samurai" because the culture to which it referred was most noticeable among the samurai class'.[60] His physical isolation from the metropole contributed to the anachronistic feel of *Bushido: The Soul of Japan* to Japanese readers when it was first published. Whereas *bushidō* discourse had become considerably more nationalistically confident by 1900, Nitobe portrayed his book as a response to a foreign stimulus, just as Ozaki and Uemura's early *bushidō* theories were responses to traits they believed to have identified in Western culture. Nitobe credited a question asked by a Belgian jurist regarding the nature of Japanese ethics with prompting him to compose his *bushidō* theory, and he sought foreign equivalents for every aspect of his *bushidō* (or vice versa). In comparison, when Nitobe's contemporaries discussed European chivalry or other foreign ethical systems, they tended to insist that Japanese *bushidō* existed entirely independently of these traditions, and was in no way a response to them.

Bushido: The Soul of Japan blended different sources, arguments, and observations so as to attribute virtually the entire range of human emotion and behaviour to the influence of the warrior class. *Bushidō* was far more than a class ethic, Nitobe claimed, and was manifested in all Japanese behaviour: 'What Japan was she owed to the samurai. They were not only the flower of the nation, but its root as well. All the gracious gifts of Heaven flowed through them'.[61] In addition, 'There was no channel of human activity, no avenue of thought, which did not receive in some measure an impetus from Bushido. Intellectual and moral Japan was directly or indirectly the work of Knighthood'.[62] According to Nitobe,

⁶⁰ Ota Yuzo (1995), 'Mediation between Cultures', in John Howes (ed.), *Nitobe Inazō: Japan's Bridge Across the Pacific* (Boulder: Westview Press), pp. 242–43.
⁶¹ Nitobe Inazō, *Bushido: The Soul of Japan*, p. 167.
⁶² Nitobe Inazō, *Bushido: The Soul of Japan*, p. 169.

bushidō 'permeated all social classes', eventually becoming a 'moral standard' for the entire nation.[63] It was still the nation's 'animating spirit' and 'motor force' in the modern period, and as 'the maker and product of Old Japan, [*bushidō*] is still the guiding principle of the transition and will prove the formative force of the new era'.[64] Nitobe confidently wrote that 'The transformation of Japan is a fact patent to the whole world. Into a work of such magnitude various motives naturally entered; but if one were to name the principal, one would not hesitate to name Bushido'.[65]

Bushido: The Soul of Japan is an often frustrating work filled with generalizations and tautologies, and Nitobe tended to qualify characteristics of *bushidō* to the point of meaninglessness or subsequently contradict his own statements. With regard to honour, Nitobe stated that 'Our sense of honour is responsible for our exaggerated sensitiveness and touchiness; and if there is the conceit in us with which some foreigners charge us, that, too, is a pathological outcome of honour'.[66] This heightened sensitivity should not be dismissed as a fault, however, for 'as in religious monomania there is something touchingly noble as compared with the delirium tremens of a drunkard, so in that extreme sensitiveness of the samurai about their honour do we not recognise the substratum of a genuine virtue?'[67] In contrast, regarding 'self-control' Nitobe wrote that:

> The discipline of fortitude...and the teaching of politeness...combined to engender a stoical turn of mind, and eventually to conform it into a national trait of apparent Stoicism...It was unmanly for a samurai to betray his emotions on his face. 'He shows no sign of joy or anger', was a phrase used in describing a great character.[68]

In other words, if a Japanese person were quick-tempered and reacted impulsively to some insult, this was a manifestation of their *bushidō*-founded sense of honour. If, instead, they stoically bore the same provocation with great patience, this should be attributed to their *bushidō* composure.

Nitobe's discussion of loyalty is similarly problematic: 'The individualism of the West, which recognizes separate interests for father and son, husband and wife, necessarily brings into strong relief the duties owed by one to the other; but Bushido held that the interest of the family and of the members thereof is intact,— one and inseparable'. In spite of this emphasis on the family:

> Bushido never wavered in its choice of loyalty. Women, too, encouraged their off-spring to sacrifice all for the king...Since Bushido, like Aristotle and some modern sociologists, conceived the state as antedating the individual—the latter being born into the former as part and parcel thereof—he must live and die for it or for the incumbent of its legitimate authority.

---

[63] Nitobe Inazō, *Bushido: The Soul of Japan*, pp. 170–71, 177, 178.
[64] Nitobe Inazō, *Bushido: The Soul of Japan*, p. 179.
[65] Nitobe Inazō, *Bushido: The Soul of Japan*, p. 181.
[66] Nitobe Inazō, *Bushido: The Soul of Japan*, p. 184.
[67] Nitobe Inazō, *Bushido: The Soul of Japan*, p. 80.
[68] Nitobe Inazō, *Bushido: The Soul of Japan*, pp. 108–09.

However, Nitobe qualified, 'Bushido did not require us to make our conscience the slave of any lord or king…A man who sacrificed his own conscience to the capricious will or freak or fancy of a sovereign was accorded a low place in the estimate of the Precepts'.[69] Much of Nitobe's *bushidō* is essentially assemblages of mutually exclusive tenets.

As rationalist Tsuda Sōkichi (1873–1961) pointed out, one of the reasons for the contradictions in *Bushido: The Soul of Japan* was that Nitobe did not distinguish between places and periods of history in selecting references for his *bushidō*. Nitobe portrayed actions that occurred at any time in Japanese history, or were at least recorded in a poem or story, as manifestations of *bushidō*, in spite of the great diversity of the samurai. Other inconsistencies resulted from Nitobe's stated goal in theorizing about *bushidō*:

> I did not intend [*Bushido: The Soul of Japan*] for a Japanese audience but for foreigners who seem to think that the Japanese are really a very strange people. I wanted to show in it that the Japanese are not really so different, that you can find similar ideas to those of the Japanese even in the West, though under a slightly different guise, and that there is no East or West as far as human beings are concerned.[70]

In seeking to incorporate the greatest variety of human experience, Nitobe's *bushidō* was typically too broad to provide meaningful insights regarding Japan, although this shortcoming was simultaneously key to the success of Nitobe's book in a world that knew very little of Japan. By demonstrating that Japanese had similar emotions, hopes, and fears as Westerners, Nitobe contributed to intercultural understanding at a time when biological and psychological theories of racial difference, especially in terms of superiority or inferiority, were very much in vogue. However, by appealing not just to a universal humanity, but instead invoking *bushidō* as the motivation for Japanese behaviour, Nitobe implied that the Japanese were unique in the foundations of their common humanity, undermining his broader argument.

Aspects of *Bushido: The Soul of Japan* were reminiscent of *bushidō* discourse from the previous decade, but other characteristics were in line with contemporary intellectual currents, leading scholars to place Nitobe in the early *Nihonjin ron* tradition.[71] Nitobe's appeals to universal humanity were often simultaneously arguments for Japanese singularity: 'If what M. Boutmy says is true of English royalty—that it "is not only the image of authority, but the author and symbol of national unity", as I believe it to be, double and trebly may this be affirmed of royalty in Japan'.[72] Similarly, Nitobe cited an unnamed 'Russian statesman' on the dependence of people on social networks and the state, agreeing with his theories and claiming that they were 'doubly true of the Japanese'.[73] While some Japanese customs might strike foreign observers as being 'hard-hearted,' Nitobe wrote, 'we

[69] Nitobe Inazō, *Bushido: The Soul of Japan*, pp. 92, 93, 96–97.
[70] Ota Yuzo, 'Mediation between Cultures,' p. 250.
[71] See, for example: Minami Hiroshi, *Nihonjin ron: Meiji kara kyō made*, p. 202; and Funabiki Takeo, *Nihonjin ron saikō*.
[72] Nitobe Inazō, *Bushido: The Soul of Japan*, p. 14.
[73] Nitobe Inazō, *Bushido: The Soul of Japan*, pp. 41–42.

are really as susceptible to tender emotion as any race under the sky. I am inclined to think that in one sense we have to feel more than others—yes, doubly more— since the very attempt to restrain natural promptings entails suffering'.[74] In other words, while the Japanese were subject to the same emotions and motivations as people in other nations, they experienced these with a unique degree of intensity.

In addition to his view of Japanese uniqueness, Nitobe's attitude towards the rest of East Asia was also in line with intellectual currents following the Sino-Japanese War, when arguments against China in *bushidō* discourse took on a dimension of racial or national superiority/inferiority, often bolstered by Social Darwinist theories from abroad. Nitobe cited in full the opinion of French Orientalist Antoine Rous de la Mazaliere (1864–1937):

> the sixteenth century displays in the highest degree the principal quality of the Japanese race, that great diversity which one finds there between minds (*esprits*) as well as between temperaments. While in India and even in China men seem to differ chiefly in degree of energy or intelligence, in Japan they differ by originality of character as well. Now, individuality is the sign of superior races and of civilizations already developed.[75]

Later writings from Nitobe's time as a colonial administrator reveal a similar attitude. With regard to Koreans, Nitobe argued that they were an 'inferior race' with no 'attributes for development' and an 'insufficient capacity for nation-founding and administration' that could only continue to exist under imperial Japanese administration.[76] The fundamental goal of Nitobe's arguments was for equality between Japanese and Westerners, and he spent much of his life combating racism inherent in the European-dominated international system.[77] While excepting Japan, Nitobe internalized many of the racist theories that Western Orientalists had directed at non-Caucasian peoples.[78] Through the use of *bushidō* and Victorian social theories, Nitobe could appeal to the common humanity of Japanese and Westerners, while removing Japan from the rest of Asia.

At the time of its initial publication, Nitobe's *Bushido: The Soul of Japan* received a lukewarm reception from those Japanese who read the English edition. Tsuda Sōkichi wrote a scathing critique in 1901, rejecting Nitobe's central arguments. According to Tsuda, although Nitobe's book seemed to be popular, the author knew very little about his subject. Nitobe's equation of the term '*bushidō*' with the 'soul of Japan' was flawed, as *bushidō* could only be applied to a single class at a

---

[74] Nitobe Inazō, *Bushido: The Soul of Japan*, p. 109.

[75] Nitobe Inazō, *Bushido: The Soul of Japan*, p. 22.

[76] Asada Kyōji (1990), *Nihon shokuminchi kenkyū shi ron* (Tokyo: Mirai sha), p. 178. For a discussion of Nitobe's views of Korea and Koreans in English, see Dudden, Alexis (2005), *Japan's Colonization of Korea: Discourse and Power* (Honolulu, University of Hawaii Press), pp. 132–43.

[77] Unoda Shōya makes a similar argument, proposing that the dichotomy '*Tōzai* (East-West)' as found in Nitobe's work should more accurately be rendered '*Ōbei to Nihon* (Europe/America and Japan)'. See Unoda Shōya, 'Bushidō ron no seiritsu: Seiyō to Tōyō no aida', p. 36.

[78] Burkman, Thomas W. (2003), 'Nationalist Actors in the Internationalist Theatre: Nitobe Inazō and Ishii Kikujirō and the League of Nations', in Dick Stegewerns (ed.), *Nationalism and Internationalism in Imperial Japan: Autonomy, Asian Brotherhood, or World Citizenship?* (New York: RoutledgeCurzon), p. 108.

specific time, and Nitobe should have written his thesis on the Yamato spirit. Tsuda further chastised Nitobe for not distinguishing between historical periods, and for positing Buddhism (especially the Zen schools), Shinto, and lastly Confucianism (especially Wang Yangming's teachings), as the roots of *bushidō*. Tsuda dismissed Nitobe's assertion that Buddhism influenced the *bushi* in the Heian period (794–1185) as pure nonsense. He further argued that Confucianism was irrelevant before the Edo period, and even then the influential teachings were those of Zhu Xi and not Wang Yangming. As for *bushidō*, Tsuda described it as merely a product of the Kantō family structure that spread throughout the country. In addition, Tsuda rejected Nitobe's assertion that love of the sovereign and patriotism were part of *bushidō*, as these virtues were too great to be contained in the ethic.[79]

Also in 1901, Inoue Tetsujirō directed similarly harsh criticism at Nitobe, focusing on the latter's claim that *bushidō* 'is not a written code; at best it consists of a few maxims handed down from mouth to mouth or coming from the pen of some well-known warrior or savant. More frequently it is a code unuttered and unwritten, possessing all the more the powerful sanction of veritable deed, and of a law written on the fleshly tablets of the heart'.[80] According to Inoue, Nitobe had overlooked Yamaga Sokō's *Bukyō shōgaku* and *Yamaga gorui*, which had been popularized by Yoshida Shōin's lectures.[81] Several years later, Inoue convinced Nitobe to include references to Yamaga in his discussions of *bushidō*.[82] Tsuda and Inoue's reviews were typical of those by Japanese academics, who did not consider Nitobe's work to be sufficiently scholarly. Uemura Masahisa disagreed with what he felt to be Nitobe's overly idealistic portrayal of the samurai: 'I am sorry that Mr Nitobe in his English language work *Bushido* assumed an attitude which was excessively advocatory'.[83] Negative assessments of Nitobe's book also came from abroad, with an anonymous reviewer in *The Athenaeum* giving one of the harshest reviews.[84] This reviewer—widely thought to be Basil Hall Chamberlain—dismissed Nitobe's theories as fabrications without any historical validity, cobbled together through 'partial statement and wholesale suppression'.[85]

Nitobe's insecurity regarding the content of *Bushido: The Soul of Japan*, combined with the harsh reviews it received in Japan, kept him from publishing a Japanese translation of the work for almost a decade, by which time his book had been translated into many other languages, including Marāthī, German, Bohemian, Polish, Norwegian, and French.[86] In spite of the rapidly growing interest in *bushidō* in Japan, and the book's cachet as an international bestseller, the reception the

[79] Tsuda Sōkichi (1976), 'Bushidō no engen ni tsuite', in Shigeno Yasutsugu (ed.), *Meiji shi roshū* 2 (Tokyo: Chikuma shobō), pp. 316–18.

[80] Nitobe Inazō, *Bushido: The Soul of Japan*, pp. 1, 4–5.

[81] Inoue Tetsujirō (1901), *Bushidō* (Tokyo: Heiji zasshi sha), pp. 36–37.

[82] Tucker, John Allen, 'Tokugawa Intellectual History and Prewar Ideology: The Case of Inoue Tetsujirō, Yamaga Sokō, and the Forty-Seven Rōnin,' *Sino-Japanese Studies* 14 (2002), p. 52.

[83] Ota Yuzo, 'Mediation between Cultures', p. 249.

[84] *The Athenaeum*, Number 4060 (19 August 1905), p. 229.

[85] Ota Yuzo, 'Mediation between Cultures', p. 249.

[86] Powles, Cyril H. (1995), '*Bushido*: Its Admirers and Critics', in John Howes (ed.), *Nitobe Inazō: Japan's Bridge Across the Pacific* (Boulder: Westview Press), p. 112.

book received from Japanese critics weighed heavily on Nitobe's mind. In the fore-word for Yamagata Kōhō's 1908 *The New Bushidō*, which appeared shortly after the Japanese translation of *Bushido: The Soul of Japan*, Nitobe wrote that he resisted the Japanese translation of his book for years out of fear of what Japanese readers might think, and was only persuaded by his good friend Sakurai Ōson (1872–1929) to let him translate it. In addition, Nitobe claimed that he would probably not have published it if he had been aware of Yamagata's (superior) work.[87]

While Nitobe has become virtually synonymous with *bushidō*, most other pre-war works on the subject were ignored after 1945, reflecting the great differ-ences in the Japanese political and social climate at either end of the twentieth cen-tury. This state of affairs has also hindered the development of a balanced view of the history of *bushidō*, and many writers on *bushidō* ignore the Meiji period entirely. As *bushidō* was first widely theorized and disseminated during Meiji, examina-tions of *bushidō* without reference to modern processes are often problematic. Even those commentators who recognize the importance of modern developments tend to focus on Nitobe, without considering the reception his work received when it was originally published. Nitobe's primary role in *bushidō* discourse before the late twentieth century was as a popularizer of the concept outside Japan. With regard to the history of Meiji *bushidō*, Nitobe is most important not for his theories, but for what reactions to them reveal about the intellectual climate of the time.

INOUE TETSUJIRŌ AND THE DEVELOPMENT OF IMPERIAL *BUSHIDŌ*

By the beginning of the twentieth century, Inoue Tetsujirō was among the most influential figures in the Japanese intellectual sphere. His position as professor of philosophy at Tokyo Imperial University placed him at the centre of academia, and his close ties with the government, military, and publishing industry allowed Inoue to disseminate his ideas far beyond the ivory tower. Along with Ozaki Yukio, Inoue was one of the few Meiji *bushidō* theorists to see the start of war with the Allies in 1941. Whereas Ozaki did not engage significantly with *bushidō* in the twentieth century, however, Inoue was intensely involved with the subject from the Russo-Japanese War until his death in 1944, writing commentaries on the *bushidō* theories of Fukuzawa Yukichi, Nitobe Inazō, and others. Inoue's *bushidō* theories were not distinguished by exceptionally original content, but brought together many of the factors that influenced the evolution of the subject in the writings of other thinkers.

Recognized as intellectually gifted at a young age, Inoue received an advanced classical education before studying history, science, mathematics, and English, enrolling in a school of foreign studies at the age of twenty. In 1882, he became assistant professor of literature at Tokyo Imperial University, having graduated

---

[87] Yamagata Kōhō (1908), *Shin bushidō* (Tokyo: Jitsugyō no Nihonsha), pp. 1–2.

from the same institution two years earlier. From 1884 to 1890, Inoue studied at various institutions throughout Europe at the expense of the Japanese government, meeting many well-known scholars of the day. Although the conditions of their stays in Europe differed in important respects, Inoue shared the feeling of national inferiority found in Ozaki's early articles, and expressed it even more directly and with greater urgency. While Ozaki criticized the Japanese *shinshi* as a poor imitation of English gentlemen, Inoue went further in arguing that the Japanese lagged behind Westerners in terms of their evolutionary development, and warned of grave consequences for Japan if foreigners were allowed to live among the general populace.[88]

Inoue's views on race reflected the theories put forth by scholars such as Takahashi Yoshio, whose *Theories for Improving the Japanese Race* (1884) argued that Japanese were 'inferior to' Westerners, but could be improved through intermarriage.[89] Inoue agreed with the premise, but rejected the solution, arguing instead that foreigners should be kept in separate residential zones until the Japanese had 'caught up' evolutionarily. Inoue's 'defensive' nationalism at this time prompted him to support measures that would 'protect' the Japanese.[90] One of these measures was the promotion of a 'Japanese spirit' as an aspect of the nation's 'unique culture'. The latter should serve as the basis for nationalistic consciousness and confidence, a process that had begun several decades earlier in Germany and impressed Inoue during his visit.[91] Writing in 1890, Nitobe Inazō criticized these intellectual currents: 'The political and intellectual history of New Japan is a story of continuous destruction of old ideas and institutions; but how little of the elements of the New Regime proceeded from native brains! Even the recent reactionary so-called *national* ideas are, to a great extent, a babbling echo of German Chauvinism'.[92]

Immediately after his return from Europe, Inoue accepted a position as the first Japanese professor of philosophy at Tokyo Imperial University, and was soon approached by the government to compose an official commentary on the Imperial Rescript on Education. Contemporary witnesses recalled that Inoue's selection for this task was guided by his occupying a middle ground between idolization of the West and excessive conservativism, a reputation that reflected the feelings of many educated Japanese in the early 1890s.[93] The Rescript is often seen as a last brief victory for the Confucian revival, but subsequent commentaries and interpretations of it varied widely, with their tone often reflecting the new national confidence in native thought. Writers such as the politician Yoshikawa Akimasa (1842–1920) tied the Rescript to *bushidō*, just as the 1882 Rescript for Soldiers and Sailors was also retroactively appropriated.

---

[88] Davis, Winston, 'The Civil Theology of Inoue Tetsujirō', pp. 7–8.
[89] Minami Hiroshi, *Nihonjin ron: meiji kara kyō made*, pp. 30–31.
[90] Davis, Winston, 'The Civil Theology of Inoue Tetsujirō', p. 8.
[91] Mehl, Margaret (1992), *Eine Vergangenheit für die japanische Nation* (Frankfurt: Peter Lang), p. 282.
[92] Nitobe Inazo. *The Intercourse between the United States and Japan: A Historical Sketch*, p. 171.
[93] Gluck, Carol, *Japan's Modern Myths*, p. 128.

Inoue's writings in the early 1890s contained a similarly nuanced nationalism as Ozaki Yukio's, but by the turn of the century Inoue's nationalism was anything but defensive or subtle, and *bushidō* served as an ideal vehicle for its dissemination. Inoue's involvement would have a profound impact on the development of general *bushidō* discourse after this time, in accordance with his broader role as summarized by Winston Davis:

> The influence of Inoue Tetsujirō on the cultural life of prewar Japan can hardly be overestimated. At that time his books, unimaginative as they are, sold in the millions. As a commissioner in charge of compiling books for teaching moral education in the public schools and as an educator of educators, his impact on the Japanese school system was deep and longlasting. From his position at Tokyo Imperial University, where at one time he had over ten thousand students, he dominated the Japanese academic world politically...[94]

By the end of Meiji, Inoue was by far the most prolific author and editor in the field of *bushidō* studies, publishing until shortly before his death in 1944. This has often been overlooked in the post-war period, and most assessments after Inoue's death have been in line with Davis' description: 'Though he claimed to be the greatest philosopher east of Suez, his logic was tendentious, his arguments forced and artificial. In fact his philosophy was little more than a smorgasbord spread with the leftovers of former ideological feasts, East and West'.[95] In spite of this, Inoue's impact on modern *bushidō* was tremendous, and his early involvement with the subject was reflected in *A Collection of Bushidō Theories by Prominent Modern Thinkers* (1905), a volume of thirty-three articles on *bushidō* from the previous fifteen years, eight of which were written by Inoue.[96] Even in works he did not write himself, Inoue was quick to offer a brief preface or introduction, and many pre-war works on *bushidō* bear his mark. The addition of a few words from Inoue signified that a work was in line with the officially sanctioned imperial interpretation of *bushidō*, and therefore presumably suitable for use as educational material.

In 1901, Inoue held a lecture at the Military Preparatory School (Rikugun Yōnen Gakkō), which was subsequently published and widely distributed under the simple title *Bushidō*.[97] This lecture concisely manifested Inoue's multifarious roles in *bushidō* discourse, and also outlined themes that would become prominent in his later work in other fields. In addition to emphasizing patriotism and loyalty to the emperor, Inoue's *bushidō* activities were defined by several characteristics: a close relationship with the military as an educator and ideologist; ultranationalism and the emphasis on a unique Japanese spirit; pronounced anti-foreignism framed in the rhetoric of Japanese superiority; aggressive intolerance of other views as a self-appointed defender of imperial *bushidō* orthodoxy; and the exaltation of Yamaga Sokō as one of the most important thinkers in Japanese history.

---

[94]　Davis, Winston, 'The Civil Theology of Inoue Tetsujirō', p. 33.
[95]　Winston Davis, 'The Civil Theology of Inoue Tetsujirō', pp. 5–6.
[96]　Akiyama Goan and Inoue Tetsujirō (eds.) (1905), *Gendai taika bushidō sōron* (Tokyo: Hakubunkan).
[97]　Inoue Tetsujirō, *Bushidō*.

The *Bushidō* lecture was an introductory overview of the subject as interpreted by Inoue, and the Military Preparatory School venue demonstrated his growing relationship with the military, which he would supply with ideological ammunition through the publication of hundreds of military-related books, articles, and pamphlets. These included works commissioned and published by the military, such as the *Bushidō* lecture, as well as military publications by other authors and publishers that Inoue supplied with a boilerplate preface or introduction relating the subject matter to *bushidō*. Inoue was arguably the closest thing to an official ideologist in the employ of the government, defining 'his academic interests in ways consistent with the ideological needs of the imperial state'.[98] As these needs changed, Inoue obligingly revised his interpretations, thereby ensuring that he was able to maintain his position of influence.

The 'Japanist' (*Nippon shugi*) nationalistic ideals of Inoue's Great Japan Society were a major theme in the *Bushidō* lecture, and the contention that the 'Japanese race' possessed a divinely mandated uniqueness was a fundamental component of Inoue's *bushidō*:

> If one says that *bushidō* is an ethic consisting of things that were traditionally practised by our nation's warriors, this would include a general meaning of *bushidō*...And if one were to say what the content of this thing called *bushidō* is, then ultimately the spirit of the Japanese race is its primary principle...However, *bushidō* developed gradually, aided by Confucianism and Buddhism, and in this way gradually came to be perfected. Because of this, *bushidō* in its fully finished form is the product of a balanced fusion of the three teachings of Shinto, Confucianism, and Buddhism...It is not possible to say with accuracy in what age *bushidō* arose...If one thinks further and further back, it is possible to already discover some of the principles of *bushidō* even in the tales of the Japanese gods...The Japanese race has a spirit that primarily respects martiality, and it must be said that this is the source [of *bushidō*]. In other words, it would certainly be safe to say that *bushidō* has existed since ancient times.[99]

Inoue's relationship with the military continued to strengthen and his insistence on a unique Japanese martial spirit increased accordingly. The Japanese spirit as manifested in *bushidō* was vital to the survival and success of the nation, Inoue argued, and was the 'source of the Japanese military's great strength'. Anyone could purchase guns and machines, but the spirit necessary for their victorious operation could not simply be imported or taught.[100] At the time, the belief that a soldier's spirit was equally or more important than materiél was widespread, and inspired tragic 'over-the-top' charges against devastating new automatic weapons in the First World War. Japan did not directly experience the horrors of this conflict, however, and Inoue's belief in the superiority of the spirit became a central pillar of military policy, with *bushidō* a core theme in spiritual education.

Inoue's emphasis on a unique Japanese spirit reflected his anti-foreignism, which grew more pronounced over time. While his xenophobic warnings a decade

---

[98] Tucker, John Allen, 'Tokugawa Intellectual History and Prewar Ideology', pp. 38–39.
[99] Inoue Tetsujirō, *Bushidō*, pp. 2, 3–4, 8–9.			[100] Inoue Tetsujirō, *Bushidō*, pp. 12–13.

earlier had been prompted by concerns regarding the 'evolutionary stage' of the Japanese at the time, by 1901 Inoue framed his anti-foreign rhetoric in the context of Japanese superiority. European chivalry was an important point of comparison from the very beginning of *bushidō* discourse, but Inoue harshly dismissed European knighthood. Superficial similarities between *bushidō* and chivalry notwithstanding, *bushidō* had 'developed from a far more severe spirit' than chivalry, which Inoue derided as mere 'woman-worship'.[101] Another European thought system frequently likened to *bushidō* was Stoic philosophy, and Inoue agreed that the two contained a similar idea of self-denial, while many Stoics committed suicide like Japanese warriors. However, Inoue argued that the two were definitely not the same, for 'the practical spirit in *bushidō* was much stronger than in Stoicism', which also 'lacked the spirit of endurance of hardship and pain that could be found in *bushidō*'.[102] This anti-foreign tone increased in Inoue's subsequent writings, and his attacks on other Japanese thinkers would infer that they were 'un-Japanese' or 'Western minds in Japanese bodies'.

The criticism that Inoue directed at others was related to his role as a self-appointed defender of imperial ideology, and his aggressive intolerance of conflicting views was especially pronounced in his early works on *bushidō*. The lack of a uniform interpretation led Inoue to appropriate *bushidō* as his personal domain, positing himself as the arbiter of correctness. Inoue's desire to defend his imperial *bushidō* was evident from the beginning, and by the end of Meiji most writers on *bushidō* came to at least nominally recognize his authority in the field. While Inoue merely dismissed Nitobe's opinions, another text published the same year defended imperial *bushidō* more aggressively. Shortly before his death, Fukuzawa Yukichi finally published his *Yasegaman no setsu*, a move he had resisted for almost a decade out of concern for how his criticism of Katsu Kaishū would be received.[103] The resulting backlash validated Fukuzawa's concerns, with Tokutomi Sohō among the most vociferous critics of the text.[104] The harshest response came from Inoue in a long article that was a polemical personal attack on Fukuzawa rather than an analysis of the text. Inoue argued that although Katsu had surrendered the walls of Edo castle, Fukuzawa had committed the greater transgression of surrendering the walls of his mind to Western thought.[105] Ironically, many of the central ideas in the *Yasegaman no setsu* were not far removed from Inoue's own views on *bushidō*, especially with regard to loyalty and choosing death over surrender, and the critique was primarily motivated by Inoue's anti-foreignism and dislike of Fukuzawa.

In contrast, by dismissing Nitobe's views, Inoue was focused on promoting Yamaga Sokō as the most significant formulator and 'sage of *bushidō*'.[106] While

---

[101] Inoue Tetsujirō, *Bushidō*, pp. 6–7.   [102] Inoue Tetsujirō, *Bushidō*, pp. 4–5.

[103] Koyasu Nobukuni (2003), *Nihon kindai shisō hihan: ikkokuchi no seiritsu* (Tokyo: Iwanami gendai bunko), pp. 307, 322.

[104] Inoue Isao. 'Tokugawa no ishin: sono kōdō to rinri', p. 269.

[105] Inoue Tetsujirō (1901), 'Bushidō wo ronjiawasete *Yasegaman no setsu* ni oyobu', *Senken ronbun 2 shū* (Tokyo: Fuzanbō), pp. 85–100.

[106] Inoue Tetsujirō, *Bushidō*, p. 15.

Inoue focused on actively promoting and defending *bushidō*, rather than providing original and reasoned contributions to discourse, one area where he had a lasting impact was in his elevation of Yamaga and Yoshida Shōin as the pivotal figures in the development of *bushidō*. Yoshida was deemed important primarily for reviving Yamaga's thought in the mid-nineteenth century, while Yamaga was emphasized due to his negative opinion of China, as well as his supposed influence on the *rōnin* of Akō.[107] According to Inoue, Yamaga was 'the first person with the intellectual ability to formulate texts [on *bushidō*]'.[108] Other scholars of his day were too focused on China, but Yamaga recognized that Japan was the land of 'civilization' and 'superior to China, which was the land of revolutions'. Inoue believed that Yamaga's 'research and writings about the [Japanese] Age of the Gods were powerful works, even if viewed in the present day', and marked an important departure from the Confucians who knew only China and nothing about Japan.[109] Yamaga's views of China, and Yoshida's even more chauvinistic interpretations, resonated with nationalistic sentiment following the Sino-Japanese War.

Yamaga's role as the alleged inspiration of the Akō *rōnin* had increased significance in Meiji as the *rōnin* were adopted into the new imperial ideology, with the emperor even issuing a proclamation praising their actions and paying a publicized visit to their graves in 1868.[110] The *rōnin* steadily increased in prominence, especially in the twentieth century, and modern accounts of their exploits introduced a new theme of imperial loyalty. Ideologically 'correct' versions of the *Treasury of Loyal Retainers* were distributed as educational materials, with the military using them in spiritual education.[111] According to Inoue, who based his arguments on texts by Yoshida and select Tokugawa Confucians, the actions of the *rōnin* were 'certainly the result of the teachings that Yamaga spread in Akō over 19 years' in that domain. The Akō Incident, which was 'without parallel in world history', was 'entirely the result of Sokō's *bushidō* teachings'.[112] There is, however, no evidence for a connection between Yamaga and the Akō Incident, and—with a few prominent exceptions—Japanese historiography after 1945 has generally dismissed the notion that Yamaga taught or even influenced the *rōnin*.[113] While he emphasized Yamaga's anti-foreign sentiments, Inoue did not examine Yamaga's thought in great detail in the *Bushidō* lecture, although he lauded Yamaga's 'teaching that *bushi* must be at one with death at all times', and credited this with steeling Yoshida Shōin's resolve.[114] On the whole, Inoue tended to focus on Yamaga's supposed impact rather than on his actual writings. This was especially the case in educational materials, and Inoue

---

[107] John Tucker has provided an overview of these aspects as they appear in Inoue's 1903 *Philosophy of the Japanese Ancient Learning School* (Tucker, John Allen, 'Tokugawa Intellectual History and Prewar Ideology', pp. 42–44).

[108] Inoue Tetsujirō, *Bushidō*, p. 40.   [109] Inoue Tetsujirō, *Bushidō*, pp. 39–40.

[110] Inoue Tetsujirō, *Bushidō*, p. 41.

[111] For example: Nagahori Hitoshi (1919), *Seishin kyōiku teikoku gunjin sōsho dai-ippen: Akō gishi* (Tokyo: Tsūzoku gunji kyōiku kai).

[112] Inoue Tetsujirō, *Bushidō*, pp. 49–50.

[113] John Allen Tucker, 'Tokugawa Intellectual History and Prewar Ideology', pp. 35–36.

[114] Inoue Tetsujirō, *Bushidō*, pp. 42–43.

maintained that Yamaga 'rendered greater service to his country as an advocate of the *Bushidō* than as a moral philosopher'.[115]

Inoue spent the following decades repackaging the central themes of his *Bushidō* lecture in his voluminous outputs, and his subsequent works on *bushidō* followed patterns set in 1901. Inoue's *bushidō* became increasingly nationalistic and aggressive, sometimes contradicting his earlier writings, but many of his themes were consistent, if unexceptional. Inoue's introduction of Yamaga Sokō was arguably his most significant theoretical contribution, as it promoted the use of Edo-period writings for research into *bushidō*. Inoue expanded this approach in his 1905 *Bushidō sōsho* (*Bushidō Library*), a three-volume collection of historical documents from pre-Meiji writers, and in the thirteen-volume *Bushidō zensho* (1942) (*Complete Writings on Bushidō*). By compiling older texts, Inoue lent *bushidō* an apparent historical legitimacy that went far beyond Nitobe's vague appeals to an 'unwritten ethic'. Indeed, by the end of Meiji the historical pedigree of *bushidō* was largely accepted and, with the notable exception of Basil Hall Chamberlain, even critics of the concept tended to focus on its interpretations rather than its recent vintage.

Aside from Inoue's introduction of Yamaga Sokō, most of his arguments had been made by other writers in the preceding decade, although not as forcefully or from such a position of academic authority. The most important element of Inoue's imperial *bushidō* was absolute loyalty to the emperor, which Mikami Reiji had discussed only two years before. Under Inoue's direction, the notion that *bushidō* was encapsulated by the phrase *chūkun aikoku* (loyalty to the emperor and patriotism) became a central tenet of imperial *bushidō*, and Inoue came to dominate *bushidō* discourse with astounding rapidity after 1901. Due in no small part to Inoue's efforts, the trajectory of *bushidō* during the early twentieth century closely mirrored his own involvement in the field, and his influence was especially pronounced in the growth of *bushidō* between 1901 and 1905. Inoue's connections to official channels aided the dissemination of his ideas, and his association with the military became especially important with the outbreak of war with Russia in 1904.

THE JAPANESE SAMURAI AND THE RUSSIAN BEAR

If the Sino-Japanese War marked Japan's rise to primacy within East Asia, the Russo-Japanese War of 1904–05 signalled the nation's arrival among the great powers of the day. Both conflicts had profound effects on all facets of Japanese society, although public reactions to the war with Russia were considerably more nuanced. More developed and extensive news coverage allowed more people to

---

[115] Inoue Tetsujirō (1909), 'Japanese Religious Beliefs: Confucianism', in Marcus B. Huish (ed.), *Fifty Years of New Japan Vol. II.* (London: Smith, Elder & Co.). p. 58 (cited by John Allen Tucker, 'Tokugawa Intellectual History and Prewar Ideology', pp. 44–45).

follow the events, and the first military victories reported by the sensationalist press were accompanied by an unprecedented surge of nationalistic fervour. This was further enhanced by the fact that Russia was a European imperial power, even if it was in terminal decline and hampered by internal unrest, poor leadership, and long supply lines. On the other hand, Japan found this war a far greater challenge than the Sino-Japanese War had been, resulting in considerable opposition and disillusionment. In this sense, it is useful to distinguish between parallel discourses on the Russo-Japanese War—the official versions of the war promoted by the government and contemporary mainstream media, and the unofficial version lived and experienced by soldiers, families, anti-war activists, and others outside the public eye.

In the context of *bushidō*, if not in terms of social and moral responsibility, the 'official' version of the war was most significant, and *bushidō* was hoisted up by the national euphoria that accompanied the war. The years 1904–05 were the peak of the Meiji '*bushidō* boom', with the concept not only becoming wildly popular in Japan and abroad, but also being redefined for militaristic and propaganda purposes. By boosting national confidence, the general progress of the conflict as portrayed in the popular media had a more significant effect on *bushidō* than did specific battles, although notable events in this regard included the sinking of the *Hitachi Maru*, the Battle of Port Arthur, and the later siege and fall of Port Arthur. These became important points of reference for *bushidō* during and after the war, as the 'proper' *bushidō* conduct of Japanese troops became an issue of spirited public debate.

Just as Japan had been assured of British non-intervention in the Sino-Japanese War, the Anglo-Japanese Alliance of 1902 ensured the neutrality of other powers in case of war with Russia. Increasing Russian military buildup in Manchuria following the Boxer Rebellion made Japanese leaders apprehensive regarding the status of Korea and, by extension, Japan's own security. The decision was taken to strike against Russia before the completion of the Trans-Siberian Railway would further solidify Russia's position, and the Imperial Japanese Navy attacked the Russian Far East Fleet on 8 February 1904. A host of foreign military and press observers closely monitored the naval and land battles over the next eighteen months, as many of the devastating methods of modern warfare on hand had never before been employed. The terrible toll exacted by machine guns and artillery, as well as the horrors of modern trench warfare, were duly recorded by European observers only to be disregarded and repeated on the Western Front a decade later. The conflict ended following the defeat of the Russian Baltic Fleet at Tsushima in May 1905, when Japan successfully pushed for peace with the aid of American pressure, and the tsar reluctantly agreed to end hostilities and focus on growing domestic turmoil. The terms of the treaty signed at Portsmouth, Maine, in September 1905 gave Japan the freedom to act in Korea and South Manchuria, but failed to include monetary reparations or significant territorial gains, reflecting the fact that the war was not a comprehensive Japanese victory. Although downplayed by the nationalistic press, the financial and human cost of the war had severely stretched Japan, and military leaders realized that continuing the conflict would have had devastating consequences.

Bushidō was one of the greatest beneficiaries of the war, with articles appearing in leading periodicals, while books, lectures, and newspaper reports frequently invoked the subject. A number of important texts were brought together in December 1905 by Inoue Tetsujirō and Akiyama Goan in *A Collection of Bushidō Theories by Prominent Modern Thinkers* (*Gendai taika bushidō sōron*). While including articles dating back as far as the early 1890s, this volume focused on works written in the twentieth century, especially after the outbreak of war with Russia. In addition to contributing eight articles himself, Inoue applied his ideological approach to the selection of the other texts. The goals of the *Collection* were twofold: first, 'to collect lectures and essays on *bushidō* from famous persons of the present day, and to do comparative research into old and new *bushidō*, thereby demonstrating Japan's unique ethic'. The second aim of the work was to 'gather essays and commentary related to the Russo-Japanese War, observe currents in our nation's current ethics, and to be used as material for future national education'.[116] Tellingly, this compilation did not include any writings by Ozaki, Uemura, Nitobe, Fukuzawa, or even any of the writers featured in the *Bushidō* journal of 1898. Inoue would have deemed most *bushidō* interpretations from the 1890s to be insufficiently compatible with the nationalistic and militaristic imperial *bushidō* interpretation that was developing under his tutelage.

Instead, Inoue directed the reader to examine the *Collection* together with his *Bushidō Library* (1905), which brought together excerpts from Edo-period writers that Inoue considered particularly important to *bushidō*, including Nakae Tōju, Kumazawa Banzan, Yamaga Sokō, Kaibara Ekiken, and Daidōji Yūzan, but no writings from earlier in Meiji.[117] Inoue's selectiveness was apparent in an appendix of 'discussions relating to *bushidō* not included in this book', listing twenty-six other articles and essays, with no reference to Ozaki, Uemura, or other writers from the early 1890s. One of Nitobe Inazō's later articles was mentioned, but his more famous and controversial *Bushido: The Soul of Japan* was not. Inoue used his editorial control to promote his 'imperial' *bushidō* by ignoring works and authors he did not agree with, as well as selecting articles from journals he edited.[118] The *Collection* also contained examples of Inoue's more aggressive work, including his 1901 attack on Fukuzawa, while another essay on '*Bushidō* and Future Ethics', repeated Inoue's earlier criticisms of Nitobe and Fukuzawa.[119]

Inoue's second objective in the *Collection* was a bold statement of his ambition as a promoter of *bushidō*, especially in the fields of military and civilian education. As Inoue argued, 'Russia has three times the population and is 60 times the size of Japan, and the Japanese victory was like David's over Goliath. There are many reasons for the Japanese victory... however, there can be no doubting

---

[116] Akiyama Goan (1905), 'Jijo', in *Gendai taika bushidō sōron* (Tokyo: Hakubunkan), p. 2.

[117] Inoue Tetsujirō (ed.) (1905), *Bushidō sōsho* (Tokyo: Hakubunkan).

[118] Nakamura Yoko, *Bushidō—Diskurs. Die Analyse der Diskrepanz zwischen Ideal und Realität im Bushidō-Diskurs aus dem Jahr 1904*, p. 22.

[119] Inoue Tetsujirō. 'Bushidō wo ronjiawasete *Yasegaman no setsu* ni oyobu', pp. 59–69; Inoue Tetsujirō (1905), 'Bushidō to shōrai no dōtoku', in Akiyama Goan and Inoue Tetsujirō (eds.), *Gendai taika bushidō sōron* (Tokyo: Hakubunkan), pp. 129, 139.

that *bushidō*...played an especially important role in this victory'.[120] The core essays in the *Collection* demonstrated Inoue's desire to both promote *bushidō* in education and actively shape broader discourse. In a series of articles published primarily in the journals *Nihon* and *Taiyō* in late 1904 at the height of the war, Inoue allied with Major General Satō Tadashi (1849–1920), a Sino-Japanese War veteran and former mayor of Hiroshima, to condemn Waseda University professor Ukita Kazutami (1860–1946) for what they considered to be a disrespectful interpretation of the Japanese martial spirit. Ukita's response resulted in an extended debate demonstrating Inoue's role as apologist and defender of imperial *bushidō*.

The controversy, often called the 'POW Exchange Student Debate', centred on the obligation of Japanese soldiers to commit suicide rather than be captured. The instigation for the debates was an incident that took place on 15 June 1904, in which three Japanese transport ships, the *Hitachi Maru, Sado Maru*, and *Izumi Maru*, were attacked by Russian warships. The transports were virtually defenceless, and the two ships carrying non-combatants surrendered to the Russians. The *Hitachi Maru*, however, had almost 1,000 troops bound for the continent on board and refused to surrender despite the enemy's overwhelming firepower. The Russian ships reportedly shelled the *Hitachi Maru* for several hours before it sank, killing most of the troops and crew. According to sensationalistic Japanese newspaper reports, although a few sailors managed to escape in lifeboats and were rescued, 'most of the officers committed suicide through *seppuku* or shooting themselves with pistols' on the deck of the ship, while others threw themselves into the ocean to die rather than become prisoners of war.[121] Detailed reports purporting to describe their final moments soon appeared, and were widely used in propaganda materials until 1945.[122] At the time, although public opinion was generally supportive of the reported actions of the officers, becoming a prisoner of war was not widely condemned in Japan.[123] Over the course of the war, about 2,000 Japanese soldiers surrendered or were captured, with most of them transferred to facilities in European Russia, and their accounts indicate that conditions there were quite comfortable.[124]

The *Hitachi Maru* incident instigated a debate when Satō, who had himself lost a leg in the Sino-Japanese War, read about a lecture by Ukita defending the actions of soldiers who surrendered. This lecture, hosted by Ozaki Yukio at the Tokyo City Education Society on 18 September 1904, was summarized and published in *Taiyō*

---

[120] Inoue Tetsujirō (1905), 'Jo.', in Akiyama Goan and Inoue Tetsujirō (eds.), *Gendai taika bushidō sōron* (Tokyo: Hakubunkan), pp. 1–2.

[121] *Nihon*. 17 June 1904, p. 5. The front page of the following issue of *Nihon* lauded the behaviour of the troops, while stating that 'according to the *bushidō* of the Sengoku Period, the blame should be on the superiors' who allowed the ships to be placed in such a position.

[122] For example, *Nihon*. 19 June 1904, p. 5; *Nihon*. 22 June 1904, p. 1.

[123] Ichinose Toshiya (2004), *Meiji, Taishō, Shōwa guntai manyuaru: hito ha naze senjō he itta no ka* (Tokyo: Kōbunsha), pp. 95–99.

[124] Hata Ikuhiko (1998), *Nihon no horyo: Hakusonkō kara Shiberia yokuryū made* (Hara shobō), pp. 14–15.

shortly thereafter. Ukita argued that one should not needlessly commit suicide, but live as long as possible to fight for one's country. In any case, Ukita continued, becoming a prisoner of war was not shameful, but rather an opportunity to learn about another country similar to a foreign exchange student.[125] Satō's response in *Nihon* described Ukita as follows:

> I have heard that he is held in esteem by scholars in education...However, in this talk he demonstrated mistaken views that can truly not be allowed in a scholar and educator.
>
> Ukita attacked the fact that we Japanese believe that dying in battle is honourable, and becoming a prisoner of war is the greatest embarrassment. He also criticized the fact that we hold the ideal that we can commit suicide in order to preserve our honour. He states that it is possible to die out of duty, but not for honour, and that many of the suicides on the battlefield are for the sake of honour, which is barbaric and not courageous.[126]

Satō also attacked Ukita's other views as being contrary to *bushidō*, stating that 'Ukita claims that as long as you have personnel, matériel, and technology, you will win wars. However, this is nonsense. What if both armies have these things? There must be a non-material, non-technological "true cause" of our victory. This is the essence of our military spirit'. According to Satō, the Russians were not inferior in terms of men and equpment, but lacked Japan's martial spirit. The Russians merely fought out of a sense of duty, but the Japanese fought for the honour of their ancestors and nation. While Satō admitted that 'giving one's most valuable life for the imperial nation is also a duty', focusing on this aspect would inevitably lead to failure. Satō reasoned that Europeans were more advanced in military arts and technology, and Japan would certainly have lost if wars were entirely technological. Instead, continued Satō, whereas Europeans fight with technology, the Japanese fight with spirit, leading to Japan's victory. In conclusion, Satō described Ukita as most dangerous due to his position as an educator. If he were merely a private individual, his mistaken views could simply be dismissed, but permitting scholars to teach this sort of disinformation would severely weaken the country and make it impossible to win great victories.[127]

Inoue joined the debate with his own essay in *Nihon*, which he presented as an objective overview. According to Inoue, Ukita's reasoning was entirely academic, his distinction between honour and duty was incorrect, and he was guilty of conflating 'lower' forms of suicide (for reasons of poverty, illness, etc.) and the 'higher' suicide of soldiers in battle. Inoue attributed this deficiency to Ukita 'seeing things through Western eyes' when this case clearly concerned Japan's unique 'true spirit',

---

[125] Ukita Kazutami, 'Nichiro sensō to kyōiku', *Nihon* (31 Oct. 1904), p. 4.

[126] Satō Tadashi (1905), 'Gakusha no jasetsu wo yabusu', in Akiyama Goan and Inoue Tetsujirō (eds.), *Gendai taika bushidō sōron* (Tokyo: Hakubunkan), p. 228. Originally printed in *Nihon*, 2 October 1904, p. 1.

[127] Satō Tadashi, pp. 229–34.

which prioritized suicide over surrender.[128] Inoue claimed that Ukita had been corrupted by Western ideas and was not able to understand the Japanese spirit, charges that had earlier been levelled at Fukuzawa. In both these cases, Inoue's attacks consisted of vague references to ambiguous spiritual virtues combined with limited reasoned argumentation, his primary *modus operandi* as the defender of imperial *bushidō*.

Ukita was renowned for holding fast to his principles, having resigned a position at Dōshisha University a decade earlier due to an ideological dispute. His response appeared in *Nihon* on 22 October, and briefly noted criticisms by Satō and segments of the press before turning to Inoue. According to Ukita, a *Mainichi shinbun* editorial by Shimada Saburō (1852–1923) had already demonstrated that there was no fundamental difference between Ukita and Satō's views on the reasons for dying in battle for one's country, and that the actual points of contention were Inoue and Ukita's differing views of suicide.[129] In this regard, Ukita found Inoue's characterization of his arguments to be misleading, with Inoue falsely accusing him of advocating ready surrender with the goal of travelling abroad as a prisoner of war. Ukita denied that his views encouraged surrender, but merely criticized needless suicide for the sake of honour.[130] If *bushidō* made long-term victory impossible by requiring one to commit suicide for short-term honour, Ukita argued the following week, then the 'future form of *bushidō* would have to be revised'.[131]

Ukita's invocation of Shimada's conciliatory editorial did not placate Satō and Inoue, and the former responded with another personal attack. According to Satō, Ukita's negative view of committing suicide in an unfavourable position was a result of Ukita having learned his *bushidō* from Westerners. Moreover, the idea that one could easily become a prisoner of war and go on 'foreign exchange' originated in Ukita's 'Christian individualistic survivalism'.[132] Satō wrote that 'Ukita physically appears Japanese, but his spirit is that of a Westerner', making Ukita 'not Japanese', which was why Ukita condoned 'Japanese soldiers losing their [honour-valuing] spirit and becoming as weak as Americans and Europeans'. In closing, Satō denounced Ukita's arguments for peace and diplomacy, demanding that the government take action to protect the youth from his 'dangerous' and 'foolish' ideas.[133]

Inoue's next response in *Nihon*, 25 October, was no more conciliatory, as he reiterated that Ukita's criticism of suicide was made from a Western perspective,

---

[128] Inoue Tetsujirō (1905), 'Ukita Satō ryōshi no ronsō ni tsuite', in Akiyama Goan and Inoue Tetsujirō (eds.), *Gendai taika bushidō sōron* (Tokyo: Hakubunkan), pp. 236–38. Originally printed in *Nihon*, 18 October 1904, p. 7.

[129] Ukita Kazutami (1905), 'Bungaku hakase Inoue Tetsujirō kun no hihyō ni tou', in Akiyama Goan and Inoue Tetsujirō (eds.), *Gendai taika bushidō sōron* (Tokyo: Hakubunkan), p. 243. Originally printed in *Nihon*, 22 October 1904, p. 1.

[130] Ukita Kazutami, pp. 244–45.

[131] Ukita Kazutami, 'Nichiro sensō to kyōiku', *Nihon*, 31 October 1904, p. 4.

[132] Satō Tadashi (1905), 'Futatabi Ukita shi no benron ni tsuite', in Akiyama Goan and Inoue Tetsujirō (eds.), *Gendai taika bushidō sōron* (Tokyo: Hakubunkan), p; 248. Eida Takahiro, 'Hankotsu no genron nin Ukita Kazutami: Waseda daigaku sōsōki no kyojin'.

[133] Satō Tadashi, 'Futatabi Ukita shi no benron ni tsuite', pp. 249, 250, 252, 254–55.

and that Japanese *bushidō* demanded suicide in certain situations.[134] In Ukita, Inoue had met an adversary who refused to concede to the pressure applied by the ultranationalists, and Ukita's position at Waseda allowed him to challenge government-promoted interpretations to a greater degree than most other scholars. At the time, many academics would have yielded to attacks from influential figures such as Inoue, Satō, Katō Hiroyuki, and others whose critiques of Ukita were included in the *Collection*.[135]

Inoue was unable to convince Ukita to retract his claims, although he energetically fulfilled his role as a defender of imperial *bushidō*. Ukita's resistance was the primary reason that such an extensive exchange occurred in print, and most others would have engaged in self-censorship or withdrawn controversial ideas. Inoue's actions in this situation, and his alliance with Satō, foreshadowed conditions three decades later, and another essay by Satō in the *Collection* is filled with imagery that would be widely used in the 1930s. Satō argued that 'the most important element of war is a martial spirit, which is similar to *shinigurui* (death madness), which in turn involves charging through bullets without fear and enjoying battle'. Furthermore, Satō believed that 'death in battle was the flowering of soldiery', invoking aesthetic imagery that would become closely associated with the suicidal tactics of the Pacific War.[136] The insistence on suicide over surrender was tied to *bushidō* from the Russo-Japanese War onward, with Inoue playing a vital role in this development.

The POW Exchange Student Debates reveal Inoue's attempts to impose an orthodox imperial view of *bushidō*, as well as the challenges that this project faced. *Bushidō* was still a young and developing ideology brought out of the realm of elite discourse by the Russo-Japanese War. Ten years earlier, victory over the Qing had been credited to Japan's status as a modern and civilized nation, at least relative to China, but *bushidō* and the Japanese spirit were invoked to explain the defeat of a Western power. *Bushidō* was closely tied to the emerging trends of cultural chauvinism that were increasingly spreading to broader society, especially after 1905. Sakurai Tadayoshi's *Human Bullets* (*Nikudan*), the most famous popular account of the war, attributed the victory to the 'invincible spirit called *Yamato-damashii*, disciplined under the strict rule of military training'.[137]

During the war, *bushidō* was used to describe and contextualize events, but there is little evidence that it influenced behaviour. As Yoshida Kenryū (1870–1943) wrote in his 'Stoic Philosophy and *Bushidō*', 'It is commonly believed that *bushidō*

---

[134] Inoue, Tetsujirō (1905), 'Ukita shi no kōben wo yomu', in Akiyama Goan and Inoue Tetsujirō (eds.), *Gendai taika bushidō sōron* (Tokyo: Hakubunkan), pp. 256–64. Originally printed in *Nihon*, 25 October 1904, p. 2.

[135] Katō Hiroyuki (1905), 'Satō tai Ukita ron ni suite', in Akiyama Goan and Inoue Tetsujirō (eds.), *Gendai taika bushidō sōron* (Tokyo: Hakubunkan), pp. 265–72.

[136] Satō Tadashi (1905),'Ōi ni shiki wo shinsaku seyo', Akiyama Goan and Inoue Tetsujirō (eds.), *Gendai taika bushidō sōron* (Tokyo: Hakubunkan), pp. 224–25. For a discussion of this imagery, see Ohnuki-Tierney, Emiko (2002), *Kamikaze, Cherry Blossoms, and Nationalisms: The Militarization of Aesthetics in Japanese History* (Chicago: University of Chicago Press).

[137] Sakurai Tadayoshi (1908), *Human Bullets: A Soldier's Story of Port Arthur* (London: Archibald Constable), p. 10.

spread among the people through heroic tales told by storytellers at festivals in the countryside. I grew up in a farming family, and I can say from personal experience that farmers rarely have time to listen to such tales, and therefore it would not have been possible to impress *bushidō* as a moral consciousness'. According to Yoshida, although prominent politicians believed that the national morality was disseminated through storytellers rather than ethics instruction, this merely demonstrated their ignorance of rural conditions. For this reason, Yoshida continued, 'one should reject the notion that the successful popularization of *bushidō* contributed to victory in the war [with Russia]'.[138] Stuart Lone argues that 'the stereotypes of the Japanese people as uniquely regimented (I use the word deliberately) and predisposed to this will-to-sacrifice were formulated in the early wars of the 1890s and 1900s'.[139] According to Lone, while 'There were, undoubtedly, many attempts by the central authorities to spread the values of the military among civilians... these attempts repeatedly fell far short of their original goals'.[140] As the debates on POWs demonstrate, Inoue's desired indoctrination of the public with imperial *bushidō* was still in its infancy, but idealized descriptions appearing during and after the conflict helped the Russo-Japanese War become a key event in the development and dissemination of modern *bushidō*, which would rely heavily on this conflict for its heroes, narratives, and symbols.

[138] Yoshida Kenryū (1905), 'Sutoa tetsugaku to *bushidō*', Akiyama Goan and Inoue Tetsujirō (eds.), *Gendai taika bushidō sōron* (Tokyo: Hakubunkan), pp. 488–89; Nakamura Yoko (2008), *Bushidō – Diskurs. Die Analyse der Diskrepanz zwischen Ideal und Realität im Bushidō-Diskurs aus dem Jahr 1904* (PhD thesis at the University of Vienna), pp. 177–78.

[139] Lone, Stewart (2010), *Provincial Life and the Military in Imperial Japan: the Phantom Samurai* (Abingdon: Routledge), p. 2.

[140] Lone, Stewart, p. 3.

4

The Late *Bushidō* Boom, 1905–1914

BUSHIDŌ IN CONTEXT

Japan's success in the Sino-Japanese War greatly increased national confidence and unity, encouraging the development of *bushidō*, but the situation was considerably more ambiguous after the war with Russia. On the one hand, the latter victory was widely considered more significant and would shape Japanese military tactics for decades, while giving militarists a resounding success to refer to in debates concerning military budgets and the involvement of the army in civilian life.[1] On the other hand, Japan entered the war against Russia with greater internal divisions than a decade earlier. There were no significant domestic peace movements or other organizations questioning Japan's actions against China in 1894 and few signs of popular dissatisfaction.[2] Incidents such as the massacres reported after the fall of Port Arthur led to post-war disillusionment, however, and a number of individuals subsequently opposed war in 1904. Some, including Uchimura Kanzō, objected on religious grounds, while others were more influenced by socialist and other leftist ideals.[3] Opposition voices were in the minority, but were given force by the unprecedented human and economic costs of the war, which made the conflict with China pale in comparison. According to one account, General Nogi's ill-conceived attacks on Port Arthur resulted in 60,000 Japanese casualties, followed by a further 41,000 at Mukden in the final two months of the war, bringing the total number of Japanese casualties to well over 100,000.[4] While the government and press lauded these as noble sacrifices, the devastating losses experienced by soldiers and their families bred resentment towards those who conducted the war. As literary critic Higuchi Ryūkyō (1887–1929) wrote:

---

[1] See MacKenzie, S. P. (1999), 'Willpower or Firepower? The Unlearned Lessons of the Russo-Japanese War', in David Wells and Sandra Wilson (eds.), *The Russo-Japanese War in Cultural Perspective, 1904–05* (London: MacMillan Press), pp. 30–40; Wilson, Sandra and David Wells (1999), 'Introduction', in David Wells and Sandra Wilson (eds.), *The Russo-Japanese War in Cultural Perspective, 1904–05* (London: MacMillan Press), pp. 19–20.

[2] Banno, Junji (1983), 'External and Internal Problems After the War', in Harry Wray and Hilary Conroy (eds.), *Japan Examined: Perspectives on Modern Japanese History* (Honolulu: University of Hawaii Press), p. 164.

[3] For a discussion of left-wing responses to the war, see Wilson, Sandra (1999), *The Russo-Japanese War in Cultural Perspective, 1904–05* (London: MacMillan Press), pp. 168–75.

[4] MacKenzie, S. P., 'Willpower or Firepower? The Unlearned Lessons of the Russo-Japanese War', p. 32. According to Sandra Wilson's 'The Russo-Japanese War and Japan: Politics, Nationalism and Historical Memory', in the same volume, Japanese losses totalled slightly less than 90,000 (p. 161).

the terrible destructive force of modern weapons claims hundreds of precious lives with a single shell and in a flash produces the tragedy of mountains of bodies and rivers of blood. Even if it is said to be for emperor and country, among the relatives of many war dead are those who sink into such misery that one cannot meet their eyes.[5]

The 1894–95 and 1904–1905 wars also differed with regard to public perceptions of their conclusions and repercussions. Both wars were followed by dissatisfaction with the meagre spoils obtained, as the domestic press had portrayed the conflicts as unbroken successions of overwhelming victories. In both cases, foreign diplomatic pressure forced Japan to relinquish some of its demands on the 'vanquished' foe. The Tripartite Intervention of 1895 was viewed as further proof of the Western powers' heavy-handedness, uniting Japanese against a perceived continuation of foreign injustice. Criticism was also levelled at the Japanese government for its concessions, but, on the whole, patriotism and martiality defined the dominant mood for several years after 1895.[6] In contrast, the negotiations at Portsmouth in 1905 provoked an entirely different reaction, as most Japanese blamed domestic factors for the failure to obtain an indemnity or greater territorial concessions from the Russians. In a speech on 30 July 1905, the right-wing activist Ogawa Heikichi blamed the poor state of the army, interference on the part of the ruling oligarchs, the incompetence of treaty delegation leader Komura Jutarō, and apathy on the part of the populace.[7]

These criticisms did not consider that Japan's military was stretched to the breaking point while Russia had large numbers of reserves in Europe, and a long-term continuation of the conflict would almost certainly have resulted in Japan's defeat.[8] As few people in Japan were aware of the precariousness of the military situation, the diplomatic 'capitulation' at Portsmouth provoked anger towards Japan's leadership. The press fuelled this outrage until it boiled over in the Hibiya Riots of September 1905, when over 350 buildings were destroyed, 17 people were killed, 1,000 injured, and more than 2,000 arrested.[9] The scholar Ōtsuka Yasuji (1869–1931) summarized the sense of uncertainty in a December 1905 lecture on the 'national spirit', arguing that Japanese society was dissolving into two anti-national streams: one of self-centred individualism, and another of internationalism promoted by the growing leftist movements.[10]

The two wars also differed in their economic impact. Japan had been able to fund the Sino-Japanese War on its own primarily through internal bonds without raising taxes, but the cost of the Russo-Japanese War was more than

---

[5] Hiraoka Toshio (1985), *Nichirō sengo bungaku no kenkyū* (Tokyo: Yuseido), p. 17.

[6] Paine, S. C. M. (2003), *The Sino-Japanese War of 1894–1895: Perceptions, Power, and Primacy* (Cambridge: Cambridge University Press), pp. 287–90; Gluck, Carol (1985), *Japan's Modern Myths* (Princeton: Princeton University Press), pp. 223, 150.

[7] Wilson, Sandra (1999), 'The Russo-Japanese War and Japan: Politics, Nationalism, and Historical Memory', p. 178.

[8] Wilson, Sandra, and David Wells (1999), 'Introduction', p. 13.

[9] Okamoto Shumpei (1982), 'The Emperor and the Crowd: The Historical Significance of the Hibiya Riot', in Tetsuo Najita (ed.), *Conflict in Modern Japanese History* (Princeton, NJ: Princeton University Press), pp. 262–65.

[10] Hiraoka Toshio, *Nichirō sengo bungaku no kenkyū*, p. 9.

seven times greater, requiring the government to finance it primarily through foreign loans, while also raising land taxes substantially.[11] Moreover, between 1903 and 1907 the total Japanese national debt more than quadrupled, with external debt increasing almost twelvefold.[12] This left the government unable to provide sufficient support for local administrations, instead beseeching them to reduce expenditure and look for alternative sources of revenue while maintaining the same level of service.[13] With regard to the general economy, some scholars describe the period between 1906 and 1913 as one of 'fitful economic growth' (Kinmonth), while others call it a 'slump' (Banno).[14] Different sectors of the economy fared better than others, but the prevailing uncertainty provided fertile ground for the growth of socialism, anarchism, and other thought feared by the establishment. Massive industrial unrest at mines, factories, and shipyards rocked the country in 1907, which has been labelled the 'year of the strike'.[15] Uprisings seemed to break out at a moment's notice for a host of reasons, leading some to call the years between 1905 and 1918 'a period of urban mass riot'.[16] Changes in education policy resulted in almost one hundred violent incidents in rural Japan between the end of the war with Russia and 1911, while the difficulties many graduates faced in finding employment led to widespread feelings of hopelessness.[17]

The disparate causes and effects of unrest were the result of and contributing factors to a pronounced feeling of uncertainty, and the very state of the nation was called into question. As David Titus describes the dynamic after 1905:

> ... where was the nation to go now? What was to be the new national purpose? Into the void of national purpose left by the very success of Meiji modernization rushed every conceivable social and political theory—from Japanist reactionism to revolutionary Marxism, from Shinto obscurantism to Christian internationalism, from bureaucratic statism to liberal democracy.[18]

In a similar vein, Oka Yoshitake sees the 'supreme order of the state' since 1868 as 'the consolidation of national independence', to which end 'the ruling class had sought to marshall and direct the energy of the people, and it was likewise

[11] Allen, G. C. (1946), *A Short Economic History of Modern Japan, 1867–1937* (London: George Allen & Unwin Ltd.), pp. 43–44.

[12] Allen, G. C., *A Short Economic History*, p. 187.

[13] Gluck, Carol, *Japan's Modern Myths*, p. 193.

[14] Kinmonth, Earl H. (1981), *The Self-Made Man in Meiji Japanese Thought: From Samurai to Salary Man* (Berkeley: University of California Press), p. 280. Banno Junji, 'External and Internal Problems After the War', p. 165.

[15] Gluck, Carol, *Japan's Modern Myths*, p. 175.

[16] Quote from Miyachi Misato and Masumi Junnosuke, cited by Okamoto Shumpei, 'The Emperor and the Crowd; the Historical Significance of the Hibiya Riot', p. 268.

[17] Gluck, Carol, *Japan's Modern Myths*, p. 167; Kinmonth, Earl H., *The Self-Made Man*, pp. 212–14, 227.

[18] Titus, David A. (1983), 'Political Parties and Nonissues in Taishō Democracy', in Harry Wray and Hilary Conroy (eds.), *Japan Examined: Perspectives on Modern Japanese History*, (Honolulu: University of Hawaii Press), p. 181.

for that purpose that the people were expected to spare no devotion or sacrifice'.[19] Oka, like Titus and others, argues that the defeat of Russia accomplished this goal. Banno Junji characterizes the period 1905–14 as defined by serious conflicts within and between the military power structure, financial circles, and increasingly influential popular—or at least party—power.[20] In a sense, the decade after 1905 can be defined and delineated by the very turbulence that frustrates concise summaries.

IMPERIAL *BUSHIDŌ* AFTER THE RUSSO-JAPANESE WAR

After Portsmouth, Inoue Tetsujirō and other proponents of imperial *bushidō* faced several challenges that fundamentally changed the nature of discourse. The end of the war made the wide dissemination of a martial code less urgent, but new difficulties arising from popular unrest, the spread of socialist and anarchist thought, and other perceived social malaise kept producers of official ideologies on their guard. As the nation faced different, internal crises, *bushidō* continued to play an important role in attempts to mould public behaviour. *Bushidō* was more thoroughly disseminated by the government through school and military education texts and a larger ideological system best-known as the teachings of National Morality (*kokumin dōtoku*). As *bushidō* reached new heights in popular discourse, the firm establishment of the 'imperial' interpretation in the nation's barracks and schools meant that deviating interpretations posed a relatively minor threat, and the defence of *bushidō* seemed less necessary. After 1905, Inoue moved into new fields considered more immediately essential to preserving domestic order, although *bushidō* continued to feature prominently in his writings. In addition, Inoue continued to confer his seal of approval in the form of forewords to texts that corresponded with the imperial interpretation of *bushidō*, such as *Eastern Ethics: Models for Character Development* (1909). He also continued to discuss *bushidō* in articles on other themes, including Japanese views of mortality or the swordsman Miyamoto Musashi.[21]

In 1908, Inoue began a series of articles on the structure of the 'national family', leading to a series of lectures and the publication of the *Outline of National Morality* (*Kokumin dōtoku gairon*) in 1912.[22] Whereas the nationalistic and militaristic

[19] Oka Yoshitake (1982), 'Generational Conflict after the Russo-Japanese War', in Tetsuo Najita (ed.), *Conflict in Modern Japanese History* (Princeton, NJ: Princeton University Press), p. 201.

[20] Banno Junji, 'External and Internal Problems After the War', pp. 168–69.

[21] Iwashi Junsei and Toyoshima Yōzaburō (eds.) (1909), *Tōyō rinri: shūyō hōkan* (Tokyo: Hakubunkan); Inoue Tetsujirō, '<Shi no kenkyū> bushidōgaku namida no shiseikan', *Chūō kōron* Vol. 28 (Oct. 1913); Inoue Tetsujirō, 'Miyamoto Musashi to bushidō' *Tōyō tetsugaku* Vol. 21, No. 1 (1914). An early example of Inoue's approval of a text was Adachi Ritsuen (1901), *Bushidō hattatsu shi,* (Tokyo: Tsujimoto shugaku dō).

[22] Fridell, Wilbur M., 'Government Ethics Textbooks in Late Meiji Japan', *The Journal of Asian Studies* 29:4 (Aug. 1970), p. 829.

sentiments arising from the Russo-Japanese War, channelled into *bushidō* and the Yamato spirit, helped to forge most of the nation into a patriotic whole in 1905, appeals to these ideologies seemed incapable of resolving the domestic turmoil that gripped much of the nation after Portsmouth. This was reflected in a 1911 *Taiyō* article that dismissed *bushidō* as an anachronism because 'we have to compete with the powers, and all the samurai had to do was be frugal'.[23] Generous government support for Inoue's National Morality movement moved it beyond academia to having real influence on the development of national consciousness and identity. National Morality was intended as a modern system that, while heavily dependent on traditional values, could counteract the ills of socialism, anarchism, and a perceived lack of patriotic feeling among the populace. Imperial loyalty, filial piety, and patriotism were portrayed as uniquely Japanese, and spread through textbooks, lectures, and official proclamations.[24] Government sponsorship of the project resulted in the publication of dozens of works over a decade, while lectures by Inoue and others at schools and teacher training institutions were intended to instill the ideology at all levels of society.[25] The roots of National Morality were evident in Inoue's earlier ethics texts, such as his *Ethics and Education* (1909), which defined *bushidō* as the 'spirit of revering the emperor and loving the nation' and provided an overview of the concept that foreshadowed its later treatment in the *Outline*.[26]

National Morality was constructed around a desire to redefine Japanese society in terms of a 'national family' with the emperor at its head as the benevolent father figure. Individual families were incorporated into the larger national family so as to combine the two traditionally competing elements of loyalty and filial piety. The primacy of loyalty to a lord or filial devotion to parents was an issue of long-standing debate, especially in Meiji discussions of samurai ethics. Filial piety was most often associated with Confucianism, whereas loyalty to a lord was generally viewed as a core aspect of *bushidō*, and therefore a more distinctly 'Japanese' virtue. Points of emphasis varied, but dismissing either concept meant disparaging either one's family or the emperor, neither of which was a socially acceptable stance. National Morality sought to resolve this dilemma by fusing filiality with loyalty and then combining the whole with patriotism. By positing the state as a family, the emperor became the focus of the 'great principle of loyalty and filialty'. As stated in an ethics textbook, 'Our country is based on the family system. The whole country is one great family, and the Imperial House is the Head Family. It is with the feeling of filial love and respect for parents that we Japanese people express our reverence toward the Throne of unbroken imperial line'.[27] This argument was then extended to include patriotism as part of the comprehensive whole

[23] Gluck, Carol, *Japan's Modern Myths*, p. 153.
[24] Reitan, Richard, 'National Morality, the State, and "Dangerous Thought": Approaching the Moral Ideal in Late Meiji Japan', *Japan Studies Review* 5 (2001), p. 23.
[25] Reitan, Richard, 'National Morality, the State, and "Dangerous Thought"', pp. 27, 40.
[26] Inoue Tetsujirō (1908), *Rinri to kyōiku* (Tokyo: Kōdōkan), p. 431.
[27] Translation from Fridell, Wilbur M., 'Government Ethics Textbooks in Late Meiji Japan', p. 831.

represented in *chūkun aikoku* (loyalty to the emperor and patriotism), a concept that became increasingly synonymous with imperial *bushidō*.[28]

Bushidō featured prominently in texts on National Morality, especially those penned by Inoue himself. A cumbersomely titled book, *Theories and Realization of Propriety and Etiquette that are the Focus of National Morality*, stressed *bushidō* because, 'in ancient times, *bushi* valued righteousness more than anything'. However, while the military—and Germans—valued righteousness, 'in everyday Japanese society there are many people who do not know honorific speech, and respect for one's superiors has almost completely disappeared'.[29] A renewed emphasis on *bushidō* was seen as a method of resolving the perceived problems with contemporary propriety and etiquette, and Inoue's *Outline* included a fifty-page chapter on the 'history, special characteristics, and future of *bushidō*'. Inoue divided the history of *bushidō* into four successive periods, as he had done in other works.[30] Following discussions of *bushidō*'s roots in Japan's pre-history and its manifestations through the sixteenth century, the third age of *bushidō* was the Tokugawa period, when '*bushidō* was developed through education'. Inoue addressed what he considered the pivotal roles of Yamaga Sokō, the loyal retainers of Akō, and Yoshida Shōin, echoing his first lecture on the subject more than a decade earlier. The fourth age of *bushidō* began in 1868, and comprised two-thirds of Inoue's discussion of the subject.

Inoue began his analysis of modern *bushidō* by arguing that, although *bushidō* was greatly influenced by the feudal age, it had existed before that time and did not perish with the samurai class. Inoue reasoned that *bushidō* was actually stronger in the non-feudal ages, as it was not monopolized by a single class, but rather spread throughout all of society. Inoue thus established a spiritual link between the Meiji period and an idealized ancient Japan before the introduction of foreign thought such as Confucianism or Buddhism. On the other hand, Inoue credited the samurai with refining and upholding *bushidō* until Meiji, when the role of guardians of the *bushidō* spirit and model for the nation was transferred to the Japanese military, as encapsulated in the Imperial Rescript for Sailors and Soldiers.[31] In a passage published only a few weeks before Nogi Maresuke's suicide, Inoue addressed the issue of suicide in general, and *seppuku* in particular, reiterating his 1901 argument that while times had changed, the 'spirit' of being willing to die for one's lord and country was still an essential part of *bushidō*.[32]

Much of Inoue's National Morality *bushidō* was rehashed from previous works, but a new section on 'trends that destroy the *bushidō* spirit' dealt with issues that were affecting the moral fibre of the nation. One major factor that undermined

[28] M. Fridell, Wilbur, 'Government Ethics Textbooks in Late Meiji Japan', p. 831.

[29] Kokumin reihō chōsakai (ed.) (1912), *Kokumin dōtoku wo chūshin to shitaru reigi sahō no riron to jissai* (Tokyo: Meiseikai), pp. 150, 156. *Bushidō* remained an important part of National Morality discourse, and large sections are devoted to it in later texts. For example, see Yoshida Sei'chi (1916), *Kokumin dōtoku yōryō* (Tokyo: Tokyo hinbunkan), pp. 249–325.

[30] For example, Inoue Tetsujirō, *Rinri to kyōiku*, pp. 426–31.

[31] Inoue Tetsujirō, *Rinri to kyōiku*, pp. 163–69.

[32] Inoue Tetsujirō, *Rinri to kyōiku*, pp. 176–77.

bushidō was the 'development of industry and commerce', which Inoue associated with the unfortunate growth of individualism. In a departure from his earlier writings, Inoue claimed that 'commerce and industry are not necessarily incompatible with *bushidō*', and success required *bushidō* values such as 'modesty, honesty, and courage'. 'As everyone knows, during the Russo-Japanese War, Japan's *bushidō* was greatly celebrated overseas, but at the same time Japanese business and industry were harshly criticized' because the lack of honesty and ethics among Japanese business people meant that foreigners had no trust or confidence in them. For this reason, Inoue argued, *bushidō* had to be introduced into the Japanese business world, a contention made by Ozaki Yukio two decades earlier. Inoue also partially revised his views on individualism, stating that while it was 'naturally opposed to *bushidō*', both individualism and 'national polity-ism' had their strengths and weaknesses. According to Inoue, 'One should not only head towards individualism. Also, it may not always be beneficial to insist on national polity-ism, so evidently there is a necessity to harmonize and strengthen the two. National polity-ism is necessary, and individualism is necessary'.[33] Inoue did not specify how this amalgamation was to be accomplished, but his views on commerce and individualism had become significantly more accommodating.

A similarly conciliatory approach can be seen in Inoue's comments on other elements that were 'destroying *bushidō*'. Inoue considered excessive interest in arts and literature detrimental to the spirit, but qualified this by stressing the importance of a balance between *bun* and *bu*, thereby making a certain amount of culture, such as military marching music, not only tolerable, but necessary.[34] Another phenomenon 'often viewed as a *bushidō*-destroying influence' was 'foreign religions, i.e. Christianity and others'. Inoue had been one of the harshest critics of Christianity in the early 1890s, but had revised his views:

> I do not think that Christianity is entirely incompatible with *bushidō*. In Christianity, the very heroic martyr spirit has been passed down. This refers to giving one's life for one's religion. Aspects of this are very similar to *bushidō*. The only difference is that they act for their religion, while we act for our lord. This means that if they prioritize their religion and take their country lightly, it will be very damaging. However, if Christianity can become Japanese and transfer the martyr spirit to the spirit of the Japanese race, I think it is possible for Christianity to become able to support *bushidō* in exactly the same way that Buddhism supported *bushidō*.[35]

The change in Inoue's views of Christianity in the *Outline* also attests to the great efforts of Meiji Christians to demonstrate their patriotism over the previous two decades.

In contrast, Inoue was not accommodating towards the types of 'dangerous thought' that made the National Morality project seem necessary in the first place.[36]

---

[33] Inoue Tetsujirō (1912), *Kokumin dōtoku gairon* (Tokyo: Sanseidō), pp. 184–91.
[34] Inoue Tetsujirō, *Kokumin dōtoku gairon*, pp. 192–94.
[35] Inoue Tetsujirō, *Kokumin dōtoku gairon*, p. 195.
[36] For an overview of the direct backgrounds to the development of the National Morality project, see Reitan, Richard, 'National Morality, the State, and "Dangerous Thought"', pp. 33–36.

According to Inoue, 'the importation of incomplete, sick thought' such as socialism, naturalism, destructionism, and anarchism was entirely opposed to *bushidō*. These thought systems, like 'extreme individualism', threatened to 'destroy *bushidō*' and could not be tolerated. To combat these dangerous influences, Inoue called for the increased study and practice of *bushidō*, 'the most unique aspect of the Japanese race', while future 'educators must take utmost care with regard to the development of *bushidō*'.[37] These criticisms seem harsh, but the *Outline* presented Inoue's views on *bushidō* in an almost conciliatory manner when compared with his earlier writings. The *Outline of National Morality* was certainly the most important task Inoue had undertaken, and was far more influential than his earlier commentaries on the imperial rescripts. The tone of the *Outline* reflects the enormity of the project. Whereas Inoue's earlier views on *bushidō* had often been in the context of lectures to military officers or students, or polemics attacking those individuals he deemed to be insufficiently patriotic, National Morality was directed at the entire nation. As such, it had to be considerably more inclusive if it was to have the desired effect—bringing the nation together as a family and leading the people away from the spectres of socialism and anarchism. At the same time, the promotion of *bushidō* had become less urgent. By 1912, the concept had become firmly established in Japanese society, with Inoue's imperial interpretation a key component of the military education system and on the verge of assuming a similar role in civilian ethics education.

APPLYING *BUSHIDŌ* TO SPIRITUAL EDUCATION

Before 1900, military education in Japan was largely devoid of ideological components, and the introduction of imperial *bushidō* in Inoue's 1901 lecture to army officers set an important precedent. From the establishment of the modern military until after the Sino-Japanese War, the content of officers' education was primarily copied from French models, and focused on practical subjects such as tactics and weaponry.[38] Almost one third of regular recruits were estimated to be illiterate in 1900, making the efficacy of spiritual education materials before this point questionable at best.[39] More pressing demands on the military, such as bringing the troops up to certain physical and educational standards, meant that issues such as inculcation of loyalty to the emperor ranked behind physical training for most of Meiji.[40] As Yoshida Yutaka has pointed out, even by 1910 only 0.8 per cent of military recruits had worn Western-style clothing before joining the army, and reversed shoes and trousers worn backwards were common sights when uniforms

---

[37] Inoue Tetsujirō, *Kokumin dōtoku gairon*, pp. 196–99.

[38] Inoue Tetsujirō, *Kokumin dōtoku gairon*, p. 24.

[39] Yoshida Yutaka (2002), *Nihon no guntai: heishi tachi no kindai shi* (Tokyo: Iwanami shinsho 816), p. 103. Carol Gluck mentions an illiteracy rate of 24.9 per cent in 1902, decreasing to 5.5 per cent by 1912; Gluck, Carol, *Japan's Modern Myths*, p. 172.

[40] Hirota Teruyuki (1997), *Rikugun shōkō no kyōiku shakaishi: risshin shusse to tennōsei* (Tokyo: Seori shobō), pp. 176–77.

were distributed.[41] Other 'civilizing' influences in the army included smoking and drinking, habits taken up by, respectively, 80 per cent and 90 per cent of soldiers leaving the army in 1892, when only 8 per cent and 12 per cent of new recruits indulged in these activities before being conscripted.[42]

Around the turn of the century, with the successful prosecution of a major war proving a certain degree of capability, the military began to introduce the more educated officer corps to elements of what would come to be called spiritual education (*seishin kyōiku*). This was quite informal at first, with Inoue Tetsujirō and others invited to give talks at the military academies. Anarchist Ōsugi Sakae (1885–1923) recalled a lecture on *bushidō* by an ethics instructor at the Cadet School in Nagoya as the only thing that made an impression during his time there between 1899 and 1901. Ōsugi devoted considerable time to studying the subject, although he also confessed to sneaking out at night and engaging in smoking and other 'distractions from *bushidō*' with older boys, including one of General Nogi's sons.[43] From informal beginnings, the content and regularity of ideological lessons grew, with *bushidō* becoming an important part of the curriculum. The military was instrumental in spreading *bushidō* during and after the Russo-Japanese War, as soldiers began to take an interest in it beyond formal education. As Ninagawa Tatsuo introduced his 1907 *History of Japan's Bushidō*: 'Since the Russo-Japanese War, *bushidō* has become a great issue and subject of research both among Japanese and foreigners. Whether politicians or business people, soldiers or scholars, people of all types have joined in *bushidō* research'. As for his own interest, Ninagawa wrote, 'during 1904–5 I served in the Imperial Guards, where I gladly received the army's military education and greatly benefited from training and nurturing my mind and body. During my time in the army, I was most impressed by *bushidō* and decided to research its roots'.[44] While attesting to the effectiveness of *bushidō* education in the military, Ninagawa also indicated that *bushidō* had not reached all Japanese before the war. The army promoted ideological elements such as the emperor system in its educational curriculum more actively after 1905, leading to the increased dissemination of these ideologies among the general populace.[45]

Another result of the war with Russia was that the Japanese army distanced itself from most of its European advisors, assuming that the deciding difference in future military action would be the mental toughness of a nation's soldiers, rather than military technology, which many believed could not be greatly improved. To this end, in addition to shifting from European management standards to a more traditional family structure, the revised military regulations of 1908 introduced spiritual education on a large scale.[46] The army's penal code reflected the stricter

---

[41] Yoshida Yutaka, *Nihon no guntai: heishi tachi no kindai shi*, pp. 34–35.

[42] Coox, Alvin D. (1975), 'Chrysanthemum and Star: Army and Society in Modern Japan', in David MacIsaac (ed.), *The Military and Society: The Proceedings of the Fifth Military History Symposium* (Darby, PA: Diane Publishing), p. 42.

[43] Ōsugi Sakae (2001), *Ōsugi Sakae jijoden* (Chūō bunko biblio 20 seiki), p. 119.

[44] Ninagawa Tatsuo (1907), *Nihon bushidō shi* (Tokyo: Hakubunkan), pp. 2–3 of preface.

[45] Yoshida Yutaka, *Nihon no guntai: heishi tachi no kindai shi*, p. 117.

[46] Humphreys, Leonard A. (1995), *The Way of the Heavenly Sword: The Japanese Army in the 1920s* (Stanford: Stanford University Press), p. 14.

new ideology, making surrender punishable by death, or imprisonment in those cases where the commander had 'done his best'.[47] Policymakers went further the following year, changing the manuals for every branch of the army to agree with the new overall strategy laid out in the most important infantry manual. According to Leonard Humphreys:

> [i]nfantry attack with small-arms fire followed by a bayonet charge was the doctrine in which army tactics centred. The activities of other branches were strictly peripheral to this main action. By its very nature, this doctrine emphasized [spirit] and almost automatically relegated technology to a secondary role.[48]

This approach formed the core of Japanese tactics through 1945, despite having been discredited in Europe after the First World War.[49] With the exception of some of the more technologically dependent services such as later aerial and motorized units, spirit was placed before matériel, and *bushidō* was one of its most important components.

By the end of Meiji, the army was confident of its role as the 'school of the people', and military education was intended to instill *bushidō* into the general populace. After 1905, draftees were increasingly drawn from the growing metropolitan areas, often with an elementary education. This combination provided the educational basis necessary for effective spiritual education, as well as a perceived need for 'correcting' the spiritual corruption considered to be endemic in urban society.[50] The influence of the military education system reached far beyond the army due largely to the efforts of Tanaka Giichi (1864–1929), and the Imperial Military Reserve Association he founded in 1910 allowed the army to extend its ideological influence throughout the entire country.[51] Roughly half of the members of the Reserve Association had never served on active duty, and after the establishment of youth and women's organizations in subsequent decades, well over ten million people in Japan would have been within the direct reach of the military education system.[52]

The imperial *bushidō* that entered military education in the decade after 1904 placed the greatest emphasis on the virtues of loyalty, duty, and self-sacrifice. The rapid development of *bushidō* into a formal subject of study was driven by the

---

[47] Coox, Alvin D. (1985), *Nomonhan: Japan Against Russia, 1939* (Stanford: Stanford University Press), p. 958. As Beatrice Trefalt has argued, 'The idea of the impossibility of surrender for Japanese soldiers was not, contrary to what was hammered into the heads of recruits, a practice stemming from the mists of time...it is more than likely that the discourse of *Bushidō* is the origin of the Japanese Army's concept of the ignominy of surrender'. Trefalt, Beatrice (2003), *Japanese Army Stragglers and Memories of the War in Japan, 1950-1975* (London: RoutlegeCurzon), p. 20.

[48] Humphreys, Leonard A., *The Way of the Heavenly Sword*, p. 15.

[49] Fujiwara Akira (1961), *Gunjishi* (Tokyo: Tōyō keizai shinpōsha), pp. 147–48.

[50] Humphreys, Leonard A., *The Way of the Heavenly Sword*, p. 14.

[51] Under Tanaka's direction, 'Japan's ground forces were transformed from the principal tool of Japanese imperialism into a spiritual guide for the entire nation'. Dickinson, Frederick R. (1999), *War and National Reinvention: Japan in the Great War, 1914–1919* (Cambridge, MA: Harvard University Press), p. 68.

[52] Smethurst, Richard J. (1974), *A Social Basis for Prewar Japanese Militarism: The Army and the Rural Community* (Berkeley: University of California Press), p. xiv.

1908 military reforms, and most texts on the subject appeared after this time. One significant earlier work was *Spiritual Training for Soldiers*, which was compiled by Makise Goichirō in 1907 and emphasized loyalty to the *kokutai* and emperor.[53] Makise, a professor at the Central Military Preparatory School and a noted scholar of psychology and education, traced the history of *bushidō* to the ancient Mononobe family. Inoue's influence was apparent in the discussion of *bushidō*, as well as in the inclusion of a quote from Izawa Banryū's 1715 *Bushi kun*, a relatively obscure text included in Inoue's 1905 *Bushidō Library*.[54]

By 1909, the Military Education Association had geared up for the new educational directives and the mobilization of *bushidō* for spiritual education was fully under way. Texts such as *A Discussion of Soldier Bushidō* were 'compiled for the purposes of spiritual education', and focused on the importance of *bushidō* to soldiers, the people, and especially the imperial house.[55] Other texts published by the Military Education Association took a similar approach. *The Mirror of Bushidō* was published in 1910 by Takahashi Seiko, who would compile a collection of Nogi Maresuke's *bushidō* commentaries for the Military Education Association in 1913.[56] Raku Yōsei's 1910 *Individual Drills for Spiritual Training* explained the task of spiritual education as instilling the spirit of *bushidō* into the general populace.[57] Raku described the role of the military as giving people vigour and nourishing their spirit, and more than a mere training ground for combat. The military 'is a school that promotes *bushidō* and polishes the Yamato spirit. It is the *dōjō* that exercises the ultimate truth of loyalty to the emperor and love for the country, as well as the great duty of offering one's self and dying for the nation'.[58]

Books published directly by the Military Education Association were complemented by many more texts written and disseminated by instructors at the military colleges in cooperation with other publishers.[59] For example, Tomoda Yoshikata, a well-known Japanese-language (*kokugo*) instructor, published his 1908 *Bushidō Training* through Tokyo's Ōno Shoten. This book was primarily an overview of imperial *bushidō* focused on the Akō vendetta, and prominently displayed Tomoda's 'Army Professor' status on its front cover.[60] *Bushidō* also filled the pages of materials printed for the Imperial Military Reserve Association, such as a 1912 text that used *bushidō* to explain controlled breathing techniques for students, housewives, and workers, indicating that *bushidō*-based military education was also designed

[53] Hirota Teruyuki, *Rikugun shōko no kyōiku shakaishi: risshin shusse to tennōsei*, p. 180.
[54] Hirota Teruyuki, p. 183.
[55] Tōgō Kichitarō (1909), *Gunjin bushidō ron* (Tokyo: Gunji kyōiku kai), p. 1.
[56] Takahashi Seiko (1910), *Bushidō kagami* (Tokyo: Gunji kyōiku kai).
[57] Raku Yōsei (1912), *Seishinteki kakko kyōren* Vol. 1 (Tokyo: Gunji kyōiku kai), p. 22.
[58] Raku Yōsei, p. 24.
[59] Examples of spiritual education texts published by publishers with close connections to the military include: Gunjingaku shishinsha (1912), *Hohei no honryō* (Tokyo: Gunjigaku shishinsha); Kaneko, Kūken and Kitamura, Daisui (1912), *Bujin hyakuwa seishin shūyō* (Tokyo: Teikoku gunji kyōkai shuppanbu); Gunju Shōkai (ed.) (1916), *Gunjin seishin kyōiku to kōgeki seishin to no rensa* (Tokyo: Tōkyō Gunju Shōkai).
[60] Tomoda Yoshikata (1908), *Bushidō kun* (Tokyo: Ōno shoten).

to influence broad sections of civilian society.[61] Other texts used military spiritual education as a basis for inculcating a military spirit in the home, specifically through channeling the spirits of the fallen soldiers from the Russo-Japanese War.[62]

The development of spiritual education in the Imperial Japanese Army has been better researched than its naval counterpart, also because the sharp divide and competition between the two services extended to their education systems. The traditional view holds that the navy's supposed cosmopolitanism and necessary reliance on technology meant that spiritual education was conducted with less vigour than in the army, but the materials used for naval education after the Russo-Japanese War reveal similar themes to those found in army ideological training. For example, the *Naval Reader* published by the Navy Education Department in 1905 discussed *bushidō* as a vital teaching that is 'not just the spirit of the *bushi*, but the spirit of all Japanese'.[63] In an overview of the history of *bushidō*, this text argued that rural fighters had always been valued more highly than those from urban areas.[64] This belief in the strength of the countryside, where traditions such as Japan's martial spirit supposedly still existed relatively uncorrupted by industrialization and modern ideas, was a core tenet of army policy throughout the pre-war period, leading to considerable discrimination against soldiers from urban centres.[65]

Parallels between *bushidō* ideology in the army and navy are especially clear in texts such as *Bukkyō shōgaku, Bukkyō honron, Bukkyō kōroku, Shikinokugadachi* (1910), published by the naval research and cultural organization Suikōsha. This book was compiled by the army under orders from Nogi Maresuke for purposes of spiritual education and then adopted by the navy.[66] Another such adoption was *Cultivating the Spirit of Military Men*, published by naval academy professor Iwasa Shigekazu in 1913, emphasizing *bushidō* virtues such as honour and loyalty to the emperor.[67] A detailed examination of spiritual education in the Japanese navy is beyond the scope of this study, but the many parallels between army and navy policies and treatments of *bushidō* indicate wider cooperation between the two. This process continued into early Shōwa, when navy discourse on *bushidō* was dominated by Captain Hirose Yutaka (1882–1960), who composed dozens of texts on *bushidō*, Yamaga Sokō, Yoshida Shōin, and imperial loyalty.[68]

Bushidō was not emphasized as strongly in civilian education as in the military during Meiji and Taishō, but nevertheless became a recurring theme in textbooks after

---

[61] Shimano Sōsuke (1912), *Kokyū seizajutsu bushidō shin eisei* (Hokkaido: Teikoku zaigō gunjin kai osamunai bunkai).

[62] Hardacre, Helen (1998), 'Asano Wasaburo and Japanese Spiritualism', in Sharon Minichiello (ed.), *Japan's Competing Modernities: Issues in Culture and Democracy 1900–1930* (Honolulu: University of Hawai'i Press), p. 139.

[63] Kaigun kyōiku honbu (1905), *Kaigun dokuhon* Vol. 4 (Tokyo: Kaigun kyōiku honbu), p. 12.

[64] Kaigun kyōiku honbu, pp. 10–11.

[65] Humphreys, Leonard A., *The Way of the Heavenly Sword*, pp. 13–14.

[66] Chihara Masatake. *Bukyō shōgaku, Bukyō honron, Bukyō kōroku, Shikinokugadachi.* (Supplement to *Suikōsha kiji* 7:3 (Sept. 1910)).

[67] Iwasa Shigekazu (1913), *Gunjin seishin no shūyō* (Tokyo: Kōbundō shoten).

[68] The role of Hirose is discussed in greater depth in Chapter 6 within this volume.

1910. Whereas the military gradually phased in *bushidō*-related material from 1901 and then at an accelerated rate after 1908, the government did not revise school textbooks between 1903 and 1910, meaning that they were relatively unaffected by the militaristic fervour surrounding the Russo-Japanese War, although some secondary school textbooks did introduce *bushidō* themes into language and history lessons.[69] After 1890, the government '...increasingly manipulated the Imperial Rescript on Education to exercise a conservative, ultranationalistic emphasis upon native and Confucian values, but it did not formulate a rigid conception of domestic attitudes and values until 1910 at the earliest'.[70] The school textbooks issued in 1903 were considerably more progressive than most others before 1945, to the point that they were subjected to considerable criticism for their 'lack of emphasis on national values'.[71]

This criticism grew over time and included calls for the introduction of *bushidō* into schools. A 1905 article on '*Bushidō* and Future Education' by the legal scholar and later Diet member Tomizu Hirondo (1861–1931) called for *bushidō* and the Russo-Japanese War to be instilled into Japan's children through the education system.[72] Three years later, kendo master Chiba Chōsaku insisted in his *Japanese Martial Arts Teaching Methods* that 'our most earnest desire is that texts with suitable explanations and examples concerning *bushidō* must be added to today's national education at all costs, thereby deeply instilling the *bushidō* spirit into the minds of children'.[73] The textbook revision undertaken in 1910 was intended to correct many of the perceived shortcomings with regard to patriotic and moralistic content. As textbook revision did not occur until this late point, *bushidō* did not feature as prominently as it might have, as Inoue Tetsujirō and other establishment figures had started to shift their focus towards projects such as National Morality. Although *bushidō* was an important part of National Morality discourse, it was only one of several ideological components, and *bushidō* also occupied this position in school textbooks from 1910.

Adult education adapted more quickly than the schools, as private textbook publishers competed for lucrative contracts. The most significant of these in the context of *bushidō* was Hakubunkan, a 'publishing empire' that built on the great commercial success of its reporting during the Sino-Japanese War and expanded its influence by publishing the magazine *Taiyō*.[74] Hakubunkan moved into the textbook market with especially nationalistic offerings that stressed loyalty and the

[69] See, for example, Kyōiku gakujutsu kenkyūkai (ed.), *Rekishika kyōjūryō kaitei kokutei kyōkasho* (vol. 2) (Tokyo: Dōbunkan, 1910); Kyōiku kenkyūkai (ed.), *Chūtō kyōka meiji dokuhon teisei jikai* (vol. 2) (Tokyo: Tōundō Shoten, 1909); Kyōiku kenkyūkai (ed.), *Shintei chūtō kokugo tokuhon jikai* (vol. 4) (Tokyo: Tōundō, 1909); Ochiai Naobumi (ed.), *Chūtō kokugaku dokuhon 9* (Tokyo: Meiji Shoin, 1913).
[70] Wray, Harold J., 'A Study in Contrasts. Japanese School Textbooks of 1903 and 1941–5', *Monumenta Nipponica* 28:1 (spring 1973), p. 69.
[71] Fridell, Wilbur M., 'Government Ethics Textbooks in Late Meiji Japan', p. 826.
[72] Tomizu, Hirondo (1905), 'Bushidō to kongo no kyōiku', in Akiyama Goan and Inoue Tetsujirō (eds.), *Gendai taika bushidō sōron* (Tokyo: Hakubunkan), p. 219.
[73] Chiba Chōsaku (1908), *Nihon budō kyōhan* (Tokyo: Hakubunkan), p. 43.
[74] Richter, Giles (1997), 'Entrepreneurship and Culture: The Hakubunkan Publishing Empire in Meiji Japan', in Helen Hardacre (ed.), *New Directions in the Study of Meiji Japan* (Leiden: Brill), pp. 597–98.

importance of the imperial rescripts.[75] In this vein, Hakubunkan became an important vehicle for the promotion of imperial *bushidō* ideology, with Inoue Tetsujirō a frequent author and editor who published many of his most significant texts on *bushidō* through the company. The number of *bushidō*-related publications on the Hakubunkan lists increased considerably during and after the Russo-Japanese War, including a variety of educational materials on history and language.[76]

Materials by other publishers also invoked *bushidō* for a variety of purposes, including texts directed at housewives. In his 1908 *Women's Bushidō*, which had originally been serialized in the *Hōchi shinbun*, the journalist Kumata Ijō (Shūjirō; 1862–1940?) explained that, just as all men had become *bushi* and contributed to the victories over China and Russia, all women had become the wives and mothers of warriors, and had to follow their forebears in fulfilling this essential role.[77] Two years later, Ōhata Hiroshi's *Bushidō and the Household* took a similar approach in discussing the home lives of famous warriors and the influence their wives had on their husbands' successes. According to Ōhata, women not only took care of the household, but they were also responsible for giving their men encouragement and a suitable send-off.[78] No matter how strong or brave a warrior was or how excellent his weapons, he would be unable to succeed if he had to think of home affairs when he went off to battle. This would have a detrimental effect on the warrior, his house, and his country, Ōhata argued, portraying domestic chores as a patriotic exercise.[79] While the efforts to introduce *bushidō* into Japan's households may not have been as effective as in the barracks, they were another manifestation of the rapid and increasingly thorough dissemination of the ideology to all areas of society.

BUSHIDŌ IN LITERATURE IN LATE MEIJI AND EARLY TAISHŌ

The year after the Russo-Japanese War, 1906, was important in the history of Japanese literature, with the appearance of groundbreaking works by Natsume Sōseki, Shimazaki Tōson, and others signalling the dawn of a new age. These writers, especially Sōseki and Tōson, have been credited with uniting the written and spoken languages, thereby creating the linguistic prototype for modern Japanese realistic novels.[80] At the same time, popular fiction, often based on traditional

[75] Kinmonth, Earl H., *The Self-Made Man in Meiji Japanese Thought: From Samurai to Salary Man*, p. 135.

[76] Mitsukuri Genpachi (1907), *Rekishi sōwa* (Tokyo: Hakubunkan); Shirakawa Jirō (1912), *Jidai no bushi meishō itsuwa* (Tokyo: Hakubunkan); Ueda Kazutoshi (1908), *Kokugogaku sōwa* (Tokyo: Hakubunkan); Watanabe Yosuke (1913), *Musashi bushi* (Tokyo: Hakubunkan).

[77] Kumata Ijō (Shūjirō) (1908), *Onna bushidō* (Tokyo: Tenchidō).

[78] Ōhata Hiroshi (1910), *Bushidō to katei* (Tokyo: Seirindō), p. 3.

[79] Ōhata Hiroshi, p. 6.

[80] McClellan, Edwin (1971), 'Tōson and the Autobiographical Novel', in Donald Shively (ed.), *Tradition and Modernization in Japanese Culture* (Princeton, NJ: Princeton University Press), p. 376.

storytelling, increasingly drew its material from the nation's pre-Meiji past or at least a modern interpretation of the same. This resulted in a flourishing of historical novels and resurrection of traditional themes, including a '*gishi* boom' based on the Akō Incident.[81] The rediscovery of Japan's martial past had begun almost two decades before, but received additional impetus and apparent legitimacy from the victory over Russia. After 1905, *bushidō* played a prominent role in popular historical novels and adventure stories, as well as in ambitious new forms of literature and literary criticism, while also finding favour among the 'literary giants' of late Meiji.

The decade to 1914 saw many writers and publishing houses attempt to profit from *bushidō*, and the long-delayed Japanese translation of Nitobe Inazō's *Bushido: The Soul of Japan* finally appeared in 1908. The opportunistic exploitation of *bushidō* was apparent in a number of works published around the time of the Russo-Japanese War that were dubiously attributed to the prominent swordsman Yamaoka Tesshū (1836–88). The enigmatic publisher of Yamaoka's works, Abe Masato, credited Yamaoka with a series of lectures on *bushidō* delivered shortly before Yamaoka's death in 1888, supposedly attended by many of his prominent friends, including the statesman Inoue Kowashi (1843–95).[82] Abe claimed to have compiled and edited the works before soliciting commentary on them from Yamaoka's old friend Katsu Kaishū.[83] The collection was published in 1902, when nationwide interest in *bushidō* was growing rapidly, and the following year Abe published *The Way of Women*, attributed to Yamaoka's wife Eiko.[84] Abe published a mass of other writings concerning the Yamaokas in late Meiji, while the lecture notes went through nine printings in ten years, and the continuing popularity of his texts in the twenty-first century indicates that his cottage industry of Yamaoka-related publications was quite lucrative.[85]

Considerable doubt has been cast on the authenticity of these works, however, and all persons cited as contributors or as having attended the lectures were dead by the time of publication. In the preface to the 1907 *Record of Tesshū's Words and Deeds*, Yamaoka's eldest son, Naoki (1865–1927), thanked Abe for compiling his parents' writings for the youth of the world, but Naoki was widely portrayed as a black sheep by Tesshū's biographers and the veracity of his statement is questionable.[86] Yamaoka Naoki drew on his father's prestige on a number of occasions, as in an 1895 note commemorating the founding of the Dai Nihon kōbu kan (Great Japan Martiality Promotion Society). In this text, Naoki pledged to 'continue [my] late father Tesshū's sense of loyalty to the emperor and patriotism, and to support

[81] Smith II, Henry D., 'The Trouble with Terasaka: The Forty-Seventh Rōnin and the *Chūshingura* Imagination,' *Japan Review* 16 (2004), p. 30; Hyōdō Hiromi and Henry D. Smith II, 'Singing Tales of the Gishi: Naniwabushi and the Forty-seven Rōnin in Late Meiji Japan', *Monumenta Nipponica* 61:4 (2006), pp. 459–508.
[82] Yamaoka Tesshū; Kuzū Yoshihisa (ed.) (1997), *Kōshi Yamaoka Tesshū: denki sōsho 242* Part II (Tokyo: Ozorasha), p. 67.
[83] Katsube Mitake (2003), *Yamaoka Tesshū no bushidō* (Tokyo: Kakegawa sofia bunko), p. 9.
[84] Abe Masato (ed.) (1903), *Joshidō: Tesshū fujin Eiko danwa* (Tokyo: Daigakukan).
[85] Katsube Mitake (2003), *Yamaoka Tesshū no bushidō* (Tokyo: Kakegawa sofia bunko), p. 9.
[86] Abe Masato (1907), *Tesshū genkō roku* (Tokyo: Kōyūkan).

bushidō...', although there is no reference to Tesshū's *bushidō* theories or lectures in this early work.[87] Research based on Yamaoka's extant writings and accounts left by his acquaintances indicates that Abe heavily edited Yamaoka's lecture notes, and may well have forged them entirely.[88] Even after the work became a popular commercial success, Yamaoka's *bushidō* was largely disregarded by other writers on the subject, but Abe Masato's efforts demonstrate the marketing opportunities *bushidō* provided.

By the end of the Russo-Japanese War, *bushidō* had become an important element in popular writing, due to its patriotic credentials, fashionability, and suitability as a literary device. *Bushidō* offered a transcendent moral norm that provided conflict when characters were placed in situations in which other obligations, e.g. to their family, were irreconcilable with its strict demands. Similar plot arrangements, typically involving tragic heroes, had been in use before the development of *bushido*. The best-known examples were tales concerning the Akō Incident, and twentieth-century editions of the *Treasury of Loyal Retainers* tended to frame the narrative in the context of *bushidō*.[89] Depending on the interpreter, the actions of the forty-seven loyal samurai were framed in the context of *bushidō* duties towards their deceased lord, his house, their families, society, the shogunate, the emperor, Confucian ideals, Buddhist morality, and other factors. The introduction of *bushidō* served to reduce the earlier ambiguity regarding moral valuation of the Akō Incident.

While public confidence in the government and military declined in late Meiji, the nation's achievements on the world stage simultaneously increased national pride. Developments in publishing capacity and a tremendous increase in the number of literate consumers combined with patriotic sentiments to drive exponential growth in the number of works with historical themes. In addition, temporal separation from the realities of pre-Meiji society contributed to increased nostalgia for what was believed to have been a simpler, more honest age.[90] These sentiments had been building gradually and, while the sense of nationalistic nostalgia focused on the recent past of Edo, it was not strictly limited to this period. In the context of *bushidō*, the most significant themes related to pre-1600 history were the so-called war tales that had become increasingly popular throughout the Meiji period, as well as works concerning important figures from the late Sengoku period.

Fictionalized accounts of historical events for popular consumption often concerned military exploits and adventures, and with the exception of the Akō vendetta and events surrounding the fall of the shogunate, this type of material tended

---

[87] Supplement to Mikami Reiji (1899), *Nihon bushidō* (Tokyo: Kokubunsha).

[88] Anshin, Anatoliy, 'Yamaoka Tesshū no zuihitsu to kōwakiroku ni tsuite', *Chiba daigaku Nihon bunka ronsō* 7 (June 2006), pp. 104–92.

[89] For example: Takeda Izumo and Namiki Sōsuke; Miyazaki Sanmai (ed.) (1906), *Kanadehon Chūshingura* (Tokyo: Fuzanbō), p. 5.

[90] Writing about the years 1910–30, Carol Gluck has argued that 'Edo became a refuge' for many Japanese intellectuals disillusioned by a perceived acceleration of materialistic trends that carried them from their 'true culture'. Gluck, Carol (1998), 'The Invention of Edo', in Stephen Vlastos (ed.), *Mirror of Modernity: Invented Traditions in Modern Japan* (Berkeley: University of California Press), pp. 270–71.

to be set in the centuries preceding the Tokugawa peace. The popularity of medieval history could also be seen in national language education, which introduced a large number of medieval war tales from the 1890s onward.[91] As accounts of warrior activity from the medieval period tended to be defined by heroic individualism rather than selfless loyal sacrifice, however, textbook editors walked a fine line when selecting texts.[92] Individualistic sentiments may have reflected the order of pre-modern Japan, but they were not deemed useful to the goal of constructing a monolithic emperor-centred state. In spite of these misgivings, a careful selection of warrior narratives formed an important part of the educational canon until the end of Meiji, by which time the modern nation had two major military victories of its own to mine for educational material.

Japanese youth exposed to medieval war tales in the 1890s contributed to the dramatic increase in the appearance of these themes in popular literature after the Russo-Japanese War. *Bushidō* aided this development by contextualizing classical and classically themed texts, giving them relevancy to the present. *Bushidō* found use in popular literature from an early stage of its modern development, as in the 1892 'Mirror of the Moon: A Political Tale' by prominent storyteller San'yūtei Enchō (1839–1900). In this story, one of many historical pieces composed by San'yūtei, a character accused of a crime in 1750s Japan refuses to divulge his lord's name as this would bring shame to his lord and domain and therefore be 'against *bushidō*'.[93] *Bushidō* also found early use in translated popular works, such as the prolific Kuroiwa Ruikō's (1862–1920) 1897 Japanese rendition of Fortune du Boisgobey's mystery novel *Les Cachettes de Marie-Rose*.[94] As Kuroiwa's mention of *bushidō* in this translation shows, the concept was beginning to enter popular culture by this point, but had not yet been clearly defined or associated exclusively with Japan. Similarly, Natsume Sōseki's 1906 short story 'The Phantom Shield' demonstrated the flexibility of interpretations among popular writers even after the Russo-Japanese War. This story was set in the England of King Arthur and the Knights of the Round Table, and included a scene in which a character at a banquet regales the party with tales of battle, in the course of which he lists 'the crimes against *bushidō*' committed by a certain castle lord.[95] Natsume assumed that his readers were sufficiently aware of *bushidō* to include it, but was also comfortable applying *bushidō* to a medieval European context.

Bushidō-related popular literature grew most quickly after 1908, with the appearance of major publications such as Ryūbunkan's *Complete Collection of Bushidō Novels*, a historical fiction series written by Watanabe Katei (1864–1926). This series continued until 1910, and included accounts based on pre-modern warlords

[91] Shirane Haruo (2000), 'Curriculum and Competing Canons', in Haruo Shirane (ed.), *Inventing the Classics: Modernity, National Identity, and Japanese Literature* (Stanford: Stanford University Press), p. 237.

[92] Bialock, David T. (2000), 'Nation and Epic: *The Tale of the Heike* as a Modern Classic', in Haruo Shirane (ed.), *Inventing the Classics: Modernity, National Identity, and Japanese Literature* (Stanford: Stanford University Press), pp. 159–60.

[93] San'yūtei Enchō (1975), *San'yūtei Enchō zenshū* 2 (Tokyo: Kakugawa shoten), p. 594.

[94] Kuroiwa Ruikō (trans.) (1897), *Bushidō ichimei himitsubukuro* (Tokyo: Fusōdō).

[95] Natsume Sōseki (1951), *Rondon tō / Maboroshi no tate* (Tokyo: Iwanami shoten), p. 53.

Katō Kiyomasa, Gotō Mototsugu, and Kusunoki Masanori. Hakata Seishōdō's more extensive 'Bushidō Pocketbooks' series followed in 1912, including an almost obligatory rendition of the Akō Incident, as well as accounts of historical figures such as Sakamoto Ryōma and the White Tigers of Aizu. Significantly, 'Bushidō Pocketbooks' also included events from Japan's recent wars. Titles relating to the Russo-Japanese War included *The Bloodstained Regimental Colours, Height 203, The Bloodstained Turret*, and *Suicide Corps in the Siege of Port Arthur*, reflecting the growing view that *bushidō* was responsible for Japan's modern victories.[96]

The most popular series with a *bushidō* theme was the Tachikawa Bunko, which continues to be republished in various formats even in the twenty-first century. The Tachikawa Bunko, 'in which fictional Edo heroes lived by sincerity and the sword', comprised about 200 small paperbacks published in Osaka between 1911 and 1925.[97] Most of these were versions of tales told by *kōdan* storytellers, and the nationwide popularity of the series among youth has been compared to that of recent manga.[98] Initially read by young workers in Osaka, the Tachikawa Bunko soon spread to elementary and middle-school students, and its impact was reflected in the nationwide interest in ninja inspired by Tachikawa's *Sarutobi Sasuke* in early 1914.[99] Titles were loosely organized into several themed series on subjects such as 'famous ninja', 'loyal retainers of Akō', and 'masterpieces of horror', as well as various series on Sengoku warlords. One of the most popular early series was titled the 'Flower of *Bushidō*', which contained at least forty-four books appearing between 1911 and 1916.[100] Paperbacks in this series were generally devoted to one or two historical figures each, and included famous individuals such as Ōishi Kuranosuke, Miyamoto Musashi, Saigō Takamori, Nogi Maresuke, and Takeda Shingen and Uesugi Kenshin. Pocketbook publishers prospered throughout the late Meiji and Taishō periods as increasing literacy rates, especially among the youth, opened up new possibilities for the distribution of popular tales, but by the mid-1920s, larger firms dominated the market and many of the smaller, family-run publishing houses were no longer able to compete.[101]

On the whole, mass-produced texts for popular consumption were formulaic and adhered to the imperial interpretation of *bushidō* that was increasingly disseminated in the education system. Some writers, especially those affiliated with

---

[96] *Bushidō bunko* titles: *Chizome no rentaiki* (1912), *Nihyakusan no kōchi* (1913), *Chizome no hōtō* (1913), *Ryojun kōi kesshi tai* (1913).

[97] Gluck, Carol, *Japan's Modern Myths*, p. 172; Adachi Ken'ichi, *Tachikawa bunko no eiyūtachi*, p. 12.

[98] Namekawa Michio (1977), 'Taishūteki jidō bungaku zenshi toshite no "tachikawa bunko"', in Nihon bungaku kenkyū shiryō kankōkai (ed.), *Jidō bungaku* (Tokyo: Yuseido), p. 162.

[99] Adachi Ken'ichi, *Tachikawa bunko no eiyūtachi*, p. 13.

[100] Seven texts were published in the '*Bushidō no seika*' series in 1911, six in 1912, eight in 1913, fifteen in 1914, six in 1915, two in 1916, and none thereafter. These figures are based on a list of works compiled by Adachi, Ken'ichi and, while it is the most complete available, it is missing a few works and some bibliographical information for the period after 1918, due to the fact that the lists of prior publications included in the paperbacks themselves were often contradictory. (Adachi Ken'ichi, *Tachikawa bunko no eiyūtachi*, pp. 195–208.)

[101] Namekawa Michio, 'Taishūteki jidō bungaku zenshi toshite no "tachikawa bunko"', pp. 162–63.

Hakubunkan, were partially motivated by a desire to convey moral lessons to their readership, but the majority of popular texts were written to sell and make money, and the occasional confluence of the two goals was a happy coincidence. Popular writers tended to go with the flow, and their adoption of *bushidō* in late Meiji reflected the growth of general interest in the subject, which they in turn helped stoke and maintain through their widely distributed works. When the mood began to shift away from *bushidō* in early Taishō, writers and editors looked elsewhere for subject matter, and most *bushidō*-related series soon disappeared. The *Yomiuri shinbun*, for example, printed a daily series of historical profiles entitled 'Bushidō Biographies' beginning in July 1910, replacing the long-running 'Tales of the Loyal Retainers of Akō' series, which had been appearing daily for almost two years. With the exception of a few brief intervals, such as its temporary replacement by the column 'Biography of General Nogi' in the autumn of 1912, 'Bushidō Biographies' could be found in almost every issue of the *Yomiuri shinbun* until the feature was finally dropped in favour of the short-lived 'Biographies of Other Loyal Retainers' in February 1914.

In addition to its wide dissemination in popular culture, *bushidō* also became a frequently discussed subject in literary and intellectual circles, which included a few critical voices. Writers were in general agreement that the Russo-Japanese War would mark a major turning point in Japanese literature, but were divided as to whether its impact would be positive or negative. Natsume Sōseki was full of confidence, optimistically comparing the war to the destruction of the Spanish Armada inspiring the flowering of Elizabethan literature.[102] Other writers were more cautious, wondering whether the recent conflict would usher in an era of world-class Japanese literature, or whether it would result in 'mere island-mentality writing'.[103] Writer and critic Ueda Bin feared that chauvinistic currents would dominate the post-war period, resulting in a disregard for foreign thought and an increase in *bushidō*-related navel-gazing.[104] Ultimately, all of these predictions were fulfilled to some degree. The last years of Meiji were marked by a proliferation of nationalistic publications, but they are better remembered for the emergence of a sophisticated and modern national literature, with the works of Natsume, Nagai Kafū (1879–1959), and Shimazaki Tōson separated from what came before by their content, complex characters, and modern language.[105]

Treatments of *bushidō* by literary figures after 1905 were varied, with some writers such as naturalist Iwano Hōmei (1873–1920) accepting its historical validity. In his most highly regarded work of literary criticism, a 1906 essay 'Mystical Half-Beastism', Iwano laid out his own philosophy in response to Emerson, Swedenborg, Schopenhauer, and others.[106] Discussing Emerson's essay 'Compensation', Iwano stated that Emerson's American background might

---

[102] Hiraoka Toshio, *Nichirō sengo bungaku no kenkyū*, p. 12.
[103] Hiraoka Toshio, p. 13.   [104] Hiraoka Toshio, p. 15.
[105] McClellan, Edwin, 'Tōson and the Autobiographical Novel', pp. 356–57.
[106] Keene, Donald (1984), *Dawn to the West: Japanese Literature of the Modern Era (Vol. 1, Fiction)* (New York: Holt, Rinehart, and Winston), pp. 290–91.

make his writings seem somewhat unpleasant to Japanese readers whose 'point of view is coloured by *bushidō*'.[107] In this essay, Iwano promoted his own theory of 'half-beastism' as the reason for Japan's victory in the Russo-Japanese War, for without this supporting force, *bushidō*, Japanism, and other national characteristics would not be able to unfold their full strength.[108] Another prominent modern literary figure who relied on the imperial interpretation of *bushidō* was Mori Ōgai (1862–1922). In his historical drama *The Vendetta of Gojin Plain* (1913), which concerns a samurai revenge killing, protagonist Yamamoto Kurōemon applies for permission to carry out a vendetta. Fortunately for Yamamoto, the official to whom he applies is a man 'deeply inscribed by *bushidō*' and hears his request immediately.[109] Mori understood *bushidō* as a historical moral norm dictating warrior behaviour and the death of Nogi Maresuke inspired a nostalgic desire to compose a series of feudal tales.[110]

Views of *bushidō* in modern literary fiction and criticism often differed considerably from those found in works churned out by popular publishers. The clearest difference was an implicit criticism of *bushidō* found in many more intellectually ambitious works. *Bushidō* permeated the entire social and political spectrum by the end of Meiji, at least with regard to the idea that a universally accepted warrior ethic existed in earlier Japanese history, but doubts remained regarding the applicability of such a moral code to the modern age. Poet Ishikawa Takuboku (1886–1912) accepted *bushidō* as a historical component of the Japanese character, but also criticized it as an anachronistic relic of an earlier time. He wrote in an essay of 1920 lamenting the 'Impatient Thought' of his countrymen: 'speaking of old things, that thing called *bushidō*...can be said to be one of the most impatient ethics in the entire world'.[111] Similarly, Uchida Roan (1868–1929) argued that *bushidō* would have disappeared after 1868 if the former samurai class had not had their hereditary positions protected by the new government.[112] Romanticist Izumi Kyōka (1873–1939) also saw *bushidō* as an anachronism, and his 1912 article 'Indian Saraca' criticized both *bushidō* and Japanese traditional society in general.[113] The same ideas were implicit in Izumi's 1913 play *Yaksa Lake*, in which a character professing *bushidō* explained the concept as condoning the killing of women and children for the sake of one's country.[114]

After 1914, interest in *bushidō* among literary figures declined, and criticism of the subject became more pronounced, with Akutagawa Ryūnosuke (1892–1927) going beyond mere portrayal of *bushidō* as an anachronism to questioning its legitimacy. In his 1916 short story 'The Handkerchief', a thinly disguised satire

---

[107] Iwano Hōmei (1965), *Meiji bungaku zenshū 71: Iwano Hōmei shū* (Tokyo: Chikuma shobo), p. 332.

[108] Iwano Hōmei, p. 354.

[109] Mori Ōgai (1955), *Gojiin ga hara no katakiuchi* (Tokyo: Iwanami shoten), p. 12.

[110] Mori Ōgai, pp. 99–100.

[111] Ishikawa Takuboku (1970), 'Sekkachi na shisō', *Meiji bungaku zenshū 52: Ishikawa Takuboku shū* (Tokyo: Chikuma shobo) p. 254.

[112] Uchida Roan, 'Nijūgonenkan no bunjin no shakaiteki chii no shinpo', p. 146.

[113] Izumi Kyōka (1926), 'Indo sarasa', *Kyōka zenshū 9* (Tokyo: Shun'yōdō), p. 324.

[114] Izumi Kyōka (1926), 'Yasha ga ike', *Kyōka zenshū 14* (Tokyo: Shun'yōdō), p. 455.

of Nitobe Inazō and his views on *bushidō*, Akutagawa describes an aging professor visiting the mother of one of his former students, who tells him about the death of her son. The professor is moved by her stoicism and detachment, which he attributes to *bushidō*, a subject in which he is much interested. It is only near the end of her matter-of-fact account that he notices the handkerchief the woman has been grasping tightly and wringing as an apparent silent outlet for her suppressed emotions. The Nitobe figure is more impressed than ever with the power of *bushidō* after this encounter. Later that day, however, he happens to read in a Western book a criticism of poor acting techniques, one of which is the showing of internal tension by tearing a handkerchief in two while maintaining a smiling countenance.[115] Akutagawa was highly critical of Nitobe's *bushidō* in this text, reducing it, as Roy Starrs puts it, 'to a mere mannerism out of an old-fashioned sentimental melodrama'.[116]

Akutagawa's work contained an implicit questioning of *bushidō*, as in 'The Battle of the Monkey and the Crab' (1923). In this story, a lawyer for a crab accused of killing a monkey mounts a defence that sees the crab's actions as being in line with *bushidō*, but there 'is no way that anyone would lend an ear to this type of outdated argument'.[117] The lawyer is portrayed as a drunken fool, and there are rumours that his position was motivated not by higher ideals but spite towards the monkey resulting from an unpleasant incident between the two many years earlier. Similarly, in the closing lines of Akutagawa's 'From Yasukichi's Notebook', a tough-talking military officer ostensibly strikes a match for the protagonist's cigarette, but his real motivation is to allow the latter to 'observe his *bushidō* in its light'.[118] In this case as well, Akutagawa reduced *bushidō* to an affected expression that stood out against the thoroughly modern subject matter of the rest of the story.

The use of *bushidō* in literature, criticism, and popular writing after the Russo-Japanese War was strongly influenced by earlier trends, but it also played an important role in embedding the concept in the popular consciousness. Writers of popular fiction did not greatly contribute to the content of *bushidō* and generally adhered to the 'imperial' interpretation. In this way, the majority of Japanese became familiar with the concept and came to believe that *bushidō* was a historically valid moral code that guided samurai behaviour. In addition, the idea that *bushidō* was wholly or partially representative of a 'Japanese spirit' gained wide acceptance, in spite of claims to the contrary by a handful of dissenting voices. Acceptance of *bushidō* was also conversely promoted by the few works that were

---

[115] Akutagawa Ryūnosuke (1953), 'Hankechi', in *Meiji bungaku zenshū 26: Akutagawa Ryūnosuke shū* (Tokyo: Chikuma shobo), pp. 27–31.

[116] Starrs, Roy (1998), 'Writing the National Narrative: Changing Attitudes towards Nation-Building among Japanese Writers, 1900–1930', in Sharon Minichiello (ed.), *Japan's Competing Modernities: Issues in Culture and Democracy 1900–1930* (Honolulu: University of Hawai'i Press), p. 219.

[117] Akutagawa Ryūnosuke (1990), 'Saru kani gassen', in *Kumo no ito / toshi shun / torokko / hoka 17 hen* (Tokyo: Iwanami shoten), pp. 259–62.

[118] Akutagawa Ryūnosuke (1953), 'Yasukichi no techō kara', in *Meiji bungaku zenshū 26: Akutagawa Ryūnosuke shū* (Tokyo: Chikuma shobo), pp. 198–203.

seemingly critical of the subject, such as the writings of Ishikawa Takuboku and Izumi Kyōka. By focusing their criticism of *bushidō* on its alleged incompatibility with the modern age, literary figures in late Meiji and early Taishō implicitly (and sometimes explicitly) gave *bushidō* historical legitimacy. In the later Taishō period, this characterization of *bushidō* as authentic yet anachronistic would dominate discourse, providing fertile ground for *bushidō* revivalists in the 1930s.

BUSHIDŌ FOR HISTORICAL AND PATRIOTIC LEGITIMIZATION

As *bushidō* became a widely accepted and fashionable concept during and after the Russo-Japanese War, it was adopted by a broad spectrum of institutions and social groups to promote sports, religious orders, and other causes. In this context, *bushidō* was used to give foreign ideas and activities a native Japanese connection and, ironically, provide relatively recent constructs with apparent historical legitimacy stretching back centuries or even millennia. As in the case of popular literature, *bushidō* was used for commercial purposes; the sales of a text could be improved by adding *bushidō* to the title. This frequent invocation of *bushidō* was based not only on the pervasiveness of the concept at the time, but also its largely unquestioned patriotic credentials. Generally, these opportunistic appropriations of *bushidō* as a catchphrase or brand were superficial, and did not deal with *bushidō* in great depth. One significant exception was the widespread use of *bushidō* by followers of religious groups, especially Christians and Buddhists, whose patriotism and devotion to the national cause were often called into question. When using *bushidō* to prove their 'Japaneseness', promoters of 'foreign' religions did not simply accept the Shinto-influenced imperial interpretation put forth by nationalists such as Inoue, and instead formulated their own interpretations. The use of *bushidō* ideology by groups and individuals whose goals seemed to bear no direct relation to—or even appeared to contradict—mainstream *bushidō* discourse reflected the breadth of appeal of *bushidō* at the time.

From an early stage, *bushidō* featured prominently in discourse on the martial arts, many of which were only codified and developed into their modern forms during the Meiji period. The publication of the *Bushidō* journal by the Great Japan Martial Arts Lecture Society in 1898 was a clear early link between *budō* and *bushidō*, and promoters of kendo and judo often discussed the subject. These sports began to be organized into associations during mid-Meiji, and the nationalistic fervour that accompanied the Sino-Japanese War caused the number of students joining martial arts associations to increase rapidly.[119] The inherent martial character of *bushidō* meant that it soon came to be used to promote sumo and other martial arts with less obvious connections to the samurai, as well as imported sports such as baseball. *Bushidō* was invoked to lend patriotic and historical legitimacy to these sports and help to counter criticism from judo and kendo supporters who saw them as unwelcome competition.

---

[119] Sakaue Yasuhiro, *Nippon yakyū no keifu gaku*, p. 99.

In the case of sumo, many aspects of the current form of the sport are products of the late Meiji period, and the time of greatest change coincided with the late *bushidō* boom. In 1909, referees began to wear colourful robes and headwear rather than traditional dress, wrestlers became obliged to wear *haori* and *hakama* rather than casual clothing to the tournaments, the first national sumo stadium was completed at Ryōgoku, and the rank of *yokozuna* was first recognized by the Sumo Association, which also unilaterally designated sumo as the national sport of Japan.[120] *Bushidō* was appropriated to help sumo's rapid growth, and Kitagawa Hakuai's 1911 mythologized history of the sport, *Sumo and Bushido*, used *bushidō* to raise the book's profile and lend the sport historical legitimacy. Echoing Inoue's imperial *bushidō*, Kitagawa wrote, 'Japan has been a martial land since the Age of the Gods, giving it a long history in the world. For three thousand years, *bushidō* has been the essence of Japan. The national spirit was trained by *bushidō*, and is the crystallization of the Yamato spirit'. However, *bushidō* also had to be trained by strengthening the physique and completing the spirit. Fortunately, Kitagawa provided a simple method for doing this: sumo. 'The fact that sumo has a great deal of force in the training of *bushidō* is already best illustrated by our nation's ancient history. From this we can say that sumo is the *bushidō* of our nation'.[121] According to Kitagawa, sumo was the 'oldest *bushidō* of Japan', having been practised for at least five or six thousand years. During the Tokugawa period, sumo wrestlers were permitted to wear swords, demonstrating that 'sumo was respected as a type of *bushidō*, and wrestlers were equal to outstanding *bushi*'.[122] The *bushidō* inherent in sumo, wrote Kitagawa, could be seen in an incident in Aizu in the late sixteenth century, when the warlord Gamō Ujisato insisted on a match with a great wrestler among his retainers. The retainer, Nishimura Samanosuke, pulled no punches and handily defeated his lord not once but two times. Kitagawa described this single-minded focus on defeating one's opponent, even if he was one's lord, as 'true *bushidō*'.[123] Sumo and *bushidō* could not be separated, Kitagawa concluded, and it was a patriotic duty for Japanese to support and participate in sumo.[124]

While promoters of sumo stressed their sport's Japanese historicity, baseball faced a much stiffer challenge. Martial arts practitioners and nationalists attacked the foreign origins of the sport from the time of its introduction, and much promotional work was required for it to gain popular acceptance. As *bushidō* gained in popularity, it was increasingly cited by promoters of baseball, resulting in a situation where supporters of various athletic activities claimed *bushidō* as their own so as to capitalize on its high profile. Baseball was linked with *bushidō* from an early stage and a handful of articles mentioning the two subjects appeared soon after the

---

[120] Thompson, Lee A. (1998), 'The Invention of the *Yokozuna*', in Stephen Vlastos (ed.), *Mirror of Modernity: Invented Traditions in Modern Japan* (Berkeley: University of California Press), pp. 177–78.
[121] Kitagawa Hakuai (1911), *Sumō to bushidō* (Tokyo: Asakusa kokugi kan), p. 4.
[122] Kitagawa Hakuai, pp. 6, 7.   [123] Kitagawa Hakuai, p. 48.
[124] Kitagawa Hakuai, pp. 195–96.

Sino-Japanese War.[125] The sudden growth of martial arts after 1895 presented a problem for 'civilizational' (i.e. Western) sports such as baseball, and its promoters decided to seize the initiative with regard to patriotic legitimacy, a course taken with great success. As author and critic Takayama Chogyū argued in 1898, the martial arts were effective for instilling courage in the individual and 'baseball was also superb for spiritual training'. Unlike the martial arts, which focused on man-to-man combat, baseball 'brought two groups of nine individuals together into a team unit, where they attacked and defended together over the course of nine battles'. In the context of inter-civilizational struggles, Takayama continued, it was essential that individuals abandon self-interest for the good of the group. In Takayama's view, the problem facing Japan was that 'the people of our country have always had a very strong individual spirit, but have been wanting in their communal spirit', making it essential for Japan to adopt baseball in order to succeed in the age of imperialistic competition.[126]

Following Takayama, other writers argued for the promotion of baseball in terms of its team-building effects and usefulness as a spiritual training tool. The spiritual aspects of baseball were expounded by writers such as Hirano Masatomo, who argued in 1903 that baseball was equally or more capable than the martial arts of fostering a martial spirit, a development that Sakaue Yasuhiro refers to as 'samurai baseball'.[127] The combination of 'native' martial virtues with 'civilizational' baseball reached a peak after 1905, when the wide dissemination of *bushidō* led to its increased use in sports discourse. In the introduction to Hashido Shin's (Makoto) *Recent Baseball Techniques* (1905), former Waseda player Oshikawa Shunrō provided a *bushidō* framework for baseball in Japan:

Japan's *bushidō*, which is unparalleled in the world, is partly a product of spiritual training, and partly a product of martial training and the strengthening of courage... By training martiality and strengthening the physique, by strengthening the physique and refining the spirit, and to this adding mental power, one will not fear anyone under heaven. This is the origin of Japan's *bushidō*...

In Japan, from ancient times there have been kendo, judo, and techniques for mounted archery, and these have been used to train the physique and form the spirit for over three thousand years... However, martial skills that train the physique and form the spirit are not necessarily limited to those that use the sword and spear, but also include football, rowing, and baseball. These are originally products of the West, and although I do not know what the Westerners used these skills to prepare for, when these skills are brought to Japan and we apply our true Japanese *bushi*-like spirit to them, with regard to training the physique and forming the spirit, they bear comparison with our ancient martial skills. Baseball, especially, is truly a civilizational martial skill, and at the same time a *bushi*-like sport.[128]

In the decade after 1905, baseball became ever more closely identified with *bushidō*, resulting in what Ariyama Teruo calls '*bushidō* baseball'. Ariyama cites an editorial

---

[125] Sakaue Yasuhiro, *Nippon yakyū no keifu gaku*, p. 101.
[126] Sakaue Yasuhiro, pp. 82–83.   [127] Sakaue Yasuhiro, pp. 88–89.
[128] Sakaue Yasuhiro, pp. 111–12.

from the 20 November 1908 edition of *Baseball Monthly* as arguing that, in spite of the American origins of baseball, 'our nation's baseball techniques are a complete departure from the old forms, and pure Japanese *bushidō* baseball techniques can be expected to eventually become the champion of the world'.[129] The *bushidō* baseball established after the Russo-Japanese War was of long duration, and the patriotic legitimacy bestowed by *bushidō* was key to baseball's expansion and the development of a national championship in the Taishō period.[130] The idea of a unique Japanese 'samurai baseball' would last well beyond the *bushidō* boom and into the twenty-first century.

BUSHIDŌ AND BUDDHISM

The quest for patriotic legitimacy was also important to followers of 'foreign' religions, as the establishment of state Shinto presented a serious challenge to Christianity and Buddhism.[131] Buddhism suffered the greater shock during this process as its institutions went from being the official registries of all Japanese households during the Tokugawa period to being persecuted, disowned, and even disbanded. The government policies against Buddhism met with widespread protest, with the military dispatched to quell uprisings in parts of Japan. The state soon realized that the harshest policies were not tenable, and measures of limited reconciliation and incorporation of Buddhism into the state Shinto structure prevented further major outbreaks of violence. Buddhism remained distinctly second-class relative to Shinto in official eyes throughout the Meiji period and beyond, but continued to dominate religious life in many areas. For their part, following the protests of early Meiji, many Buddhists shifted to a policy of almost aggressive conformation in order to prove that Buddhism could play a useful role within the new emperor-centred order. This approach was reflected in the founding of organizations such as the United Movement for Revering the Emperor and Revering the Buddha, formed in 1889 to 'preserve the prosperity of the imperial household and increase the power of Buddhism'.[132] As a part of this process, Buddhists focused on the long history of their religion in Japan, an argument that also conveniently separated them from more recently arrived Christianity, and *bushidō* was invoked to bolster appeals to the supposedly inseparable roots of Buddhism and the Japanese national character.

The effectiveness of Buddhist efforts to connect with patriotic themes and traditional culture is evident in many of the writings on *bushidō* that appeared during and after the Sino-Japanese War. As early as 1894, Uemura Masahisa argued that

---

[129] Ariyama Teruo (1997), *Kōshien yakyū to Nihonjin: media no tsukutta ibento* (Tokyo: Yoshikawa kobunkan), p. 55.

[130] This is discussed in greater depth in Chapter 5 within this volume.

[131] Hardacre, Helen (1989), *Shinto and the State, 1868–1988* (Princeton, NJ: Princeton University Press).

[132] Victoria, Brian Daizen (2006), *Zen at War* (Oxford: Rowman & Littlefield), p. 18.

'[t]o understand chivalry, you must know Christianity. To understand *bushidō*, you must know Buddhism and Confucianism'.[133] Similarly, Mikami Reiji's *Nihon bushidō* (1899) described Buddhism and Confucianism as important sources of *bushidō* along with Shinto and Shingaku.[134] Inoue Tetsujirō acknowledged the influence of Buddhism on imperial *bushidō*, stating that '*bushidō* in its fully finished form is the product of a balanced fusion of the three teachings of Shinto, Confucianism, and Buddhism'.[135] The movement to link Buddhism with *bushidō* drew a response from Christian Ebina Danjō (1856–1937), who argued that *bushidō* was created by Japanese for Japanese, and if promoters of foreign belief systems such as Buddhism and Confucianism had a right to comment on it, then Christians did as well.[136]

Connections between *bushidō* and Buddhism became most pronounced during and after the Russo-Japanese War, when *bushidō* had become firmly established in the popular consciousness, and a number of Buddhists increasingly relied on *bushidō* to promote their faith and causes. In a 1905 article in *Chūō kōron*, 'Concerning the Relationship between *Bushidō* and Buddhism', Buddhist scholar Nanjō Bun'yū (1849–1927) wrote that 'people commonly say that the basis of Buddhism is mercy, and therefore it not only provides no benefit to *bushidō*, but there is even a danger that it will weaken the warrior spirit'. Nanjō argued that this was only a very superficial understanding of Buddhism, and discussed Prince Shōtoku, Kusonoki Masashige, and Commander Hirose Takeo as brave men who derived strength from Buddhism. 'Our *bushidō* has received the Buddhism of causality spanning the past, present, and future, and even if the body dies the spirit continues, so one will be reborn as a human for seven lives' in order to reach the long-cherished goals of repaying the nation's kindness and supporting the imperial house.[137] Nanjō used *bushidō* as a tool to promote Buddhism beyond sectarian boundaries, an approach that could also be seen in the activities and works of writers such as Shimaji Mokurai (1838–1911). Shimaji's 'The Future of *Bushidō*' (1905), which was included in Inoue and Akiyama's authoritative *Collection*, is a representative example of this approach.[138]

Patriotic activities by Buddhists paid dividends by the end of Meiji, although the costs could be high. Buddhist sects assisted in the colonization of Hokkaido and the other northern territories, sent missionaries and medical workers to the wars with China and Russia, and spread morale-boosting information and collected

[133] Uemura Masahisa (1966), 'Kirisutoyō to bushidō', *Uemura Masahisa chosakushū* 1 (Tokyo: Shinkyō shuppansha), p. 394.

[134] Mikami Reiji (1899), *Nihon bushidō* (Tokyo: Kokubunsha), p. 11.

[135] Inoue Tetsujirō (1901), *Bushidō* (Tokyo: Heiji zasshi sha).

[136] Ebina Danjō, 'Shin bushidō', *Shinjin* 2:10 (May 1902), pp. 1–2.

[137] Nanjō Bun'yū (1905), 'Bushidō to bukkyō no kankei ni tsuite', in Akiyama Goan and Inoue Tetsujirō (eds.), *Gendai taika bushidō sōron* (Tokyo: Hakubunkan), pp. 416–19.

[138] Shimaji Mokurai (1905), 'Bushidō no shōrai', in Akiyama Goan and Inoue Tetsujirō (eds.), *Gendai taika bushidō sōron* (Tokyo: Hakubunkan) pp. 411–15.

donations and supplies on the home front.[139] By 1912, Buddhists and Christians, who made similar efforts, had been accepted by the state to the point that they were included by the Home Ministry in a 'Meeting of Three Religions' designed to promote national morality.[140] This progress did not lead to complacency, however, and Buddhists continued to invoke *bushidō* and expound their patriotic credentials. In *Bushidō and Buddhism* (1913), Nakatani Togetsu attributed the nation's great victory in the Russo-Japanese War to the emperor and to the loyalty and bravery of the nation's soldiers, which were founded on *bushidō* and the Japanese spirit. According to Nakatani, the origins of *bushidō* were the same as the origins of the Japanese race, and the ethic had been refined and developed until it was distilled in the Imperial Rescript to Soldiers and Sailors in 1882.[141] In recent times, however, dangerous thought had been imported into Japan, causing the people to forget the foundations of their 'national morality' and to turn to materialistic civilization. This made it necessary to again spread Buddhism, for 'since ancient times, Buddhism has harmonized with our national polity and thus helped strengthen *bushidō*'.[142]

Even within Buddhism, points of emphasis in the promotion of *bushidō* varied. In a lecture on 'Nichiren Buddhism and *Bushidō*', naval strategist and future admiral Ogasawara Naganari (1867–1958) explained the supposed historical ties between these two. According to Ogasawara, Buddhism was often seen as overly passive due to the characteristics of some schools, but this did not apply to the teachings of Nichiren. Instead, Nichiren 'not only insisted vehemently on *Lotus Sutra*-ism, but also read the Buddha's teachings to conclude that "the world is the Japanese nation"'. In addition, argued Ogasawara, the most fundamental virtue of both *bushidō* and Nichiren Buddhism was the concept of *taigi meibun* ('higher principles'), giving them identical, uniquely Japanese roots.[143] Militaristic *bushidō* interpretations could also be found among promoters of Pure Land Buddhism, such as Ōsuga Shūgō (1876–1962) and Okano Ryōgan (dates unknown), who edited a collection of articles on Buddhism and the Russo-Japanese War.[144]

Appeals to *bushidō* were strongest among promoters of Zen, and this activity continues to influence popular perceptions. The historical connections drawn between Zen and the samurai were tenuous, but this did not prevent prominent figures from presenting arguments to the contrary.[145] The writings of samurai who were also Zen followers, especially Suzuki Shōsan (1579–1655), Takuan Sōhō (1573–1645), and Yamamoto Tsunetomo, were frequently presented as evidence that Zen represented the true spirit of the samurai. Zen was credited with providing

---

[139] Ketelaar, James Edward (1993), *Of Heretics and Martyrs in Meiji Japan: Buddhism and its Persecution* (Princeton, NJ: Princeton University Press), p. 133.

[140] Gluck, Carol, *Japan's Modern Myths*, p. 135.

[141] Nakatani Togetsu (1913), *Bushidō to Bukkyō* (Tokyo: Kendō shoin), pp. 3–4.

[142] Nakatani Togetsu, p. 5.

[143] Ogasawara Naganari (1911), 'Nichiren shugi to bushidō', *Miho kōen shū* 1 (Tokyo: Shishiō bunko), pp. 8–9.

[144] Ōsuga Shūgō (1905), *Senji dendō taikan* (Kyoto: Hōzōkan); Okano Ryōgan (ed.) (1905), *Senji Bukkyō* (Toyama: Kobayashi Shinchūdō).

[145] For a discussion of Zen's relationship with the samurai, see Colcutt, Martin (1981), *Five Mountains: The Rinzai Zen Monastic Institution in Medieval Japan* (Cambridge, MA: Harvard

the oft-heralded Stoic or even welcoming attitude towards death and killing that was believed to define Japanese warriors, even though the views of samurai thinkers were considerably more nuanced than portrayed by their modern interpreters.[146]

The connection between Zen and *bushidō* was supported by influential figures in *bushidō* discourse, which played a more important role in the broad dissemination of this theory than did any historical evidence. In his *Zen and Bushidō* (1907), Akiyama Goan observed that although *bushidō* and Zen had a very close relationship, most people were not aware of the reasons behind this.[147] Akiyama focused on the idea that the period of Zen Buddhism's greatest growth in Japan coincided with the establishment of warrior power, when Kamakura warriors developed a powerful connection with Zen. Later, when their lives were 'constantly at risk' during the Sengoku period, the 'affinity between Zen and *bushidō* became ever closer'.[148] Akiyama dismissed the notion that warrior patronage of Zen institutions was primarily due to secular reasons, and denied that other, more popular Buddhist schools could have had a strong influence on *bushidō*. With regard to the Pure Land and Tendai schools of Buddhism, Akiyama derided these as mere 'superstition' and 'reasoning', respectively, which 'absolutely did not have the power to cultivate and nurture Japan's unique ethic, i.e. the *bushidō* spirit'.[149] Instead, Akiyama argued that Zen was the key to the effectiveness of *bushidō*, and 'just as Kamakura Zen worked with Kamakura *bushidō*, we need to strive to combine Meiji Zen with Meiji *bushidō*'.[150] *Bushidō* was an important tool for Akiyama and others to promote Zen Buddhism's nationalistic credentials.[151] Many Zen figures promoted the idea that warriors should completely lose themselves and not think about death, and Rinzai master Shaku Sōen (1860–1919) applied this reasoning to modern soldiers in 1909.[152] Other texts further reinforced the connection between Zen and *bushidō*, such as Arima Sukemasa's (1873–1931) 'About Bushidō', Katō Totsudō's (1870–1949) *Zen Observations* (1905), and Yamagata Kōhō's (1868–1922) *New Bushidō* (1908).[153]

Zen Buddhism's patriotic legitimacy was bolstered by the patronage of General Nogi Maresuke, who had become a living symbol of *bushidō* by the end of the

University Press) and 'Musō Soseki', in Jeffrey P. Mass (ed.), *The Origins of Japan's Medieval World* (Stanford: Stanford University Press), pp. 261–94; Grossberg, Kenneth Alan (2001), *Japan's Renaissance: The Politics of the Muromachi Age* (Ithaca: Cornell University Press); Bielefeldt, Carl, 'Koken Shiran and the Sectarian Uses of History', in Jeffrey P. Mass (ed.), *The Origins of Japan's Medieval World* (Stanford: Stanford University Press), pp. 295–317; Bielefeldt, Carl (2003), *Yoshimasa and the Silver Pavillion: The Creation of the Soul of Japan* (New York: Columbia University Press); Victoria, Brian Daizen, *Zen at War*.

[146] For example, the *Hagakure* explicitly states that Buddhism is something for old men, not warriors, and Yamamoto Tsunetomo is generally seen to have retired to a Zen temple primarily as a symbolic suicide and withdrawal from the world, rather than as a devoted practitioner. See Victoria, Brian Daizen, *Zen at War*, p. 229.

[147] Akiyama Goan (1907), *Zen to bushidō* (Tokyo: Kōyūkan), p. 1.

[148] Akiyama Goan, pp. 77–85.   [149] Akiyama Goan, p. 292.

[150] Akiyama Goan, p. 293.

[151] For other discussions of Zen and *bushidō* from this period, see Katō Totsudō (1905), *Zen kanroku* (Tokyo: Ireido), pp. 22–60; Yamagata Kōhō (1908), *Shin bushidō* (Tokyo: Jitsugyō no Nihonsha), pp. 167–223.

[152] Shaku Sōen (1909), *Sentei roku* (Tokyo: Kōdōkan), pp. 154–86.

[153] Arima Sukemasa (1905), 'Bushidō ni tsuite', *Gendai taika bushidō sōron* (Tokyo: Hakubunkan), pp. 273–84; Yamagata Kōhō, *Shin bushidō*, pp. 167–223; Katō Totsudō, *Zen kanroku*, pp. 22–60.

Russo-Japanese War.[154] Nogi was introduced to Rinzai Zen master Nakahara Nantembō (1839–1925) in 1887 and studied his teachings with such dedication that Nantembō attested to Nogi's enlightenment and named him as a successor.[155] Some aspects of Nogi's interest in Zen and *bushidō* reflect the selective revisionism practised by many *bushidō* theorists in late Meiji. Nogi was a keen student of Inoue Tetsujirō's *bushidō* theories and described Yamaga Sokō as the 'sage of *bushidō*' and single most important exponent of the warrior ethic, with Yoshida Shōin a close second. Although the actual writings of Yamaga and Yoshida were highly critical of Zen, such inconsistencies were generally overlooked in the name of *bushidō*, and the efforts of modern promoters had more sway than ancient texts.[156]

Another figure who relied heavily on *bushidō* as a vehicle for promoting Zen was Suzuki Daisetsu (1870–1966).[157] Suzuki's early writings on the connections between *bushidō* and Zen during the period immediately after the Russo-Japanese War set a pattern that would mark his work for over half a century. Suzuki was one of the most significant disseminators of a Zen-based *bushidō*, and was also highly influential outside Japan. On the Sino-Japanese War, Suzuki wrote that in the face of the challenge from China, 'In the name of religion, our country refuses to submit itself to this. For this reason, unavoidably we have taken up arms... This is a religious action'.[158] Suzuki's willingness to combine Zen with militarism became more pronounced thereafter, as in a 1906 article in the *Journal of the Pali Text Society*:

> The Lebensanschauung of Bushido is no more nor less than that of Zen. The calmness and even joyfulness of heart at the moment of death which is conspicuously observable in the Japanese, the intrepidity which is generally shown by the Japanese soldiers in the face of an overwhelming enemy; and the fairness of play to an opponent, so strongly taught by Bushido—all these come from the spirit of Zen training...[159]

These views would have resonated with Nogi Maresuke, under whose headship Suzuki taught at the Peers School in 1909. In spite of recent criticism, Suzuki's influence on popular conceptions of Zen Buddhism is still strong and continues to contribute to the belief that Zen formed a broad spiritual foundation for the samurai in general and *bushidō* in particular.[160]

---

[154] Foulk, T. Griffith (2006), ' "Rules of Purity" in Japanese Zen', Steven Heine and Dale S. Wright (eds.), *Zen Classics: Formative Texts in the History of Zen Buddhism* (Oxford University Press), pp. 158–59.

[155] Victoria, Brian Daizen, *Zen at War*, pp. 36–37.

[156] Yoshida Shōin (1940), *Yoshida Shōin zenshū* 4 (Tokyo: Iwanami shoten), p. 240.

[157] For a discussion of Suzuki, see Kirita Kiyohide (1994), 'D. T. Suzuki on Society and the State', in James Heisig and John Maraldo (eds.), *Rude Awakenings: Zen, the Kyoto School, & the Question of Nationalism* (Honolulu: University of Hawai'i Press), pp. 52–74.

[158] Translation by Christopher Ives. Found in Ives, Christopher (1994), 'Ethical Pitfalls in Imperial Zen and Nishida Philosophy: Ichikawa Hakugen's Critique', in James Heisig and John Maraldo (eds.), *Rude Awakenings: Zen, the Kyoto School, & the Question of Nationalism* (Honolulu: University of Hawai'i Press), p. 17.

[159] Victoria, Brian Daizen, *Zen at War*, p. 105.

[160] Van Meter Ames discusses the early connection of Zen and *bushidō* in the West in Josiah Royce's 1908 *The Philosophy of Loyalty*, published by Macmillan and Co., New York. Ames, Van Meter (1962), *Zen and American Thought* (Honolulu: University of Hawaii Press), pp. 175–81.

Nukariya Kaiten (1867–1934) reaffirmed the connections between Zen and *bushidō* for a foreign readership in *Religion of the Samurai* (1913), which, by discussing Zen's mixed fortunes in Meiji, inadvertently highlighted the relatively recent history of this relationship.

> After the Restoration of the Mei-ji (1867) the popularity of Zen began to wane, and for some thirty years remained in inactivity; but since the Russo-Japanese War its revival has taken place. And now it is looked upon as an ideal faith, both for a nation full of hope and energy, and for a person who has to fight his own way in the strife of life. Bushido, or the code of chivalry, should be observed not only by the soldier in the battle-field, but by every citizen in the struggle for existence.

According to Nukariya, being a samurai was what separated men from 'beasts' and he looked to a bright future for Zen and *bushidō*, portraying this as a return to a traditional order that contrasted with the turmoil these 'so closely connected' thought systems had suffered since 1868.[161]

BUSHIDŌ AND CHRISTIANITY

Japanese Christians, including Uemura Masahisa, Nitobe Inazō, and Uchimura Kanzō were among the strongest promoters of *bushidō* from a very early point, while the 1898 *Bushidō* journal had several Christian contributors, such as Ebara Soroku, Kataoka Kenkichi, and Ōi Kentarō. Scholars often differentiate the work of Christian *bushidō* theorists from non-Christian interpretations, as in Kannō Kakumyō's division of Meiji *bushidō* into 'Christian' and 'nationalistic' types.[162] Similarly, Matsumae Shigeyoshi focuses on Christian writers in his discussion of modern *bushidō*.[163] A closer reading of the sources reveals, however, that connections between Christian *bushidō* theories and theorists were far more limited than these categorizations suggest. For example, Uemura was one of the first modern commentators on *bushidō*, as well as an outspoken Christian activist, but Nitobe did not mention his work and claimed to be unaware of any other discussion of *bushidō* when he composed his own theories. Many Christians were attracted to *bushidō* by similar factors as Japanese Buddhists writing on the subject. In the officially Shinto-dominated order of Meiji Japan, *bushidō* was seen as a non-religious, authentically Japanese spirit that was 'the best stock on which to engraft the gospel', to use Uchimura and Nitobe's metaphor.[164] By emphasizing the similarities between *bushidō* and Christianity, a task which generally entailed redefining *bushidō*, Japanese Christians endeavoured to combine their foreign religion with a 'native' spirit. In this way, they hoped to overcome some of the difficulties they

[161] Kaiten Nukariya (1913), *Religion of the Samurai: A Study of Zen Philosophy and Discipline in China and Japan* (Tokyo), pp. 50–51.

[162] Kanno Kakumyō (2004), *Bushidō no gyakushū* (Tokyo: Kōdansha gendai shinsho), pp. 260–61.

[163] Matsumae Shigeyoshi (1987), *Budō shisō no tankyū* (Tokyo: Tōkai daigaku shuppankai).

[164] Howes, John F. (2005), *Japan's Modern Prophet: Uchimura Kanzo 1861–1930* (Vancouver: UBC Press), p. 315.

faced in the increasingly nationalistic climate of late Meiji, as well as making Christianity more suitable for proselytization in Japan.

In the *Bushidō* journal, Kataoka Kenkichi advocated increasing Japan's Christian population to equal the number of *bushi* that had ruled the country, creating a new model of *bushidō* leadership rooted in the Bible and Confucian classics. In 1902, Christian educator Ebina Danjō (1856–1937) proposed a 'New *Bushidō*' that could serve the nation's future.[165] Ebina described Tokugawa samurai as violent knights errant who terrorized the weak and were *bushi* only in name, having lost the true *bushidō* spirit of compassion for the less fortunate. Furthermore, their loyalty was embarrassingly narrow in scope, as true *bushi* loyalty was similar to the Christian heart in demanding love for the nation and all of its people. The primary duty of Ebina's 'true *bushi*' was respecting the gods, while fighting for one's name or family was a shameful activity.[166] In spite of this disparaging view of the former samurai, Ebina also portrayed them as martyrs of a sort. After the Meiji Restoration, he wrote, some *bushi* killed one another in the turmoil, while others gave up their roles to become merchants and artisans. The *bushi* disappeared and *bushidō* was lost. Here, Ebina argued that just as the spirit of Christ entered many people after his martyrdom, the sacrifice and disappearance of the *bushi* should create many followers of *bushidō*.[167] Ebina's interpretation of *bushidō* was among the most explicitly Christian, and he criticized those aspects of samurai behaviour that were not compatible with his Christian ideals. Ebina's emphasis on compassion broke with dominant *bushidō* discourse, and was among the most anti-samurai views of samurai ethics.

If Ebina's *bushidō* was notable for its idealism, the *bushidō* described by Anglican John Toshimichi Imai (1863–1919) was among the least idealistic, Christian or otherwise. Whereas Ebina—more than Uchimura or Nitobe—saw compassion as a central characteristic of *bushidō*, Imai rejected this assertion. In *Bushido in the Past and Present* (1906), Imai portrayed *bushidō* as a simple set of 'practical ethics' that had easily combined with Japanese religions in the past, and could be combined effectively with Christianity in the future:

> ...it is not always easy to separate what is purely Bushido from the teachings of religion and philosophy. But this is only because Bushido was a simple thing, nothing but a peculiar characteristic energy of the Japanese affected by whatever was the spirit of the times. It had no special doctrine of its own but appropriated from the prevailing forms of religion or philosophy whatever was fit to harmonize with itself or to help in elevating its practical ethics.[168]

> Shintoism and Bushido nevertheless are not to be confused; for the former is a religion while the latter embodied the practical ethics of the Feudal times. If Bushido could go hand in hand with Shintoism, it was equally open to it to pay its adieus to its religions [sic] elder sister and form alliance with Buddhism or Confucianism or Taouism,—then, why not also with Christianity?[169]

[165] Ebina Danjō, 'Shin bushidō', pp. 1–2.　　[166] Ebina Danjō, pp. 11–12.
[167] Ebina Danjō, p. 4.
[168] Imai, John Toshimichi (1906), *Bushido in the Past and Present* (Tokyo: Kanazashi), p. 7.
[169] Imai, John Toshimichi, *Bushido in the Past and Present*, p. 9.

In Imai's view, joining together Christianity and *bushidō* was a natural progression not because of parallels between the two in terms of humanitarian virtues or respect for enemies, as Nitobe had argued, but rather because of the very absence of these elements in samurai thought and behaviour. Imai warned: '[l]et us not be misled for a moment into supposing that the Bushido spirit could ever have originated institutions like the Red Cross Society, or could have lifted into principles such as humanity to prisoners, generosity to the conquered, refraining from loot, and respect for female virtue'. Imai contended that these characteristics came to Japan through interaction with the West, and Christianity in particular.[170] According to Imai, *bushidō* was not only compatible with Christianity, but even required it to become a complete and practical ethic for the modern age.[171]

Imai's relatively critical approach resulted from his desire to dispel misconceptions among British Anglicans fascinated with *bushidō* during and after the Russo-Japanese War.[172] Through his affiliation with the Society for the Propagation of the Gospel in Foreign Parts, Imai was able spend a year studying in the UK, including stays at Oxford and Cambridge.[173] In a 1905 article on *bushidō* in the *South Tokyo Diocesan Magazine*, Imai contended that the 'soul of Japan' was the Yamato spirit, while *bushidō* was merely a class-specific practical ethic with little relevance in the modern world beyond the officer corps of the army.[174] *Bushido in the Past and Present* moved beyond mere criticism to outline a *bushidō* that reflected the sensibilities of his British Anglican acquaintances rather than the sensationalistic militarism that dominated discussions of *bushidō* in the Western press during the Russo-Japanese War. At the same time, Imai's attacks on the *bushidō* theories of Nitobe and other Christians were motivated also by hostility towards their ties to the United States.

Imai's critique of Nitobe's *bushidō* theories relied heavily on reviews published earlier by Inoue Tetsujirō, an unusual choice given Inoue's history of anti-Christian activism and the militaristic tone of his writings. Although Imai must have been aware of Inoue's significant contributions to the flaring of anti-Christian sentiment fifteen years earlier, he did not mention this in *Bushido in the Past and Present*. Due to his reliance on Inoue's work, Imai's *bushidō* contained more references to the military than the theories of other Christian

---

[170] Imai, John Toshimichi, *Bushido in the Past and Present*, p. 71.

[171] Another 1906 text presented precisely the opposite argument to Imai's view of the Red Cross. The authors of *The History of the Development of the Japanese Red Cross Society* stated that while Christianity may have formed the basis for the European Red Cross, the Japanese Red Cross developed purely from the principles of *bushidō* and the Yamato spirit, which were one and the same. Teikoku haihei isha kai (ed.) (1906), *Nihon sekijūjisha hattatsu shi* (Tokyo: Teikoku haihei isha kai).

[172] Holmes, Colin and A. H. Ion. 'Bushido and the Samurai: Images in British Public Opinion, 1894–1914', *Modern Asian Studies* 14:2 (1980).

[173] Pinnington, Adrian (2008), 'Introduction', in Peter O'Connor (ed.), *Critical Readings on Japan, 1906–1948: Countering Japan's Agenda in East Asia* 1 (Tokyo: Edition Synapse), pp. xlii–xliv.

[174] Imai, John Toshimichi, 'Bushido', *South Tokyo Diocesan Magazine* 9:28 (Dec. 1905), pp. 78–84. Cited in Ion, A. Hamish (1990), *The Cross and the Rising Sun: The Canadian Protestant Missionary Movement in the Japanese Empire, 1872–1931* (Waterloo: Wilfrid Laurier University Press), p. 150.

writers. After the dissolution of the feudal system, Imai wrote, '... where could [*bushidō*] find a new abode other than in the barracks and beneath the uniforms? So the officers in our army are to-day the heirs of Bushido; it is preserved in the military life but has had to adapt itself to strange new conditions'. Imai rejected the notion advanced by Ebina and others that *bushidō* had passed from the samurai into all Japanese, stating that '... Bushido in khaki is alive but it sleeps away in other dresses'.[175]

The target of Imai's criticism, Nitobe Inazō, is often grouped with other Meiji Christians writing on *bushidō*, but there was a fundamental difference that set his approach apart. Nitobe tended to define himself more as a Japanese among Westerners than as a Christian among Japanese, and his *bushidō* theories were motivated by a desire to create a bridge between cultures by showing parallels with Western thought and religion. Many other Meiji Christians argued for the compatibility of Christianity with Japanese culture, while Nitobe argued for the compatibility of Japanese values with Western ones. A similar approach could be seen in the early writings of Nitobe's schoolmate Uchimura Kanzō, who is frequently discussed in connection with 'Christian *bushidō*'. After gaining national notoriety through his refusal to bow to the Imperial Rescript on Education, Uchimura's activism caused him to resign another post in 1903, when his open advocacy of absolute pacifism in the face of mounting militarism made him unable to continue working for the *Yorozu chōhō* newspaper.[176]

Uchimura and Nitobe's *bushidō* commentaries had significant similarities as well as differences, and their respective views evolved considerably throughout late Meiji and early Taishō, reflecting developments in *bushidō* discourse, as well as changes in broader society and their personal situations. Uchimura and Nitobe's *bushidō* also varied according to the nationality of their audiences, and Nitobe's most important role in this context was as a cultural ambassador explaining Japan to Westerners. Uchimura Kanzō's earliest writings on samurai ethics were also directed at an American audience and differed significantly from his later essays published in Japan. In January 1886, Uchimura published a one-off article on samurai ethics in the American journal *The Methodist Review*. In 'Moral Traits of the Yamato Damashii,' Uchimura did not use the still-unusual term '*bushidō*', but his arguments foreshadowed later *bushidō* discourse by explaining Japanese culture and society as being defined by the samurai class, reflecting the curiosity of his American audience regarding this particular Japanese institution. This text listed the three basic characteristics of Japanese as '1. filial piety, 2. loyalty to higher authorities, 3. love for inferiors', and Uchimura used famous narratives to illustrate these traits.[177] Uchimura selected the tale of the revenge of the Sōga brothers to explain filial piety, and an idealized account of the Akō Incident as an example of

---

[175]　Imai, John Toshimichi, *Bushido in the Past and Present*, pp. 61–62.

[176]　Imai, John Toshimichi, *Bushido in the Past and Present*, pp. 153–54.

[177]　Uchimura Kanzō (1980–84), 'Moral Traits of the Yamato Damashii', in *Uchimura Kanzō zenshū* 1 (Iwanami shoten), p. 114.

the Japanese spirit of loyalty, which he argued was not limited to the samurai.[178] On the subject of Japanese compassion and love for inferiors, Uchimura credited the influence of Buddhism.[179]

Many of the 'Japanese' behaviours Uchimura sought to explain to his foreign audience were universal aspects of the human experience, and the ambitious scope of the essay resulted in problems with logical consistency and historical accuracy that would also affect Nitobe Inazō's work. For example, after arguing for the primacy of filial piety in Japanese ethics—'for Japanese no relation can be greater than the sacred relation of child to parent'—Uchimura explained that loyalty to one's lord was the most important duty: 'a man may leave his parents and follow his master, but he cannot do the opposite'. Much of this text focused on the samurai class, but Uchimura's discussion of Japanese compassion towards inferiors used a parable of a self-sacrificing farmer, presumably due to the scarcity of samurai tales related to this virtue.[180]

Just as Nitobe Inazō would do later, Uchimura sought to demonstrate to his Western readers that the range of human morality and emotion also existed in Japan, but couched it in culturally unique terms such as 'Yamato spirit' and 'samuraism'. As Uchimura was writing for a foreign readership, he formulated his ideas differently than for a domestic audience, who would have viewed his arguments as naïve, at best. When he revisited the subject of Japanese morality in an 1897 essay published in Japan and titled 'Lack of Japanese Morality', Uchimura criticized idealistic views similar to those he had himself put forth in *The Methodist Review* a decade earlier:

> One most conspicuous lack of Japanese Morality is that it teaches too much of the duty of the inferior towards the superior, and too little, if any, of the duty of the superior towards the inferior. Its two cardinal principles CHŪ and KŌ are nothing more than the submissive obedience of the subject to his sovereign and of the child to his parents... For a child to disobey his father is a capital sin; for a father to neglect his child is a sin only towards the society upon which may fall the burden of its sustenance, but *not* towards the child itself. Adultery on the husband's side is no adultery at all; the term has its sense only in the case of the wife. A man is a rebel, a renegade, who slights his master's command; the latter goes unpunished for slighting the gravest of Heaven's commands. We are bound upwards, and free downwards. Stiff in head, and loose in feet, the society built upon such principles must necessarily be very unsteady.[181]

Uchimura was a dedicated social and political critic, and his attack on traditionalism, written for an audience in Japan, displayed radically different views from his earlier commentary for an American audience.

Uchimura did not write on samurai ethics for several years following his 1886 article, and only joined Japanese *bushidō* discourse with dedicated essays when

---

[178] Uchimura Kanzō, 'Moral Traits of the Yamato Damashii', pp. 116, 124–26.
[179] Uchimura Kanzō, 'Moral Traits of the Yamato Damashii', p. 127.
[180] Uchimura Kanzō, 'Moral Traits of the Yamato Damashii', pp. 115, 122, 131.
[181] Uchimura Kanzō (1980–84), 'Lack of Japanese Morality', in *Uchimura Kanzō zenshū* 4 (Iwanami shoten), p. 68.

it had already become firmly established. When he began to write on *bushidō* in the twentieth century, Uchimura portrayed it as an integral part of the Japanese character, emphasizing sincerity, courage, and ethical prescriptions.[182] As he summarized in later articles:

> We can solve nearly all of the problems in our lives by relying on *bushidō*. For honesty, noble-mindedness, tolerance, the keeping of promises, not going into debt, not chasing fleeing foes, not taking pleasure in the misfortune of others, for these things we do not need to rely on Christianity. To solve these problems without failure we can rely on the *bushidō* that has been handed down from our ancestors. However, with regard to our duties towards God and our future judgment, *bushidō* does not teach us about these things... Those who cast aside *bushidō* or take it lightly have no chance of becoming virtuous like Christ's disciples. The individuals that God has demanded from among the Japanese people are those who allow Christ to dwell within the soul of a *bushi*.[183]
>
> *Bushidō* is the greatest product of the Japanese nation, but *bushidō* itself does not have the power to save Japan. Christianity grafted to the stock of *bushidō* is the world's greatest product, and has the power to not only save the Japanese nation but the entire world.[184]

In many ways, Uchimura was more ostensibly traditional than other Christian writers on *bushidō*, and Mark Mullins has discussed the 'Confucian' structure of Uchimura's Non-Church movement and his insistence on the superiority of men to women.[185] At the same time, while certainly nationalistic, his interpretation of *bushidō* rejected the militarism of contemporary mainstream commentators on the subject. Instead, Uchimura relied on *bushidō* and his reading of Yōmeigaku to justify his resistance to the war with Russia in the face of popular opinion.[186] Uchimura's disassociation with the foreign churches and strong criticisms of his own government resulted in his alienation from much of society, but his amalgamation of Christian faith and *bushidō* presented a possibility for reconciling the frequently conflicting 'Japanese' and 'foreign' aspects of his life.

The *bushidō* of Ukita Kazutami, a member of the Protestant Kumamoto Band, is significant because of his direct challenge to the imperial *bushidō* of Inoue Tetsujirō during the Russo-Japanese War. Ukita was not fundamentally opposed to the concept of *bushidō*, however, and even contributed to the development of *bushidō* discourse after the war. For Ukita, as for many Japanese Christians, *bushidō* had greater relevance outside the military sphere, and should be implemented to improve ethics in other fields. In this context, Ukita desired to introduce *bushidō*

---

[182] Uchimura Kanzō, 'Lack of Japanese Morality', pp. 315–16.

[183] Uchimura Kanzō, 'Untitled', *Seisho no kenkyū* No. 210 (1916). Reproduced in Matsumae Shigeyoshi, *Budō shisō no tankyū*, p. 92.

[184] Uchimura, Kanzō. 'Untitled', *Seisho no kenkyū* No. 186 (10 Jan. 1916). Reproduced in Matsumae Shigeyoshi, *Budō shisō no tankyū*, p. 91.

[185] Mullins, Mark (1998), *Christianity Made in Japan: A Study of Indigenous Movements* (Honolulu: University of Hawai'i Press), pp. 64–66.

[186] For an overview of Uchimura's interest and reliance on the teachings of the Japanese Wang Yangming school, see Kojima Tsuyoshi (2006), *Kindai Nihon no Yōmeigaku* (Tokyo: Kōdansha sensho metier), pp. 72–92.

into the world of commerce to shore up Japan's business ethics, much as Ozaki Yukio had almost two decades earlier.[187] Writing the editorial in the July 1910 edition of *Taiyō*, Ukita surveyed three contemporary *bushidō* interpretations that he considered to be the most dominant. The first of these centred on the notion that *bushidō* and the *kokutai* were one and the same; the second interpretation rejected *bushidō* and was intent on replacing it with a different ideology for serving the emperor and strengthening the country; and the third accepted the historical value of *bushidō* but sought to create a superior 'national morality' for the future.[188]

Ukita claimed to adhere to this third position and outlined what he saw to be the three major problems with mainstream *bushidō*. The first problem was that *bushidō* did not 'value character' sufficiently and ignored all virtues that were not martial. The second problem was that *bushidō* caused 'genius to atrophy', for unless a person's abilities were in a military field, they were not regarded. Thirdly, and most importantly to Ukita, *bushidō* did not currently apply to the business world, which would determine the nation's future. In Ukita's words, 'As the people of a martial nation, the Japanese have astounded the world. However, for some reason our credentials as a nation of business people are in a state that the level of trust is even lower than among the Chinese. One cannot avoid saying that this is truly a matter of national shame for Japan'. According to Ukita, the solution to Japan's problems in commerce could be solved by adapting *bushidō* to this non-military purpose, resulting in economic success and the creation of a new national spirit even greater than *bushidō*, which could 'truly nurture the qualifications of a great cultural people'.[189]

The diversity of Christian opinion during the late *bushidō* boom is apparent in the writings of Saeki Yoshirō (1871–1965), an influential Sinologist who rose to prominence in 1908 with a study of the Nestorian stele of Xi'an. The history of Christianity in East Asia was the focus of Saeki's long academic career and his influential, if sometimes unorthodox theories included an argument that the Japanese had Jewish ancestry resulting from a Jewish community that had settled on the outskirts of Kyoto in the fifth century.[190] Saeki's emphasis on the historical connections between Japan and the continent made his thought popular among pan-Asianists, and he also sought the roots of *bushidō* in the interaction between cultures. As Saeki wrote in *Research on the Nestorian Monument* (1911):

> Chinese Buddhism changed to become Japanese Buddhism. The Chinese learning of the Nara period became the Japanese literature of the Kamakura period. The Great Buddhist art of the Nara period became the filigreed art of Kannon figures. The service of Wen Tianxiang and Xie Bingdei in the name of Chinese Confucian morality became Japan's unique "Japanese spirit, Chinese learning"; it became the Yamato spirit; it became *bushidō*. It is not difficult to speculate on these processes.[191]

[187] Ukita outlined these opinions in 1908 and 1910 articles in the magazine *Taiyō* (Gluck, Carol, *Japan's Modern Myths*, p. 223).
[188] Ukita Kazutami, 'Bushidō ni kansuru sanshu no kenkai', *Taiyō* 16:10 (July 1910), p. 1.
[189] Ukita Kazutami, 'Bushidō ni kansuru sanshu no kenkai', pp. 5–7.
[190] Goodman, David G. and Miyazawa Masanori (1995), *Jews in the Japanese Mind: The History and Uses of a Cultural Stereotype* (New York: The Free Press), pp. 64–65.
[191] Saeki Yoshirō (1911), *Keikyō hibun kenkyū* (Tokyo: Tairō shoin), p. 6.

While acknowledging the influence of Chinese thought and civilization on Japan, Saeki also presented nationalistic arguments in line with mainstream Japanese thought at the time. In chapter six of his *Research*, entitled 'The thing called *bushidō* and Confucian morality', Saeki opined that the unique innate characteristic of 'our superior race of the Land of the Gods' is the ability to absorb and digest first Chinese and now Western culture and civilization.[192] In accordance with this spirit of amalgamating foreign ideas, Saeki argued elsewhere in 1908, even with *bushidō* it was still necessary for Japan to adopt Christianity.[193] For Saeki, *bushidō*, like the *Yamato damashii*, was a unique characteristic arising from Japanese interaction with other peoples, rather than a divinely ordained racial trait, and he also saw the combination of *bushidō* with Christianity as essential. While the latter portion of this argument accorded with the views of other Christian writers on *bushidō*, Saeki's pan-Asian ideals and valuation of China differentiated him from most other *bushidō* commentators including Nitobe and Uemura, and Saeki's *bushidō* was among the least chauvinistic at the time.

As with Buddhist writers on *bushidō*, the broad appeal that the concept had to Japanese Christians in the modern period often masks the diversity of 'Christian' *bushidō* theories, which often differed more from one another than they did from non-Christian interpretations. For both Christians and Buddhists, *bushidō* was seen as an 'ideal stock' because of its largely secular nature. While some promoters of *bushidō*, especially the imperial interpretation, traced the concept back to the Age of the Gods, many other Meiji theorists identified it primarily with the rise to national power of the warrior families in the Kamakura period (1185–1333), thereby making *bushidō* a national character that had developed through historical processes rather than divine providence. In contrast, the *Yamato damashii*, which was often equated to or compared with *bushidō*, was tightly interwoven with Shinto beliefs, making its adoption by adherents of 'foreign' religions more problematic.

CONSIDERING THE LATE *BUSHIDŌ* BOOM

The Sino-Japanese and Russo-Japanese Wars bookended a long decade of *bushidō* growth and development, but the end of the Meiji *bushidō* boom cannot be specified with similar precision. In the decade after 1905, interest in *bushidō* waxed and waned depending on the context in which it was used. The number of publications on *bushidō* declined slightly immediately following the Treaty of Portsmouth, but the war had firmly established the concept in the popular mind. From roughly 1907 onward, the nature of writings on *bushidō* also began to change, with the number of academic works remaining relatively steady as the number of *bushidō*-themed works for popular consumption increased. At the same time, *bushidō* appeared in

---

[192] Saeki Yoshirō, pp. 8–9.
[193] Ion, A. Hamish (1995), 'Japan Watchers: 1903–31', in John Howes (ed.), *Nitobe Inazō: Japan's Bridge Across the Pacific* (Boulder: Westview Press), p. 85.

a rapidly expanding variety of contexts, as authors and organizations sensed that invoking it could increase sales and/or awareness of their causes.

By 1906, the emperor-centred *bushidō* posited and vigorously defended by Inoue Tetsujirō and others provided a broadly accepted foundation for discussion. Although most writers on *bushidō* remembered the recent past before *bushidō* was popularized, few criticized or attempted to radically redefine the concept. The imperial *bushidō* that dominated discourse after the Russo-Japanese War retained a degree of vagueness that give it considerable resilience. Imperial *bushidō* broadly equated the samurai ethic with the Yamato spirit or at least portrayed it as the most important manifestation of the latter. The origins of *bushidō* were traced to ancient history or mythical pre-history, especially the Age of the Gods and the Plain of High Heaven. While these interpretations moved closer to a 'warrior' *bushidō* predating the samurai, there was a simultaneous trend towards the use of carefully selected historical sources for the legitimization of modern theories. Imperial *bushidō* was also portrayed as a uniquely Japanese ethic with no equivalent in other cultures or nations, although European knighthood and other ideals could serve as foils for comparison. Most importantly, imperial *bushidō* called for absolute loyalty to the sovereign and nation, and sought to instill a willingness or desire to die for these causes. The notion of 'loyalty to the emperor and love for the nation' was closely tied to *bushidō*, contributing to the rapid popularization of the warrior ethic during wartime, and many *bushidō* theorists came to accept the basic framework of imperial *bushidō*.

There was a widespread view that excessive 'worship of the West' had weakened *bushidō* in the early decades of Meiji, but that the wars with China and Russia demonstrated its resurgence and vitality. Japan's uncertain economic and political state meant there was no room for complacency, however, and concentrated effort and considerable changes were required to maintain the spirit demonstrated during the wars. The *bushidō* boom peaked at the end of the Russo-Japanese War, but imperial *bushidō* became a key component of military and civil ethics education by 1914, especially in National Morality teachings. The dissemination of *bushidō* through the education system and military gave it recognition and legitimacy, but there was still leeway for other interpreters to adapt the concept. At the same time, parallel *bushidō* discourses in other countries gave the concept even greater influence, and it became a central theme for discussing Japanese culture and society. *Bushidō* discourse in other countries was given considerable coverage in Japan, reflecting national pride and a desire for international recognition for what was increasingly perceived as the 'soul of Japan'. In spite of domestic criticism of Nitobe's *Bushido: The Soul of Japan*, its international success was widely celebrated, while a 1904 article in *The Times* praising the virtues of *bushidō* was repeatedly translated and cited throughout the following decade.[194]

The great popularity of *bushidō* during the late *bushidō* boom meant that it was appropriated by many different causes and individuals in a reciprocally influencing

---

[194] For example, Abram Smythe-Palmer's 1908 *The Ideal of a Gentleman* included the article in a section on 'Gentlemen of Other Nations'.Smythe-Palmer, Abram (1908), *The Ideal of a Gentleman, or A Mirror for Gentlefolks* (London: George Routledge & Sons Limited), pp. 485–87.

cycle that continued into early Taishō. The development of *bushidō* was both market-driven and market-driving. The deployment of *bushidō* as a marketing device in late Meiji extended beyond native concepts and organizations, as the use of *bushidō* in works translated from Western languages, especially those dealing with chivalry, demonstrates. One such text was the Japanese version of Louis Albert Banks' moralistic tome *Twentieth Century Knighthood: A Series of Addresses to Young Men* (1900), rendered *20 seiki no bushidō* (*Twentieth-Century Bushidō*) in Japanese.[195] Banks used examples from the recent past to demonstrate how the ideals of medieval European chivalry could be successfully applied to the modern age.[196] Another example of this sort, published by Hakubunkan and endorsed by Nitobe Inazō, was *Occidental Bushidō* (*Seiyō no bushidō*) (1909), a translation of Léon Gautier's 1884 history of medieval European chivalry.[197] Neither of these works had any direct relation to Japan, but rather than use the term '*kishidō*', the standard translation for 'chivalry', the publishers used '*bushidō*' in order to improve sales. This equation would certainly have displeased Inoue Tetsujirō, who derided European chivalry, but this diversity was essential to the rapid growth and popularity of *bushidō* in late Meiji, which in turn aided the dissemination of institutional interpretations.

As a committed supporter of constitutional government, Ozaki Yukio was bemused by many of the chauvinistic and militaristic *bushidō* interpretations that would follow his own, and his contribution to *bushidō* discourse in the twentieth century was minimal. When Ozaki revisited *bushidō* in *On Politics and Education* (1913), he noted his considerable amusement at the recent popularity of the subject, as he had already written about *bushidō* three decades earlier. Ozaki repeated many of his original arguments from both *Shōbu ron* and his *bushidō* articles, including the tale of the Thames boatmen, reflecting his continuing fondness for the English and their gentlemanship.[198]

[195] Banks, Louis Albert (1907), *20 seiki no bushidō* (Tokyo: Naigai shuppan kyōkai).
[196] Lupack, Alan and Barbara (1999), *King Arthur in America* (Cambridge: D. S. Brewer), pp. 59–60.
[197] Maeda Chōta (trans.) (1909), *Seiyō bushidō [Leon Gautier* La Chevalerie *no yakuhon]* (Tokyo: Hakubunkan).
[198] Ozaki Yukio (1913), *Seiji kyōiku ron* (Tokyo: Tōkadō), pp. 192–217.

5

The End of the *Bushidō* Boom

NOGI MARESUKE AND THE DECLINE OF *BUSHIDŌ*

The end of Meiji was one of the most symbol-laden conclusions to an imperial reign in Japanese history. Over the course of less than half a century, Japan transformed itself from an insular state unable to resist the demands of the Western powers to the dominant force in Northeast Asia with its own colonial possessions. The Meiji emperor personified this change, and his death signalled the transition from an era of rapid progress to an age of uncertainty concerning the nation and its direction. After the Russo-Japanese War, the spectres of socialism and anarchism came to haunt those in power, culminating in the Great Treason Incident of 1910. The actual extent of this alleged leftist plot to assassinate the emperor is debatable, but it shocked many people for whom the very possibility of such an action was inconceivable. In this sense, both the reported attempt on the sovereign's life, as well as his passing two years later, signified a break with the past and a chance to reflect. This feeling was brought to a point on the day of the imperial funeral by the dramatic suicides of General Nogi Maresuke and his wife Shizuko (b.1859).[1] If the emperor symbolized the nation in its entirety, including its modernization and development, General Nogi was seen as the embodiment of Japan's traditional virtues and sense of honour, and was referred to as the 'flower' and 'epitome' of *bushidō*. His death by *seppuku* had a tremendous impact on *bushidō* discourse, and the debates that followed served as an exclamation point marking the end of the *bushidō* boom.

Nogi Maresuke was born the third son of a high-ranking retainer of the Mōri clan of Chōshū. After his two older brothers died at a young age, Nogi became heir of the main Nogi house, a role he seems to have accepted reluctantly. Accounts of his youth portray Nogi as a frail and bullied child, one of whose nicknames was 'crybaby', a situation exacerbated by his greater interest in literature than military matters. At fifteen, Nogi ran away from home to study under Yoshida Shōin's uncle Tamaki Bunnoshin (1810–76), a renowned scholar and founder of the Shōka Sonjuku school.[2] Though Nogi's motivations were primarily academic, he became

---

[1] There are still uncertainties regarding the circumstances around the death of the Nogis, as the subsequent investigation revealed that Shizuko died before her husband. This has led some to speculate that she was either killed by him or committed suicide first to spur him into action. For an overview of the arguments in English, see Bargen, Doris G. (2006), *Suicidal Honor: General Nogi and the Writings of Mori Ōgai and Natsume Sōseki* (Honolulu: University of Hawai'i Press), pp. 70–74.

[2] Bargen, Doris G., *Suicidal Honor*, pp. 34, 37.

involved in the armed conflicts of the late 1860s when a number of Shōka Sonjuku students and alumni assumed prominent roles in the imperial loyalist cause. In 1869, Nogi was transferred to the Imperial Guard, and gradually moved up the army ranks to become aide-de-camp to Yamagata Aritomo in 1875, a connection that proved decisive in Nogi's later career.

The first major crises in Nogi's professional life were his roles in putting down rebellions in his own domain of Chōshū in 1870 and again in 1876, and his younger brother's death on the opposing side of the latter conflict has been put forth as a possible motivation for Nogi's later suicide.[3] The year after his brother's death, Nogi suffered another shock when he rashly attacked a vastly superior rebel force during the Satsuma Rebellion, losing the imperial banner in the process. This incident greatly shamed Nogi, and he referred to it in the first line of his final farewell letter.[4] After an eighteen-month spell in Germany in the late 1880s to study Prussian military techniques, Nogi was placed in charge of the Imperial Guards and then the Fifth Infantry Brigade in Nagoya. To widespread bewilderment, Nogi briefly resigned from the military in 1892, with one theory holding that this action was prompted by young officers ridiculing Nogi when, while on horseback, his dentures fell out and were trodden on by his mount.[5]

Nogi was summoned back to the army in 1893, but his further rate of promotion slowed considerably, reportedly due to Nogi's lack of strategic knowledge and leadership ability. Indeed, scholars have attributed Nogi's promotions primarily to his roots in Chōshū and close personal relationships with Yamagata and exceptional soldiers, including Katsura Tarō (1848–1913) and Kodama Gentarō (1852–1906). According to Ōhama Tetsuya, Nogi's tactics were essentially limited to direct frontal assaults, allowing Kodama and other colleagues to consistently rout his forces on the training fields.[6] This single-minded and seemingly reckless approach resulted in the loss of the imperial banner in 1877, but it made Nogi an instant national hero in 1894, when his forces took the supposedly indomitable fortress of Port Arthur in a single day. There had been considerable unrest within the fortress following the Japanese victory at Dalian shortly before, and morale among the defenders was reportedly so low that Chinese soldiers were looting the town before the attack. The Chinese officers fled aboard two small ships, abandoning their men and effectively surrendering the fortress.[7] The deplorable conditions in the fortress meant that Nogi's frontal assault met with little resistance, and there is a debate as to whether this victory should be attributed to good intelligence or good fortune.

The notion that this success was a one-off was reinforced by events ten years later, when recently promoted General Nogi attempted the same feat again, this time against Russian forces holding Port Arthur. His direct, 'human bullet' approach

---

[3] Bargen, Doris G., pp. 40–43.

[4] Nogi Maresuke, 'Nogi taishō yuigonsho', *Shimin* 7:8 (7 Oct. 1912), p. 57.

[5] Bargen, Doris G., *Suicidal Honor*, p. 48.

[6] Ōhama Tetsuya (1988), *Nogi Maresuke* (Tokyo: Kawade shobō), pp. 104–09.

[7] Paine, S. C. M. (2003), *The Sino-Japanese War of 1894–1895: Perceptions, Power, and Primacy* (Cambridge: Cambridge University Press), pp. 207–09.

cost tens of thousands of lives, including those of both of his sons, over several months.[8] Nogi was finally relieved by Kodama Gentarō, who succeeded in taking the fortress after several more weeks of fighting. In spite of this, the victory was ascribed to Nogi, who conducted the surrender ceremony with the Russian general Stessel. In the interest of wartime morale, the Japanese government decided against exposing the internal wrangling in the military and, as an established hero, Nogi was useful for domestic and international propaganda purposes. Celebrated as the hero of Port Arthur once again, Nogi was fully aware of his failure and the practical considerations behind the bestowed honours. These dynamics, combined with the deaths of his sons, are also cited as important factors in his desire to commit suicide for atonement and release.[9] The last years of Meiji were especially difficult for Nogi, as he was under pressure to maintain the pretense of being a heroic and able commander, while he and his peers were aware of his failings. After the war, Nogi again left active duty and the government gave him headship of the Peers School in order to maintain 'popular respect for his image as hero of Port Arthur while excluding the failed general from the inner circles of power'.[10]

Nogi's powerful public image also strongly influenced discourse on *bushidō*, which he had been interested in from early in the *bushidō* boom. *Bushidō* appeared in Nogi's diaries as early as 1901, when he mentioned borrowing a book on the subject from fellow general Terauchi Masatake (1852–1919).[11] According to Inoue Tetsujirō, an unexpected visit from Nogi in the same year requesting a lecture sparked Inoue's interest in *bushidō*, and Nogi unfailingly attended Inoue's weekly lectures at the Peers School.[12] Under Inoue's tutelage, Nogi also pushed for the founding of a society for the promotion of Yamaga Sokō, whose works he eagerly read, and was actively involved in their publication and distribution.[13] Anecdotes concerning Nogi's promotion of Yamaga abound, including presenting his works to the crown prince and ensuring that Yamaga was posthumously awarded high imperial ranks.[14] Nogi followed Inoue in closely identifying Yamaga with *bushidō*, and published several articles on the subject.[15] Biographers have argued that Nogi's involvement with the Shōka Sonjuku would have exposed him to the teachings

---

[8] Yoshihisa Tak Matsusaka points out that Japanese military doctrine closely followed European models in the late 1890s and did not favour massed infantry attacks, arguing that Nogi's tactics at Port Arthur 'must be understood as a discretionary judgment and not the product of a combat doctrine steeped in the cult of the bayonet, whether attributed to Major Meckel or *bushido*'. Matsusaka, Yoshihisa Tak (2005), 'Human Bullets, Nogi, and the Myth of Port Arthur' in John W. Steinberg et al. (eds.), *The Russo-Japanese War in Global Perspective: World War Zero* (Leiden: Brill), p. 187.

[9] Bargen, Doris G., *Suicidal Honor*, pp. 57–59.

[10] Fujii, James A. (1993), *Complicit Fictions: The Subject in the Modern Japanese Prose Narrative* (Berkeley: University of California Press), p. 135.

[11] Fujii, James A., pp. 107–08.

[12] These claims were made after Nogi's death, and the extent to which they represent Nogi's motivations, or are simply self-aggrandizement on the part of Inoue, is debatable.Inoue Tetsujirō (1915), 'Yamaga Sokō sensei to Nogi taishō', *Nihon kogakuha no tetsugaku* (Tokyo: Fuzanbō), pp. 801–02, 804.

[13] Inoue Tetsujirō, 'Yamaga Sokō sensei to Nogi taishō', pp. 798–99.

[14] Tucker, John Allen, 'Tokugawa Intellectual History and Prewar Ideology: The Case of Inoue Tetsujirō, Yamaga Sokō, and the Forty-Seven Rōnin', *Sino-Japanese Studies* 14 (2002), pp. 50–51.

[15] For example, Nogi Maresuke (1907), 'Bushidō mondō', *Shiyū* (Tokyo: Gunji kyōiku kai).

of Yamaga Sokō and his interpreter Yoshida Shōin, but there is no conclusive evidence linking Nogi to *bushidō* at that time, nor of a lasting influence. According to Ōhama Tetsuya, it was Nogi's later encounter with German thought emphasizing cultural traditions that caused him to go back to the texts he had studied in his youth, which had already been incorporated into modern *bushidō* discourse.[16]

Headlines after Nogi's dramatic death highlighted his connection with *bushidō*, leading to a surge in interest that lasted for well over a year.[17] Opinions regarding Nogi's actions were divided, however, even among the majority of commentators who interpreted his suicide in terms of *bushidō*. As Carol Gluck outlines the general situation in 1912, 'Neither Meiji nor modernity met with universal approval. The devoutest wish of some progressive youth was to be quickly quit of Meiji so that modernity could move ahead, while the direst fear of many of their elders was that Meiji's end would enable modernity to swamp the remains of their familiar world'.[18] In this light, Nogi following his lord in death (*junshi*) provoked both strong approval and condemnation for various reasons. Nogi's suicide was broadly agreed to be representative of *bushidō*, and debates centred on the nature of the *bushidō* that it manifested, as well as its suitability for the modern age.

Inoue Tetsujirō led those Nogi supporters who saw his action as the ultimate realization of *bushidō*, and quickly amended his earlier criticism of *seppuku* as an anachronistic custom. Speaking at the Yamaga Sokō Society less than two weeks after Nogi's death, Inoue argued:

> There are many different opinions with regard to Nogi's *junshi* suicide. Although General Nogi cannot be completely removed from discussions concerning the allowance or rejection of suicide, especially *junshi*, this situation should be examined separately.
>
> Many of the suicides in the world are of extremely foolish origins. They are born of personal failures, hopelessness, and disappointment resulting in the necessity of suicide. For this reason, many of the world's suicides should be condemned, but there are other cases in which great and outstanding individuals carefully plan and calculate their suicide. Rather, when viewed objectively this can have very positive results. If General Nogi had continued to live, he would certainly have contributed to society in beneficial ways. However, as he wrote in his will, at 64 years of age he did not feel he had long to go, and did not think he could be of great use to society, so by giving himself up and committing *junshi* suicide, the result truly shook heaven and earth. This powerful influence was then transmitted to all of society. If one thinks of the grand aspects of this effect, this suicide can certainly not be rejected...Although it cannot be said that suicide is good, or that *junshi* is good, in the case of General Nogi it was truly a magnificent end. It was a glorious end to a *bushi*'s life that would have satisfied General Nogi. In fact, if one considers General Nogi's usual thought, it was an event worth celebrating. However, if one considers losing a great man such as this, one must be deeply saddened. Our thought has these two sides. In any case, the *junshi* suicide

---

[16] Ōhama Tetsuya, *Nogi Maresuke*, p. 112.

[17] 'Bushidō no seika', *Yomiuri shinbun*, 17 Sept. 1912, p. 5.

[18] Gluck, Carol (1985), *Japan's Modern Myths* (Princeton, NJ: Princeton University Press), p. 226.

of General Nogi truly demonstrated the great strength of the *bushidō* of our Japan. I believe it will certainly still produce great effects from now on.[19]

This eulogy was largely representative of conservative thought concerning Nogi's death, although Inoue's role as a formulator of official educational and social ideology meant that he had to temper his enthusiasm in order to discourage imitators and reinforce the government's suicide-prevention messages that followed a perceived spate of self-inflicted deaths a decade earlier.

Other commentators dispensed with such qualifying statements. Okada Ryōhei (1864–1934), a former head of Kyoto University, member of the House of Peers, and future education minister, lauded Nogi's action unequivocally as the 'realization of *bushidō*'. In an article published in October 1912, Okada wrote of Nogi's admiration for the '*bushidō* of the Yamaga Sokō school', drawing comparisons with the leader of the loyal retainers of Akō:

> Ōishi Yoshio was truly a person who embodied and realized the Yamaga school [of *bushidō*]. Towards his lord, he demonstrated the great spirit of *junshi* known as 'with death repaying the lord's favour'. However, the death of General Nogi must be seen as superior even to the death of Yoshio. With his death, Yoshio repaid the favour of his lord, but the General dedicated his death to the sacred son of heaven who had bestowed great blessings higher than the mountains and deeper than the sea. The times are different, so it is unavoidable that the General's death has been compared to Yoshio's and has taken its place.[20]

Nitobe Inazō also praised Nogi's act, calling it the 'complete manifestation of our nation's *bushidō* spirit' and a 'superb *bushi*-like end' that would hopefully lead to the further spread of *bushidō* not only in Japan, but throughout the world.[21] In addition to a flood of newspaper and magazine articles, at least twenty-eight volumes on Nogi were published by the end of 1912, and the *naniwabushi* genre of narrative ballads 'rode to the peak of their popularity in 1912 and 1913 on the crest of an interest in the tale of General Nogi that knew no social distinctions'.[22]

The Zen popularizer and *bushidō* promoter Nukariya Kaiten provided foreign audiences with a positive assessment of Nogi in *The Religion of the Samurai* (1913). According to Nukariya, '[w]e can find an incarnation of Bushido in the late General Nogi, the hero of Port Arthur, who, after the sacrifice of his two sons

---

[19] Inoue Tetsujirō, 'Yamaga Sokō sensei to Nogi taishō', pp. 827–29. For a summary of this lecture in English, see Tucker, John Allen, 'Tokugawa Intellectual History and Prewar Ideology', pp. 46–48.

[20] Okada Ryōhei (2005), 'Nogi taishō no bushidō jitsugen', in Horiuchi Ryō (ed.), *Okada Ryōhei hōtoku ronshū* (Tokyo: Dai Nihon hōtokusha), p. 45.

[21] Yamamuro Kentoku (2007), *Gunshin: kindai Nihon ga unda "eiyū" tachi no kiseki* (Tokyo: Chuōkōron shinsha), pp. 111–12.

[22] Gluck, Carol, *Japan's Modern Myths*, 224–25. Publications from these two years included *A Record of Sayings by General Nogi* (Ōbuchi Rō, *Nogi shōgun genkō roku*. Kyoto: Shinshindō Shoten, 1912); *General Nogi: Songs of the Flower of Bushidō* (Muramatsu Seiin, *Nogi taishō shōka bushidō no hana*. Tokyo: Sanmeisha Shoten, 1912); *The Flower of Bushidō: General Nogi* (Hitomi Tecchō, *Bushidō no hana Nogi taishō*. Tokyo: Hiyoshidō Shoten, 1912); *General Nogi's Bushidō Dialogues* (Takahashi Seiko, *Nogi taishō bushidō mondō*. Tokyo: Gunji Kyōiku Kai, 1913); *The Epitome of Bushidō: General Nogi* (Kōno Masayoshi, *Bushidō no tenkei Nogi taishō*. Tokyo: Tōkyō Kokumin Shoin, 1913), and many others in a similar vein.

for the country in the Russo-Japanese War, gave up his own and his wife's life for the sake of the deceased Emperor'. Nukariya was optimistic regarding the effect of Nogi's act, hoping that it would 'inspire the rising generation with the spirit of the Samurai to give birth to hundreds of Nogis'.[23] Hope for an inspirational effect on the nation's youth was repeated by a number of commentators, focusing on the virtues that the idealized figure of Nogi symbolized in life, although the reception of his suicide was considerably more nuanced.

The responses to Nogi's suicide were not all positive, and while patriotism and respect for the deceased prevented most writers from attacking Nogi directly, the value and meaning of his action were widely questioned. Critical works were also generally couched in discussions of *bushidō*, which had become even more closely linked with Nogi immediately after his death. An article in the *Tōkyō asahi shinbun* on 15 September summed up the position of many critics: 'General Nogi's death marked the completion of Japan's bushidō of old. And while emotionally we express the greatest respect, rationally we regret we cannot approve. One can only hope that this act will not long blight the future of our national morality. We can appreciate the General's intention; we must not learn from his behavior' (translation by Carol Gluck).[24] For progressives, Nogi's actions represented many of the problems with the old order and were an international embarrassment that damaged Japan's developing image as a 'civilized' society. Those Japanese who had despaired at their nation being defined in terms of militaristic *bushidō* around the time of the Russo-Japanese War were especially perturbed by these developments, which once again brought *bushidō* to the fore. With even Inoue Tetsujirō pressed to qualify his praise for Nogi, the incident presented great difficulties for those Christians and other *bushido* commentators who argued against the imperial interpretation.[25] An article on 'Theatrical *Bushidō*' by Uemura Masahisa in the *Fukuin shinpō* on 24 October 1912, stated that Nogi was a great man but his interpretation of *bushidō* was in need of revision. Uemura argued that soldiers had always been disposed to the theatrical in any country and this was especially true of *bushidō*. Uemura speculated that 'if someone arose to create a Japanese Don Quixote, I believe that it would have many benefits towards the reform of *bushidō*, the teaching of our nation's people', for it would excite a much-needed debate on the subject.[26] Similarly, Ukita Kazutami's assessments of the incident alternated between praising Nogi's resolve and lamenting his actions as a tragic anachronism.[27] Christian journalist and politician Shimada Saburō (1852–1923) argued in an article in the *Tōhi* on 17 September that 'if all people under heaven learn from General Nogi and commit *junshi*, there is no way the nation could

[23] Kaiten Nukariya (1913), *Religion of the Samurai: A Study of Zen Philosophy and Discipline in China and Japan* (Tokyo), p. 50–52.

[24] Gluck, Carol, *Japan's Modern Myths*, p. 222.

[25] For an overview of the debates following Nogi's death, see Yamamuro Kentoku, *Gunshin: kindai Nihon ga unda 'eiyū' tachi no kiseki*, 111–134; Sugawara Katsuya, '20 seiki no bushidō: Nogi Maresuke jijin no hamon', *Hikaku bungaku kenkyū* 45 (April 1984), pp. 90–116.

[26] Uemura Masahisa (1966), *Uemura Masahisa chosakushū* 1 (Tokyo: Shinkyō shuppansha), pp. 426–27.

[27] Gluck, Carol, *Japan's Modern Myths*, p. 223.

exist'. On the same day, an article in the *Ōsaka mainichi shinbun* pointed out that 'Through General Nogi, *junshi* became allowable for the first time. If another person had done this, it would be affectation, theatricalism, and a foolish and laughable incident'.[28]

The Meiji *bushidō* boom ended around 1914, after the commotion surrounding Nogi's suicide had subsided. Anecdotes concerning Nogi's life were widely used in popular literature, school textbooks, and government campaigns, but the divisiveness of Nogi's act was clearly evident in the responses that followed.[29] At the same time, the dramatic incident and subsequent debates led to the decline of *bushidō* discourse around this time. Nogi had demonstrated a strong interest in *bushidō* in the decade before his death, which certainly influenced his decision to conclude his life in the manner he chose. While Nogi had been identified with the concept even before 1912, death by *junshi* made his person inseparable from *bushidō* in the popular consciousness. *Bushidō* had enjoyed great popularity since the Russo-Japanese War and, Inoue Tetsujirō's efforts notwithstanding, discourse on the subject remained diverse. Nogi's suicide changed this by creating a template for *bushidō* that attracted the attention of the entire nation. *Bushidō* theorists had to address this incident and most felt compelled to agree that Nogi was motivated by *bushidō*, for better or for worse.

Nogi's prominence and subsequent lionization notwithstanding, the majority of people took note of his suicide, but saw it as an unusual event with no direct relation to them.[30] As the driving force behind Nogi's death, *bushidō* experienced a similar dynamic. Although virtually all people in early Taishō were aware of *bushidō*, their understanding of it was typically as something equal or comparable to the similarly vague Yamato spirit; i.e. as a source of national identification and imperial loyalty, and therefore key to the nation's military successes, but generally without immediate relevance to everyday life. Nogi's death cast a very tangible interpretation of *bushidō* into the spotlight, and many people were surprised at what they saw. The anachronistic sense of detachment from the modern age alarmed many progressives, and people with only a passing knowledge of *bushidō* were bemused by this noble yet tragic act. When Nogi seemingly became the manifestation of *bushidō* through his suicide, *bushidō* was also joined with Meiji in the public consciousness. As a result, as the nation moved on from Meiji, it also moved on from *bushidō*, drawing the *bushidō* boom to a close.

---

[28] Yamamuro Kentoku, *Gunshin: kindai Nihon ga unda 'eiyū' tachi no kiseki*, pp. 114–15.

[29] For example, Mori Ōgai's story 'Okitsu Yagoemon' is widely viewed as a tribute to Nogi. Starrs, Roy (1998), 'Writing the National Narrative: Changing Attitudes towards Nation-Building among Japanese Writers, 1900–1930', in Sharon Minichiello (ed.), *Japan's Competing Modernities: Issues in Culture and Democracy 1900–1930* (Honolulu: University of Hawai'i Press), pp. 210–11; Nogi's loyalty to the emperor was invoked by industrialists to instill loyalty in employees through the creation of 'Nogi Societies'. Gordon, Andrew (1985), *The Evolution of Labor Relations in Japan: Heavy Industry, 1853–1955* (Cambridge, MA: Harvard University Press), p. 226; Nogi also became one of the most prominent figures in elementary school texts in pre-war Japan. Gluck, Carol, *Japan's Modern Myths*, p. 225.

[30] Gluck, Carol, *Japan's Modern Myths*, p. 225.

DEMOCRACY, INTERNATIONALISM, AND *BUSHIDŌ*

The notion that Japan was moving beyond Meiji was one of a number of factors that influenced *bushidō* discourse during Taishō (1912–26). The death of the Meiji emperor was not as immediately significant to *bushidō* as that of General Nogi, but the imperial succession soon caused ideological difficulties. The close identification of *bushidō* with the virtues of patriotism and imperial loyalty centred on the strong figure of the Meiji emperor as embodiment of the nation. In contrast, the Taishō emperor had readily apparent physical and neurological ailments, preventing him from being a prominently public figure as his father had been. The perceived weakness of the new sovereign contributed to a shift in emphasis from the person of the emperor to the abstract concept of 'national polity' (*kokutai*) in the military, amid similar developments in the popular realm.[31] Insofar as loyalty to the emperor was an important component of most modern *bushidō* interpretations, this contributed to the decline of the warrior ethic during Taishō.

The loss of such a symbolically powerful unifying figure also exacerbated rifts in Japanese discourse on nationalism, and Kevin Doak and Thomas Havens discuss the conflicts between 'statists' and 'nationalists' in the 1910s and 1920s. While 'statists' accepted the legitimacy and authority of the state, many 'nationalists' attacked the governing structure in the name of the people, and one of the government's great concerns was reunifying these factions as they had been in Meiji.[32] The anti-government sentiments of many popular nationalists adversely affected government-sponsored ideologies such as National Morality or *bushidō*, while the growing split between nationalists and the state was accompanied by a weakening of nationalism in general as dissatisfaction with the government and military spread. As an ostensibly martial ethic, the fortunes of *bushidō* were closely tied to those of the Japanese military, and popular attitudes towards the two generally mirrored one another.

The Taishō political crisis of 1912–13 dealt a major blow to the popularity of the military in Japan when the army brought down the government by refusing to provide a war minister to the cabinet of Saionji Kinmochi. This high-handed approach was widely resented, provoking nationwide protests and anti-military feelings that remained strong for a decade. Further violent protests followed in 1914 over the Siemens Affair, in which senior naval officers accepted bribes from the German firm over the construction of warships. This corruption scandal not only compromised the Yamamoto cabinet, but exacerbated anti-military sentiment by involving the imperial navy, which was already resented for consuming 30 per cent of the national budget.[33] By 1914, both services had reached a nadir in

[31] Yoshida Yutaka (2002), *Nihon no guntai: heishi tachi no kindai shi* (Tokyo: Iwanami shinsho 816), pp. 161–62.

[32] Doak and Havens use the terms 'statists' (*kokkashugishai*) and 'nationalists' (*kokuminshugisha*).Doak, Kevin Michael (2007), *A History of Nationalism in Modern Japan: Placing the People* (Leiden: Brill), pp. 201–02.

[33] Coox, Alvin D. (1975), 'Chrysanthemum and Star: Army and Society in Modern Japan', in David MacIsaac (ed.), *The Military and Society: The Proceedings of the Fifth Military History Symposium* (Diane Publishing), p. 47.

their popularity, and were saved from further inciting the public's displeasure only by the outbreak of the First World War, which provided a distraction and boost to the nation's economy as Japanese businesses stepped into the breach left by the distracted Europeans.

Given Japan's relatively limited military involvement in the conflict, attitudes towards the First World War were mixed. Certain segments of society welcomed the opportunities the war presented, especially in terms of economic and territorial gains, but the growing anti-military sentiment meant that there was also considerable resistance to involvement in a new conflict.[34] Ukita Kazutami warned against the militarism inherent in mainstream *bushidō* by drawing comparisons with ancient Sparta, which focused on military matters and failed to produce any great men before ultimately sinking into oblivion.[35] If the events of 1914–18 did not reconcile the military with broader society, the easy military successes and improving economic climate prevented relations from deteriorating further during the period. This brief respite for the military's public image ended in 1918, however, when the resulting inflationary pressures caused widespread unrest throughout the country. These 'rice riots' consisted of hundreds of incidents across rural and urban areas, necessitating the use of the military to restore order. The harsh crackdown that followed increased resentment of the military, and marked another low point in the popularity of the army during Taishō.[36] The Terauchi government collapsed soon afterward, ushering in a brief era of rule by political parties that were fundamentally sceptical of military influence, while the quagmire of the Siberian Expedition of 1918–22 prevented the army's reputation from recovering. At the same time, European preoccupation with the prelude to and consequences of the First World War greatly reduced the perceived military threat from the West, resulting in proposed and realized reductions in military budgets in Japan throughout the period.[37]

Dissatisfaction with the military and liberalizing trends in politics and the arts in Taishō contributed to *bushidō*'s decline after 1914, with market-driven publishers of popular fiction halting publication of *bushidō*-related series and moving to different subjects. Similar trends took place in more intellectually ambitious literary works, as later Taishō writers tried to liberate themselves from the legacy of their Meiji predecessors, who had identified more directly with the national project.[38] The identification of *bushidō* with the Meiji state—and General Nogi—affected the treatment of *bushidō* by literary and intellectual figures. Discussions of

---

[34] Frederick Dickinson focuses on the 'enthusiastic' reception the war received among some Japanese commentators while Alvin Coox contends that there 'is no evidence that World War I was popular in Japan'. Dickinson, Frederick R. (1999), *War and National Reinvention: Japan in the Great War, 1914–1919* (Cambridge, MA: Harvard University Press), pp. 34–35; Coox, Alvin D., 'Chrysanthemum and Star: Army and Society in Modern Japan', p. 48.

[35] Ukita Kazutami (1915), *Bunmei no yo* (Hakubunkan), pp. 135–36.

[36] Humphreys, Leonard A. (1995), *The Way of the Heavenly Sword: The Japanese Army in the 1920s*, p. 43.

[37] Drea, Edward (2009), *Japan's Imperial Army: Its Rise and Fall, 1853–1945* (Lawrence: University Press of Kansas), p. 130.

[38] Starrs, Roy, 'Writing the National Narrative', p. 215.

bushidō became rarer and more nuanced, especially during the 'Taishō democracy' of the early 1920s, when the identification of *bushidō* with reactionary politics led writers to openly criticize the subject. Akutagawa Ryūnosuke summed up this attitude in a 1920 note on the tendency of 'Passing Trends', to transform into conservative forces over time. According to Akutagawa, the damaging potential these defunct trends posed to scholarship and the arts declined with age, meaning that the recent 'humanist' and 'naturalist' movements posed the greatest threats to progress. In comparison, he argued, the conservative attempts to impede progress made by anachronistic '*bushidō*-ists' were no more significant than the actions of mischievous children.[39]

Thinkers influenced by Western political thought were especially critical of *bushidō* and the establishment with which it was linked. Keiō University economist Horie Kiichi (1876–1927), who had received an extensive education at top schools in the United States and Europe, saw the influence of *bushidō* and veneration of the samurai manifested in the many riots and mass disturbances that rocked Taishō. According to Eiko Maruko Siniawer, observers such as Horie and philosopher and critic Miyake Setsurei (1860–1945) interpreted the prevalent political violence of the early 1920s as a rejection of modernity and a return to the country's 'feudal' past, when strong men controlled society. The ruffians' role models might be late Tokugawa 'men of spirit' or warriors from much earlier periods, and commentators considered the widespread and misguided romanticization of the samurai past to be a key factor in this development.[40]

Another Keiō figure, professor and literary critic Togawa Shūkotsu (1870–1939) was also critical of *bushidō* and addressed the decline of popular discourse on the subject. Revisiting his own 'non-*bushidō* theory' in late Taishō, Togawa wrote that the subject had been very popular when he originally commented on it fifteen or sixteen years earlier, but times had changed and no one spoke of *bushidō* in public. Togawa compared *bushidō* to the idea of 'good wives, wise mothers', (*ryōsai kenbo*) which he had earlier considered to be 'the most insipid concept in existence'. At the time, Togawa recalled, he thought that *bushidō* was nothing special and certainly not worthy of the extensive discussions it provoked. Togawa considered much of *bushidō* to have been so obvious as to be beyond debate, but the growth of industry and an increased focus on wealth in society meant that traditional values had all but disappeared, and *bushidō* was no longer self-evident.[41] Togawa's original 'non-*bushidō* theory' was highly critical of the class-based elements of *bushidō*, and he referred to it as a 'slave morality'. According to Togawa, although *bushidō* was being credited by both Japanese and foreigners for victory in the war with Russia, it was an 'antique' concept with little use in the present day.[42]

---

[39] Akutagawa Ryūnosuke (1955), 'Ryūzoku', in *Akutagawa Ryūnosuke zenshū 10* (Tokyo: Iwanami Shoten), pp. 35–36.

[40] Siniawer, Eiko Maruko, 'Liberalism Undone: Discourses on Political Violence in Interwar Japan', *Modern Asian Studies*, 45:4 (2011), pp. 989–90.

[41] Togawa Shūkotsu (1926), *Bonjin sūhai* (Tokyo: Arusu), pp. 170–77.

[42] Togawa Shūkotsu, 'Hi bushidō ron', *Jidai shikan* (1908), pp. 132–33.

Even with regard to military matters, Togawa argued, *bushidō* had limited relevance in modern wars. The rejection of business and money by the samurai meant that their children were not taught mathematics and accounting, but warfare had developed in a way that made these essential skills. Togawa further described *bushidō* as 'a teaching of death' that focused on how one should die and kill, thereby inducing people to take their lives lightly. As a result, *bushidō* caused warriors to become excessively passive in combat as they did not value life, making *bushidō* counterproductive as a martial spirit. In addition, Togawa saw the promotion of *bushidō* as dangerous to broader society given the rash of suicides among the nation's youth, and wrote that it could only be damaging to 'dig up such an antique relic and make it today's morality'.[43] In the 1920s, Togawa still felt that *bushidō* was unsuited to the modern age and that its followers were irresponsible, but he conceded that certain elements of it could help improve society. While something like Nitobe's book was nothing more than a plaything, Togawa wrote, he held out hope that a splendid and useful *bushidō* theory might emerge sometime in the future.[44]

In Taishō, the feeling that the nation had 'arrived' on the world stage reached all levels of society, and the feeling of competition with other nations that had defined much of Meiji thought lost its urgency. As *bushidō* discourse originated in and was driven by efforts to define and position the nation relative to foreign 'others', it lost momentum as the gap between Japan and Western powers became less pronounced and Japanese scholars were better able to relativize the West. The First World War contributed to this process by distracting Western nations militarily while fuelling an economic boom in Japan, which supplied the warring parties and also stepped into the Asian markets they had vacated. In spite of a post-war slump, Japan emerged from the conflict with its position in the world strengthened considerably.

Interest in Western thought and the importation of foreign ideas and trends continued to grow during Taishō, encouraged by the perception that Japan was able to introduce foreign concepts 'freely' from a position of cultural strength and autonomy. This confidence could be seen in changes in domestic scholarship on Japan, which went from defining the nation as a whole using concepts such as *bushidō* (Nitobe, Inoue), 'teaism' (Okakura Tenshin), or climate (Shiga Shigetaka), to examining regional differences (Yanagita Kunio) or taking a more international perspective (Okakura). As Funabiki Takeo has argued, the most important figures in Meiji *Nihonjin ron* moved beyond the framework of Japan in Taishō, with issues of national identity appearing to be temporarily resolved.[45] Funabiki defines *Nihonjin ron* as explaining the insecurities of readers and writers in the context of comparisons with foreign countries, a description that applies to many early writings on *bushidō* in Meiji. He further argues that the relative lack of insecurities regarding Japanese identity between 1910 and 1930 made *Nihonjin ron* seem less necessary.[46]

[43] Togawa Shūkotsu, 'Hi bushidō ron', pp. 138–44.
[44] Togawa Shūkotsu, *Bonjin sūhai*, pp. 170–77.
[45] Funabiki Takeo (2003), *Nihonjin ron saikō* (Tokyo: NHK Publishing), pp. 79–80.
[46] Funabiki Takeo, pp. 84–85.

Discourse on Japanese cultural identity during the Taishō period was marked, if not by insecurity, then certainly by a greater degree of scepticism regarding the theories formulated in Meiji. Minami Hiroshi has described the 1910s as a period in which the established myths came under increasing scrutiny, and *bushidō* was no exception.[47] In contrast with its decline in popular culture, however, a somewhat reduced *bushidō* discourse developed among intellectuals and social commentators. This new *bushidō* challenged the sweeping generalizations of mainstream discourse, taking a more nuanced approach that attempted to situate the ideology in historical and social contexts, rather than in mythical pre-history. Tsuda Sōkichi, for example, sought the origins of *bushidō* in the social structure of early modern warrior society in his 1901 criticism of Nitobe's *Bushido: The Soul of Japan* and expanded this argument in his *Inquiry into the Japanese Mind as Mirrored in Literature*, published in installments from 1916. According to Tsuda, the notion that Japanese patriotism was founded in *bushidō* was historically inaccurate, as *bushidō* was merely a social construct. In fact, he argued, the Japanese were traditionally the least martial of races, as war had always been internecine and therefore carried out in a less ruthless manner. This lack of 'interracial' conflict also prevented a pronounced national spirit from developing among the Japanese.[48]

In 1912, writer and historian Shirayanagi Shūko (1884–1950) revisited the accepted view of *bushidō* from a historical perspective, stating that while he was reluctant to discuss its shortcomings, he felt it necessary to bring up a very dangerous side to *bushidō*. Shirayanagi pointed out that many famous Meiji scholars equated *bushidō* with the ethic of *chūkun aikoku*, but that Japanese history threw up many examples of warrior treachery, such as the betrayal of Oda Nobunaga by his vassal Akechi Mitsuhide.[49] In addition, there were considerable differences between *bushi* in different historical periods and their loyalty was often contingent on receiving compensation. In this sense, Shirayanagi argued, *bushi* were concerned with money and, like today's workers, expected compensation for their services.[50] Ukita Kazutami's 1915 criticism of *bushidō* also adopted the historicist approach, arguing that *bushidō* was a product of the feudal period that had been reinterpreted in Meiji, when it was idealized and projected back on the past. Ukita argued that *bushidō* was no more than the fashion of a defunct class and had originally been fundamentally opposed to the idea of imperial rule. Furthermore, *bushidō* only valued military ability and considered women and commoners to be worthless, ideas that had resulted in the modern Japanese predilection to worship bureaucrats and soldiers.[51]

The popularity of internationalist, democratic, and anti-militarist currents during Taishō was especially detrimental to the fundamentally martial and loyalistic

---

[47] Minami Hiroshi (2006), *Nihonjin ron: Meiji kara kyō made* (Tokyo: Iwanami gendai bunko), pp. 79–81.

[48] Minami Hiroshi pp. 99–100, Tsuda Sōkichi (1917), *Bungaku ni arawaretaru waga kokumin shisō no kenkyū* (Tokyo: Rakuyōdō).

[49] Shirayanagi Shūko (1912), *Oyabun kobun: eiyū hen* (Tōadō shobō), p. 7.

[50] Shirayanagi Shūko, pp. 280–82.   [51] Ukita Kazutami, *Bunmei no yo*, pp. 124–35.

ethic of *bushidō*. To be sure, 'progressive' revisions of samurai history had existed since late Meiji, such as Tokutomi Sohō's early portrayal of Yoshida Shōin as a republican revolutionary. Historian and literary critic Yamaji Aizan (1864–1917), who wrote for Tokutomi's Min'yūsha, reinterpreted the role of Satsuma in a 1910 biography of Saigō Takamori. According to Yamaji, Satsuma's strength derived from the weaker class consciousness among its samurai, which kept them from becoming as degenerate as their peers in other domains.[52] In addition to its social aspects, Yamaji's argument also reflected the use of *bushidō* to promote regional exceptionalism while keeping the local firmly integrated into the national whole. In a 1919 essay that keyed into the new intellectual currents, Nitobe Inazō extolled the virtues of 'the way of the common people (*heimindō*)', deeming this to be a superior translation for the English term 'democracy' in an attempt to show that participatory government was not incompatible with Japanese traditions. Nitobe stated that *heimindō* (democracy) could be seen as an expansion and continuation of the warrior ethic, and was more relevant than *bushidō* in the current age.[53] By mid-Taishō, even Nitobe, who maintained great affection for 'his' *bushidō*, acknowledged that it was being superseded by democracy and internationalism. The same year, the socialist editor of the series *Compendium of Writings on Common People*, Uno Chūjin, argued that *heimindō* was merely an extension of *bushidō*. According to Uno, while terms often changed, the fundamental ideas stayed the same; the character '*shi*' had lost its purely martial connotations and been extended to lawyers, scholars, and other learned professionals. The conscription order then extended *bushidō* to all Japanese by making everyone responsible for national defence, not just the *bushi* class.[54]

The relationship between *bushidō*, democracy, and the military was given a new angle by former Lieutenant General Satō Kōjirō (1862–1923), a veteran of the Russo-Japanese and First World wars who had studied in Germany early in his career. Writing in 1920, Satō argued that the military had to 'return to the past', but his nostalgia for earlier values reflected the new values of Taishō democracy. Satō credited the Meiji Restoration and victory in the Sino-Japanese and Russo-Japanese wars to Japan's unique *bushidō* spirit, but warned that this had been corrupted in recent times. According to Satō, Japanese armies had historically been private entities with essentially democratic organizational structures, but the admiration for foreign militaries in Meiji—particularly the worship of the Prussian General Jakob Meckel's ideas—had robbed the Japanese military of its traditional democratic structure. Since the disaster of the First World War, Satō wrote, the German army had become more democratic than before, and Japan needed to make similar reforms to reintroduce the ancient spirit of self-determination into the military.[55]

[52] Miyazawa Seiichi (2005), *Meiji ishin no saisōzō: kindai Nihon no 'kigenshinwa'* (Tokyo: Aoki shoten), p. 47.

[53] Nitobe Inazō, 'Heimindō', *Jitsugyō no Nihon* 22:10 (1 May 1919), pp. 17–20.

[54] Uno Chūjin (1919), *Nihon kokumin to demokurashii* (Tokyo: Funasaka Yonetarō), pp. 43–46.

[55] Satō Kōjirō (1920), *Kokubō jō no shakai mondai zusho (Gendai shakai mondai kenkyū 18)* (Utsunomiya: Tōkasha), pp. 161–77.

Among the revisionist interpretations that dominated the limited elite *bushidō* discourse of late Taishō, a minority of commentators used the new approaches to maintain imperial ideals. Shortly before his death, statesman Ōkuma Shigenobu (1838–1922) lamented the decline of *bushidō* since the late Tokugawa, stating that the 'spirit of the military must be the crystallization of the *Volksgeist*'. The Japanese national spirit, which Ōkuma equated with the Yamato spirit and *bushidō*, was a spirit of sacrifice that obliged people to be ready to die at the proper time. This was epitomized by the *Hagakure*, which expressed the virtue of willingly dying a dog's death when necessary for the greater good of the nation and people. According to Ōkuma, in the fifteen years since *bushidō* had become popular, some thinkers tried to trace it back to Song Confucianism. This, Ōkuma claimed, was a mistaken assumption as the Confucians were weak, and the imperial regalia proved that *bushidō* was far older.[56]

In 1923, Naruse Kanji (1888–1948), who later achieved considerable fame with a controversial book that demythologized Japanese swords by studying their disappointing practical performance in the Second Sino-Japanese War, invoked *bushidō* to counter the liberalizing currents of Taishō.[57] Naruse believed that Japan had demonstrated the strength of its *bushidō* spirit in the wars with China and Russia, which had stunned the West and provoked anti-Japanese legislation and Yellow Peril rhetoric in the United States and Germany. Unfortunately, Naruse wrote, although *bushidō* had still been capable of ensuring Japanese victory in these conflicts, it had been weakened considerably from its ancient peak. The establishment of the new education system in early Meiji eliminated the idea of class differences and *bushidō* was discarded, while Shinto and Confucianism were mixed with Western thought. As a result, the twenty-year period from 1870 until the promulgation of the Imperial Rescript on Education was one with no moral foundation in education. At the same time, the samurai themselves fell into a terrible plight of impoverishment and unemployment, until the Satsuma Rebellion ended their influence completely. Although the Restoration had been accomplished with the blood of *bushi*, it simultaneously represented their downfall.

According to Naruse, *bushidō* had long been challenged by another ethic that had developed from the tension between commoners and samurai. This 'way of the commoner', or *chōnindō*, was a 'moral of gold-worship' that led people to forget national concerns. Naruse saw its equivalent in the 'morality that governs Jews', which he blamed for both the Russian Revolution and the collapse of Germany, and this 'Jewish morality' had come to dominate Japan in the form of *chōnindō*. During the three centuries of Tokugawa rule, Naruse explained, the *bushi* had become 'drunk on peace' and allowed 'commoner morality' to become strong, creating a powerful new force in society. In 'a great moral revolution' in 1868, the great merchant houses—including Mitsui, Iwasaki, Yasuda, and Sumitomo—became the new rulers in place of the *daimyō*, while the order of the classes was turned on

---

[56] Ōkuma Shigenobu (1922), *Ōzei wo takkan seyo* (Hōbundō), pp. 597–603.
[57] See also Naruse's study of Japanese swords in warfare: Naruse Kanji (1940), *Tatakau Nihontō* (Jitsugyō no Nihonsha).

its head to relegate the *shizoku* to the bottom of society. Recently, however, Naruse wrote, there had been positive signs of the revival of the *shizoku*, especially in the bureaucracy and military, where most high officers were *shizoku*. Believing that the 'non-capitalist classes' had already announced a war on the 'capitalists', Naruse was optimistic regarding *shizoku* plans to destroy commoner morality and restore *bushidō*. Throughout Japanese history, he maintained, the *bushi* had always managed to come back from adversity and revive the nation.[58]

SPORTS AND *BUSHIDŌ* IN TAISHŌ

In spite of the decline in popular interest in *bushidō* in Taishō, the imperial interpretation of the ideology continued to be disseminated on a major scale in sports and education, and connections between these discoursal spheres were close. As in Meiji, *bushidō* was an important ideological component of both native and imported sports, which were becoming increasingly popular in schools. At the same time, institutional emphasis on *bushidō* remained constant or even increased during Taishō, as the slow pace of bureaucratic change meant that the introduction of new concepts into schools lagged considerably behind popular trends. The content of public education was not significantly reformed until 1910, and *bushidō* entered the civilian classroom from this period onward. Conversely, the resistance of the education system to rapid change meant that once established, a concept such as *bushidō* was not easily removed from the curriculum, and *bushidō* remained a part of civilian education even in the relatively anti-military environment of Taishō. In this study, 'institutional *bushidō*' refers to the *bushidō* taught in public institutions, both military and civilian. While this was generally the same as imperial *bushidō*, and the two evolved together over time, the lag between the production and implementation of a new ideology meant that differences existed at certain periods.

Promoters of sports in Meiji explored all possible means to popularize their activities, with *bushidō* used after the Sino-Japanese War to confer patriotic legitimacy on both native and foreign sports. The tremendous efforts of bringing sport to the public paid off on a grand scale in Taishō, when many organized sports became established in mainstream society in their modern forms. The dissemination of modern sports was assisted significantly by two interrelated factors: promotional activities by the increasingly popular print media and the inclusion of sports into the school curriculum on a national scale. The impact and timing of these varied with regard to 'Japanese' and 'foreign' sports, but the competition for national attention brought sports into the public domain on a large scale in the 1910s. Western sports were introduced into Japanese education early in Meiji, a period when most 'traditional' martial arts had not yet been standardized or organized in structures that would permit broad dissemination. Baseball, tennis, boating, football (soccer), field hockey, and athletics could all be found in Japanese schools before 1880 on at least a recreational level, with baseball the

---

[58] Naruse Kanji (1923), *Shizoku* (Seibunsha), pp. 36–54.

most widely practised.[59] The number of middle schools with baseball programmes was 218 in 1900, growing to 311 by the end of 1910.[60] In contrast, major lobbying efforts by martial arts organizations from 1896 notwithstanding, judo and kendo were rejected for inclusion in the school curriculum by the Ministry of Education as less suitable than Western 'scientific' forms of exercise. It was only in 1908 that the Imperial Diet overruled the education bureaucracy to incorporate martial arts into middle and upper schools, a policy that was finally and reluctantly instituted in 1911.[61] Emotional appeals to *bushidō* were instrumental in convincing politicians to intercede on behalf of the martial arts, and also played a key role in the explosive growth of baseball in the first decade of Taishō.

Baseball faced a last Meiji hurdle to its popular acceptance in 1911 when the *Tōkyō asahi shinbun* instigated a major debate on its detrimental effects. A number of prominent contributors, including Nitobe Inazō, criticized the increasingly popular pastime for distracting students from their studies and creating an artificial hierarchy that rewarded athletes. Other points of contention were the commercialization of the sport through the introduction of spectator entrance fees, as well as fundamental moral issues stemming from underhanded tactics such as 'stealing' bases or heckling opponents. Critics claimed that Japanese baseball had degraded from the earlier *bushidō* ideals that guided play at the First Higher School, while defenders of contemporary developments also defended baseball in terms of *bushidō*, arguing that although the sport had originated in the United States, it had now become a 'pure Japanese *bushidō* baseball'. The critics were accused of having misinterpreted changes such as the charging of admission, which was supposedly necessary to sustain the sport and not a sign of creeping commercialization.[62] Baseball's popularity made it an easy target for criticism, which was primarily driven by a desire to increase newspaper circulation through the creation of controversy.

Commercial considerations were also behind the major breakthrough of school baseball in Taishō, when the *Ōsaka asahi shinbun* staged the first national middle school baseball tournament in 1915. Appeals to the national interest were an integral part of the marketing campaign, which also responded to the earlier criticisms. As Nakao Wataru of the sponsoring newspaper stated, 'the games of this tournament are not a direct translation of the increasingly corporate American baseball, but rather the Japanese baseball founded in the *bushidō* spirit'.[63] Reports of the national tournament tended to ignore that it was a game played by middle school students, and instead invoked *bushidō* and samurai imagery in their portrayals of the matches as battles between medieval warriors. The *bushidō* spirit was also integrated into the game itself through the introduction of uniquely

[59] Maguire, Joseph and Masayoshi Nakayama (eds.) (2006), *Japan, Sport, and Society: Tradition and Change in a Globalizing World* (London: Routledge), p. 18.
[60] Ariyama Teruo (1997), *Kōshien yakyū to Nihonjin: media no tsukutta ibento* (Tokyo: Yoshikawa kobunkan), p. 46.
[61] Guttman, Allen and Lee Thompson (2001), *Japanese Sports, A History* (Honolulu: University of Hawai'i Press), p. 116.
[62] Ariyama Teruo, *Kōshien yakyū to Nihonjin: media no tsukutta ibento*, p. 47–67.
[63] Ariyama Teruo, p. 86.

'Japanese' greeting rituals, while emphasis was placed on players sacrificing themselves for the team and the importance of character-building rather than victory.[64] In spite of a widespread belief that baseball's resonance with traditional values led to its popularity, the documentary evidence strongly indicates that baseball's success in Japan was founded primarily on its 'modern' and 'international' character, with 'traditional' virtues such as *bushidō* applied retroactively.[65] In *Athletic Competitions and National Characters* (1923), educator Shimoda Jirō (1872–1938) argued that as the Japanese had learned baseball from the United States, the fans behaved in a similarly excited and loud manner as American fans. Had they adopted their sporting culture from the more reserved English, on the other hand, Japanese fans would certainly behave in a more subdued manner. According to Shimoda, the stratified character of Japan's feudal society meant that its sports were more individual, but adopting Western team sports was a natural part of the modernization process that made communal activity more important.[66]

The role of the media in the popularization of 'traditional' sports in Taishō was similarly important. The establishment of the professional sumo structure as it exists today is largely a product of this period, evolving from mutual efforts by print media and promoters of the sport.[67] The role of the Great Japan Martial Virtue Society and other organizations was considerable and they framed their arguments in nationalistic terms. As Irie Katsumi has pointed out, even during the more liberal years of Taishō, sports continued to be bastions of nationalistic and even chauvinistic thought.[68] As the self-appointed guardians of ostensibly ancient Japanese traditions, martial arts organizations were often founded by nationalistic groups or maintained close ties with them.[69] *Bushidō* provided a useful link between the martial arts and the goals of nationalists, as in the *Bushidō* journal of 1898. This connection was also reflected in Uchida Ryōhei's 1903 book, *Jūdō*, published by the Amur River Society, and included a foreword on the relationship between judo and *bushidō*.[70] Kanō Jigurō, the founder of Kōdōkan judo, contributed to both of these publications and in 1918 co-authored a military physical training textbook that incorporated lessons in *bushidō*. Similar to other military educational materials, this text relied on imperial *bushidō*, strongly emphasizing patriotism and loyalty to the emperor, and frequently referring to National Morality.[71] While Kanō used *bushidō* to his advantage when it could help his promotional activities, he generally tended to stress the 'scientific' basis of judo as a modern sport rather than its more limited nationalistic aspects, as in discussions about having the sport recognized by the International Olympic Committee.

---

[64] Ariyama Teruo, pp. 87–97.
[65] Guttman, Allen and Thompson, Lee, *Japanese Sports, A History*, pp. 89–90.
[66] Shimoda Jirō (1923), *Undō kyōgi to kokuminsei* (Yūbunkan), pp. 210–16.
[67] Thompson, Lee A. (1998), 'The Invention of the *Yokozuna*', in Stephen Vlastos (ed.), *Mirror of Modernity: Invented Traditions in Modern Japan* (Berkeley: University of California Press), pp. 177–78.
[68] Irie Katsumi (1986), *Nihon fashizumu shita no taiiku shisō* (Tokyo: Fumaido shuppan).
[69] Guttman, Allen and Thompson, Lee, *Japanese Sports, A History*, p. 106.
[70] Uchida Ryōhei (1903), *Jūdō* (Kokuryūkai shuppanbu).
[71] Kanō Jiguro and Watari Shōzaburō (1918), *Shinsen shihan shūshin sho 4* (Kinkodō).

The approval of the martial arts for use in the education system by the Ministry of Education in 1911 was a major victory for the martial arts in their struggles with sports of foreign origin. For many nationalists, physical education was fundamentally a form of military drill, and German—after 1913, Swedish—gymnastics were believed to be best-suited to this purpose due also to their 'scientific' pedigree. Promoters of baseball also alluded to its potential benefit for national defence, as it trained the coordinated movements and teamwork required by the modern military. In 1917, the Imperial Diet passed new objectives for the physical education of middle school students, specifically outlining military aims and the inculcation of a martial spirit.[72] This official sanction was reflected in the number of textbooks published for martial arts education, which increased dramatically and remained at a high level until 1945.

The importance of the martial arts for the nation's spiritual health was a persuasive argument, with noted kendo instructor Chiba Chōsaku (1861–1935) discussing 'the nation's vitality and *bushidō*' in a 1916 text promoting his sport.[73] The many texts on martial arts education in late Taishō stressed the connections between the warrior spirit and their sports, especially kendo and judo, although the causal relationship was not always clear. Ōgawa Yoshiyuki, for example, argued that 'Our nation's kendo is the wellspring of the *bushidō* that is the glory of our country', giving swordsmanship primary importance.[74] Similarly, Shimokawa Ushio stated that the practice of kendo has long been a way of encouraging spiritual training and was a core aspect of the great development of *bushidō*.[75] Continuities between ancient practices and modern sports were created and emphasized, with the notion that kendo had been a professional sport in the Edo period becoming widespread. As Shimoda Jirō argued, kendo and judo had declined after the sword ban of early Meiji, but were regaining popularity.[76] With regard to judo, educator Shingyōji Ryōsei warned in 1926 that even though Western sports had been introduced, the beautiful and unique practices of Japan's ancient warriors should not be allowed to deteriorate. Shingyōji discussed the importance of self-sacrifice and the other virtues of Japan's ancient and unique *bushidō*, explaining that 'Kendo is the most suitable method for learning this *bushidō*'.[77]

BUSHIDŌ AND TAISHŌ EDUCATION

Sport was not the only area of the education system in which *bushidō* retained a high profile, and it was also disseminated through civilian and military curricula during Taishō. In civilian education, the Ministry of Education was directly or indirectly

---

[72] Guttman, Allen and Thompson, Lee, *Japanese Sports, A History*, p. 153.
[73] Chiba Chōsaku (1916), *Kokumin kendō kyōhan* (Tomida Bun'yōdō), p. 7.
[74] Ōgawa Yoshiyuki (1918), *Kendō taikan: seinen kyōiku* (Bunbukan), p. 5.
[75] Shimokawa Ushio (1925), *Kendō no hattatsu* (Dai Nihon butokukai), p. 270.
[76] Shimoda Jirō, *Undō kyōgi to kokuminsei*, pp. 214–15.
[77] Shingyōji Ryōsei (1926), *Gakkō kagai taiiku yōgi* (Bunkyō shoin), pp. 224, 269.

responsible for the content of primary and middle school textbooks, with the production of the latter undertaken by private publishers working to strict government guidelines. The long periods between curricular revisions meant that, throughout the 1910s and 1920s, textbook content was strongly influenced by the ideals of late Meiji, and Japan's achievements in the Sino-Japanese and Russo-Japanese wars played a prominent role. For example, for thirty years from 1911 onward, the considerable military content in music-related school textbooks was directly related to the Russo-Japanese War.[78] Ienaga Saburō recalled that not only music texts, but materials for the study of history, ethics, language, and many other subjects were filled with tales of the modern wars and designed to inculcate a military spirit.[79] One 1913 middle school language textbook for second-year students included vocabulary sections on the 'establishment of *bushidō*' in order to teach essential Tokugawa names and concepts, such as 'Yamaga Sokō', 'Itō Jinsai', and 'militarism'.[80] The death of General Nogi was another popular theme, although school texts focused on Nogi's loyal *bushidō* spirit rather than his actual suicide.

The greater dominance of patriotic and nationalistic themes in Taishō education relative to Meiji inspired reformist movements seeking to liberalize and internationalize the curriculum. A significant number of educators in organizations such as the International Education Movement were reluctant to implement some of the government-mandated teachings, but were ultimately unable to force any changes.[81] Inoue Tetsujirō's National Morality programme remained a powerful influence in formal education and imperial *bushidō* expanded its significance in the classroom throughout Taishō and beyond. In *Fundamental Problems of History Instruction* (1922), Ōkubo Kaoru cited Inoue in outlining the tasks of elementary history teachers, the most important of which was conveying to the students the meaning and value of Japan's unique national polity.[82] Addressing the new trends towards individualism and personal freedom that had supposedly entered Japan during Meiji, Ōkubo wrote that these values were not necessarily opposed to the nation's *bushidō* character, but had to be treated carefully to ensure that they were in line with Japan's inherent values, especially that of loyalty to the imperial house.[83] In this way, while reinforcing the patriotic aspects of *bushidō*, primary and middle school education in Taishō at least superficially engaged with progressive ideas before dismissing most of them. Stressing continuities with Japan's mythical past on the one hand, public education portrayed *bushidō* as an adaptable ethic that had been strengthened through a modernization process which eliminated class divisions, suicide, and other negative 'feudal' elements. In *Ethics and National*

---

[78] Yamamuro Kentoku, *Gunshin*, p. vii.

[79] Ienaga Saburō, 'The Glorification of War in Japanese Education', *International Security* 18:3 (Winter 1993/94), pp. 118–19.

[80] Kokugo Kenkyūkai (ed.) (1913), *Chūgaku kokubun kyōkasho sankōsho: dai 2 gakunen yō* (Seibidō shoten), pp. 37–38.

[81] For an overview of the International Education Movement, see Lincicome, Mark E., 'Nationalism, Imperialism, and the International Education Movement in Early Twentieth-Century Japan', *The Journal of Asian Studies* 58:2 (May, 1999), pp. 338–60.

[82] Ōkubo Kaoru (1922), *Kokushi kyōju no konpon mondai* (Tōkyō: Hōbunkan), pp. 58–60.

[83] Ōkubo Kaoru, pp. 90–115.

Morality (1916), for example, Fukasaku Yasubumi discussed new and old forms of *bushidō*, outlining the ways in which the new ethic had to incorporate modern ideas such as humanism and human rights, while not losing its ancient spirit of self-sacrifice, loyalty, and actionism.[84]

Bushidō was present in almost all fields of civilian education in Taishō, but the centrality of its role should not be overestimated. In contrast to its role in popular culture in late Meiji, or in the military curriculum, *bushidō* was rarely a central theme outside National Morality-based ethics education. Within this field, *bushidō* played a central role and was a subject of examination for instructors at the middle, higher and normal schools.[85] *Bushidō* functioned primarily as a tool for teaching other subjects, such as music, history, and the duties of imperial subjects. In this sense, the most enduring effect of *bushidō* in civilian education before 1925 was to familiarize new generations with the concept and to maintain its profile even when it faded from popular discourse.

These dynamics established a receptiveness to *bushidō* that aided its rapid spread following the introduction of military officers into schools in 1925. It also conditioned students to *bushidō* when they encountered it in other contexts, such as the materials used by the Imperial Military Reserve Association and various popular education initiatives. The methods in which educational materials were used are not always precisely understood, but their volume and number of reprints indicate that they were widely distributed to students.[86] This applies especially to texts composed by military figures and published by private publishers as study guides for entrance exams to military academies. These exam aids would have had a significant and concentrated readership, and the prominent role of *bushidō* in these materials strongly indicates that it was a subject of examination.[87]

During most of Taishō, the military faced a greater threat from domestic critics than from foreign armies, and the successful action against German possessions in China reduced pressure for institutional reform. Changes in the military during the 1910s were essentially reductions and doctrine was not modified. It was not until well after the First World War that information from this conflict began to have a major impact on military policy. Japanese military leaders continued to be under great financial pressure, although many realized that the militaries of the West had made great technological progress between 1914 and 1918. The politically embattled military forces of the 1910s were preoccupied with shrinking budgets and fiscal retrenchment, while the troops were still short of average educational standards that would make comprehensive spiritual education beyond the officer class seem an effective investment of resources.

---

[84] Fukasaku Yasubumi (1916), *Rinri to kokumin dōtoku* (Kōdōkan), pp. 623–40.

[85] Meiji kyōikusha (ed.) (1916), *Bunken juken yō kokumin dōtoku yōryō* (Meiji kyōikusha), pp. 231–78.

[86] Hirota Teruyuki (1997), *Rikugun shōkō no kyōiku shakaishi: risshin shusse to tennōsei* (Tokyo: Seori shobō), p. 181.

[87] For example, see author and playwright Wakatsuki Shiran's (1879–1962) 1920 *Complete Training Materials*, focusing on the 'war god' Lieutenant Hirose and prefaced by an introduction by Tanaka Giichi himself. The subject of the first chapter is the 'establishment of *bushidō*—the flower of the Japanese spirit'. Wakatsuki Shiran (1920), *Shūgyō sōsho 2* (Shingetsu Sha).

The end of the First World War and bold pronouncements at Versailles convinced many that war would become obsolete, and concern regarding these ideas prompted the army to implement a questionnaire to this effect in the course of the 1923 conscription survey.[88] Russia and China were not deemed immediate threats due to their own internal turmoil, making it difficult for the army to justify postponing further cuts, while the Washington Naval Treaty limited potential growth in that department.[89] Arms reductions in 1923–24 cut the army by almost 60,000 men and, minor technological advances relating to machine guns, artillery units, and aircraft notwithstanding, the relief efforts for the Kantō Earthquake swallowed funds that could have enabled significant constructive reforms. These financial constraints forced considerable changes in military policy regarding spiritual education, as this was seen as a most cost-effective method of compensating for technological deficiencies and boosting morale among troops suffering from extremely low wages and hostility from the civilian population.

Military leaders were also concerned by shifts in Japan's demographics that were exacerbated by the spread of socialism and other dangerous thought. While over three-quarters of conscripts in 1888 had agricultural backgrounds—and were therefore considered most suitable for service due to their supposed physical strength and lack of contamination by urban vices—by 1920 that figure had declined to roughly half of recruits.[90] In addition, the expansion of the public education system and the increasingly high standards the army set for recruits made these cohorts more receptive to spiritual education programmes than previous generations. The complexity of modern warfare required a certain degree of literacy and numeracy, and the ideal Taishō recruit had a primary education. These recruits were assumed to have necessary basic skills, but not to have been exposed to the problematic liberal thought encountered by those with higher levels of education.[91]

By the early 1920s, recruits were familiar with concepts such as *bushidō, kokutai,* and other nationalistic ideals that had been introduced into the education system on a large scale in Taishō. In this sense, the content of spiritual education materials did not change significantly over the period, and the emphasis on 'attack spirit', loyalty to the emperor, and the spiritual heritage of the samurai remained largely constant, as outlined in texts such as the 1916 *Linking Military Spiritual Education and the Attack Spirit.*[92] Throughout Taishō, the more general educational materials used for troops and students in the Imperial Military Reserve Association often relied on popular stories to convey ideological concepts, with *bushidō* and the Akō Incident playing

[88] Yoshida Yutaka, *Nihon no guntai: heishi tachi no kindai shi,* p. 136.
[89] Humphreys, Leonard A., *The Way of the Heavenly Sword: The Japanese Army in the 1920s,* pp. 45–46.
[90] Yoshida Yutaka, *Nihon no guntai: heishi tachi no kindai shi,* pp. 159–60.
[91] Yoshida Yutaka, p. 118.
[92] Gunju Shōkai (ed.) (1916), *Gunjin seishin kyōiku to kōgeki seishin to no rensa* (Tokyo: Tōkyō Gunju shōkai).

central roles.[93] The Russo-Japanese War also remained an important source of material, and concepts such as 'human bullets' continued to be described as the 'true spirit of Japan's *bushidō*' in educational texts even after the First World War had discredited the idea of human wave attacks in Europe.[94]

Materials for officer education in early Taishō were similar to those from late Meiji, and addressed many of the same themes. In a 1915 text for students studying for the Army War College entrance exams, Saitō Ryū (1879–1953) outlined the principles of National Morality, and especially the relationship of *bushidō* and the Yamato spirit. According to Saitō, *bushidō* was the Yamato spirit as manifested in ancient warriors and should be upheld by modern soldiers as their spiritual heirs.[95] In late Taishō, materials used for elite officer education became more nuanced, and engaged more directly with broader intellectual and social currents such as democracy and individualism as these became more of a concern for the army leadership. These prominent issues could not simply be ignored and the use of the army against labour and socialist movements exposed soldiers to 'dangerous' thought while carrying out their duties. Although treatments differed in some ways, elite education in the military focused on the same themes as that for reservists and regular troops. The emperor and imperial family were strongly emphasized throughout the education system, and Yoshida Yutaka contends that there was no fundamental change in the imperial ideology during Taishō.[96] One significant factor that set students in the elite academies apart in this regard was their identification with the imperial family, who, for elite officers, were not just an abstract and distant focal point of loyalty, but classmates and regular attendees at graduation ceremonies and other events.[97]

Hirota Teruyuki portrays pre-war officer education as a balance between the emperor system ideology and the striving for personal success, and questions the effectiveness of spiritual education in general. Based on his analysis of diaries of student cadets in late Taishō, Hirota argues that the officers came to identify more closely with the imperial family and nation, but that their initial priorities of personal success remained largely unchanged. Identification with the greater good was significant, but was most pronounced when it simultaneously furthered personal goals. As the many appeals to new methods of spiritual education indicate, there was considerable concern that indoctrination was not entirely successful, and leading officers admitted as much. As Hirota puts it, it was possible to tell all recruits what to think, but impossible to make them actually think it.[98] Shortcomings in the military education programme became apparent in the young officers' movements of the 1930s, which, while using the same emperor-, nation-, and *bushidō*-focused terminology found in spiritual education materials, were motivated by an entirely

---

[93] For example: Nagahori Hitoshi (1919), *Seishin kyōiku teikoku gunjin sōsho dai-ippen: Akō gishi* (Tokyo: Tsūzoku gunji kyōiku kai); Chapter One on '*Bushidō* and Soldiers' in Tsūzoku Kyōiku Kenkyūkai (ed.) (1912), *Tsūzoku kyōiku kokumin jōshiki kōwa* (Meiseikan shobō).

[94] Miyaoka Naoki (1922), *Kimi ni sasagete* (Gunji Kyōikukai).

[95] Saitō Ryū, *Seinen shōkō no shūyō*, pp. 100–02.

[96] Yoshida Yutaka, *Nihon no guntai: heishi tachi no kindai shi*, p. 169.

[97] Hirota Teruyuki, *Rikugun shōkō no kyōiku shakaishi: risshin shusse to tennōsei*, pp. 228–38.

[98] Hirota Teruyuki, pp. 253–301.

different and nonconformist ideology. In this sense, the cumulative exposure to certain concepts in Taishō education would have a profound effect throughout early Shōwa, but not always the ones intended by the formulators of educational policy.

CONSIDERING THE END OF THE MEIJI *BUSHIDŌ* BOOM

In the wake of Nogi Maresuke and Shizuko's deaths, the whole nation was again made aware of *bushidō*, and many were shocked and disturbed by what was generally seen as a noble, yet tragic and anachronistic act. The identification of General Nogi with *bushidō* and the simultaneous identification of Nogi with Meiji also linked *bushidō* to the Meiji past. After the initial furor over Nogi's death had passed, people looked forward and moved away from Meiji, setting aside *bushidō* and other trappings of the earlier period. On the other hand, in spite of the negative impact that Nogi's death had on the popularity of *bushidō* in the short-to-medium term, by taking certain samurai-inspired ideals to their final conclusion, Nogi further contributed to the perceived historical legitimacy of *bushidō* in the long term.

Between 1895 and 1912, *bushidō* developed from a little-known concept to a widely accepted ideology used to define Japan's national character, both at home and abroad, a transformation facilitated by a reciprocally strengthening combination of institutional support and popular interest. During the Taishō period, the balance of these two factors shifted and *bushidō* suffered a significant decline in many public spheres. The close association between *bushidō* and the military that had been established around the time of the Russo-Japanese War proved problematic between 1913 and 1925, when the popularity of the military declined to its lowest levels before 1945. As a result, *bushidō* was primarily neglected or criticized during this period, especially by intellectuals, although some took advantage of its inherent flexibility and reinterpreted *bushidō* in line with popular democratic and internationalist trends. This was accomplished by selecting other historical sources or events that supported the ideal of a democratic tradition among the samurai, or by emphasizing the capacity for change that *bushidō* had supposedly demonstrated over the past centuries. Mainstream popular culture did not revisit the subject on a large scale until the late 1920s, but imperial *bushidō* was established as a significant theme in civilian and military education during the same period. The changes in *bushidō* discourse during most of Taishō were due to a complex interplay of factors, including shifts in thought concerning nationalism, Japan's status in the world, the person of the emperor, and the role of the military in society.

At the same time, institutional promotion of *bushidō* maintained an awareness of the concept and gave it greater legitimacy through collective exposure, creating the conditions for its later resurgence in early Shōwa. This institutional influence was reflected in the matter-of-fact nature of much of Taishō *bushidō* discourse, as the ideology no longer required dedicated propagandists to promote its legitimacy, either in Japan or abroad. It remained prominent in nationalistically evocative fields such as sport, which became increasingly popular. Both *bushidō* and sport served as vehicles for bringing Japan's regions into the national whole, especially after the establishment of the school baseball championships. Regional teams competed on the basis of local strengths, but the greatest distinction was between Japanese *bushidō* baseball and its American counterpart. Pride in regional and national sporting accomplishments helped nurture *bushidō* through a difficult period in its history, ensuring its relevance in the popular mind.

The acceptance of *bushidō* at the highest levels in mid-Taishō can be seen in statements such as the remarks by Foreign Minister Uchida Yasuya (Kōsai, 1865–1936) in the debates over the founding of the League of Nations in late 1918: 'The "noblesse oblige" of the West or the "bushido" of the East must permeate and guide the action of any such league. Distrust and suspicion must be left outside its door'.[99]

---

[99] Burkman, Thomas W. (2008), *Japan and the League of Nations: Empire and World Order, 1914–1938* (University of Hawaii Press), p. 40.

6

The Shōwa *Bushidō* Resurgence

THE *BUSHIDŌ* REVIVAL OF EARLY SHŌWA

From the late 1920s, *bushidō* began to revive in public discourse through a concert of social, economic, and geopolitical factors that influenced the character of Japanese nationalism. Nationalistic feeling increased along with Japanese activities in China and diplomatic conflicts with Western nations, while the role and popular perceptions of the military changed considerably. These developments were influenced by *bushidō* and also contributed to *bushidō's* evolution. Dissatisfaction over the limitations imposed on Japan by the Washington Naval Treaty of 1922 and the subsequent dissolution of the Anglo-Japanese Alliance reflected the growing clash of interests between Japan and the Western powers. The restrictions placed on Japanese immigration by the US Immigration Act of 1924 caused outrage in Japan, and even the usually pro-American Nitobe Inazō vowed to not set foot in the US until it was repealed. *Bushidō* also received a boost as popular opinion of the military improved amidst the deteriorating international situation, while the army's handling of the aftermath of the Great Kantō Earthquake in 1923 drew praise from the populace.[1]

Japan's growing international isolation fanned nationalistic sentiments, further increasing receptiveness to *bushidō*. Japanese activities in China, beginning with the two Shandong Expeditions of 1927 and 1928, the assassination of the warlord Zhang Zuolin in the latter year, and the Manchurian Incident of 1931 all contributed to this process. Heavy-handed approaches to China by Japan, Britain, and the United States stirred anti-imperialist activities there from 1925 onwards, but after the Western powers recognized the Chinese Nationalist government in 1928–29, Japan became the sole focus of Chinese resentment. Tensions with the West were further exacerbated by the London Naval Conference of 1930, which left Japan seriously disadvantaged relative to the US and UK.[2]

Global economic, cultural, and technological trends also heavily influenced Japanese society in early Shōwa, as the stock market crash of 1929 resulted in a worldwide economic depression. The subsequent economic turmoil and hardship in Japan increased resentment against capitalists and democratic institutions—especially the parties—that seemed to be responsible for the crisis, and

---

[1] Humphreys, Leonard A. (1995), *The Way of the Heavenly Sword: The Japanese Army in the 1920s* (Stanford: Stanford University Press), pp. 52–53, 88.

[2] Minami Hiroshi (1987), *Shōwa bunka 1925–1945* (Tokyo: Keisō shobō), pp. 9–23.

this sentiment increased when many banks made staggering profits by playing the markets as the population suffered. Foreign influences and institutions were widely blamed, adding to nationalistic feelings. When Japan's economy improved in the early 1930s, aided by the invasion of Manchuria and new industrial controls supported by military leaders, popular support for the armed forces increased further. Meanwhile, technological innovations such as radio spread throughout the country, while increased literacy rates helped the publishing industry reach an unprecedented percentage of the population. The establishment of new media and forms of distribution more quickly and thoroughly disseminated national ideals and Western-influenced popular culture. The Kōdansha publishing house was one of the greatest drivers and beneficiaries of these trends, with its flagship magazine *Kingu* (*King*) becoming arguably the most influential periodical of its day. As Satō Takumi points out, the importance of Kōdansha in early Shōwa (*c.*1926–37) was so great that sholars have labelled the pre-war period as one of 'Kōdansha culture'.[3] Satō compares Kōdansha's role in forming Japanese culture and ideology with Nazi *Gleichschaltung*, and examines *Kingu* as a vehicle for disseminating fascist ideology in the 1930s.[4]

As nationalistic sentiment and disenchantment with certain aspects of modernity grew, samurai epics became increasingly popular, acting as carriers of a broader *bushidō*. On the kabuki stage, *A Treasury of Loyal Retainers* alone was staged well over one hundred times between 1931 and 1945, typically emphasizing 'samurai' virtues such as loyalty and self-sacrifice.[5] Popular novels such as Yoshikawa Eiji's (1892–1962) *Miyamoto Musashi*, serialized in the *Asahi shinbun* between 1935 and 1939, responded to the demand for samurai themes. *Bushidō* again became a popular marketing and promotional device as it had been in late Meiji and was linked to a wide variety of causes. The Sacred Sword Society (Kenseikai), for example, promoted kendo by distributing a collection of essays in 1933 entitled *Essential Ideas of Bushidō* (*Bushidō yōi*).[6] This high-quality production was an eclectic collection of mainly Edo-period texts and also included calligraphy by General Araki Sadao and an article by Nitobe Inazō, some of whose writings that year drew parallels between *bushidō* and emperor-worship.[7]

The reconvergence of popular ideas and military aims in the nationalistic climate of early Shōwa provided the conditions for a *bushidō* resurgence, which was further aided by the presence of a new and stronger emperor who was better suited as the object of *chūkun aikoku* ideology. The institutionalization of imperial *bushidō* that began in late Meiji ensured the survival of the concept through Taishō and provided the conditions for its revival. Whereas the *bushidō* boom of late Meiji

[3] Satō Takumi (2005), *'Kingu' no jidai: kokumin taishū zasshi no kōkyōsei* (Tokyo: Iwanami shoten), p. xi.

[4] Satō Takumi, *'Kingu' no jidai:*, Parts 3 and 5.

[5] Brandon, James R. (2009), *Kabuki's Forgotten War: 1931–1945* (Honolulu: University of Hawaii Press), pp. 3–5.

[6] Kenseikai (ed.) (1933), *Bushidō yōi* (Kenseikai).

[7] Ohnuki-Tierney, Emiko (2002), *Kamikaze, Cherry Blossoms, and Nationalisms: The Militarization of Aesthetics in Japanese History* (Chicago: University of Chicago Press), p. 118.

was driven primarily by popular sentiments and grassroots nationalism with limited formal encouragement from the government, *bushidō* received considerable additional support from official policies in early Shōwa.

INSTITUTIONAL *BUSHIDŌ* IN EARLY SHŌWA

Bushidō remained a part of military and civilian education throughout the Taishō period and was positioned to become a central theme when major changes to the army in the mid-1920s brought spiritual education to the fore. A series of military retrenchments beginning in late Taishō reduced considerably the size of the active forces, and were accompanied by increased investment in technology such as machine guns, artillery, tanks, and aircraft, although the implementation of this technology remained far below European levels. Probably the most influential retrenchment occurred in 1925 under the direction of General Ugaki Kazushige (1868–1956), who realized that Japan's military had to keep pace with the great advances in military technology that Europe had made during the the First World War.[8] Ugaki's efforts were frustrated by reactionary elements in the army, however, as well as by a lack of funds, and instead the military turned increasingly to relatively cost-effective spiritual education programmes along the lines of those initiated by Tanaka Giichi after the Russo-Japanese War. This approach defined imperial army policy through 1945, and officers who expressed the need for improved weaponry rather than spiritual conditioning were harshly rebuked.[9]

In addition to this emphasis on spirit, the military strengthend its ties with local communities through the expansion of the Imperial Military Reserve Association and the establishment of organizations such as the network of Youth Training Centres created in 1926. These centres provided general and military education for youths between sixteen and twenty years of age, and were intended to 'clarify the national idea and the true principles of constitutionalism', while rural military schools worked to inculcate the military spirit to counteract the worldwide spread of 'chaotic ideas' after the First World War.[10] The perceived necessity for increased military influence in civilian life and education was bolstered by the widely held belief that Germany's recent defeat had been caused not by strategic failings, but by a collapse in the fighting spirit of the German people; the so-called *Dolchstoßlegende* often mentioned in connection with Erich Ludendorff (1865–1937).[11] In a 1927 book on military reform, educator Matsushima Kō (Tsuyoshi;

---

[8] Humphreys, Leonard A., *The Way of the Heavenly Sword*, p. 90.

[9] Drea, Edward J. (1998), *In the Service of the Emperor: Essays on the Imperial Japanese Army* (Lincoln: University of Nebraska Press), p. 13.

[10] For more information, see Ishizu Masao, 'Seinen kunrenjo ni kansuru taiiku shiteki kenkyū'; Minami Hiroshi (1988), *Taishō bunka, 1905–1927* (Keisō shobō), p. 378; Hirota Teruyuki (1997), *Rikugun shōkō no kyōiku shakaishi: risshin shusse to tennōsei* (Tokyo: Seori shobō), p. 175.

[11] Humphreys, Leonard A., *The Way of the Heavenly Sword*, p. 80. See also Schivelbusch, Wolfgang (2003), *Die Kultur der Niederlage- Der amerikanische Süden 1856, Frankreich 1871, Deutschland 1918* (Frankfurt: Fischer), pp. 227–49.

1854–1940) warned that the difficult conditions imposed on the military would 'destroy *bushidō*'. According to Matsushima, the lack of public support and poor pay in the military led potential recruits to injure themselves to avoid the draft, while low morale drove soldiers to commit crimes and ruin the image of the imperial military.[12] By the end of the 1920s, these foreign and domestic concerns combined to revive popular interest in *bushidō*. As Sawada Ken observed in a discussion of '*Bushidō* and Popular Education' in 1927, 'when considering Japanese morality, many people think of *bushidō*'.[13]

The process of change in the army continued into early Shōwa, with regulations altered in 1927 to further emphasize spiritual training, while orders by General Araki Sadao in 1928 removed 'negative' terms such as 'surrender', 'retreat', and 'defence' from the *General Principles of Strategic Command*.[14] As early as 1922, decorated army officer Satō Kōjiro wrote that 'The military education of many foreign countries makes much use of battlefield movements, but I could not recognize any sign of extreme efforts to cultivate the soldier's spirit and martial lore to a similar extent that our nation does'.[15] Writing in the official organ of the Imperial Japanese Army officer's association (*Kaikōsha*) in 1927, Infantry Lieutenant Okada Meitarō mentioned his previous writings on the national polity and the nation's unique spirit before turning his attention to the promotion of *bushidō* in military education. According to Okada, the unity of *bun* and *bu* manifested in *bushidō* was the most important concept for the modern age, and must be taught in the military.[16] In 1929, Nitobe Inazō, who still saw himself as the inventor of *bushidō*, wrote with considerable pride that 'Currently, *bushidō* is being commonly taught in schools. In addition, virtually all sections of the military, including the army education and training organizations, can be described as "higher schools of *bushidō*". Irrespective of rank, whenever a group of officers gather, the subject of their conversations is 90 per cent *bushidō*'.[17] Nitobe may have overstated the situation, but it reflected the role of the military in driving the resurgence of *bushidō* in early Shōwa.

As Hirota Teruyuki points out, the Meiji military order of physical training over imperial loyalty had been completely reversed by 1931. The memorization of imperial rescripts by the troops began in early Shōwa, while the army was more regularly referred to as the 'emperor's' army rather than the 'nation's'.[18] James Crowley argues that 'this revitalization of the mystique of *bushidō* tended to downgrade the importance of tanks, planes, means of communication, and a greatly improved industrial capacity'.[19] Spirit was emphasized even in cases where technological superiority was unquestionably of primary importance, especially in naval and aerial warfare. This

---

[12] Matsushima Tsuyoshi (1927), *Heieki kakushinron okudzuke* (Yamato shōten), pp. 70–75.
[13] Sawada Ken (1927), *Gendai Nihonron okudzuke* (Dainihon yūbenkai kōdansha), pp. 106–08.
[14] Humphreys, Leonard A., *The Way of the Heavenly Sword*, p. 106.
[15] Katō Yōko (1996), *Chōheisei to kindai Nihon* (Tokyo: Yoshikawa kōbunkan), p. 5.
[16] Okada Meitarō, 'Bushidō rinri no shiteki kenkyū (1)', *Kaikōsha kiji* 640 (1927), pp. 3–28; Okada Meitarō, 'Bushidō rinri no shiteki kenkyū (2)', *Kaikōsha kiji* 641 (1927), pp. 1–23.
[17] Ōta Yūzō (1986), *Taiheiyō no hashi toshite no Nitobe Inazō* (Tokyo: Misuzu shobō), p. 77.
[18] Hirota Teruyuki, *Rikugun shōkō no kyōiku shakaishi: risshin shusse to tennōsei*, pp. 176–77.
[19] Crowley, James B. (1966), *Japan's Quest for Autonomy: National Security and Foreign Policy 1930–1938* (Princeton, NJ: Princeton University Press), p. 204.

was not a uniquely Japanese phenomenon, however, and romantics in the West also lamented the increased mechanization of warfare. Economist and legal scholar Narasaki Toshio (1891–1972) discussed this trend with regard to the evolution of aerial warfare over the course of the First World War in Europe. In a 1926 article on '*Bushidō* and the Legality and Practice of Aerial Warfare', Narasaki equated *bushidō* with European chivalry and examined the influence of the knightly ideal on the methods of aerial combat that had developed during the war. Narasaki examined a wide variety of reports on the chivalric interactions between airmen on the Western Front, especially early in the war, and how these high ideals declined as the air war lost much of its earlier glamour. Citing a certain Lieutenant W. Noble's statement from 1920, Narasaki wrote: 'There is, unfortunately, no chivalry of the air which forbids the bagging of a single machine by three or four should the fortune of war deliver a "lame duck" into their hands'.[20] Narasaki revealed the problems of integrating an existing chivalric spirit with new technology in the West, but his views had little impact on military education.

One of the most important military education texts of early Shōwa was the 1930 *Moral Training for Soldiers* (*Bujin no tokusō*), a two-volume set designed primarily for officer training, although its frequent reprints and continued availability indicate that it found much wider use. The authors of the *Moral Training for Soldiers* sought to 'relaunch' *bushidō* to combat the recent spread of corrupting thought in the military, and the first volume was devoted entirely to the warrior ethic. The preface by Imperial Japanese Army General Hayashi Nariyuki (1877–1944) lamented the rapid spread of 'Occidental civilization' in society from Meiji onward, which caused people to focus on theorizing rather than practising virtue. The beautiful aspects of the national character were being lost, Hayashi argued, and this deleterious trend was in danger of infiltrating the military. *Moral Training for Soldiers* was intended to counteract these trends and to restore the health of the 'emperor's army' by introducing examples of great soldiers who had gone before and provided invaluable guidance with their blood.[21]

The stated task of *Moral Training for Soldiers* was to enable student officers to realize the continuation of the ancient imperial warrior spirit in their future roles as leaders of the army. The first volume focused on the history and characteristics of *bushidō*, illustrating these with examples from the ancient and recent past. As *Moral Training for Soldiers* was intended for officer education—especially the elite who would fill key positions in Central Command—it did not merely prescribe passages for memorization, but took an unusually nuanced view for an official text. It introduced broad characteristics of *bushidō*, followed by specific examples for thought and discussion. The authors explicitly stated in the guidelines to the text that they did not necessarily advocate the worship of all characteristics of the protagonists in the provided examples. These materials were intended for reference and further research, and some of the examples were certainly not suitable for all

---

[20] Narasaki Toshio, 'Kūsen naishi kūsen hōki to bushidō', *Hōgaku shinpō*, 36:9 (1926), pp. 58–75.
[21] Hayashi Nariyuki (1930), 'Jo', in Kyōiku sōkan bu (ed.), *Bujin no tokusō* (Tokyo: Kaikōsha), p. 1–3.

situations.[22] This approach differed from most spiritual education materials for regular troops, which did not typically encourage discussion. *Moral Training for Soldiers* reflected the relatively high educational level of its intended audience, as well as a perceived necessity to engage with *bushidō* on a more sophisticated level in 1930, by which time the subject had been invoked in many different contexts.

The history of *bushidō* outlined in *Moral Training for Soldiers* was similarly nuanced and focused on the examination of selected source materials. *Bushidō* was divided into two broad types: a practical *bushidō* that was lived by Japan's warriors from ancient times, and a theoretical *bushidō* codified by Confucian scholars in the Tokugawa period. The former was considered far more significant due to its basis in practice rather than theory and was seen as Japan's true spirit. As such, the roots of *bushidō* were as ancient as the very founding of the country, and the eighth-century *Man'yōshū* poetry anthology supposedly revealed a number of original *bushidō* virtues from the time before the arrival of corrupting foreign thought. In the peaceful Heian period (794–1185), Japan's national spirit atrophied and became weak and effeminate, and *bushidō* suffered a decline. It was only at the end of the period that the appearance of great warriors in the northeast led to a revival of *bushidō*, and its practical manifestation became the dominant ethic of the Kamakura period (1185–1333). In the later turmoil of Sengoku, culture was destroyed and only *bushidō* remained strong as other types of moral thought were discarded. The wars aided the development of *bushidō* by demonstrating its necessity and resulted in the publication of many warrior house codes containing both practical and moral advice, including the important *bushidō* virtues of unified loyalty and filial piety, politeness, bravery, and austerity. These virtues also made up four of the five major section headings in *Moral Training for Soldiers*, reflecting the symbolic importance of Sengoku to modern military educators.

The 'warfare that should be seen as the mother of *bushidō*' gave way to peace in the Tokugawa period, and *bushidō* might also have disappeared if not for the establishment of the warrior class atop society. The political and social order naturally deepened the importance of *bushidō*, and Tokugawa *bushidō* became complete through the contributions of scholars, the most important of whom was Yamaga Sokō. In addition to strategists such as Yamaga, martial arts practitioners, National Learning scholars, and members of the Mito school all contributed to Tokugawa *bushidō*, which was finally brought together and completed by Yoshida Shōin. *Moral Training for Soldiers* highlighted Yoshida's emphasis on the unity of imperial loyalty and filial piety as the ancient and unique Japanese way, which 'could certainly not be observed in other countries'.

After the Meiji Restoration, the *bushi* class was eliminated as the 'feudal system' collapsed, but the Conscription Ordinance soon transformed all Japanese into soldiers. According to *Moral Training for Soldiers*, these troops then internalized the directives of the Imperial Rescript for Soldiers and Sailors, and took these ideals back to the villages every year. In this way, 'the previous *bushidō*, i.e. the soldier's spirit, became entirely like National Morality'. The first two decades of Meiji were

---

[22] Kyōiku sōkan bu (ed.) (1930), 'Shogen', *Bujin no tokusō* (Tokyo: Kaikōsha), p. 2.

also marked by an influx of Western ideas, which were countered by less prominent movements towards nationalistic thought. After the succession of victories
in the Sino-Japanese War, however, the world noticed Japan with great surprise
and began to investigate its history and culture. Foreigners identified *bushidō* as
the reason for Japan's success and many Japanese also began to consider it for the
first time. Nitobe Inazō's work introduced the concept to the world, and this was
followed by Inoue Tetsujirō's discussions of the subject. *Moral Training for Soldiers*
described the Russo-Japanese War as the greatest stimulant of *bushidō*-related
activity, resulting in an explosion of *bushidō*-based stories, picture books, novels,
and performances that continued on into the present with no signs of abating.
A four-page bibliography of modern works on *bushidō* reflected this view, and
listed only texts published in the twentieth century.[23] *Moral Training for Soldiers*
acknowledged the role of the West in the development of modern *bushidō* in the
case of Nitobe, but did not mention any texts from the 1880s or 1890s, which
were the most directly influenced by foreign ideas and an awareness of Japan's
position in the world. Three decades into the twentieth century, *Moral Training for
Soldiers* portrayed Nitobe as the initiator of modern *bushidō* discourse and this idea
remains most influential.

Relying on 'the principles of the imperial rescripts and elementary education
texts', *Moral Training for Soldiers* used the writings and theories of previous ages
as a basis for researching the characteristic values of *bushidō*. Fifteen characteristic virtues were classified into five broad categories: loyalty, politeness, bravery,
faithfulness, and austerity.[24] The first and most important category included the
virtues of imperial loyalty and patriotism, as well as filial piety, and was illustrated by materials including the farewell letters of forty-five submariners whose
vessel sunk off Sasebo in 1924. Each section of the text was prefaced by a brief
overview of the characteristic virtue in question, followed by a series of historical examples taken from the late Heian period to the present. The materials
were selected to convey the importance of practice over theory in *bushidō*, and
only a handful were taken from the Kamakura and Tokugawa periods, while the
Sengoku period was represented by almost fifty tales of famous warlords. The
period after 1868 was by far the most important in this context, with well over
one hundred examples of *bushidō* in practice in modern Japan. These were taken
especially from the conflicts with Russia and China, but also included the First
World War, smaller expeditions, and incidents outside combat operations. The
illustrative examples were as recent as possible, helping officers studying *Moral
Training for Soldiers* to identify with them. Sections were arranged chronologi-
cally, so the reader first encountered a famous historical figure before reading
about his modern spiritual heirs, who were given considerably more coverage. In
this way, students would be able to relate to the examples, and ideally also see the
actions of ordinary soldiers valued as highly as those of great warlords, inspiring
them to similar deeds.

---

[23] Kyōiku sōkan bu (ed.) (1930), *Bujin no tokusō* (Tokyo: Kaikōsha), pp. 1–30.
[24] *Chūsetsu, reigi, buyū, shingi, shisso.*

BUSHIDŌ AND THE BLURRING OF CIVILIAN AND MILITARY LIFE

The institutional promotion of *bushidō* in Taishō and early Shōwa had a strong influence on the broader development of the concept, especially after the introduction of military officers into public schools. The involvement of civilian academics in military education originated in Meiji, as did the use of military themes and examples in civilian curricula. Inoue Tetsujirō's activities were an early example of this interaction, but the early Shōwa period saw an unprecedented unification of civilian and military education, as key concepts were implemented in both spheres. The ideals of National Morality provided the backbone for military ethics education, while military materials were edited and published for civilian use. Interchanges between the two became increasingly frequent and complex as the government aspired to the total militarization of society; historian Ienaga Saburō later attested to the militaristic content of pre-war school textbooks, especially after 1932. According to Ienaga, educational materials for ethics and history in the 1920s drew heavily on the Sino-Japanese and Russo-Japanese wars, and in the 1930s turned to justifying the expanding war in China.[25]

Bushidō was especially important as a bridge linking military and civilian discourses. Two writers whose activities reflected this interaction were Imperial Japanese Navy Captain Hirose Yutaka (1882–1960) and Tokyo Imperial University professor Hiraizumi Kiyoshi (1895–1984), whose influence went far beyond their respective fields. Hirose lectured at naval acadamies and officer training institutes before reaching national prominence by producing materials for the army and the general public. Published through the *Bushidō* Research Society, Hirose's works went through dozens of printings between the late 1920s and 1945, becoming an integral part of the military's efforts to blur the lines between it and civilian society. In the preface to Hirose's 1928 *On Soldier Morality* (*Gunjin dōtoku ron*), the head of the Imperial Japanese Naval Academy, Tosu Tamaki (1877–1949), credited 'soldier morality' with Japan's victories in the Sino-Japanese and Russo-Japanese wars. According to Tosu, this soldier morality formed the basis for the nation's morality, demonstrating the importance of the military in everyday life. Tosu criticized the evils of material civilization, as well as the misconception that soldiers had become mere technicians with little need for spiritual strength, an idea that he felt had spread in Japan since the First World War.[26]

Hirose's ambitious goals were evident in the 1934 eleventh edition of his *Small Training for Soldiers* (*Gunjin shōkun*). In this text, originally published in 1927, Hirose discussed the wide readership of his work and thanked high-ranking officers of both services for their support. According to Hirose, the 'crisis of the empire' had made it necessary for him to revise the text, primarily to include the works

---

[25] Ienaga Saburō, 'The Glorification of War in Japanese Education', *International Security* 18:3 (Winter 1993/94), pp. 118–22.

[26] Tosu Tamaki (1928), 'Jo', in Hirose Yutaka, *Gunjin dōtoku ron* (Tokyo: Bushidō kenkyūkai).

of Yoshida Shōin, 'the leading figure of modern *bushidō*'.[27] The encroachment of dangerous thought from the West since Meiji had contributed to a misunderstanding of the nature of warfare and the role of the military. Loosely citing the Imperial Rescript for Soldiers and Sailors, Hirose argued that although the original meaning of martiality was to pacify the country with force, the important aspects of military expeditions and punitive missions were often neglected. These were especially significant in the current age of domestic peace, when the role of the military was to stop heinous disturbances in other countries in a manner similar to an international police force. This, Hirose wrote, was the meaning of warfare in Japan from ancient times.

Hirose explained that warfare had recently been portrayed as the method by which humanity advanced and evolved in the world of fierce and merciless competition. These theories had become widespread in Japan since their importation from the West in Meiji, leading to the mistaken belief that warfare was a terrible thing and inspiring pacifists to criticize it. In fact, Hirose argued, Japan was the only 'lord's country' and the only '*bushidō* country' in the world, and therefore uniquely understood the meaning of sacred military expeditions. As shown in the Sino-Japanese and Russo-Japanese wars, Hirose wrote, it was most difficult for evil to defeat justice, and Japan's mission in the world was to deeply consider the global meaning of the use of force for the benefit of humanity. While the nations of the West considered the role of the state to be to increase the wealth of the nation and people, this was a hedonistic approach that was against the past and future of humanity. Instead, the goal of the state was to ensure benevolence and righteousness, as Mencius had realized. Japan's national mission was founded on the unique qualities of its people, Hirose argued, and this 'heavenly task' was to spread righteousness in the world. In the fierce international environment, this could only be accomplished with sufficient military strength founded on 'Japan's traditional life force, the Yamato spirit, also known as *bushidō*'.[28]

Hirose's imperial *bushidō* strongly emphasized imperial loyalty and patriotism, and he was one of the greatest Shōwa exponents of Inoue Tetsujirō's model of seeking *bushidō* in the writings of Yoshida Shōin. Following the *Small Training for Soldiers*, Hirose went on to become one of the most prolific writers on Yoshida, and also edited an edition of his complete works.[29] While Inoue's *bushidō* theories inspired Hirose to study Yoshida, he soon departed from his mentor's views. Inoue's interest in Yoshida was primarily as a teacher and conduit of Yamaga Sokō's samurai ethics, but Hirose saw Yoshida's role as more significant. According to Hirose, Yamaga's *bushidō* had grown out of Confucian thought and typically struck twentieth-century readers as very Chinese. This was an inevitable result of Yamaga's time, Hirose wrote, and while Yamaga had striven to escape from Chinese thought

[27] Hirose Yutaka (1927), *Gunjin shōkun* (Tokyo: Bushidō kenkyūkai), p. 1.

[28] Hirose Yutaka, *Gunjin shōkun*, pp. 13–27.

[29] Hirose's writings on Yoshida include: Hirose Yutaka, *Gunjin shōkun*, p. 144; Yoshida Shōin, Hirose Yutaka (ed.) (1940), *Yoshida Shōin zenshū* (Tokyo: Iwanami shoten); Hirose Yutaka (ed.) (1943), *Kō-Mō yowa* (Tokyo: Iwanami shoten).

and understand Japan's original spirit and national polity, he was ultimately unable to overcome the age in which he lived. This task was left to Yoshida, whose *bushidō* theories relied most heavily on Yamaga's work, but Yoshida's theories excelled these in scholarship and, more importantly, in practice. Hirose saw this departure in Yoshida's use of the Japanese term '*bushidō*', while Yamaga had persisted with the Chinese concept of *shidō*.

For Hirose, 'the core spirit of *bushidō* must truly be the idea of revering emperor', which had existed in Japan since the founding of the nation. From the Kamakura period onward, however, this spirit was condensed into a more limited type of vertical relationship between lords and vassals, and survived in this reduced form until the end of the Tokugawa period, when Yoshida was able to grasp and teach the 'Way of the Japanese people'. The unity of loyalty and filial piety had also been understood by ancient Chinese sages, Hirose wrote, but was only ever realized in Japan. Yoshida himself lamented having to use Chinese terminology to express the Japanese way of reverence for the imperial country, and Hirose saw this as the one flaw in his work. In order to understand the pure Japanese spirit of *bushidō*, Hirose argued, it was necessary to return to the ancient past before the advent of Chinese influences.[30]

Historian Hiraizumi Kiyoshi took a similar approach to Yoshida and Japan's pre-history in his own imperial *bushidō* teachings, which rivalled Hirose's impact across civilian and military education. Hiraizumi's father was the head priest at Hakusan Shrine in Fukui Prefecture, an especially significant place in the context of early Shōwa imperial *bushidō*. The shrine was closely tied to Japan's mythical pre-history through its patron deity Izanami no Mikoto, who was believed to have created the Japanese islands together with her husband Izanagi, and, perhaps more importantly, it was also the final resting place of the legendary fourteenth-century warrior and imperial loyalist Kusunoki Masashige. Hiraizumi's later historical research at Tokyo Imperial University focused on Shinto shrines in the medieval period, and his *bushidō* theories also incorporated elements from the imperial founding myths.[31] As assistant professor from 1926 and full professor after 1935, Hiraizumi was a dominant presence in the history department until the end of war, with even his senior colleagues hesitant to express opinions that might challenge his nationalistic views.[32] His ideas became even more radical during a trip to Europe and the United States, when Hiraizumi was especially impressed by the attempts of German historians to spiritually strengthen the youth through nationalistic

---

[30] Hirose Yutaka (1941), 'Yoshida Shōin no bushidō', in Bushidō gakkai (eds.), *Bushidō shinzui* (Tokyo: Teikoku shoseki kyōkai), pp. 204–24. Texts on Yoshida and Yamaga published by Hirose in the wartime period of the early 1940s include: Hirose Yutaka (ed.), *Kō-Mō yowa* (Tokyo: Iwanami Shoten, 1943); Hirose Yutaka (ed.), *Yamaga Sokō heigaku zenshū* (Tokyo: Kyōzaisha, 1943); Hirose Yutaka (ed.), *Yamaga Sokō zenshū* (Tokyo: Iwanami shoten, 1942).

[31] Brownlee, John S. (1997), *Japanese Historians and the National Myths, 1600–1945* (Vancouver: UBC Press), p. 168.

[32] A number of renowned scholars recalled Hiraizumi's tenure in the Department of History with dread, including Ienaga Saburō and Inoue Mitsusada: Brownlee, John S., *Japanese Historians*, pp. 173–75.

education.[33] Commenting on the German model following his return to Japan, Hiraizumi noted the revival of nationalistic education in Germany through the use of Gottlieb Fichte (1762–1814), whose *Reden an die deutsche Nation* (1807–1808) provided inspiration for generations of German nationalists.[34] Hiraizumi further recalled having been encouraged by an elderly German woman, who lamented the relatively young Germany's still 'unrefined' spirit, as compared to Japan's exalted virtue rooted in its ancient history.[35]

Thus inspired, Hiraizumi set about the task of promoting the national spirit in the early 1930s, publishing a number of educational texts and holding lectures at civilian and military institutions, including museums, police academies, and universities.[36] In Hiraizumi's new role as a public promotor of nationalistic ideology, *bushidō* became one of his most important tools for combating societal evils such as individualism, materialism, freedom, and socialism. One of his most influential texts was *The Revival of Bushidō* (*Bushidō no fukkatsu*), a collection of essays published in December 1933 that went through six printings in as many months. Hiraizumi opened this work with a warning of the crisis that had overcome Japan and Asia, as Western dominance and materialism had become so complete that Asia had ceased to exist. Japanese scholars had a long-standing tendency to worship foreign ideas, he wrote, and this was especially problematic in the case of Western materialistic thought, which was incompatible with Japan's fundamentally spiritual nature. A similar process had occurred throughout Asia, Hiraizumi contended, and Japan was the only hope not only for itself, but for the rest of the continent. According to Hiraizumi, Asia could only recover by rediscovering its Asianness, and Japan first had to become 'Japanese' again in order to lead Asia down this difficult path.[37]

Hiraizumi saw the recovery of the Japanese spirit as essential to the nation's revival, and closely linked this to the recovery of *bushidō*. *Bushidō* was not entirely the same as the Japanese spirit, Hiraizumi wrote, but was the most superior distillation of the finest aspects of the latter. In order to revive the Japanese spirit, it was essential to lay the foundations by first evoking the *bushidō* spirit.[38] *The Revival of Bushidō* stressed the importance of loyalty and knowing one's time to die, citing both Yamaga and Yoshida in line with the imperial *bushidō* interpretation. Another common element was Hiraizumi's contention that all Japanese became soldiers in Meiji, when the *bushi* were not eliminated, but rather expanded to include the whole nation with *bushidō* becoming the nation's morality. In this sense, Hiraizumi and Hirose agreed that *bushidō* had become condensed during

[33] Brownlee, John S., *Japanese Historians*, pp. 171–73.

[34] The usage of Fichte's work often disregarded its historical context and philosophical aspects, as Stefan Reiss points out, but it nonetheless proved a powerful tool: Reiss, Stefan (2006), *Fichtes 'Reden an die deutsche Nation' oder, Vom Ich zum Wir* (Berlin: Akademie Verlag)).

[35] Hiraizumi Kiyoshi (1933), *Bushidō no fukkatsu* (Tokyo: Shibundo), pp. 90–96.

[36] Wakai Toshiaki (2006), *Hiraizumi Kiyoshi: mikuni no tame ni ware tsukusanamu* (Mineruva shobō), pp. 11, 168.

[37] Hiraizumi Kiyoshi, *Bushidō no fukkatsu*, pp. 1–4.

[38] Hiraizumi Kiyoshi, *Bushidō no fukkatsu*, pp. 5–6.

the periods of warrior rule before being revived in Bakumatsu and early Meiji.[39] In addition to Yoshida Shōin, Hiraizumi also credited the influence of Bakumatsu activist Hashimoto Sanai (1834–59), who 'recognized the sacred nature of Japan over other countries' and had a strong influence on Saigō Takamori.[40]

Hiraizumi and Hirose also agreed on the negative influence of Chinese thought and Hiraizumi criticized Mencius' views of the sovereign, comparing these to Rousseau's idea of the social contract.[41] According to Hiraizumi, the ancient Japanese had known how to deal with the Mencian heresy, but people later became enamoured with Chinese and other foreign thought. This was often subconscious, Hiraizumi argued, as in the case of referring to the 'Meiji Revolution,' a label which fundamentally misunderstood the significance of 1868. One of Hiraizumi's favourite subjects was criticism of the French Revolution, and he considered the concept of 'revolution' to be wholly alien to Japan.[42] Repeating an argument put forth by Yamaga and other Tokugawa scholars, Hiraizumi identified revolutions with China, as dynasties had changed often over the millennia. In contrast, Japan had never experienced dynastic change from the time of Emperor Jimmu onward, and Hiraizumi considered the introduction of the concept of 'revolution' a most dangerous development.[43]

The Revival of Bushidō was frequently republished over the next decade, and pre-war copies continue to be widely available in Japan, with the publisher Kinseisha issuing reprints of the original text in 1988 and again in 2011. The book's sales in the year following its appearance at the end of 1933 were boosted by Hiraizumi's high profile as organizer of activities commemorating the 600th anniversary of Emperor Go Daigo's (1288–1339) Kenmu Restoration, which Hiraizumi portrayed as a failed attempt to revive Japaneseness and bring the country's focus back to the imperial house.[44] This interpretation of Go Daigo's goals echoed the central argument of *The Revival of Bushidō*, and Hiraizumi often combined the two subjects. In 1935, Hiraizumi became a full professor at Tokyo Imperial University and simultaneously took a leading role in public history education. As a founding member of the History Education Seminar, Hiraizumi exerted considerable influence on the content of history textbooks and contributed a number of chapters himself. *Bushidō* featured especially in lessons on medieval history, and students were encouraged to compare the development of *bushidō* as reflected in the activities of Kamakura *bushi* with the Imperial Rescript for Soldiers and Sailors.[45]

That same year Hiraizumi responded to the tremendous success of *The Revival of Bushidō* with a sequel intended to introduce a wide audience to what he

---

[39] Hiraizumi Kiyoshi, *Bushidō no fukkatsu*, pp. 6–9.
[40] Hiraizumi Kiyoshi, *Bushidō no fukkatsu*, pp. 11–42.
[41] Hiraizumi Kiyoshi, *Bushidō no fukkatsu*, pp. 343–44.
[42] Hiraizumi Kiyoshi, *Bushidō no fukkatsu*, pp. 113–204.
[43] Hiraizumi Kiyoshi, *Bushidō no fukkatsu*, pp. 343–49.
[44] Brownlee, John S., *Japanese Historians*, p. 176.
[45] On the role of the History Education Seminar, which also shows the use of materials related to *bushidō* in teaching medieval history, see Fukuda Yoshihiko. 'Shōwa senzenki ni okeru rekishi kyōiku jōhō no juyō to shōtō kyōin no shishitsu keisei: *Rekishi kyōiku kōza* no kōsei to sono tokushoku no kentō kara' *Ehime daigaku kyōiku gakubu kiyō* 58 (2011) pp. 191–208. Hiraizumi's contributions

considered to be the most important texts on the subject. This work, *The Bushidō Textbook* (*Bushidō kyōhon*), began with a discussion of Yoshida Shōin before examining writings by Daidoji Yūzan, Yamaga, the newly popular *Hagakure*, and finally the *Analects* of Confucius.[46] The broad scope of Hiraizumi's activities was also reflected in his contributions to a number of police education materials, including a volume on *The Japanese Spirit* (*Nihon seishin*) published by the Osaka City Police Department Office in 1937.[47] At the same time, Hiraizumi's ties with the military grew closer, and he held lectures and contributed to military education materials used by the army and navy.[48] With the outbreak of hostilities with the United States, Hiraizumi helped spread the militarists' message to the general public, publishing an explanation of the declaration of war in 1942 and contributing to special wartime education texts for youth groups until the end of the war.[49]

The growing interrelation between military and civilian education subjects after the Manchurian Incident was reflected in the large number of textbooks on *bushidō* that appeared after this time. *The Japanese Spirit and Bushidō* (*Nihon seishin to bushidō*), 'a book designed for youth education' published by Admiral Tōgō Heihachirō's (1848–1934) biographer Niki Shōha in 1934, collected anecdotes concerning Edo-period thinkers commonly associated with the Wang Yangming school as well as prominent Bakumatsu 'men of action' such as Yoshida Shōin, Saigō Takamori, and others.[50] According to Niki, these men had made great sacrifices for the imperial nation and were loyal in exceptional times similar to those currently faced by the empire. In contemporary Japan, Niki wrote, there were two types of thought: one was in line with the Japanese spirit that sought to spread supreme righteousness to the four seas, while the other 'clings to the spirits of Russia and the United States and destroys the empire from the inside'.[51] Dangerous ideas such as 'American' liberalism and 'Russian' socialism were threatening the Japanese spirit, while 'money-worship' led to people 'becoming slaves to individualism'.[52] By relating recent military heroes such as Commander Hirose Takeo to pre-Meiji thinkers, *The Japanese Spirit and Bushidō* also reflected the nativization of Confucian ideas in modern Japan, especially the notion that Wang Yangming's philosophy of action was most clearly manifested in *bushidō*.[53] Unlike Hiraizumi and Hirose Yutaka,

---

can be found in textbooks such as: Kōfūkan Hensanjo (eds.) (1935), *Chūgaku kokubun kyōkasho kyōju bikō 5 (23rd ed.)* (Kōfūkan Shoten); Nihon Toshokan Kyōkai (eds.) (1935), *Ryōsho hyakusen 2* (Nihon Toshokan Kyōkai); Toyamabō Hensanbu (eds.) (1938), *Kokugoka Kyōju no jissai: teikoku jitsugyō dokuhon teiyō 5* (Toyamabō).

[46] Uwa shichō gakumuka (ed.) (1935), *Bushidō kyōhon*, (Uwa shichō gakumuka).

[47] Hiraizumi Kiyoshi (1937), *Nihon seishin 2* (Ōsaka-fu Keisatsubu Keimuka); Naimushō Keihokyoku (eds.) (1939), *Keisatsu kanbu yokuonkan kōwa roku* (Keisatsu Kyōkai); Keisatsu Kōshū Jo (eds.) (1943), *Keisatsu kōwa roku* (Shōkadō Shoten).

[48] See, for example, Hiraizumi's contribution to a composition book used at the military academies: Kōfūkan Hensanjo (eds.), *Shihan kokubun: dai ichibu yō kyōju bikō 7* (Kōfūkan Shoten, 1938).

[49] Hiraizumi Kiyoshi, *Sensen daishōkin kai* (Asahi Shinbunsha, 1942); Mie-Ken Seishōnendan Honbu (eds.), *Seishōnen senji kyōyō dokuhon* (Mie-Ken Seishōnendan Honbu, 1945).

[50] Niki Shōha (1934), *Nihon seishin to bushidō* (Kōbunsha), pp. 5–9.

[51] Niki Shōha, pp. 509–10.   [52] Niki Shōha, p. 14.

[53] Niki Shōha, see pp. 132–47 for a discussion of Commander Hirose Takeo.

Niki did not deny the influence of Chinese thought, even including a chapter on the Song general and scholar Wen Tianxiang (1236–83), whose resistance against the Mongols became a powerful patriotic symbol.[54]

Another 1934 textbook, Nose Hiroaki's *Patriotic Readings for Youth: On War* (*Shōnen aikoku dokuhon: sensō no hanashi*), epitomized the drive towards the militarization of society in the 1930s. Designed to explain the military's important role to children, this book brought together significant strands of historical, religious, and tactical ideology, simplifying them for a younger audience. A chapter 'On Bushidō' reminded readers that 'from the Age of the Gods, our country has never lost to a foreign nation', and stressed the *bushi* as the pinnacle of Japanese society. Given the recent popular emphasis on military virtues, Nose wrote, the young reader might counter with the argument that 'my father isn't a soldier, but he is still a great man!' While first affirming that *bushi* were the most important members of society, Nose comforted the reader by stating that people of other professions could also be useful. Fortunately, *bushidō* was the same as the *bushi* spirit, which was a manifestation of the Yamato spirit, and all Japanese were *bushi* deep down.[55] This was most important in modern war, Nose explained, for although people tended to focus on technology and technical ability, spirit continued to be the decisive factor, with the courage and loyalty handed down through history being especially crucial elements.[56] Finally, Nose's discussion of 'Future Wars' examined the probability of a 'Second Great War' occurring, as the nations of the world prepared militarily not only to attack, but also to deter one another from invading. In modern war, Nose warned, weapons were no more than toys if the country did not have the economic strength to maintain and operate them, and Japan was still a small power in this regard. All aspects of life had to be directed towards the national goal of military preparation, and the spiritual strength of the people was a most important factor in this regard. If the nation became separated from *bushidō*, it would be unable to retain its independence, but if the people strengthened their *bushidō* spirit then foreign countries would not dare to challenge Japan, even if it lacked weapons or resources.[57]

CHALLENGES FACING INSTITUTIONAL *BUSHIDŌ*

Institutional ideologists and educators saw *bushidō* as a useful tool for emphasizing the 'Japanese' virtue of loyalty at the core of key concepts in ethics education, including 'imperial loyalty and patriotism' and 'loyalty and filiality'. In order to fulfill this role, *bushidō* had to overcome several significant challenges, the most immediate of which were related to the problematic historiography on which imperial *bushidō* was based. In searching for martial precedents among pre-Meiji samurai to support their theories, thinkers who took historical

---

[54] Niki Shōha, p. 83.
[55] Nose Hiroaki (1934), *Shōnen aikoku dokuhon: sensō no hanashi* (Kōseikaku shoten), pp. 182–86.
[56] Nose Hiroaki, p. 197.   [57] Nose Hiroaki, pp. 197–203.

approaches to *bushidō* necessarily tended to rely on sources from periods in which the imperial house was under threat or even persecuted. This was especially problematic when emphasizing the 'practical' aspects of *bushidō* in the manner of many military education materials, as discussions focused on the Sengoku period. In addition, many interpretations explicitly dismissed the Nara and Heian periods as decadent, effeminate, and corrupted by Chinese influence, although these were also the periods when imperial power was arguably at its pre-modern peak. Typical solutions to this dilemma included shifting the focus to mythical pre-history and/or reinterpreting the Sengoku past to make the imperial house more important, but neither approach was satisfactory. The traditional dichotomy of court and military rulers was a major complicating factor, and the large number of different interpretations reflected the difficulty of bridging the gap with the aid of *bushidō*.

One of the most common approaches to pre-modern history taken by institutional promoters of imperial *bushidō* was to place its roots in the mythical founding age of the country, dismissing the period after the Taika reforms of 645 as excessively Chinese and marked by the illegitimate rulership of the Fujiwara clan. As Okada Meitarō argued in 1927, Taika wrenched apart the ancient unity of letteredness and martiality in Japan, and the periods that followed were the worst age with regard to *bushidō* and *taigi meibun* ('higher principles').[58] Similarly, *Moral Training for Soldiers* portrayed the Kamakura period as an age in which the warrior spirit recovered from the weak Heian age, while school textbooks such as *Patriotic Readings for Young People* criticized Nara and Heian but rehabilitated the Tokugawa as an age in which *bushidō* flourished.[59] This pattern continued through the end of the war, with Hashimoto Minoru's *Bushidō History for Young People* (*Shōnen bushidō shi*) (1942) maintaining that the Japanese spirit survived only in the warriors of the Kantō region during the Nara and Heian periods, from where it was revived in Kamakura and became instrumental in repelling the Mongol invasions.[60] In addition, Hashimoto wrote, the loyalty of Kamakura warriors to the shogun should be seen as ultimately directed towards the emperor.[61] Although critical of aspects of Tokugawa rule, Hashimoto stressed the influence of Yamaga Sokō and Daidōji Yūzan during the Edo period, and acknowledged that Confucian scholars contributed some useful ideas to the development of *bushidō* at the time.[62]

One of the few direct criticisms of these historiographical contortions came from educator Isono Kiyoshi, who wrote a number of commentaries on National Morality and the National Polity in the 1930s. In *A Detailed Discussion of Japan's Bushidō* (*Nihon bushidō shōron*) of 1934, Isono sought to correct deficiencies he saw in other studies of *bushidō*. According to Isono, most studies were too narrow, equating *bushidō* with the Japanese spirit and portraying it as a national ethic, when it was really no more than the ethic of a single class. Isono defined *bushidō*

[58] Okada, Meitarō, 'Bushidō rinri no shiteki kenkyū (part 2)', pp. 9–16.
[59] Nose Hiroaki, *Shōnen aikoku dokuhon: sensō no hanashi*, pp. 194–95.
[60] Hashimoto Minoru (1942), *Shōnen bushidō shi* (Tōkyō Ikubunsha), pp. 11–15, 100.
[61] Hashimoto Minoru, *Shōnen bushidō shi*, p. 227.
[62] Hashimoto Minoru, *Shōnen bushidō shi*, pp. 190–91.

as 'the way that *bushi* should follow exclusively', and cautioned against applying it to other groups. Confusion arose between the imprecise understanding of terms, Isono argued, with *shidō* being Chinese while chivalry was Western. Isono rejected the broad claim that *bushidō* entered all Japanese in Meiji, instead labelling the martial ethic found in the modern rescripts as 'the spirit of the emperor's army' (*kōgun seishin*), which he strictly differentiated from *bushidō*.[63] Isono avoided potential controversy over the omission of the imperial house by briefly discussing imperial loyalty, but the body of the text made it clear that he did not consider its relationship with *bushidō* to be supported by historical evidence.[64]

Another scholar who expressed his disagreement with imperial *bushidō* was Saitō Kaname, a specialist in Chinese philosophy who published widely on Kantianism, Confucianism, Japanese history, and the use of Shinto shrine materials in elementary education. In his 1937 *Reinvestigation of Japan's Bushidō* (*Nihon bushidō no saiginmi*), written to commemorate the 800th birthday of Zhu Xi, Saitō observed that many texts seeking to revive ancient traditions had recently been published on *bushidō*, which he equated to the imperial way. While acknowledging the roots of *bushidō* in the Age of the Gods, Saitō criticized the recent interpretations as extremely conservative, as they dismissed any foreign influences and sought the imperial way in a pre-historical Japanese spirit that existed before foreign ideas entered the country. Saitō rejected this approach, arguing that Confucianism and Buddhism had been grafted on to 'imperial way *bushidō*', and investigating these thought systems was essential for understanding *bushidō*. As he was not an expert on Buddhism, Saitō saw his task in the examination of Confucianism, and claimed that his interest in the subject was driven by a desire to better comprehend the Japanese spirit.[65] In a departure from mainstream *bushidō* historiography, Saitō did not dismiss early Chinese influences, positing the Ritsuryō legal system as the basis for the imperial ruling structure. In further departures, Saitō defended the Fujiwara clan for foiling the plans of the potential usurper, the monk Dōkyō (d. 772). Saitō also highlighted the Heian scholar Sugawara no Michizane (845–903), and stressed the important influence of Nara Buddhism on the development of *bushidō* at the time.[66]

According to Saitō, the *bushidō* that developed at the end of the Heian period was a mix of Japanized Buddhism, Confucianism, and the Japanese spirit, and was transmitted through the medieval period until the Edo period brought the opportunity to examine the teachings of Zhu Xi in depth, and these became the centre of *bushi* life.[67] While the 'feudal *bushidō*' of this time contained the all-important ideas of loyalty and filial piety, this was only a 'small virtue' directed towards one's lord. The Meiji Restoration finally marked the end of the feudal period, Saitō wrote, initiating a great age of 'imperial way *bushidō*', manifested especially in the Imperial Rescript for Soldiers and Sailors—the 'true spirit of Japan's *bushidō* and

---

[63] Isono Kiyoshi (1934), *Nihon bushidō shōron* (Meguro shoten), 'Introduction' pp. 2–3; pp. 1–3.
[64] Isono Kiyoshi, p. 391.
[65] Saitō Kaname (1937), *Nihon bushidō no saiginmi* (Daitō shuppansha), Preface, pp. 2–4.
[66] Saitō Kaname, pp. 87–118.   [67] Saitō Kaname, p. 150.

the core of the nation's morality'.[68] Saitō's distinction between 'feudal *bushidō*' and 'imperial way *bushidō*' was also a response to a major shift in the understanding of *bushidō* in Shōwa. The earliest modern discourse on the subject in Meiji treated *bushidō* primarily as the 'way of the samurai', and a common criticism of Nitobe's *Bushido: The Soul of Japan* was his alleged confusion of the samurai class ethic with the Yamato spirit. Interpretations extending a timeless *bushidō* to all Japanese had also been formulated in Meiji and promoted by the government and military, but it was only under the influence of Shōwa imperial *bushidō* that this view became mainstream. In this sense, the 'way of the samurai' became a much broader 'way of the warrior' that incorporated gods and legendary emperors, as well as modern soldiers.

The historical revisionism of imperial *bushidō* appeared problematic to those who looked more closely at the subject, although open criticism that might denigrate the imperial house was rare. Poet and literary critic Hagiwara Sakutarō (1886–1942) wrote extensively on the imperial house and *bushidō*, and criticized the dominant view of history mandated by imperial *bushidō*. Although he was a staunch patriot, Hagiwara was uncomfortable with the militarism inherent in *bushidō*. Like Okakura Tenshin and Tsuda Sōkichi before him, Hagiwara rejected the increasingly widespread notion that the Japanese were inherently more martial than other people. In his *Principles of Poetry* (1928), Hagiwara argued that the fraternal nature of Japanese warfare in the pre-modern age made it more personal and tragic than in other countries, where wars were often prosecuted against other nations and races. As a result, Hagiwara wrote, Japanese had a deep-rooted dislike of conflict, making Japan 'very much an exception in the world' in its lack of a *bushidō* spirit.[69]

Even as Japan's military activities in China expanded in the 1930s, Hagiwara maintained this basic line of argument. In a 1938 essay on 'Japan's Soldiers' published in the journal *Inochi*, Hagiwara wrote that Germans were the most soldier-like, while Americans and English seemed more like cowboys or sportsmen. Whereas Western soldiers typically wore flashy uniforms and strutted around with their chests thrust out, Japanese soldiers were much more simply dressed and reserved in the manner of office workers. According to Hagiwara, this also reflected the scientific nature of modern warfare, which had been stripped of romanticism. Hagiwara cited military music as evidence for the differing views of warfare between Japan and the West, with Japanese war songs and poetry inevitably laden with pathos while Western music tended to have a much more lively tone. According to Hagiwara, the lack of Japanese equivalents to wartime songs such as 'I'm on My Way to Dublin Bay' or 'It's a Long Way to Tipperary' reflected fundamentally different attitudes to warfare. The Japanese were much more aesthetically minded, Hagiwara argued, and even the country's ancient warriors valued beauty and treasured works of art. This traditional aestheticism might influence the seriousness of Japanese soldiers in the future, he wrote, as troops serving in China were

[68] Saitō Kaname, pp. 275–332.
[69] Hagiwara Sakutarō (1950), *Shi no genri* (Tokyo: Sōgensha), pp. 259–60.

listening to Western music and becoming more relaxed. They might revive the spirit of an elite group of medieval *bushi* who treated warfare as sport, Hagiwara surmised, overcoming the national exhaustion resulting from Japan's drive to catch up on centuries of civilizational change in a fraction of the time.[70]

In the late 1930s, Hagiwara's thought underwent a significant change toward greater nationalism, and by 1940 he had come to accept the ancient existence of *bushidō*.[71] Hagiwara's views of the historical pedigree and content of *bushidō* differed considerably from the 'imperial' interpretation, however, and he placed its origins in the Nara period. According to Hagiwara, Japan's *bushidō* was initially defined by courage and love in the same manner as European chivalry.[72] It was only when Confucian teachings arrived from China that love was purged from *bushidō*, a process that became especially pronounced in the Tokugawa period.[73] Throughout the Kamakura period, Hagiwara argued, *bushidō* had been most heavily influenced by Buddhism, just as chivalry had been defined by Christianity.[74] Unfortunately, he wrote, the *bushidō* being promoted in contemporary Japan was the Confucian form that had been forced on the nation by the Tokugawa, and this Sinified *bushidō* of loyalty and filial piety promoted by the government was not the pure Yamato spirit sought by Motoori Norinaga and other scholars of the National Learning school.[75] Hagiwara lamented that the government promotion of this corrupted Confucian *bushidō* caused foreigners to see the courage displayed by Japanese on the battlefield and equate the Yamato spirit with barbaric militarism, which was as ludicrous as portraying Japanese as barbarians because they enjoyed eating raw fish.[76]

Hagiwara directed much of his criticism at the history education system for promoting a militaristic view at the expense of Japan's traditional aesthetics. According to Hagiwara, the periods described as 'good ages' were those in which the *bushidō* spirit was celebrated and a steely, practical stoicism dominated the political climate. In contrast, the supposed 'bad ages' were those in which this spirit declined and martial law loosened, with a flowering of culture and a 'bookish weakening' afflicting the warriors. Textbooks were critical of the Fujiwara age, while the late Heian wars between the Taira and Minamoto clans, the Kamakura period, and the Sengoku period were all portrayed positively. Hagiwara pointed out that both the Hōjō and Ashikaga families were descended from traitors, but their treatement in history education differed completely. This was because the martial

---

[70] Hagiwara Sakutarō (1938), 'Nihon no gunjin', *Nihon he no kaiki* (Tokyo: Hakusuisha), p. 490.

[71] Dorsey, James (2007), 'From an Ideological Literature to a Literary Ideology: "Conversion in Wartime Japan"', in Dennis Washburn and A. Kevin Reinhart (ed.), *Converting Cultures: Religion, Ideology and Transformations of Modernity* (Leiden & Boston: Brill), pp. 465–83.

[72] Hagiwara Sakutarō (1936), 'Seiyō no urayamashisa', *Rōka to shitsubō* (Tokyo: Dai-ichi Shobō), pp. 293–98.

[73] Hagiwara Sakutarō, 'Seiyō no urayamashisa'; Hagiwara Sakutarō (1940), 'Yosano tekkan ron', *Kigōsha* (Tokyo: Hakusuisha), pp. 188–231.

[74] Hagiwara Sakutarō (1944), 'Nō to sengoku bushi', *Hagiwara Sakutarō zenshū 8* (Tokyo: Shōgaku Kan), pp. 313–16.

[75] Hagiwara Sakutarō, 'Seiyō no urayamashisa'.

[76] Hagiwara Sakutarō (1940), 'Nihon bunka no tokushusei', *Kigōsha* (Tokyo: Hakusuisha), pp. 3–22.

government of the Hōjō had the essential traits of a Stoic warrior spirit, simple toughness, and Confucianized Zen, whereas the Ashikaga were seen as decrepit and effeminate rulers who practised tea ceremony, poetry, and other courtly pursuits, while letting the *bushidō* spirit atrophy. This ideology, Hagiwara charged, had resulted in a history education system which only valued military heroes and almost completely ignored literary figures—including great writers such as Matsuo Bashō, Ihara Saikaku, and Murasaki Shikibu—beyond rote learning of their names.[77]

Hagiwara's criticism of *bushidō* was an early response to the increased dissemination of the concept in the late 1920s, and reflected the lingering anti-military sentiment among Taishō intellectuals. As militaristic trends increased in the 1930s, a number of writers and theorists took Hagiwara's approach of rejecting mainstream interpretations of *bushidō* and instead promoting theories regarding Japan's 'unique' aesthetic values.[78] These theories were no less nationalistic for their repudiation of militarism, and often drifted into aestheticist cultural chauvinism.[79] Significantly, many of these intellectuals ostensibly relied on European methods of historical, sociological, and philosophical inquiry in constructing their Japanese ideals.

Arguably the most significant figure in this context was philosopher Kuki Shūzō (1888–1941), whose *The Structure of 'Iki'* (*'Iki' no kōzō*) (1930) strongly influenced Japanese philosophy and aesthetics in the pre-war period and beyond. Kuki studied in France and Germany under Sartre, Heidegger, and other leading thinkers from 1921 to 1929, giving him a broad understanding of European languages and philosophy, which he employed in his arguments for Japanese exceptionalism. *Bushidō* was a cornerstone of Kuki's thought even during his time in Europe, and he described it as 'the moral ideal of Japan' that developed in response to the challenges posed by Buddhism.[80] By invoking *bushidō*, Kuki sought to set Japan apart from the West as well as from the rest of Asia. *The Structure of 'Iki'* compared the concept of '*iki*' with the French concept of *chic*, before concluding that *iki* was ethnically specific and ultimately untranslatable. According to Kuki, *iki* was a singularly Japanese spirit that defined the unique aesthetic sensibilities of his countrymen, and had been most clearly manifested in the citizens of Edo.[81] While celebrating Edo commoner culture, Kuki also described *iki* as inseparable from *bushidō*, drawing parallels between commoner extravagance and samurai frugality.[82]

[77] Hagiwara Sakutarō (1943), 'Rekishi no shashisen', *Hagiwara Sakutarō zenshū 10* (Tokyo: Shōgaku Kan), pp. 41–60.

[78] Bialock, David T. (2000), 'Nation and Epic: *The Tale of the Heike* as a Modern Classic', in Haruo Shirane (ed.), *Inventing the Classics: Modernity, National Identity, and Japanese Literature* (Stanford: Stanford University Press), p. 162.

[79] For an overview of aesthetics and cultural chauvinism, see Minami Hiroshi (2006), *Nihonjin ron: Meiji kara kyō made* (Tokyo: Iwanami gendai bunko), ch. 5.

[80] Pincus, Leslie (1996), *Authenticating Culture in Japan: Kuki Shūzō and the Rise of National Aesthetics* (Berkeley: University of California Press), p. 86.

[81] Nakano Hajimu (1990), 'Kita Ikki and *The Structure of Iki*', in Thomas Rimer (ed.), *Culture and Identity: Japanese Intellectuals During the Interwar Years* (Princeton, NJ: Princeton University Press), p. 268.

[82] Pincus, Leslie, *Authenticating Culture in Japan*, pp. 130–32.

By focusing on aesthetics and a spirit of rebellion inherent in Edo commoner culture, Kuki's early *bushidō* ran counter to mainstream interpretations. In contrast, Kuki's cultural chauvinism was very much in line with imperial *bushidō*, and he moved towards militaristic and imperialistic views as these became more widespread. In a 1937 *Bungei shunshū* article on 'Thoughts on the Times' ('Jikyoku no kansō'), Kuki argued that Japan must promote its superior aesthetics and spirit militarily: 'By vanquishing China, we Japanese must teach them in a decisive manner the spirit of Japanese philosophy. It is our cultural-historical mission to lend spiritual succor to the renewal of their mother country by imprinting our idealistic philosophy in the form of *bushidō* in the innermost recesses of their bodies'.[83] Kuki's later work moved ever closer to imperial *bushidō*, accepting the importance of Yamaga Sokō and Yoshida Shōin, while emphasizing the emperor as the unified object of loyalty and filial piety.[84] This support for imperial *bushidō* was echoed by a number of other aestheticist thinkers whose interests focused on the uniqueness of Japanese thought and culture, with Tomino Yoshikuni (1904–?) and author and critic Kishida Kunio (1890–1954) incorporating *bushidō* into their Japanist aesthetic theories.[85]

The combination of imperial *bushidō* with academic philosophy was epitomized by Watsuji Tetsurō (1889–1960), a giant in the field who became the chair in ethics at Tokyo Imperial University in 1934. The following year, Watsuji completed his influential *Climate* (*Fūdo*), in which he argued that Japan's unique climatic conditions determined the nation's character and spirit. Watsuji subsequently placed his ideas on the uniqueness of the Japanese spirit in the service of the government, with his *Japan's Way of the Subject* (*Nihon no shindō*) (1944) lending support to the imperial *bushidō* ideology. According to Watsuji, whereas Japanese warriors had always willingly given their lives for their domainal lords, a number of samurai in the sixteenth century questioned the target of their loyalty. Thinking more deeply, they rediscovered the cultural tradition of imperial loyalty that originated in the founding of the country and transcended feudal loyalties. Although the way of the samurai was influenced by Buddhist and Confucian ideals at different times, these primarily aided the warriors to become conscious of the true way of the Japanese subject, which had reached its pinnacle in the present day.[86] Watsuji further contributed to the dissemination of imperial *bushidō* in 1937 by serving on the official Compilation Committee of the *Principles of the National Polity* (*Kokutai no hongi*), and in 1940 he compiled an abridged version of the *Hagakure* for soldiers to take off to war.[87] While ethics and aesthetics could challenge the militaristic aspects of *bushidō*, or even reject the ethic as a whole, emphasis on the uniqueness of the

---

[83] Kuki Shūzō, 'Jikyoku no kansō', *Bungei shunshū* 15:12 (Oct. 1937) (trans. Leslie Pincus), cited in Pincus, Leslie, 'In a Labyrinth of Western Desire: Kuki Shuzo and the Discovery of Japanese Being', *boundary 2* 18:3 (Autumn, 1991), p. 156.

[84] Pincus, Leslie, *Authenticating Culture in Japan*, pp. 222–25.

[85] Minami Hiroshi, *Nihonjin ron: meiji kara kyō made*, pp. 205–07.

[86] Watsuji Tetsurō (ed.) (1944), *Nihon no shindō, Amerika no kokuminsei* (Chikuma shobō).

[87] Gauntlett, John Owen (trans.) (1949), *Kokutai No Hongi: Cardinal Principles of the National Entity of Japan* (Cambridge, MA: Harvard University Press), p. 5; Unoda Shōya (1997), 'Bushidō ron no seiritsu: seiyō to tōyō no aida', *Edo no shiso 7 (shisō shi no 19 seiki)* (Tokyo: Perikan sha), p. 43.

Japanese spirit and world view could easily feed into imperial *bushidō* ideology, buttressing it from new angles.

IMPERIAL DEVIATIONS FROM INSTITUTIONAL *BUSHIDŌ*

Whereas some thinkers rejected or minimized militaristic aspects of *bushidō* in their cultural theories in favour of a more aesthetically focused national character, challenges to imperial *bushidō*—and the state—also came from the other end of the political spectrum. In the 1920s and 1930s, extreme nationalist groups within and with close ties to the military took increasingly bold action with the aim of effecting a 'Shōwa Restoration' that would break the existing power structures dominated by older soldiers, bureaucrats, and industrialists. Just as the Meiji Restoration had supposedly freed the imperial house from the oppressive yoke of the Tokugawa shogunate, the new order was intended to 'restore' true imperial authority. Drawing on the restorationist model, the Shōwa activists saw themselves as the spiritual heirs of Yoshida Shōin and other 'men of action' who sacrificed themselves in the name of a great and righteous cause, and were popularly identified with *bushidō*.[88] The young officers who formed the core of the movement assassinated a number of business, military, and political leaders, including Prime Minister Inukai Tsuyoshi in May 1932. James Crowley describes Inukai's assassins as 'recent graduates of the service academies...imbued with the cult of *bushidō* and a reverence for the Imperial institution'.[89] The movement reached a climax on 26 February 1936, when 1,500 young officers seized central Tokyo and attempted to kill government figures who they believed opposed them. Several politicians were murdered by death squads, but the coup failed when the emperor demanded their surrender. The leaders of the movement were executed after secret trials, and most of the young officers involved were dispersed to other regions.

The spiritual father of the Shōwa restorationist movement was political philosopher Kita Ikki (Terujirō; 1883–1937), who was arrested and executed following the 26 February incident. Kita's *National Polity Theory and Pure Socialism* (*Kokutairon oyobi junsei shakai shugi*) (1906) written at the height of the Meiji *bushidō* boom, was highly critical of *bushidō* in general and Inoue Tetsujirō in particular. According to Kita, during the warrior-dominated period, '*bushidō* became the oppressor of the imperial house', which suffered terribly for most of Japanese history. 'Today's national polity theorists are angry at the warriors that arose along with *bushidō* and indignantly protest against the weakening of the imperial house through the warriors'. At the same time, 'they hammer on people's skulls with Japan's unbroken imperial line while shouting "*bushidō*" and "long live

---

[88] While certainly a biased view, Hiraizumi Kiyoshi attested to the popularity of late Tokugawa 'men of action' in his 1933 *Revival of Bushidō* (Hiraizumi Kiyoshi, *Bushidō no fukkatsu*, p. 11).

[89] Crowley, James B., *Japan's Quest for Autonomy: National Security and Foreign Policy 1930–1938*, p. 173.

the emperor!" ' Kita described Inoue Tetsujirō as the 'village headman' of this tribe of *bushidō* promoters. Kita argued that virtually all examples of seemingly loyal behaviour throughout Japanese history could be explained by economic relationships and the only loyal retainers the imperial house had were the aristocrats who depended on them financially.[90]

Kita's controversial *National Polity Theory and Pure Socialism* outlined his vision of a socialism rooted in Japan's supposedly communalistic ancient past, free from the later vertical economic relationships that made *bushidō* a 'slave ethic'. Inspired by the impending change in China, Kita travelled to Shanghai, where he observed the 1911 revolution first hand. Kita was impressed with many of the young activists driving the revolution, likening them to the lower-class 'slave *bushi*' from Satsuma and Chōshū who led the Meiji Restoration. After 1911, Kita spent several years between Japan and China, but was disillusioned by the revolutionaries' subsequent compromise with the warlord Yuan Shikai (1859–1916).[91] Identifying the primary problem with the Chinese revolution as the absence of a sufficiently powerful unifying figure, Kita proposed revolutionary action in Japan focused around an 'emperor of the people'. In his *Outline of Measures for Reconstructing Japan* (*Nihon kaizō hōan taikō*) (1919), Kita wrote of a great crisis facing Japan, calling for the abolition of the constitution, assemblies, and court officials in a coup d'etat that would bring the emperor closer to the people.[92] Kita believed that the reformed Japanese empire would take a leading role in freeing Asia from Western domination, a notion that appealed to many with imperialistic ideals. The *Outline* was banned several times due to its controversial and inflammatory nature, but nevertheless became the guiding text of many would-be revolutionaries in the 1920s and 1930s.

One thinker heavily influenced by Kita was ultranationalist politician Nakano Seigō (1886–1943), who advocated strong and direct government by the emperor in a populist order often compared with contemporary European fascism. Like Kita, Nakano looked to Saigō Takamori and other Bakumatsu samurai for inspiration, but did not share Kita's negative opinion of *bushidō*. Kita's view of *bushidō* was heavily influenced by his observations in late Meiji, when the ideology was promoted by the officialdom he detested. In contrast, Nakano, while critical of the government, was more willing to work within the system, siding with Ozaki Yukio and other supporters of constitutional government against the military and party oligarchs during the Taishō political crisis.[93] Nakano often invoked samurai imagery in his rhetoric and his traditionalist image characterized his legacy as a '*bushidō* politician'.[94] For Nakano, *bushidō* was not a symbol of feudal repression, but rather symbolized the restorationist spirit that drove positive change. When his

[90] Kita Terujirō (1906), *Kokutairon oyobi junsei shakai shugi* (Kita Terujirō), pp. 710–20.

[91] Kita outlined his view of the problems in China in his *Unofficial History of the Chinese Revolution*: Kita Terujirō (1921), *Shina kakumei gaishi* (Daitōkaku).

[92] Kita Terujirō (1928), *Nihon kaizō hōan taikō* (Tokyo: Nishida Mitsugi), Section 1.

[93] Oates, Leslie Russell (1985), *Populist Nationalism in Prewar Japan: A Biography of Nakano Seigō* (Sydney: George Allen), p. 11.

[94] For example, see Ōhashi Yukio (2006), *Aogeba sonshi sokoku Nihon yo: Nihon he no kenpaku isho* (Bungeisha), p. 42.

own attempts to effect this change through political means failed as the national crisis intensified, Nakano committed suicide by *seppuku* in 1943.[95]

The restorationist ideals espoused by Kita and Nakano had a powerful impact in the army, especially among the supporters of the Shōwa Restoration movement who are often labelled as the 'Imperial Way' faction. Ishiwara Kanji (1889–1949), a staff officer and architect of the Manchurian Incident, was an important influence on young rightist officers, although he ultimately opposed their attempts to seize power by force. Long before the outbreak of the Pacific War, Ishiwara was convinced that events were inevitably leading to a 'final war' between East and West, with Asia uniting behind Japan. In 1931, Ishiwara argued that Japan had to control Manchuria and Mongolia in order to become strong enough to stabilize China and challenge the West, and his involvement in the occupation of Manchuria led to his promotion to high rank. The outbreak of the Second Sino-Japanese War contributed to pan-Asianist Ishiwara's later fall from favour, although he continued to theorize from his enforced retirement. In his *Historical Overview of War* (*Sensō shi taikan*) (1941), Ishiwara stated that both China and Japan had lost much of their ancient martial abilities. China's military had been in decline since the Tang dynasty (618–907), he argued, and hoped for the sake of Japan and Asia that it would be able to revive its pre-Tang martial spirit. In Japan, Ishiwara claimed, the warriors of the Sengoku period relied on the *bushidō* founded in the national spirit to produce the phenomenal fighting strength and cunning tactics feared by the foreigners who encountered them. Sengoku *bushi* schemed and sacrificed their families if it was expedient, Ishiwara argued, but the degenerating effect of three hundred years of Tokugawa peace meant that the Japanese military was completely incapable of formulating successful tactics.[96]

One of the most significant ideological leaders of the Imperial Way group was General Araki Sadao (1877–1967), who was also one of the greatest promoters of *bushidō* in the military. Holding positions including Principal of the Army War College and later Chief of the Inspector General of Military Training Department, Araki had considerable control over the content of military education in early Shōwa. In addition to revising the *General Principles of Strategic Command* in 1928, Araki initiated trends towards the production of spiritual education materials with a new degree of sophistication, such as *Moral Training for Soldiers* (1930).[97] Araki served as War Minister in the Inukai and Saitō cabinets between 1931 and 1934, where he was even better able to force the implementation of spiritual education in the military, while invoking nationalistic concepts such as 'national polity', 'Yamato spirit', and 'emperor's army' to an unprecedented degree.[98] Military doctrine came to be marked by what Alvin Coox describes as an 'abhorrence of the defensive', with few or no provisions made for surrender or retreat.[99] Araki's

---

[95] Oates, Leslie Russell, *Populist Nationalism in Prewar Japan*, pp. ix, 45, 89.

[96] Ishiwara Kanji (1941), *Sensō shi taikan* (Chūō kōron sha), p. 70.

[97] Humphreys, Leonard A., *The Way of the Heavenly Sword*, pp. 106–07.

[98] Crowley, James B., *Japan's Quest for Autonomy*, p. 203.

[99] Coox, Alvin D. (1985), *Nomonhan: Japan Against Russia, 1939* (Stanford: Stanford University Press), p. 1084.

regime placed greater emphasis on the imperial rescripts, and an official army and navy textbook commemorating the fiftieth anniversary of the Rescript for Soldiers and Sailors included a preface from the war minister himself.[100] The activist young officers, most of whom were excluded from the highest positions due to their regional and/or educational background, were impressed by Araki's efforts to remove the oligarch-friendly Chōshū clique from power in favour of soldiers loyal to the emperor.[101]

The young officers were enamoured with *bushidō*, a major pillar of Araki's spiritual education policies, and he promoted it in educational materials and articles as well as by contributing forewords and calligraphy to approved texts on *bushidō*.[102] Araki laid out his views on *bushidō* in an article entitled 'On Loyal Retainers and Great Warriors', which was reprinted in public education texts such as the *Bushidō Handbook* (1939) and *Introduction to Bushidō* (1941), both compiled by the Bushidō Society.[103] In keeping with the imperial *bushidō* interpretation, Araki emphasized the 'uniquely Japanese virtue of loyalty', specifically the imperial loyalty demonstrated by Kusunoki Masashige. Accordingly, Araki traced the virtue of loyalty through the tales of the gods to the sun goddess Amaterasu, ancestor of the imperial house. The imperial house was indivisible from the gods and the land of Japan, and the resulting impossibility of Japanese to be apart from the imperial house was the origin of their unique loyalty. Araki also mentioned the importance of morality, which set Japanese warriors apart from the military technicians of other nations. While Alexander, Napoleon, Caesar, and Hannibal may have been brave and able, Araki wrote, they lacked virtue in the eyes of Japanese. For comparison, Araki provided examples of medieval warriors who fulfilled the Japanese warrior ideal of bravery with moral fortitude, including Kusunoki, Hōjō Tokimune, Uesugi Kenshin, and Katō Kiyomasa.[104]

Araki distanced himself from the 1936 coup attempt that his emperor-centred spiritual education measures helped inspire, and this event demonstrated the difficulties inherent in the application of imperial *bushidō*.[105] Emperor-centred *bushidō* theories typically invoked Bakumatsu loyalists such as Yoshida Shōin and Saigō Takamori, and there was a risk that their resistance against a corrupt and unjust official order might inspire students in unintended ways. This danger was encapsulated in the ideal of a Shōwa Restoration that would wash away the decadent order and restore the emperor's power and direct connection with the people. Kita Ikki held to these tenets although he rejected modern *bushidō* as a tool of the despised

---

[100] Rikugunshō, Kaigunshō (eds.) (1932), *Chokuyu kasha 50 nen shukuga kōen shū* (Rikugunshō).

[101] Humphreys, Leonard A., *The Way of the Heavenly Sword*, pp. 159–60.

[102] Araki's calligraphy forms the frontispiece of a number of texts, including a book promoting *bushidō* and swordsmanship (Kenseikai (eds.), *Bushidō yōi*).

[103] Araki Sadao (1941), 'Chūjin meishō wo kataru', in Bushidō Gakkai (ed.), *Bushidō nyūmon* (Tokyo: Futara Shobō), pp., 232–48.

[104] Araki Sadao, 'Chūjin meishō wo kataru'.

[105] John Brownlee mentions Hiraizumi Kiyoshi's little-understood connection with the rebels, which occurred when he met with the emperor's younger brother, Prince Chichibu, on 27 February as the latter travelled from Aomori to Tokyo to gauge the situation. The prince was a known supporter of the rebels, but ultimately took no action during the affair, leading to considerable speculation with regard to his discussion with Hiraizumi. Brownlee theorizes that the efforts of the young officers

state, but younger Shōwa activists exposed to *bushidō* ideology through the civilian and military education systems did not typically have such a nuanced view. To them, Yoshida Shōin's battle against tyranny was a prime example of the *bushidō* they sought to emulate in their own restoration. While the actions of the young officers were in line with their own views of *bushidō*, the military tribunals that sentenced nineteen alleged conspirators to death charged the accused with 'failing to uphold the standards of *bushidō*'.[106]

BUSHIDŌ IN THE TIME OF CRISIS

The 26 February Incident and the initiation of formal hostilities with China in 1937 marked the beginning of a period of general crisis. Conservative elements in the government and military used the public terror resulting from the failed Shōwa Restoration to implement stricter controls over dissent and social criticism in the army and broader society. The general public supported stricter controls as necessary measures in a 'time of crisis', and political pluralism effectively disappeared as the weakening political parties rubber-stamped proposals put forth by the governing bureaucrats and military leaders. The implementation of the National General Mobilization Law in 1938 gave the government sweeping powers to control almost all aspects of economic and social life in support of the war effort, although these were not fully used until the outbreak of the Pacific War. In 1940, the prime minister, Prince Konoe Fumimaro (1891–1945) dissolved the political parties and replaced them with a government organization known as the Imperial Rule Assistance Association. The totalitarian concentration of power at the centre was accompanied by massive education campaigns and propaganda activities to promote the 'New Order' against dangerous ideas including individualism, socialism, communism, and other 'un-Japanese' philosphies. As Gregory Kasza describes it, 'the unifying concept of the family nation embodied in the Emperor, the samurai's *bushidō* code, and the nationalistic Yamato spirit formed an ideal moral basis for the new state-society system'.[107] Konoe's writings reflected his strong interest in *bushidō*, including a widely reprinted article entitled 'The National Polity and Bushidō.'[108] Konoe's *bushidō* stressed the uniqueness of Japanese imperial loyalty, tracing it from pre-history to the ongoing war with China. According to Konoe, throughout Japan's modern wars, imperial soldiers proved this ancient loyalty and courage by unfailingly calling out 'long live the emperor!' as their last words when dying in battle.[109]

to 'restore' imperial power would have garnered Hiraizumi's support (Brownlee, John S., *Japanese Historians and the National Myths, 1600–1945*, p. 168).

[106] Kōno Tsukasa (ed.) (1957), *Ni ni roku jiken* (Tokyo: Nihon shūhōsha), p. 448.

[107] Kasza, Gregory J. (1988), *The State and the Mass Media in Japan, 1918–1945* (Berkeley: University of California Press), p. 203.

[108] For a 2013 reprint, see Bushidō gakkai, Kokusho kankō kai (eds.) (2013), *Bushidō dokuhon* (Kokusho Kankō Kai), pp. 235–43.

[109] Konoe Fumimaro (1941), 'Kokutai to bushidō', in *Bushidō nyūmon* (Tokyo: Futara shobō), pp. 20–27.

The dangerous ideological rifts exposed in the military in 1936 made spiritual education in the services more urgent, while the wartime situation and fear of a total war against the Allies led to a perceived necessity to similarly galvanize the populace. An important role went to the experienced Araki, who, after being placed in the reserves following the 26 February mutiny, was able to extend his influence to the whole nation during two terms as education minister. *Bushidō* was used to promote imperial loyalty, patriotism, and self-sacrifice, with the imperial interpretation undergoing significant revision during this time. In addition to even greater emphasis on imperial loyalty, wartime *bushidō* was marked by an increased reliance on the *Hagakure*, which had played a relatively minor part in earlier discourse.[110] The martial writings of Daidōji Yūzan had been used by the military at least informally since the late nineteenth century due to the importance they placed on a samurai knowing the proper place to die, but selected passages of the *Hagakure* that actively promoted self-destructive behaviour as the highest *bushidō* virtue were deemed more suitable to the desperate nature of war in early Shōwa.

Samurai and *bushidō* featured prominently in popular culture of the time, reinforcing the official line through cumulative exposure. New versions of *A Treasury of Loyal Retainers* continued to appear, both with and without an imperial storyline, and were most often introduced by their authors in terms of *bushidō*. Constant news coverage of the situation in China, especially after 1937, led to war fatigue among the populace, and forms of popular culture directly related to current events did not often attract large audiences. On the other hand, underlying nationalistic and militaristic currents in society created demand for *bushidō*-based narratives based on idealized earlier history, and roughly sixty new kabuki plays on famous wars and warriors appeared between 1931 and 1945.[111] Many popular plays dealt with medieval warlords and events from the modern wars of late Meiji. In line with imperial *bushidō* ideology, the government promoted plays about exemplary samurai, while disseminating the notion that the martial spirit entered all Japanese citizens after the Meiji Restoration. The play *All Citizens Are Soldiers* (1940), for example, discussed the effectiveness of the modern conscript armies against the samurai.[112] By 1942, it was indicated that approval for plays would not be given by the Bureau of Information if their authors were 'lacking in a new spirit of *bushidō*'.[113] *Bushidō*-themed plays based on current events appeared more frequently after the outbreak of war with the United States, and celebrated playwright Kikuchi Kan (Hiroshi; 1888–1948) commented on the attempt to sink a US ship in Sydney Harbour, in which three midget submarine crews were lost: 'Like every member of the Japanese Army and Navy... the four heroes... thought only of accomplishing their mission at any sacrifice, the goal

---

[110] First published in 1906 *Hagakure* was not immediately accepted by the establishment, and Inoue Tetsujirō felt that it was too localized and unsuitable for national purposes:Unoda Shōya, 'Bushidō ron no seiritsu: seiyō to tōyō no aida', pp. 42–43.

[111] Brandon, James R., *Kabuki's Forgotten War: 1931–1945*, pp. 55–60.

[112] Brandon, James R., *Kabuki's Forgotten War*, pp. 122–25.

[113] Brandon, James R., *Kabuki's Forgotten War*, p. 203.

of the Bushido...to find consummation of the spirit of Bushido in death'.[114] Kikuchi was a prominent supporter of imperial *bushidō*, promoting the idea that the great virtue of imperial loyalty had existed from ancient times, but had been neglected during seven centuries of warrior rule before being revived with the Meiji Restoration.[115]

Native theatre such as kabuki was forced to change in line with the wartime mood, and foreign cultural forms, such as jazz, were reformed to bring them into supposed harmony with the Japanese spirit and thereby escape government bans.[116] The integration of nativized forms of Western fashion and culture reflected the government's inability to completely 'purify' the nation of dangerous foreign thought, in spite of considerable efforts in this regard. Similarly, while institutional *bushidō* discourse moved towards the extremes that would define the concept for decades in the eyes of many foreign observers, diverging narratives continued to coexist with the wartime imperial interpretation. The severity of the crisis on both civilian and military fronts required inclusiveness in the national struggle, and diverse contributions were still appreciated. In this sense, not only the heavily Shinto-influenced imperial *bushidō*, but also Buddhist, Christian, and non-religious interpretations were useful to the dissemination and acceptance of ideology. Zen Buddhism, especially, was picked up by a number of institutional *bushidō* theorists, aided by its long-established connection with Nogi Maresuke and, increasingly, the *Hagakure*. Similarly, Aoyoshi Katsuhisa's 1941 biography of Uemura Masahisa stressed both his samurai character and the patriotic nature of Japanese Christians.[117]

PREPARATION FOR TOTAL WAR

The demise of the Imperial Way movement in the military in 1936 was simultaneously a victory for rival conservatives usually known as the 'Control Faction'. The primary concern of these thinkers, led by the wartime Prime Minister Tōjō Hideki (1884–1948), was the mobilization of the entire nation's resources for a coming war with the West. As their power and influence in the government grew, these policymakers increased military content in schools and brought the imperial *bushidō* ideals of loyalty and self-sacrifice into almost all areas of civilian life. The most important single publication in this context was *The Principles of the National Polity* (1937), produced by the Ministry of Education and printed over two million times before being explicitly banned by the Occupation authorities.

---

[114] James Brandon's translation: Brandon, James R., *Kabuki's Forgotten War: 1931–1945*, p. 232.
[115] Kikuchi Kan, 'Bushidō no hanashi', in Bushidō gakkai (eds.), *Bushidō shinzui* (Tokyo: Teikoku shoseki kyōkai), pp. 130–49.
[116] Atkins, E. Taylor (2001), *Blue Nippon: Authenticating Jazz in Japan* (Duke University Press), pp. 127–32.
[117] Aoyoshi Katsuhisa (1941), *Dr Masahisa Uemura: A Christian Leader* (Tokyo: Maruzen & Co.), pp. 17–18, 81–85.

The Principles sought to clarify the proper understanding of the *kokutai* in order to enable the public to effectively fend off damaging foreign ideas, and focused on imperial loyalty as the manifestation of the Japanese spirit, while stressing the unique unity of loyalty and filial piety in Japan. In the tradition of Inoue Tetsujirō's *Outline of National Morality, The Principles* promoted imperial *bushidō* as an important characteristic of the nation's morality that was influenced by but ultimately transcended foreign teachings such as Confucianism and Buddhism.[118]

According to *The Principles*, in spite of the difficulties faced by the imperial house in the medieval period, warriors such as Oda Nobunaga and Toyotomi Hideyoshi were only able to achieve great success by demonstrating loyalty to the emperor.[119] From the time of the first emperor, Jimmu, Japan's unique and sacred martial spirit of *bushidō* brought morality to the conduct of war, the goal of which was to make peace and give life.[120] In this way, *The Principles* did not glorify death as such, but stressed the importance of seeing life and death as one and inseparable, as *bushidō*. *Bushidō* respected death and taught that it should be accepted calmly as the fulfillment of life. '[T]o treat life and death as two opposites and to hate death and to seek life is to be taken up with one's own interests, and is a thing of which warriors are ashamed'.[121] During Sengoku, warlords took care of the common people, and this magnanimity to the lower classes, combined with reverence for the gods and ancestors above, was the spirit of *bushidō*. During the Tokugawa period, Yamaga Sokō, Matsumiya Kanzan (1686–1780), and Yoshida Shōin strived to perfect *bushidō*, which 'shed itself of the outdated feudalism at the time of the Meiji Restoration, increased in splendour, became the Way of loyalty and patriotism, and has evolved before us as the spirit of the Imperial Forces'.[122] By locating the origins of *bushidō* in Japan's mythical past, portraying its core value as imperial loyalty, focusing on Yamaga and Yoshida as the most important formulators of *bushidō*, and seeing its completion in the modern imperial military, *The Principles* outlined the core tenets of imperial *bushidō* at the outset of expanded warfare and crisis.

Commentaries on *The Principles* appeared almost immediately, including articles written by the editors of the original text. One of these was the philosophy professor Kihira Tadayoshi (1874–1949), an expert on Hegelian thought and member of the National Spirit Cultural Research Institute, an organization that contributed significantly to the *The Principles* and other texts on Japanese cultural theory.[123] Written in late 1937, Kihira's commentary expanded on the *bushidō* theme discussed in *The Principles*, and used a number of examples from Japanese history to illustrate the unity of *bun* and *bu*, including writings by Miyamoto Musashi and Yamamoto Tsunetomo. Kihira cited the *Hagakure* to promote *bushidō*, loyalty, filial piety, and compassion, arguing that Yamamoto's

---

[118] Gauntlett, John Owen (trans.), *Kokutai No Hongi: Cardinal Principles of the National Entity of Japan*, p. 145.
[119] Gauntlett, John Owen, pp. 83–84.   [120] Gauntlett, John Owen, pp. 94–95.
[121] Gauntlett, John Owen, pp. 144–45.   [122] Gauntlett, John Owen, pp. 145–46.
[123] Minami Hiroshi, *Nihonjin ron: meiji kara kyō made*, p. 166.

thought had national relevance in spite of its explicit limitation to the Nabeshima domain.[124] The *Hagakure* was sporadically included in educational materials from its initial publication in 1906 onwards, as in a 1934 textbook for higher school educators, but it was not a significant text.[125] It was only when the prospect of total war gave martial aspects of *bushidō* a new urgency that the *Hagakure* became more prominent, with the full text published for the first time in the 1930s.[126]

As interpreters of the *Hagakure* shifted their emphasis to Yamamoto's exhaltation of death, the text became more popular than ever before. The change in reception was perhaps best reflected in a series of commentaries published by Matsunami Jirō (1900–1949?). In his 1938 *Hagakure Bushidō*, which went through five reprints in as many months, Matsunami criticized previous readings of the text for focusing on virtues such as seriousness and diligence. In contrast, Matsunami claimed that loyalty was the only virtue in what he called a 'philosophy of death'. According to Matsunami, who was 'confident in this newest interpretation' and its necessity in the time of crisis, the *Hagakure* was 'pure *bushidō*' that was understood not through reason, but went directly to the cells of the body.[127] Matsunami emphasized that the *Hagakure* rejected the combined virtues of loyalty and filial piety; there was only loyalty, which included filial piety in its greater whole.[128]

In response to the great success of his work, especially among the military, Matsunami revised the text in 1940 for the new order of wartime Japan. This edition, published as *The Spirit of Hagakure Bushidō* (*Hagakure bushidō seishin*; the 1942 edition would revert to the original 1938 title), was dedicated to the success of the Greater East Asia Co-Prosperity Sphere and included three new opening chapters. Emphasizing the importance of thoroughness (*tettei*) to victory, Matsunami discussed the current holy war:

> have we not cried often at the moving and tragic tales of those whose guns broke, so they swung their swords; their swords broke, so they swung their arms; their arms broke, so they used their legs; their legs were also injured, so they used their torsos; with but one fragment of flesh, one splinter of bone remaining, they faced the enemy and fought on.[129]

Matsunami described death as essential to the transmigration of souls from one generation to the next, not as a tragedy but as a step towards eternal life.[130] According to Matsunami, *bushidō* was similarly eternal, dating from the founding of the nation. It only came to be known as '*bushidō*' in the age of the *bushi*, he wrote, and

---

[124] Kihira Tadayoshi (1944), 'Waga kokutai ni okeru wa', in Monbushō Kyōgaku Kyoku (eds.), *Kokutai no hongi kaisetsu sōsho* (Monbushō Kyōgaku Kyoku), pp. 287–89.

[125] Chūtō Kyōiku Danwa Kai (eds.), *Chūtō gakkō ni okeru kō no kyōiku* (Tokyo: Sanseidō, 1935), p. 80.

[126] Koike Yoshiaki (1999), *Hagakure: bushi to 'hōkō'* (Tokyo: Kōdansha gakujutsu bunko), pp. 42–43. John Allen Tucker provides an overview of publications related to *Hagakure* in the 1930s, focusing on connections with Yamaga Sokō and the Akō *rōnin*: Tucker, John Allen, 'Tokugawa Intellectual History and Prewar Ideology: The Case of Inoue Tetsujirō, Yamaga Sokō, and the Forty-Seven Rōnin', *Sino-Japanese Studies* 14 (2002), pp. 61–62.

[127] Matsunami Jirō (1938), 'Jo', *Hagakure bushidō* (Tokyo: Ichiro Shoen), pp. 1–2.

[128] Matsunami Jirō, *Hagakure bushidō*, p. 13.

[129] Matsunami Jirō (1940), *Hagakure bushidō seishin* (Tokyo: Ichiro Shoen), p. 3.

[130] Matsunami Jirō, *Hagakure bushidō seishin*, p. 6.

people who claimed that it had arisen at that time were Western-influenced fools. After Meiji, he charged, Western thought entered Japan like a poisonous mushroom, contaminating people with 'commoner philosophy' and distracting them from their martial spirit.[131] For Matsunami, the *Hagakure* provided a possibility to understand Japan's unique *bushidō* and the importance of loyalty and willingness to give one's life for the emperor.

Various editions of the *Hagakure* were distributed by the government as educational materials in the decade before 1945, including Watsuji Tetsurō's pocket edition.[132] *Bushidō* propagandists such as Hashimoto Minoru described the first line of *Hagakure*, which equated *bushidō* with death, as 'true *bushidō*', and many texts discussed the 'spirit of the *Hagakure* warrior'.[133] Educator Hada Takao cited the *Hagakure* in his 1940 examination of approaches to teaching imperial *bushidō* during wartime, *Bushidō and the Way of the Educator (Bushidō to shidō)*.[134] *Hagakure* came to be broadly identified with *bushidō*, and by the 1940s had been integrated into the imperial interpretation. A 1944 textbook on *The Spirit of Japanese Tank Operators* included an overview of the *Hagakure*, while a history of the Japanese temperance movement published by the Japan National Temperance Union also cited the text.[135] Due to its emphasis on loyalty, death, and self-sacrifice, as well as its suitability for selective citation of single lines, the *Hagakure* challenged the popularity of works on Yamaga Sokō and Yoshida Shōin as well as other historical texts in the *bushidō* canon during the early 1940s.

The evolution of imperial *bushidō* that allowed it to incorporate the *Hagakure* was reflected in the 1939 *Bushidō Treasury (Bushidō hōten)*, which contained a selection from Yamamoto among heavily annotated historical documents from the *Man'yōshū* through to the Edo period. Inoue Tetsujirō provided an extensive preface to the *Bushidō Treasury*, and a German review of the text in *Monumenta Nipponica* attested to its high profile.[136] Inoue's preface was largely consistent with his *bushidō* theories from almost four decades before, defining *bushidō* as the martial element of the Japanese spirit responsible for the modern military successes that had surprised the world. Inoue argued that the uniqueness of *bushidō* could be seen in the term itself. Unlike the Confucian *shidō*, *bushidō* did not exist in China and was a purely Japanese product. Nor did an equivalent to *bushidō* exist in the West. While some might refer to chivalry as 'Western *bushidō*', this was mistaken as chivalry was an ethic of 'woman-worship', Inoue maintained, revisiting one of his earliest criticisms of the West.[137]

---

[131] Matsunami Jirō, *Hagakure bushidō seishin*, p. 124.

[132] Hashimoto Minoru (1934), *Bushidō no shiteki kenkyū* (Tokyo: Yūzankaku), p. 16.

[133] Hashimoto Minoru (1943), *Bushidō shiyō* (Tokyo: Dainihon kyōka tosho), p. 331; Yamagami Sōgen (1942), *Hagakure bushi no seishin* (Tokyo: San'yūsha).

[134] Hada Takao Hada Takao (1940), *Bushidō to shidō* (Baifūkan).

[135] Takeda Yasuji (1944), *Nihon sensha no tamashii* (Kyōyōsha), p. 123; Fujiwara Gyōzō (1941), *Nihon kinshū shi* (Nihon kokumin kinshū dōmei), p. 87.

[136] Schiffer, Wilhelm, 'Bushido Hoten (Handbuch des Bushido)', *Monumenta Nipponica*, 3:1 (Jan. 1940), p. 331.

[137] Inoue Tetsujirō (1939), 'Josetsu', in Saeki Ariyoshi (ed.), *Bushidō hōten* (Tokyo: Jitsugyō no Nihonsha), pp. 1–3.

Inoue's preface centred on a discussion of six unique elements of Japan's *bushidō* that could not be found in other countries. First, when the Japanese army attacked the enemy, the latter invariably scattered and fled, Inoue wrote, mentioning the Russo-Japanese and both Sino-Japanese wars as examples. Second, Japanese pilots did not carry parachutes when they left on a sortie, as there was no reason to try and flee if one's plane had been destroyed; there was only victory or death. Third, if a Japanese plane was damaged, the pilot would crash into the enemy in a suicide attack. There were 'countless' examples of suicide missions in Japanese military history, such as the 'three-hero bomb' involving three army engineers using explosives to blast through barbed wire. According to the official version, they charged into the fortification with explosives in the knowledge that a suicidal attack was the only effective measure. According to eyewitnesses, however, the men were ordered by their commanding officer to use a defective bomb with a very short fuse that would not permit them the usual time required to clear the area before it detonated.[138]

The fourth unique element of Japan's *bushidō* was that no Japanese soldiers had ever been taken prisoner. While many Chinese had surrendered and now worked for the Japanese army, no Japanese soldier had ever surrendered. General Stessel's surrender at the end of the Russo-Japanese War would have been unthinkable in Japan, Inoue contended, and if the war had gone differently, General Nogi would certainly have committed suicide rather than surrender. Fifth, many Japanese soldiers shout 'long live the emperor' three times before they die, a phenomenon unique to Japan and a sign of the emperor's incomparable authority. Inoue compared this with Chinese soldiers, and could not imagine them yelling 'long live Chiang Kai-shek!' in a similar situation. Sixth, the Japanese army treats all its enemies with great compassion, extending to the recital of prayers over fallen foes. All of these traits, Inoue argued, were unique characteristics of Japan's *bushidō* and could not be found in other countries.[139]

The main editor of the *Bushidō Treasury*, Shinto scholar Saeki Ariyoshi (1867–1945), related *bushidō* to Japan's expansionist policies. According to Saeki, the time had come for Japanese people to advance rapidly into the Asian continent that was the new promised land. In order to realize these aims, he argued, it was most essential to grasp the *bushidō* spirit by carefully reading the documents in the *Bushidō Treasury*.[140] 'The time has come for the sacred land of Orient to be managed by Orientals', Saeki wrote, a task which required selfless devotion and spiritual strength steeled through the study of *bushidō*.[141] This study was broadened significantly in 1942, when Saeki and Inoue compiled the thirteen-volume *Complete Works on Bushidō* (*Bushidō zensho*), an extensive collection of samurai

---

[138] Earhart, David C. (2008), *Certain Victory: Images of World War II in the Japanese Media* (London: M.E. Sharpe), pp. 76–78.

[139] Inoue Tetsujirō, 'Josetsu', pp. 4–9.

[140] Saeki Ariyoshi (1939), 'Jijo', *Bushidō hōten* (Tokyo: Jitsugyō no Nihonsha), p. 4.

[141] Saeki Ariyoshi (1939), 'Bushidō hoten no sue ni daisu', *Bushidō hōten* (Tokyo: Jitsugyō no Nihonsha), pp. 304–06.

writings that was reissued by the Society for Publishing National Texts (Kokusho Kankō Kai) from 1998.[142] This text credited *bushidō* with Japan's swift victories in Singapore and Malaya, a theme found in the majority of *bushidō* writings from the time, including those of prolific researcher Hashimoto Minoru. Hashimoto had studied *bushidō* at the Graduate School of Tokyo Imperial University and claimed to have written hundreds of books and articles on the subject.[143] In his 1942 textbook, *Bushidō History for Young People* (*Shōnen bushidō shi*), Hashimoto credited *bushidō* for the attack on Pearl Harbor and subsequent victories over the Western powers. According to Hashimoto, the British government's response to Japan's startlingly rapid advance was a sheepish admission that 'We forgot that Japan has *bushidō*'.[144]

In the time of crisis, *bushidō* became 'the imperial military's most important morale-building tool'.[145] 'Samurai' virtues such as frugality, self-sacrifice, and perseverance in the face of hardship were ideally suited to a nation at war on several fronts, while the ideals of patriotism and absolute loyalty to the emperor found favour with militaristic nationalists. With the imperial interpretation increasingly dominating discourse, *bushidō* found its way into almost all works on the Japanese spirit and ethics, as well as expanding its reach into popular culture. At the same time, government radio broadcasts used the rapidly spreading new medium to further disseminate the concept among the populace.[146]

In spite of the unprecedented popularity of *bushidō*, its historiographical problems were not overlooked by all. One of the most significant criticisms of *bushidō* in the wartime period was found in the *Great Principle* (*Taigi*) of Lieutenant Colonel Sugimoto Gorō (1900–37), who fell in combat in China. Up to 1.3 million copies of Sugimoto's ultranationalistic emperor-worshipping text were printed after his death for sale and distribution in schools to spiritually condition the nation's current and future soldiers.[147] Following the publication of *Great Duty*, Sugimoto's heroic actions were celebrated in books and magazines, many of them aimed at young people, and he was revered as one of the most popular 'war gods' of early Shōwa.[148] The account of Sugimoto's death in a 1940 Kōdansha biography for children reflected the sensationalistic tone of many educational publications:

> Sugimoto was struck in the chest by an enemy bullet, and stumbled forward two or three more steps before stopping. He stuck his bloody sword into the ground and

---

[142] Inoue Tetsujirō and Saeki Ariyoshi (eds.) (1942), *Bushidō zensho* (Tokyo: Jidaisha).

[143] Some of Hashimoto's most widely distributed studies include his relatively measured 1934 *Historical Research into Bushidō*, and his militaristic and death-focused 1943 *Essential History of Bushidō* (Hashimoto Minoru, *Bushidō no shiteki kenkyū*; Hashimoto Minoru, *Bushidō shiyō*).

[144] Hashimoto Minoru, *Shōnen bushidō shi*, pp. 2–5.

[145] Victoria, Brian Daizen, 'The "Negative Side" of D. T. Suzuki's Relationship to War', *The Eastern Buddhist* 41:2 (2010), p. 136.

[146] Kasza, Gregory J. (1988), *The State and the Mass Media in Japan, 1918–1945* (Berkeley: University of California Press), pp. 257–63.

[147] Victoria, Brian Daizen. 'The "Negative Side" of D. T. Suzuki's Relationship to War', p. 124. Yamamoto Kentoku gives the number as 'more than one million': Yamamuro Kentoku, *Gunshin: kindai Nihon ga unda 'eiyū' tachi no kiseki*, p. 262.

[148] Yamamuro Kentoku, *Gunshin*, p. 261–65.

adjusted his position before saluting in the direction of the distant Japanese sky and the Emperor. As a final act of worship Sugimoto faintly cried "long live the Emperor!" before his breath silently stopped. He was still standing.

At first, the account continued, Sugimoto's men didn't notice that anything was wrong, but wondered why he had stopped. Sugimoto did not reply to their questions, and it was only when they approached him and saw his terrible wound that they realized he was dead. Amid a hail of enemy fire Sugimoto's men wept as they gently lowered his body from the inspirational standing position that his Zen training had allowed him to maintain even in death.[149]

Sugimoto's stance on *bushidō* is significant especially in light of the prominent use of his writings and legacy by government and popular ideologists. For Sugimoto, loyalty to the emperor was the only important virtue and he rejected historical *bushidō* as it was limited to loyalty to a feudal lord, which was a minor virtue at best. By placing feudal lords above the emperor, Sugimoto argued, *bushidō* was treasonous and not fit to be labelled a 'way'. Sugimoto also rejected more recent *bushidō* interpretations as attempts to revive a treasonous ethic.[150] Since loyalty to the emperor was the essence of the sacred Imperial Japanese army, Sugimoto criticized the young officers and soldiers involved in the 26 February Incident as nothing but beasts who had been corrupted by the evils of individualism and freedom, bringing shame on the military by going against the imperial decree and causing chaos in a manner similar to communists.[151]

Sugimoto's dismissal of *bushidō* as treasonous was unusual given his status as a powerful symbol of the increasingly accepted militaristic Zen interpretations. Promoters of Zen sought patriotic legitimacy by claiming historical connections with *bushidō* from late Meiji onward, and these efforts peaked in the wartime period of early Shōwa.[152] In books and articles such as 'Zen and *Bushidō*', Suzuki Daisetsu argued for the influence of Zen on Japan's great warriors, from the Kamakura period to Miyamoto Musashi to the loyal retainers of Akō.[153] The effectiveness of Zen propagandists and the causal linkages between Zen and *bushidō* have recently come under increasing scrutiny and Sugimoto's writings reflect the historiographical difficulties faced by modern ideologists attempting to connect the two.[154]

---

[149] Nakaoke Takeo (1942), *Gunshin Sugimoto Gorō chūsa: shō kokumin no Nihon bunko* (Kōdansha), pp. 244–45.

[150] Sugimoto Gorō (1938), *Taigi* (Heibonsha), pp. 69–72.

[151] Sugimoto Gorō, pp. 78–79.

[152] For an overview of broader Buddhist activities in support of the early Shōwa government, see Ives, Christopher (2009), *Imperial-Way Zen: Ichikawa Hakugen's Critique and Lingering Questions for Buddhist Ethics* (Honolulu, University of Hawaii Press), pp. 30–53. For an examination of the connections of Zen and the military, see Victoria, Brian Daizen, *Zen at War.*

[153] Suzuki Daisetz T. (1941), 'Zen to bushidō', in Bushidō gakkai (eds.), *Bushidō nyūmon* (Futara shobō), pp. 64–77.

[154] See, for example, Ives, Christopher, *Imperial-Way Zen: Ichikawa Hakugen's critique and lingering questions for Buddhist ethics*, pp. 102–07.

BUSHIDŌ AND THE BATTLEFIELD

Government support at all levels of education combined with popular interest and the unprecedented reach of new media to ensure that *bushidō* was more widely disseminated in the early 1940s than at any other time. The extent to which *bushidō*, especially the imperial interpretation, influenced behaviour is more difficult to gauge. While *bushidō* ideologists of all colours desired to change people's behaviour, it is difficult to discern which actions were motivated by *bushidō* rather than other compelling factors. In this context, the battlefield provided the most suitable arena for observing the potential practical influence of *bushidō* ideology, both because it was most thoroughly disseminated in the military, and because it presented many of the extreme situations addressed by *bushidō* theories.

Discussions of *bushidō* in wartime tend to gravitate towards two phenomena that continue to define popular perceptions of the Japanese military in the Pacific theatre: the 'suicidal' tactics increasingly adopted later in the war, and the attitudes towards prisoners of war, both Japanese and foreign. These subjects, which are discussed here primarily in relation to Japanese engagements with Western forces rather than with other Asian nations, attract considerable attention due to aspects that seem to render them unique in military history. *Bushidō* played an important role in shaping opinion towards both self-destructive tactics and the treatment of POWs, and was frequently invoked to explain and justify Japanese actions and Allied responses. *Bushidō* was used as an ideological tool by the Japanese and United States governments, and victims of state power on both sides of the Pacific also sought to defend themselves, or at least rationalize the injustices they experienced through recourse to *bushidō*.

The Japanese military used *bushidō* to shape attitudes towards death from the time of the Russo-Japanese War, with noble or brave deaths seen as manifestations of Japan's unique warrior spirit. These narratives emphasized the virtue of self-sacrifice, as in the suicide of the Hitachi Maru officers in 1904, the 'three-hero bomb', and miniature submarine attacks at Pearl Harbor and Sydney Harbour. In all of these cases and many others, sensationalistic accounts of the events that transpired glossed over tactical errors and equipment failures to glamorize the spirit of men who died in the line of duty. James Dorsey describes the technical failures and shortcomings of five midget submarines that attacked Pearl Harbor in 1941. According to Dorsey, none of the five accomplished their mission due to mechanical problems, with one submarine running aground and its only surviving crew member becoming the first Japanese POW of the war.[155] While imperial *bushidō* ideology rejected surrender or retreat as foreign ideas incompatible with the Japanese spirit, the military still considered it necessary to implement capital penalties to ensure compliance.

It was less the effect of spiritual indoctrination that kept soldiers from surrendering in hopeless situations, but rather other factors such as the immediate threat of

---

[155] Dorsey, James (2009), 'Literary Tropes, Rhetorical Looping, and the Nine Gods of War: "Fascist Proclivities" Made Real', in Alan Tansman (ed.), *The Culture of Japanese Fascism* (Durham: Duke University Press), pp. 414–15.

being shot by their comrades as soon as they attempted to do so.[156] A US military report on a group of Japanese prisoners of war compiled shortly before the end of the war revealed that 84 per cent of them were convinced that they would be tortured or executed by their Allied captors, leading the authors to conclude 'that fear of the consequences of surrender, "rather than Bushido" was the motivation for many Japanese battle deaths in hopeless circumstances'.[157] Poor to nonexistent logistical planning and insufficient supply lines, both on the continent and in the Pacific, caused desperation among the troops and led to extreme situations and actions. Japanese soldiers were often forced to purchase their own rice during the war, while health problems, bullying, and supply shortages resulted in many suicides, all of which undermined the ideals of absolute obedience to a benevolent imperial family-state.[158] In China, Japanese troops were often forced to carry their own food or scavenge, and were known as the 'locust army' for their effect on the countryside.[159] Soldiers in the Burma campaign commonly referred to captured British supplies as 'gift rations from Mr Churchill', and this precarious method of obtaining food was central to the success and failure of military objectives.[160]

On Pacific islands where there was little or nothing to scavenge and supply lines were often severed completely, the situation was even more desperate. The diversionary invasion of the Alaskan island of Attu in 1943 resulted in 2,630 men being stranded with few supplies or munitions as the Americans cut their means of transport. The majority of the Japanese troops on Attu died through starvation and sickness before their commanding officer, Colonel Yamazaki Yasuo, led the several hundred remaining men in a desperate night attack against a far greater American force.[161] Only twenty-eight Japanese soldiers survived and, inspired by romanticized coverage in Japan, this tragic event repeated itself many times over on tropical islands much further south, as the '*gyokusai* charge' (lit. 'shattering like a jewel') became a widespread practice among desperate troops.[162] Escape from these situations was almost impossible, and the mortality rates of these largely unsuccessful tactics often approached 97 per cent.[163] A telling US military report on the few Japanese prisoners of war in the Southwest Pacific in 1944 revealed that 76 per cent thought they would be executed or severely punished if they returned to Japan.[164] Becoming a prisoner of war, which had been designated a most shameful act in the *bushidō* debates during the Russo-Japanese War, became virtually

---

[156] Earhart, David C., *Certain Victory: Images of World War II in the Japanese Media*, pp. 400–01.

[157] Dower, John (1987), *War Without Mercy: Race and Power in the Pacific War* (New York: Pantheon), p. 68.

[158] Yoshida Yutaka (2006), 'Ajia-taiheiyō sensō no senjō to heishi', in *Senjō no shosō (Ajia-Taiheiyō sensō 5)* (Tokyo: Iwanami shoten), pp. 66–69.

[159] Yoshida Yutaka (2002), *Nihon no guntai: heishi tachi no kindai shi* (Tokyo: Iwanami shinsho 816), p. 174.

[160] Nunneley, John and Kazuo Tamayama (2000), *Tales by Japanese Soldiers of the Burma Campaign 1942–1945* (London: Cassell & Co), pp. 38, 76, 81, 88, 120, 171, 175.

[161] Earhart, David C., *Certain Victory: Images of World War II in the Japanese Media*, pp. 378–80.

[162] Earhart, David C., pp. 397–406.   [163] Earhart, David C., p. 400.

[164] Trefalt, Beatrice (2003), *Japanese Army Stragglers and Memories of the War in Japan, 1950-1975* (London: RoutlegeCurzon), p. 21.

unthinkable in the *bushidō*-dominated environment of the early 1940s, when it would result in social ostracization of the individual and family, assuming they were allowed to return to Japan. In this sense, indoctrination with *bushidō* was at least as thorough and effective in civilian society as in the military.

Allied forces were equally cognizant of *bushidō*, not least because of the many sensationalistic writings on the subject, with the military commissioning research reports on subjects such as 'The Warrior Tradition as a Present Factor in Japanese Military Psychology'.[165] The Tenth Corps instructed its men as follows: 'desertion is frequently regarded as more acceptable to the Bushido-trained Jap than outright surrender. It gives the cornered Jap an opportunity to rationalize his position without too much loss of face'.[166] The US diplomat John K. Emmerson, who had observed many Japanese prisoners of war, described the mental change in new POWs, who, after receiving a course of 'medical care, good food, and considerate treatment' became 'filled with gratitude for the treatment which he did not expect and rapidly sloughs off his veneer of indoctrinated Bushido. For him one life has ended and another has begun'.[167]

These findings led to a concerted American propaganda campaign to entice Japanese troops to surrender and instructed them how to do so. Calls to surrender also appealed to *bushidō*. As one US propaganda leaflet asked Japanese soldiers, 'Does Japan have two codes of bushido: One for the navy and one for the army? The navy runs away to save itself, but the army, abandoned and cut off from all aid, is expected to remain and die a useless death ... You cannot win alone'.[168] Leaflets, loudspeaker messages, and other measures were implemented to convince Japanese troops that their situation had become hopeless, but that their safety would be guaranteed if they surrendered.[169] Reports of American atrocities against surrendering troops were not baseless, as John Dower points out, and a number of massacres of defenceless Japanese were committed during the war. This was exacerbated by practices such as the collection of trophies from dead Japanese soldiers which, if not common practice, were widely reported. In many situations, the supposedly innate Japanese unwillingness to surrender became a self-fulfilling prophecy, and Allied forces often suspected that attempts to surrender must be traps and met them with lethal force. Dower also concludes, however, that the Japanese 'bore no little responsibility for the reluctance of Allied soldiers to take prisoners, for early in the war they established a practice of booby-trapping their dead and wounded, and using fake surrenders to ambush unwary foes'.[170]

The treatment of enemy, especially Western, prisoners of war was another major issue related to *bushidō*, and one that had evolved considerably since the

---

[165] Gilmore, Allison B. (1998), *You Can't Fight Tanks with Bayonets: Psychological Warfare against the Japanese Army in the Southwest Pacific* (Lincoln, NE: University of Nebraska Press), p. 132.

[166] Gilmore, Allison B., p. 111.

[167] Iriye, Akira (1981), *Power and Culture: The Japanese-American War 1941–1945* (Cambridge, MA: Harvard University Press), p. 212.

[168] Gilmore, Allison B., *You Can't Fight Tanks with Bayonets*, p. 88.

[169] For an analysis of the effectiveness of these measures in the Philippines, see ch. 7 of Gilmore, Allison B., *You Can't Fight Tanks with Bayonets*.

[170] Dower, John, *War Without Mercy: Race and Power in the Pacific War*, pp. 64–71.

Russo-Japanese War. During Meiji and Taishō, Japan had largely acted in accordance with international law concerning prisoners of war, at least with regard to the conflicts with Russia and Germany.[171] The situation changed considerably in the Pacific War, however, as the *bushidō*-influenced view of surrender as a mortal shame became dominant. While most *bushidō* interpretations contended that the refusal to surrender was uniquely Japanese, the negative image of prisoners of war also affected treatment of captured foreign combatants. To be sure, many of the fatalities arising from the terrible conditions in which the Japanese kept prisoners of war arose from a chronic lack of supplies that extended to the entire military. The army struggled to feed itself, and there was little motivation to use scarce resources to keep enemy troops in better conditions than Japanese soldiers who were often at or below the level of bare subsistence. The influence of expedient factors was especially strong among Japanese troops operating in China, where there was less concern with possible negative reactions from Western powers. As Scott Corbett mentions, Japanese treatment of prisoners of war in China was considerably different from that in other areas. According to a 1933 book published by the Infantry Academy on methods of fighting the Chinese army, there were few requirements, and Chinese POWs could be freed, deported, or killed at the discretion of the capturing troops.[172]

With regard to the intentional mistreatment of prisoners, however, *bushidō* ideology certainly contributed to condescending views of those who surrendered and found themselves in Japanese custody. At the same time, *bushidō* was invoked by propagandists criticizing treatment of Japanese by the United States government, contrasting this with the Japanese approach: 'for our part, based on the ancient code of Bushido, we treat enemy POWs justly and noncombatants as leniently as possible, which has been common knowledge worldwide since the time of the Russo-Japanese War'.[173] Appeals to *bushidō* could not long hide the reality of conditions in which prisoners of war were kept, as reflected in a House of Commons speech by British Foreign Secretary Anthony Eden, in 1942. With regard to reported atrocities committed against defeated troops and civilians following the fall of Hong Kong, Eden stated, 'The Japanese claim that their forces are animated by a lofty code of chivalry, Bushido, is a nauseating hypocrisy'.[174] This response was directed at statements such as a Japanese description of the battle for Hong Kong, according to which the *bushidō* spirit had compelled the Japanese army to generously give the British two chances to surrender before attacking with full force.[175]

---

[171] Dobson, Hugo and Kosuge Nobuko (eds.) (2009), *Japan and Britain in War and Peace* (London: Routledge), p. 46.

[172] Corbett, P. Scott (2008), 'In the Eye of a Hurricane: Americans in Japanese Custody during World War II', in Karl Hack and Kevin Blackburn (eds.), *Forgotten Captives in Japanese-Occupied Asia* (London: Routledge), p. 113.

[173] From the *Asahigraph* (42:8), cited and translated by David C. Earhart (Earhart, David C., *Certain Victory: Images of World War II in the Japanese Media*, p. 366).

[174] Flower, Sibylla Jane (2008), 'Memory and the Prisoner of War Experience: The United Kingdom', in Karl Hack and Kevin Blackburn (eds.), *Forgotten Captives in Japanese-Occupied Asia* (London: Routledge), pp. 60–61.

[175] Earhart, David C., *Certain Victory: Images of World War II in the Japanese Media*, p. 233.

Bushidō became synonymous with wartime abuses in English and Ileana Troiano's 1943 book, *Hungarian Bushido: Atrocities Committed During the Occupation of Northern Transylvania in September 1940*, had no direct relation to Japan. According to Troiano, 'Bushido, Japanese for chivalry, is the term used by the British press after the occupation of Hong Kong at the end of 1941'.[176] The identification of *bushidō* with the mistreatment of prisoners became even stronger after the war, as accounts from survivors and those who liberated POW camps reached the general public. Lea Morris, for example, described Dutch experiences in Japanese captivity in Indonesia in her 1947 *Bushido: Krijgsmanseer, de erfenis der godenzonen*, which went through several printings over the following decades.[177] *Bushidō* was considered a decisive factor in Japanese behaviour by the vast majority of observers, with texts on the subject bearing titles such as *The Knights of Bushido, Bamboo and Bushido, Blood and Bushido: Japanese Atrocities at Sea, 1941–1945,* and *The Bushido Code and a Belief in Japanese Racial Superiority: Catalysts for Brutal Treatment of American Prisoners of War*.[178] These views also reflect foreign familiarity with *bushidō* and its wide acceptance in other countries during the Second World War.

In North America, the internment of Americans of Japanese descent was largely driven by racist fears that they would ultimately remain loyal to the emperor and fight against the United States from within. Their supposed adherence to an ancient *bushidō* ethic, which had become tainted with negative connotations in the United States by the 1930s, seemed to be additional proof that US citizens with Japanese ancestry could not be trusted. A 1932 tour of North America by Nitobe Inazō, in which he fruitlessly sought to convince Americans of Japan's noble ambitions in China, reinforced popular notions of Japanese duplicity.[179] At the same time, Japanese Americans invoked *bushidō* as evidence of their loyalty to the United States. As an immigrant leader in Seattle argued, US citizens of Japanese descent had 'the spirit and virtue of Bushido in their blood', making them 'loyal and true to their country, the United States of America, the country which gave them birth, education, and protection'.[180] Howard Miyake, who was serving in the US military at the time, recalled his mother's shocked disbelief when she heard the news from Pearl Harbor: 'A country of samurai could not have made an attack like that.'[181]

---

[176] Troiano, Ileana (1943), *Hungarian Bushido: Atrocities Committed During the Occupation of Northern Transylvania in September 1940* (Oxford: I. Troiano).

[177] Morris, Lea (1947), *Bushido: Krijgsmanseer, de erfenis der godenzonen* (Amsterdam: Nieuwe Wieken).

[178] Allbury, Alfred George (1955), *Bamboo and Bushido* (London: R. Hale); Russell, Edward F. L. (1958), *The Knights of Bushido* (London: Cassell); Edwards, Bernard (1997), *Blood and Bushido: Japanese Atrocities at Sea, 1941–1945* (Brick Tower Press); Moore, Patrick Burton (2000), *The Bushido Code and a Belief in Japanese Racial Superiority: Catalysts for Brutal Treatment of American Prisoners of War* (California State University, Dominguez Hills).

[179] Oshiro, George (1995), 'The End: 1929–1933', in John Howes (ed.), *Nitobe Inazō: Japan's Bridge Across the Pacific* (Boulder: Westview Press), pp. 253–78.

[180] Azuma Eiichiro (2005), *Between Two Empires: Race, History, and Transnationalism in Japanese America* (Oxford: Oxford University Press), pp. 130–32.

[181] Coox, Masayo Umezawa and Peter Duus (trans.) (1987), *Unlikely Liberators: The Men of the 100th and 442nd* (Honolulu: University of Hawai'i Press), p. 15.

Also due to the accessibility of Nitobe's work and other English-language materials on the subject, *bushidō* was an important concept for Japanese Americans, although their views in the 1930s tended to deviate considerably from contemporary imperial discourse in Japan.

CONSIDERING EARLY SHŌWA *BUSHIDŌ*

The diversity of *bushidō* discourse complicates attempts to determine which aspects of the ethic were accepted by whom, but it is beyond doubt that *bushidō* ideology in early Shōwa had devastating effects for both Japanese and foreigners. *Bushidō* was used to rationalize terrible and tragic actions committed by both Allies and Japanese, and was also invoked to dehumanize the latter. By redefining *bushidō* as a transcendental 'way of the warrior' rather than a historicized 'way of the samurai', imperial *bushidō* became an important pillar of the larger ideological state structure that sought to mobilize the entire nation for a holy war against the West. Accordingly, regional *bushidō* interpretations were emphasized less than at other times, with the pronounced local character of the *Hagakure* downplayed to make the text suitable for national implementation. This view of early Shōwa *bushidō* often obscures the diversity of discourse, however, and does not account for the various challenges to imperial *bushidō* from across the political and social spectrum, many of which targeted its problematic revision of history. In addition, the degree to which emperor-worship was accepted by most people in Japan is debatable, and theories that traced *bushidō* to the mythical Age of the Gods met with considerable scepticism.

While many of the more fantastical elements of imperial propaganda may not have grown the deepest roots, the diversity of *bushidō* discourses meant that there was an interpretation suitable for almost any purpose, often supported by carefully selected historical texts. This adaptability contributed greatly to the popularity of the subject, and although specific manifestations of *bushidō* might differ considerably, they contributed to the cumulative exposure of the population to *bushidō*, reinforcing its apparent legitimacy. Furthermore, even when Hagiwara Sakutarō, Kuki Shūzō, and Nakano Seigō criticized certain aspects of *bushidō*, their views were coloured by cultural nationalism and pride in other characteristics of the country's warrior heritage. On the whole, *bushidō* came to be closely identified with the imperial ideologies that dominated education and much of public discourse in wartime Japan, even if its position within the complex ideological ecosystem of early Shōwa is not easily defined. As an integral part of civilian and military curricula, the legitimacy of *bushidō* as a historical ethic was largely unquestioned and imperial *bushidō* was most thoroughly disseminated during this period. On the other hand, the heritage of Meiji and Taishō *bushidō* discourses strongly influenced Shōwa theories, complicating attempts to institute a monolithic interpretation. As a result, the development of *bushidō* between the end of Taishō and 1945 was characterized by an often uneasy relationship with the emperor-focused ideological structure of the time. It is possible to identify a lowest common denominator *bushidō* which, reduced to essentials of patriotism, loyalty, self-sacrifice, and a certain fatalism, was accepted by an overwhelming majority. In this sense, *bushidō* was more deeply rooted and effective than most other aspects of imperial ideology, as would become apparent after the war.

By 1945, foreigners identified Japan more closely with *bushidō* than ever before. Japanese military activities in China were explained by *bushidō* and a bellicose national character that drove Japan towards military expansion.[182] Japan's Axis partners also became highly interested in *bushidō* as a method of grasping the Japanese psyche and for practical use in their own spiritual education and propaganda projects. The German government took particular interest in *bushidō*, with Heinrich Himmler contributing the foreword to Heinz Corazza's 1937 *Die Samurai—Ritter des Reiches in Ehre und Treue* (*The Samurai—Honourable and Loyal Knights of the Realm*), a product of the central publishing organ of the Nazi party.[183] Overseas *bushidō* discourse became even more pronounced after the attack on Pearl Harbor, and many Allied observers saw the roots of Japanese imperialism in the nation's samurai heritage. It was hoped that understanding Japan's supposedly innate martial spirit would help predict Japanese actions and devise effective tactics, but it simultaneously dehumanized the enemy into *bushidō*-driven automatons. John Dower describes arguments based on 'suicide psychology' as one of the three main lines of American thought regarding 'thoroughgoing defeat' of Japan. According to this view, the samurai spirit would prevent Japan from surrendering, and the United States military would have to kill everyone in order to end the war.[184] Conversely, as the tragic mass suicides of civilians and soldiers in Okinawa in August 1945 demonstrated, propaganda-stoked fears of the behaviour of invading US troops meant that this scenario was not entirely unthinkable.

---

[182] An early example of this trend was Taid O'Conroy (1933), *The Menace of Japan* (London: Hurst & Blackett). Also see H. J. Timperley (1942), *Japan: A World Problem* (New York: The John Day Company).

[183] Spang, Christian W. and Rolf-Harald Wippich (2006), 'Introduction—from "German Measles" to "Honorary Aryans": An overview of Japanese-German relations until 1945', in Christian W. Spang and Rolf-Harald Wippich (eds.), *Japanese-German Relations 1895–1945: War, Diplomacy, and Public Opinion* (New York: Routledge), p. 16.

[184] Dower, John, *War Without Mercy: Race and Power in the Pacific War*, p. 56.

7

Bushidō in Post-War Japan

THE REJECTION OF IMPERIAL *BUSHIDŌ*

Domestic reactions to the surrender of Japan in August 1945 varied widely, but the vast majority of people who had lived through fifteen years of increasingly devastating warfare came to see this turning point as a declaration of the ideological bankruptcy of the imperialists. Japan did not resist to the last person, as the government had maintained, and even the overwhelming majority of the 'spiritually educated' troops accepted the surrender rather than continuing to fight or committing suicide in line with the demands of imperial *bushidō*. As John Dower points out, while a few hundred military officers and others took their own lives, this was comparable to the number of German officers who committed suicide after Germany's surrender the previous year.[1] Furthermore, the emperor's historic first radio address announcing the capitulation shattered illusions of imperial divinity, to the extent that these had been accepted. As the immediate shock and practical considerations of the war's end subsided in the transition to life under American occupation, anger towards elements of the old order was rife, and managing this was an important concern for the offices of the Supreme Commander for the Allied Powers (SCAP) that controlled Japan until the Treaty of San Francisco came into force in 1952.

One target of popular resentment was *bushidō*, specifically the imperial interpretation that had provided increasingly shrill backing to the militarists' messages. Some of the harshest critics of *bushidō* were soldiers, who had, in many ways, been most directly affected. Furthermore, they had experienced the hollowness of the ideology on the battlefield, as well as its most dangerous aspects. As one war correspondent recalled: 'Victory and defeat for air units were determined by altitude, speed, and firepower. No matter how much you asserted *bushidō* there, if you didn't have the speed you couldn't escape or overtake your opponent. Japan lost because it didn't have any of them'. When criticized by his superiors for focusing on technical matters rather than spirit, he replied that the front-line soldiers would have seen through 'such stupid things' as they didn't reflect the reality of the war.[2] The later reflections of a veteran naval officer were similarly critical of the leadership's

---

[1] Dower, John (1999), *Embracing Defeat: Japan in the Aftermath of World War II* (London: Allen Lane, The Penguin Press), pp. 38–39.

[2] Cook, Haruko Taya and Theodore F. (2000), *Japan at War: An Oral History* (London: Phoenix Press), p. 210.

drive towards warfare and dismissal of risks: 'They held that if you attack, the path of opportunity will open up naturally. If you try to defend yourself, you will lose. "Advance, advance" therefore became the only objective...As in *bushidō*, whether you lived or died was not crucial. Individual autonomy or independence? *Not important*'.[3] Many veterans recalled *bushidō* as essentially synonymous with blind obedience, epitomizing the most hated aspects of their military service. Others took a more fatalistic approach, accepting *bushidō* as a core part of their identity as Japanese and as soldiers against whom circumstances had conspired.

For many, the end of the war stripped imperial *bushidō* of any relevance it may have had, while the occupation authorities banned any writings or performances with martial themes, largely eliminating possible vehicles for a revival of *bushidō* even if a popular appetite for such had existed. The disappearance of *bushidō* from popular culture, combined with the immediacy of more practical concerns and challenges, meant that *bushidō* was generally ignored rather than explicitly criticized in the early post-war period. One exception to this was the writers often described as belonging to the Burai literary movement ('the decadents') around novelist Dazai Osamu (1909–48).[4] Burai works expressed the widespread disillusionment within society at the time and addressed the strong identification of *bushidō* with the emperor system and militarism. Sakaguchi Angō (1906–55) achieved fame in 1946 with the publication of 'On Decadence', an attack on both cultural icons and reductionist attempts to distill a 'Japanese spirit' that struck a deep resonance with the prevailing *zeitgeist*.[5]

In seeking to break down staid traditions, Sakaguchi targeted the samurai image that had been promoted so heavily in the preceding decade. Sakaguchi questioned the historical accuracy of *bushidō*, arguing that the Japanese people were among the most conciliatory and least likely to bear a grudge, and supposed samurai obligations such as taking lethal vengeance seemed implausible. Furthermore, the history of Japanese warfare was not a history of *bushidō*, but rather a history of negotiations, and fighting a war with Japanese troops would have been impossible without regulations stipulating that it was shameful to be captured alive. The Japanese tended to follow regulations, Sakaguchi continued, even when their true intentions were entirely opposed, and he criticized both *bushidō* and the emperor system as very Japanese political creations. Sakaguchi described *bushidō* as 'inhumane and anti-humanitarian' due to its prohibitive prescriptions against human urges and instincts, while it was precisely the piercing result of these prohibitions that made *bushidō* an entirely human thing.[6] Sakaguchi's views had not softened three years later, when he described *bushidō* as the 'most misguided bias' and those who cited it as 'mentally ill'.[7]

---

[3] Cook, Haruko Taya and Theodore F., p. 80.
[4] Keene, Donald (1984), *Dawn to the West: Japanese Literature of the Modern Era (Vol. 1, Fiction)* (New York: Holt, Rinehart, and Winston), p. 1023.
[5] Dorsey, James, 'Culture, Nationalism, and Sakaguchi Ango', *Journal of Japanese Studies* 27:2 (Summer, 2001), pp. 349.
[6] Sakaguchi Angō, 'Daraku ron', *Shinchō* 43:4 (1 April 1946).
[7] Sakaguchi Angō, 'Interi no kanshō', *Bungei shunjū* 27:3 (1 March 1949), pp. 27–30.

Tanaka Hidemitsu (1913–49), a disciple of Dazai Osamu who is also often described as a Burai writer, was even more critical of *bushidō* ideology. Writing in 1949, Tanaka's 'Sayōnara' cited the death-focused famous opening line of the *Hagakure* as epitomizing imperial Japan's ruling ideology. According to Tanaka, the Japanese were taught that, 'when standing on the line between life and death, it is correct to choose death'. The deaths of General Nogi, the Akō *rōnin*, the victims of suicide charges, and the rebellious officers of the 1930s were celebrated, while the authorities handed out poison that could kill ten people at once as part of this exaltation of death. To the 'foolish Japanese people', who 'love and respect suicidal individuals and assassins like gods', Tanaka wrote, 'the shallow nihilism of [the casual parting expression] *"sayōnara"* was most fitting'.[8]

Strong anti-*bushidō* sentiment notwithstanding, discourse on the subject began to revive as the US occupation came to an end. Censorship of the media and culture by the American occupation authorities extended to many popular spheres that had been carriers of *bushidō* ideology in the decades before 1945. Targets of bans included films that were considered to be 'militaristic' or 'propagating feudalism'.[9] As the *Daily Mail* reported in October 1945, 'the only film which has been completed since the occupation, an historical production called "General Beggar" was banned by MacArthur's censors because it boosted Bushido, or the martial spirit of the Japanese'.[10] The latter designation was especially crucial for cultural products related to *bushidō*, with its unquestionably 'feudal' character, and period pieces were essentially banned unless they omitted 'sword fighting scenes or when they explicitly criticized Bushido, revenge, and other feudal ideals'.[11] Influenced also by their own wartime propaganda, including films such as the 1945 *Know Your Enemy—Japan*, Americans tended to see the samurai and other martial themes as inseparable from the events of early Shōwa, and therefore in need of suppression.[12]

Many people in Japan held similar views, and the *bushidō* brand had been seriously damaged as a result of the war, but there was also an awareness that the discredited imperial interpretation was not the only *bushidō*, especially before the 1930s. In spite of the institutional and popular dominance of imperial *bushidō*, discourse on the subject had retained some diversity through the end of the war, providing possible alternatives shorn of militarism and other more problematic elements. The notion that imperial *bushidō* was an aberration was widespread, and people from all areas of public life soon began to look for 'true' *bushidō* in earlier samurai history and symbols. This was also a means of dealing with the wartime trauma, as it shifted blame away from 'normal', 'traditional' culture to the distorted wartime ideology and its promoters. Attempts to invoke 'true' *bushidō* were already seen in

---

[8] Tanaka Hidemitsu (1956), 'Sayōnara', *'Sayōnara' hoka sanpen* (Tokyo: Kadokawa shoten), pp. 35–66.

[9] Hirano, Kyoko (1992), *Mr. Smith Goes to Tokyo: Japanese Cinema under the American Occupation, 1945–1952* (Washington: Smithsonian Institution Press), p. 6.

[10] McDonald, Lachie, 'MacA Puts Back the Glamour', *Daily Mail*, (19 Oct. 1945), 3.

[11] Yoshimoto Mitsuhiro (2000), *Kurosawa: Film Studies and Japanese Cinema* (Durham: Duke University Press), p. 223.

[12] Dower, John (1987), *War Without Mercy: Race and Power in the Pacific War* (New York: Pantheon), pp. 18–23.

the sessions of the Imperial Diet, which continued to meet until the implementation of the post-war constitution in 1947. In a meeting of the House of Peers on 1 December 1945, Toki Akira (1892–1979) stated that the traditional Japanese viewpoint of *bushidō* meant that Japan would live up to its responsibilities as a defeated nation. Unfortunately, Toki continued, the inability of foreigners to understand this fact resulted in difficulties in negotiations with the occupation authorities. Similar arguments regarding the incomprehensibility of *bushidō* to non-Japanese have proved resilient, and are often used in response to criticism from abroad. Within Japan, the pace at which *bushidō* recovered varied greatly in different spheres, with an important factor being its previous history in a field of discourse.

BUSHIDŌ AND POST-WAR POPULAR CULTURE

The complex relationship of *bushidō* to the militarist period left a troubled legacy in post-war popular culture, including film, which the imperial government had used with mixed success in its attempts to promote militarism. As Aaron Gerow points out, some of the best-known attempts to promote 'Japaneseness' through cinema, such as Mizoguchi Kenji's 1941–42 film *Genroku Chūshingura* (*The Genroku Treasury of Loyal Retainers*), had been commercial and critical failures.[13] Unlike Mizoguchi's wartime effort, dramatizations of the Akō vendetta in the post-war period were positively received, beginning with a sanitized Kabuki version in 1947.[14] Film adaptations began to be produced regularly soon after the end of the occupation, laying the groundwork for what Henry D. Smith describes as the later 'ritualization' of the genre on television from the 1960s onward.[15] This reflects the significant disconnect between imperial *bushidō* and the samurai in the early post-war popular consciousness, with only the former linked to the discredited militaristic regime. In contrast, a genre of period pieces categorized as 'samurai films' by foreign critics soon came to dominate Japanese post-war cinema until the late 1960s, when a combination of changing tastes and the diffusion of television led to their ultimate decline. The classification 'samurai films' has proved enduring, if contentious, as the films classed in this genre are those most often discussed in relation to *bushidō*.[16] In contrast, Japanese film critics and scholars tend to see these films as part of a larger genre of 'period pieces' (*jidaigeki*), while using other subgenre classifications such as 'sword fight films' (*chanbara eiga*).

Problems of categorization are inevitable given the number and diversity of 'samurai films' in the immediate post-war period, reflecting not only changes in broader politics and society in Japan. Films from this period are often portrayed as direct

[13] Gerow, Aaron (2009), 'Narrating the Nation-ality of a Cinema: The Case of Japanese Prewar Film', in Alan Tansman (ed.), *The Culture of Japanese Fascism* (Durham: Duke University Press), pp. 186–87.
[14] Hirano, Kyoko, *Mr Smith Goes to Tokyo*, p. 66.
[15] Smith II, Henry D. (2006), 'The Media and Politics of Japanese Popular History: The Case of the Akō Gishi', in James C. Baxter (ed.), *Historical Consciousness, Historiography, and Modern Japanese Values* (Kyoto: International Research Center for Japanese Studies), p. 88.
[16] Yoshimoto Mitsuhiro, *Kurosawa: Film Studies and Japanese Cinema*, pp. 212–13.

responses to contemporary political events, and just as early modern artists evaded Tokugawa restrictions on discussing current events by ostensibly situating their works in the distant past, post-war filmmakers minimized political difficulties by seeking refuge in Sengoku or Tokugawa. Film critics and other commentators, especially in other countries, often describe post-war samurai films as a reaction against *bushidō* as it had been promoted in early Shōwa, and David Desser writes of a 'revision' and even 'vilification' of *bushidō* in this context.[17] The seemingly contradictory notion that samurai films were used to criticize the way of the samurai highlights the post-war continuation of the typically uneasy relationship between images of *bushidō* and the samurai, which marked discussions on the subject from the late nineteenth century.

The popularity of samurai films in the immediate post-war period can be attributed to a number of factors. These films resurrected popular earlier trends, they were familiar in a time of great uncertainty and upheaval, they facilitated escapism from the difficulties of everyday life, and they were relatively inexpensive to produce. On the other hand, they were invariably characterized by conflict and violence, albeit to varying degrees, and dealt with themes for which one would suspect the public might have little appetite so soon after the most devastating war in its history. The clear temporal distance between the setting of the samurai film and the post-war reality was certainly a significant factor in their popularity, with *bushidō* linking the two worlds. Even if directors did not always seek to make the connection explicit, audiences and critics made it inevitable that the post-war samurai film would at least indirectly engage with *bushidō* in subsequent debate.

In light of the recent past, one important task of the early post-war samurai films was to remove the samurai from (imperial) *bushidō*, and restore them as acceptable subjects for entertainment. This undertaking was accompanied by a complementary movement to strip *bushidō* from the samurai, and to deal with it on its own terms. Director Kurosawa Akira's 1954 *Seven Samurai* reflects his desire to create period films that were closer to the historical reality than the idealistic works of early Shōwa; he presented an unorthodox view of the samurai relative to the pre-war *bushidō* ideal, portraying them not as social models, but as ruffians and criminals with questionable motivations.[18] In a critique that applies to many other Japanese films and directors of the period, Yamamoto Mitsuhiro questions those critics that seek 'samurai values in Kurosawa films...because there is a tradition of "samurai discourse" in the colonial domestication of Japan by the West'. Yamamoto sees greater utility in an examination of the role criticism of Kurosawa's work has played in 'the dissemination of samurai discourse since the 1960s', a point valid for other films as well.[19]

---

[17] Desser, David (1992), 'Toward a Structural Analysis of the Postwar Samurai Film', in Arthur Nolletti, Jr. and David Desser (eds.), *Reframing Japanese Cinema: Authorship, Genre, History* (Bloomington: Indiana University Press), p. 147. Desser proposes four categories of post-war samurai film, all of which run counter to the views of *bushidō* dominant during the wartime period.

[18] Yoshimoto Mitsuhiro, *Kurosawa: Film Studies and Japanese Cinema*, p. 204; Nygren, Scott, *Time Frames: Japanese Cinema and the Unfolding of History*, p. 91.

[19] Yoshimoto Mitsuhiro, *Kurosawa: Film Studies and Japanese Cinema*, pp. 72–73.

Just as the genre of 'samurai film' has been largely missing from the vocabulary of Japanese film critics, explicit references to *bushidō* were not common within the films themselves. On the one hand, many of the films followed formulas established decades earlier, rendering explanations of cinematic samurai behaviour unnecessary to experienced viewers. On the other hand, the presence of *bushidō* was assumed in the cultural backgrounds of the films, viewers, and critics. As a recent interpretation of Kobayashi Masaki's 1962 *Seppuku* (Eng. *Harakiri*) describes the film's climactic scene:

> The armour is symbolic of the Ii household's ancestors and the traditions of *bushidō* that the film's humanist position challenges. The fact that Tsugumo Hanshirō (Nakadai Tatsuya) picks up this armour and hurls it at his opponents in the final moments of his protracted solitary battle with members of the Ii clan towards the end of the film is symbolic of his attack on the ideology of *bushidō*. The restoration of the armour to its original pedestal after Tsugumo's death is equally symbolic of the *bushidō* ideology's ability to withstand such attacks by individuals.[20]

Although unspoken in the film and certainly not identified in such a clear manner by the vast majority of viewers, *bushidō* was nonetheless seen as something that had to be addressed, ideally in terms of affirmation or rejection. The liberation of the post-war celluloid samurai from *bushidō* symbolism would not occur simply through silence.

Instead, removing *bushidō* from the samurai and treating it on terms of its Meiji heyday provided a way of saving both the concept and Japan's modernity. Nostalgia for the supposedly more innocent Meiji period combined with a desire to save aspects of Japan's modernity to drive the success of Watanabe Kunio's 1957 blockbuster *Meiji Tennō to Nichi-Ro daisensō* (*The Meiji Emperor and the Great Russo-Japanese War*). The film was wildly popular among audiences and even received praise from many Japanese critics, although some attributed its success largely to the use of the rapidly growing widescreen technology. The film was an unabashedly nationalistic look at the events of fifty years before, and also broke ground through its depiction of the sovereign, with the Meiji emperor portrayed as an exceptionally humane figure who cared most about the well-being of his troops. In spite of its length, its unsophisticated plot, and relatively primitive special effects, the film set the annual record for revenue and by itself saved the Shintōhō studios that produced it.[21]

Responses to *The Meiji Emperor and the Great Russo-Japanese War* were overwhelming, with a *Yomiuri shinbun* editorial describing 'the outpouring of nostalgic sentiments from the hearts of the people' in the cinema.[22] The Tokyo correspondent of *The Times* analyzed the phenomenon as follows:

> What is the secret of this film's success? Critics emphasize that audiences are deeply stirred by the spectacle constantly before their eyes of Emperor, military, government, and people, one in mind and spirit, working for the greatness of Japan. In a sense, the

---

[20] Standish, Isolde (2006), *A New History of Japanese Cinema: A Century of Narrative Film* (New York: Continuum), p. 289.

[21] Anderson, Joseph L. and Donald Richie (1982), *The Japanese Film: Art and Industry* (Princeton: Princeton University Press), pp. 250–52.

[22] *The Times*, 'Japan Deeply Moved By War Film,' *The Times*, Wed. 29 May 1957. p. 3.

film is militaristic; but its militarism is that of Admiral Togo, or General Nogi—not of Tojo and the leaders of the last war. It is a militarism suffused with the traditional Japanese virtues of *bushido*, the way of the warrior, and deeply tinged with humanity. Unconsciously, audiences compare the chivalrous behaviour of General Nogi, the commander-in-chief of the land forces at Port Arthur, who lost both his sons in the fighting, holding out his hand to General Stoessel, the Russian Commander, when he came to surrender, with that of General Yamashita at Singapore in 1942.[23]

This description was based on the dominant opinions in the Japanese press at the time, with the *Asahi Weekly* writing that 'The Emperor and the General must have appeared as true leaders to those who had known the pre-war unscrupulous, fascist, and arrogant militarists'.[24] According to *The Times* correspondent, the film caused people to face the spiritual fallout of the more recent war, with the post-war recovery 'providing no substitute' for 'traditional values and belief'.[25] The invocation of Meiji presented an opportunity to rescue both *bushidō* and modernity from the corruption of Shōwa militarists, while the Russo-Japanese War had lost none of its symbolic importance in a Japan on the front lines of the Cold War.

The modernity represented by Meiji was viewed as healthier also due to its proximity to the traditional morality of the Tokugawa period. In contrast, Taishō and Shōwa Japan were portrayed has having lost this moral anchor, leading to the disastrous events of the 1930s and 1940s. Popular nostalgia for an idealized nineteenth-century world of samurai values was most pronounced in—and in no small part driven by—the works of Japan's most prominent author of historical fiction, Shiba Ryōtarō (1923–96). Shiba's most productive period began in the 1960s, when many of his novels were also turned into films and television series. His 1960 novel of Bakumatsu samurai, *Zeeroku bushidō* (*Kansai Bushidō*), inspired two separate television productions that decade, while his 1969 masterpiece *Saka no ue no kumo* (*Clouds Above the Hill*) became the most expensive and elaborate period series (*Taiga dorama*) ever produced by Japan Broadcasting Corporation, airing between 2009 and 2011. Tracing the lives of three characters from the city of Matsuyama in Western Japan through the Meiji period to their heroic accomplishments in the Russo-Japanese War, *Saka no ue no kumo* exemplifies Shiba's fascination with *bushidō*, which he credited with Japan's successful modernization. According to Shiba, *bushidō* was the 'backbone of Japan', and the samurai spirit had to be revived if the nation was to successfully face the world again as it had in Meiji.[26] Although Shiba was not a historian, many readers gravitate towards his books in order to learn history, and his impact on the popular understanding of certain aspects of Japan's history should not be underestimated.[27] Also through the aid of *bushidō*, Shiba's work skilfully wove regional histories into the greater national story, bringing together samurai narratives situated in all parts of

---

[23] *The Times*, p. 3.   [24] *The Times*, p. 3.   [25] *The Times*, p. 3.

[26] Vinh, Sinh (2006), 'Shiba Ryōtarō and the Revival of Meiji Values', in James C. Baxter (ed.), *Historical Consciousness, Historiography, and Modern Japanese Values* (Kyoto: International Research Center for Japanese Studies), pp. 144–45.

[27] Fogel, Joshua A. (2006), 'On Translating Shiba Ryōtarō', in James C. Baxter (ed.), *Historical Consciousness, Historiography, and Modern Japanese Values* (Kyoto: International Research Center for Japanese Studies), pp. 153–55.

Japan. The popularity of Shiba's voluminous writings, packed with historical names and dates, has prompted cities and towns throughout Japan to open museums and tourist attractions dedicated to the figures he made famous, and Shiba's contribution to the rehabilitation of a pre-Shōwa *bushidō* in the popular mind from the 1960s onward has been significant.

Interest in Shiba's works reflected broader shifts in society as rapid economic growth fed into a resurgence of nationalistic sentiment. Japan's GNP reached pre-war levels by 1955 and continued on an upward trajectory.[28] The 1964 Tokyo Olympics symbolized the nation's recovery and its ongoing rehabilitation into global society, and US pressure helped to normalize official relations with Korea the following year. These developments did not meet with unanimous approval in Japan, however, and the 1960s also saw unprecedented unrest in opposition to the Treaty of Mutual Cooperation and Security signed with the United States in 1960. This agreement placed Japan firmly in the US camp in the Cold War, dashing the hopes of many who hoped to maintain a neutrality that could keep Japan out of military conflicts and help improve its status in Asia. These feelings and fears were exacerbated with the intensification of the widely unpopular war in Vietnam, as Japan (including Okinawa) hosted a great number of US forces and facilities. At the same time, US military spending brought a significant boost to the economy, and the 1960s also saw the growth of a new nationalism and even right-wing terrorism in response to leftist activities.[29] The situation reached a critical point at the end of the decade, as student activism swept through Japan along with many other countries, and the celebrated nationalist writer Mishima Yukio believed that riots in 1968 would bring a conclusive showdown between right and left.[30] As the centennial of the Meiji Restoration, 1968 was an especially powerful symbol for rightists seeking to recover Japan's 'lost morality and carry out that ill-defined goal of the military extremists of the 1930s, the Shōwa Restoration', although their grand plans for action were generally intended for 1970, the year the Security Treaty with the US would come up for renewed debate.[31]

The year 1970 became one of the two most eventful years in post-war *bushidō* discourse, as some of the most problematic elements of wartime *bushidō* were brought dramatically and briefly into the spotlight. In November of that year, Mishima Yukio led his personal, emperor-worshipping militia to seize offices of the Self-Defense Forces in Tokyo in an ostensible attempt to overthrow the government and create a nationalistic and militaristic new order. Mishima called on the troops to join him in this endeavour, but, failing to garner any broader support, he and his closest associate committed *seppuku* following an extended standoff with the authorities. Mishima had long been fascinated by the military, which in turn hoped to use his 1967 enlistment for much-needed publicity.[32] The sincerity

---

[28] Tsuzuki, Chishichi (2000), *The Pursuit of Power in Modern Japan 1825–1995* (Oxford: Oxford University Press), p. 379.

[29] Tsuzuki, Chishichi, pp. 395–96.   [30] Tsuzuki, Chishichi, p. 412.

[31] Jansen, Marius, 'Japan Looks Back', *Foreign Affairs*, 47:1 (Oct. 1968), pp. 45–50.

[32] Frühstück, Sabine (2007), *Uneasy Warriors: Gender, Memory, and Popular Culture in the Japanese Army* (Berkeley: University of California Press), p. 1.

of Mishima's attempted coup has been widely questioned, and given the level of detail with which he stage-managed the event, it is highly unlikely that he expected it to succeed.

In the popular view, Mishima's actions, particularly the manner of his suicide, were immediately tied to his fascination with the samurai and the death-focused imperial *bushidō* ideology of the wartime period, which had intensified in the last years of his life. In 1966, Mishima wrote *The Voices of the Heroic Dead*, in which the emperor is attacked by the spirits of Special Attack Force pilots for denying his own divinity, thereby rendering their sacrifice in vain.[33] The following year, Mishima published *A Primer on the Hagakure* (*Hagakure nyūmon*), echoing its use for military spiritual education a few decades before.[34] Mishima criticized modern society for becoming artificially detached from death, describing mindfulness of death as essential for mental health.[35] The year 1968 saw the appearance of the series 'Talks on Spirit for Young Samurai', one of a number of political texts that helped cement his identification with the samurai spirit in the popular mind.[36]

On one level, Mishima's dramatic suicide had a similar effect on popular views of *bushidō* as did Nogi Maresuke's death sixty years before, with the dominant sentiment being bewilderment at his seemingly anachronistic act. The prime minister at the time, Satō Eisaku, attributed the incident to Mishima's having gone 'mad', a view shared by many observers.[37] This was an important difference in the reactions to Nogi and Mishima in the context of *bushidō*. Nogi was viewed as the embodiment of *bushidō*, and criticisms tended to portray both him and the ethic as relics of an earlier time.[38] While Mishima's death was also seemingly driven by *bushidō* and met with bemusement, many people also saw it as a throwback to the 'corrupted' *bushidō* of early Shōwa, and his legacy was rejected by both the left and right.[39] This was more problematic for the latter, as many rightist politicians shared important ideals with Mishima and saw him as a cultural figurehead.[40]

The almost universal condemnation of Mishima also had the effect of motivating various scholars to elucidate their interpretations of 'true' *bushidō* in response. Popular historians and other writers focused increasingly on earlier history in composing *bushidō* theories that sought to set the proverbial record straight, but tended to hold fast to the basic conceptual framework of historicized *bushidō* that had developed from late Meiji onward. Mishima's influence on public perceptions of *bushidō* moved the journalist Morikawa Tetsurō (1924–82) to 'reassess the heritage

---

[33] Keene, Donald, *Dawn to the West: Japanese Literature of the Modern Era* (*Vol. 1, Fiction*), p. 1182.

[34] Mishima Yukio (1967), *Hagakure nyūmon* (Tokyo: Kōbunsha).

[35] Mishima Yukio: Kathryn Sparling (trans.) (1977), *Yukio Mishima on Hagakure: The Samurai Ethic and Modern Japan* (Souvenir Press), pp. 28–29.

[36] Keene, Donald, *Dawn to the West: Japanese Literature of the Modern Era* (*Vol. 1, Fiction*), p. 1189.

[37] Otomo Ryoko, '"The Way of the Samurai": Ghost Dog, Mishima, and Modernity's Other', *Japanese Studies* 21:1 (2001), p. 38.

[38] As Chushichi Tsuzuki points out, '…Mishima has been studied more by foreigners than by his compatriots, for whom he has become a taboo or an irrelevance': Tsuzuki, Chushichi, *The Pursuit of Power in Modern Japan: 1825–1995*, p. 460.

[39] 'The Man Japan Wants to Forget', *The Economist* (Saturday, 11 November 1995), pp. 143–44.

[40] Babb, James, 'The Seirankai and the Fate of its Members: The Rise and Fall of the New Right Politicians in Japan', *Japan Forum* 24:1 (2012), p. 78.

of the Japanese national spirit' in his *History of Japanese Bushidō* (*Nihon bushidō shi*) in 1972.[41] The following year, Morikawa followed Mishima's example and published his own *A Primer on the Hagakure* (*Hagakure nyūmon*), one of many *Hagakure* commentaries that appeared in the years following Mishima's death.[42]

POST-WAR HISTORIANS AND THE REDISCOVERY OF *BUSHIDŌ*

The task of liberating the samurai from imperial *bushidō* was not limited to fields of popular culture. One of the first groups to revisit *bushidō* in a substantial way during the post-war period was academic historians, especially scholars of early modern and pre-modern Japan. For many students of Japanese history in the 1930s and early 1940s, these earlier periods represented an escape from the militaristic present or, after 1945, the militaristic recent past. As long as they steered clear of controversial subjects such as the medieval imperial succession, pre-war historians could often pursue their study in relative peace. On the other hand, innocent mistakes regarding the imperial house could have serious consequences for even the most established patriots, as Inoue Tetsujirō experienced when he was forced to resign from the House of Peers in 1926 for questioning the authenticity of the imperial regalia.[43] Many of the major scholars of Japanese history in the post-war period had been students during the 1930s, including Ienaga Saburō, later one of the harshest and best-known critics of militarism. Ienaga recounted being made responsible for the publication of a summary of activities on a mandatory research trip to Ise Shrine led by Hiraizumi Kiyoshi. Although Ienaga attempted to take a broader historical approach, heavy editing of his report by the editors responsible removed everything that wasn't founded on myth-based imperial history.[44]

As a result, historians often added token references to imperial ideology to their work, especially when it was on related subjects.[45] These references were often not central to their arguments, and were often little more than garnish intended to prevent problems with editors and publishers. Much of this research was reissued after 1945 with these 'imperial' elements removed, as in the case of the *bushidō* theories of historian Kawakami Tasuke (1884–1959). In a 1938 article on 'The Origins of *Bushidō*', Kawakami sought the roots of 'Japan's unique *bushidō* spirit' in the late Heian period among the warriors of Eastern Japan, who had not been corrupted by the foreign influences that had weakened the court in Kyoto. Kawakami compared the breakdown of order after the Tang dynasty with conditions in Japan, arguing that the presence of the warriors and their *bushidō* allowed Japan to avoid

---

[41] Morikawa Tetsurō (1975), *Hagakure nyūmon* (Nihon bungeisha).

[42] Morikawa Tetsurō, *Hagakure nyūmon*.

[43] Tucker, John Allen, 'Tokugawa Intellectual History and Prewar Ideology: The Case of Inoue Tetsujirō, Yamaga Sokō, and the Forty-Seven Rōnin', *Sino-Japanese Studies* 14 (2002), p. 48.

[44] Brownlee, John S. (1997), *Japanese Historians and the National Myths, 1600–1945* (Vancouver: UBC Press), pp. 174–75.

[45] Brownlee, John S., p. 175.

the disorder that periodically engulfed China, where martial skills were not traditionally esteemed. Basing his arguments on what he considered to be the more historically reliable *Azuma kagami*, rather than the *Heike monogatari*, Kawakami held that *bushidō* reached a high point of refinement during the Kamakura period (1185–1333).[46]

This article was not especially controversial at the time, and Kawakami followed the imperial *bushidō* line by referencing the legendary figures of Emperor Keikō and his son, the famous warrior prince Yamato Takeru, both of whom supposedly lived in the first century CE.[47] Furthermore, Kawakami wrote, from the viewpoint of the nation's morality, the major flaw with Kamakura *bushidō* was the fact that the warriors lost their direct connection with the emperor, and that instead loyalty was directed through the shogun. It was not until the Meiji Restoration that this 'contradiction' was resolved, as the demise of the shogunate finally allowed the warriors to properly put their devotion to the emperor into practice. Although the samurai class was soon eliminated, Kawakami argued, their *bushidō* spirit passed into all Japanese, where it became the basis for the nation's morality and the key to victories over the Qing and Russia, as well as current successes in China.[48]

The dominant imperial ideology was not central to Kawakami's argument, as he demonstrated by publishing an article in the same journal in 1952, this time in English. The post-war version, entitled 'Bushido in its Formative Period', maintained essentially the same arguments as the 1938 edition and lauded Kamakura warriors, for '*bushidō* prohibited plunder and ursurpation'. This was a 'striking contrast to Chinese [provincial governors] who have been most severely criticized by historians for their avarice and selfishness'.[49] While Kawakami's view of *bushidō* was still idealistic, the second article left out any mention of mythical figures or imperial loyalty. Kawakami remained consistent in describing Edo *bushidō* as becoming the 'cornerstone of national morals', but did not repeat his claims that it had passed into all Japanese after Meiji, that it was the basis of imperial loyalty, or was the key to Japan's modern military victories.[50] The removal of 'imperial' elements by historians in their post-war *bushidō* studies was a common practice that, as these were often not central to the respective arguments, did not significantly alter most interpretations. For example, in his broad 1956 survey, *Japan's Bushidō* (*Nihon no bushidō*), medieval historian Fuji Naotomo (1903–65) left out connections to imperial ideology of the sort that had appeared in his 1943 article on '*Bushidō* and the Spirit of the Emperor's Nation' ('Bushidō to kōkoku seishin').[51]

In contrast to those historians who quietly made the necessary adjustments to their *bushidō* theories, noted medievalist and founder of the Japan Historical

---

[46] Kawakami Tasuke, 'Bushidō no genryū', *Hitotsubashi ronsō* 1:6 (1938), p. 777.
[47] Kawakami Tasuke, 'Bushidō no genryū', p. 767.
[48] Kawakami Tasuke, 'Bushidō no genryū', p. 782.
[49] Kawakami Tasuke, 'Bushido in its Formative Period', *The Annals of the Hitotsubashi Academy* 3:1 (1952), p. 75.
[50] Kawakami Tasuke, 'Bushido in its Formative Period', p. 83.
[51] Fuji Naotomo (1956), *Nihon no bushidō* (Osaka: Sōgensha); Fuji Naotomo, 'Bushidō to kōkoku seishin', *Chisei* 6:11 (Nov. 1943), cited in Hasegawa Ryōichi (2006), *15 nen sensō ki ni okeru*

Society, Takayanagi Mitsutoshi (1892–1969), attacked *bushidō* research. Takayanagi rejected the central tenets of imperial *bushidō*, arguing that virtues such as loyalty and frugality were products of the Edo period, while indirect loyalty of the sort directed toward the emperor was a modern phenomenon. According to Takayanagi, *bushi* loyalty was a direct and reciprocal relationship before the Edo period, and one's own life was invariably valued more highly than that of one's lord.[52] When *bushidō* theorists during the Pacific War demanded absolute loyalty to the emperor, Takayanagi continued, this was a perversion of *bushi* culture as the prescribed relationship was neither direct nor reciprocal.[53] Takayanagi described attempts to trace *bushidō* to the unique Japanese spirit and the military exploits of mythical gods and emperors as 'ludicrous', as martial traits were universal human characteristics.[54] With regard to *Hagakure*, Takayanagi dismissed this as a strange anachronism even in the Edo period, as it misrepresented the Sengoku period that it idealized. According to Takayanagi, death was an everyday event in Sengoku, and one did not have to 'find' it as *Hagakure* prescribed.[55]

The deficiencies of *bushidō* research had serious consequences even in the post-war period, Takayanagi argued, recounting an occasion when he was summoned to Yokohama as an expert witness at the trial of men accused of Class B war crimes. The case involved men who had decapitated severely injured prisoners of war, and Takayanagi's task was to explain the role of *kaishaku*—delivering the releasing fatal blow following *seppuku*—in order to demonstrate that the actions of the accused could not necessarily be simply equated with murder. According to Takayanagi, he was preceded as a witness by a certain Dr N., who presented a *bushidō*-based argument that held no sway with the American judges. Takayanagi surmised that the *bushidō* explained by Dr N. would have been the standard version accepted by Japanese historians at the time, and it would have been impossible for Westerners to take it seriously as it was entirely without evidence.

In contrast, Takayanagi brought a stack of historical materials to illustrate his arguments regarding *kaishaku*, including images, and these seem to have been accepted by the court as the defendants were given unusually light punishments. Takayanagi credited this success with his reliance on historical evidence, which lent him credibility that the *bushidō* theorists lacked. 'With regard to those *bushidō* theories, they were not argued using specific facts illustrating *bushidō*, but merely involved explaining that "*bushidō* is like this" in an idealistic way. This type of *bushidō* must have struck the court as pure nonsense'. Takayanagi was amazed that the existing *bushidō* discourse was satisfied with mere repetition of idealistic concepts with no foundation. 'Sometimes, specific facts or actions by historical figures were taken up, but these were virtually all fabrications. It must be said that these *bushidō* theories are entirely without value'.[56]

Monbushō no shūshi jigyō to shisō tōsei seisaku: iwayuru 'kōkoku shikan' no mondai wo chūshin toshite (Chiba University Graduate School Institute of Social and Cultural Sciences), pp. 90, 125.

[52] Takayanagi Mitsutoshi (1960), *Bushidō: Nihon bunka kenkyū 8* (Tokyo: Shinchōsha), pp. 7–15.
[53] Takayanagi Mitsutoshi, p. 18.   [54] Takayanagi Mitsutoshi, p. 49.
[55] Takayanagi Mitsutoshi, pp. 35–37.
[56] Takayanagi Mitsutoshi, pp. 51–52.

The majority of historians writing on *bushidō* before 1945 were able to remove imperial ideology from their arguments without great difficulty after the war, indicating that the more fantastical elements of imperial *bushidō* had not struck deep roots among those scholars. In contrast, as one of the most prominent promoters of the imperial *bushidō* that Takayanagi later criticized, Hiraizumi Kiyoshi resigned his post at Tokyo Imperial University and retired to Fukui prefecture even before the occupation began. He spent much of late 1945 and 1946 travelling between Tokyo and Fukui giving lectures, before settling down as the temple priest of Hakusan Shrine in Katsuyama. Hiraizumi was banned from public office by the occupation authorities between 1948 and 1952, but this did not greatly impact his activities as he continued to lecture and publish widely on his vision of an idealized emperor-focused Japan. The wartime experience did not alter the extreme nationalism Hiraizumi espoused, and he attacked the post-war order as a 'foreign' construct unsuitable to the Japanese spirit.

Perhaps Hiraizumi's greatest influence in the post-war period was through his close connection with Yasukuni Shrine, where he lectured on history and the Japanese spirit on a number of occasions.[57] Hiraizumi was especially fond of the controversial theories of historian Charles A. Beard, who accused Roosevelt of having forced Japan into attacking Pearl Harbor as part of a secret plan to sell the war to a reluctant populace.[58] This historical revisionism was especially important in the context of Hiraizumi's influence on his disciple, Matsudaira Nagayoshi (1915–2005), a fellow native of Fukui. The two had been closely acquainted from Matsudaira's youth, when he boarded with the much older Hiraizumi while attending school in Tokyo.[59] After a highly successful career in the military, Matsudaira retired in 1968 following a bout of serious illness, and returned to direct the Fukui City Museum. In 1978, Matsudaira was called back to the capital to become the new head priest at Yasukuni Shrine, and one of his first acts on appointment was to enshrine a group of Class A war criminals. Matsudaira's predecessor had long resisted this move, and some scholars argue that Matsudaira was appointed precisely with this task in mind.[60] This action was entirely in line with Hiraizumi's teachings, as he rejected the judgments of the 1946–48 International Military Tribunals of the Far East ('Tokyo Trials'). Furthermore, in lectures both before and after the war, Hiraizumi insisted that Japan's youth did not desire to return home, but rather sought to give their lives for the emperor and be celebrated at Yasukuni.[61]

Hiraizumi continued to influence public opinion after the war through lectures and publications, although the latter were not nearly as successful as his efforts before 1945. One publication that did have a considerable impact was a Japanese history textbook written by Hiraizumi in 1970, entitled *Japanese History*

---

[57] Mainichi shinbun 'Yasukuni' shuzai han (2007), *Yasukuni sengo hishi: A kyū senhan wo gōshi shita otoko* (Mainichi shinbun sha), pp. 47–49.

[58] Beard, Charles Austin (1948), *President Roosevelt and the Coming of the War, 1941: Appearances and Realities* (Transaction Publishers); Hiraizumi Kiyoshi (1977), *Nihon no higeki to risō* (Hara Shobō).

[59] Mainichi Shinbun 'Yasukuni' Shuzai Han, *Yasukuni sengo hishi: A kyū senhan wo gōshi shita otoko*, pp. 47–49.

[60] Mainichi Shinbun 'Yasukuni' Shuzai Han, pp. 52–54.

[61] Mainichi Shinbun 'Yasukuni' Shuzai Han, pp. 48–49.

for Young People (*Shōnen Nihon shi*). This comprehensive work surveyed Japanese history from the age of the mythical Emperor Jimmu to the Second World War, and was unusual for the time in its treatment of the early emperors as historical figures. While not overtly promoting *bushidō*, Hiraizumi used the same periodization and structure as in his pre-war works on the subject, with chapters on Kusunoki Masashige, the Kenmu Restoration, Yamaga Sokō, Hashimoto Sanai, Yoshida Shōin, and Saigō Takamori. Hiraizumi's emphasis on imperial loyalty and the superiority of Japan shone through strongly in *Japanese History for Young People*, the tenth edition of which was published by Kōgakkan University Press in 2010.[62] At the same time, while original copies of Hiraizumi's 1933 *The Revival of Bushidō* continued to be widely available, demand spurred the publisher Kinseisha to reprint the text beginning in 1988.[63]

Increased popular interest in *bushidō* from the 1980s, especially, has been accompanied by a variety of treatments by academic historians specializing in fields of pre-modern history. In his 1986 three-volume *History of Bushidō*, historian Takahashi Tomio examined many individuals and schools of thought, linking them through the use of labels such as 'the *bushidō* of Mito domain', 'the *bushidō* of Aizu domain', 'nature *bushidō*', etc.[64] A specialist in pre-modern history, Takahashi seeks *bushidō* in this period, and his brief discussion of modern events places the greatest importance on Nitobe Inazō, praising *Bushido: The Soul of Japan* as being fundamentally distinguished by 'an outstanding understanding and organization of *bushidō*'.[65] More recently, early modern historian Kasaya Kazuhiko has argued for *bushidō* as the basis for the contemporary Japanese social structure, as well as the key to an indigenous meritocratic tradition.[66] Kasaya has been one of the most prolific academic promoters of *bushidō*, also acting as Regular Executive (*jōmu riji*) of the *Bushidō* Association launched in early 2008.[67]

In contrast, historian Gomi Fumihiko opens his 1997 work on the medieval samurai with a brief discussion of the distorting effect of *bushidō* ideology on the study of early history, pointing out that *bushidō* only came to be closely scrutinized in the Meiji period. According to Gomi, *bushidō* was 'thought up' in detachment from the samurai, and he argues that mixing samurai and *bushidō* in discussions of the Japanese people is a 'major error'.[68] From late Meiji on, treatments of *bushidō* by academic historians have followed similar trends in that critical voices such as Gomi's have been in a distinct minority, with scholars either ignoring *bushidō* as an irrelevance or insisting on its pre-modern historical legitimacy and devising their own theories regarding its content. The reluctance among historians to critically

---

[62] Hiraizumi Kiyoshi (2005), *Shōnen Nihon shi* (Ise: Kōgakkan Daigaku Shuppan).

[63] Hiraizumi Kiyoshi (1988), *Bushidō no fukkatsu* (Kinseisha).

[64] Takahashi Tomio (1986), *Bushidō no rekishi* (Tokyo: Shinjinbutsu ōaisha).

[65] Takahashi Tomio, *Bushidō no rekishi 3*, pp. 238–53; Takahashi Tomio (1991), *Bushi no kokoro, Nihon no kokoro 2* (Tokyo: Kondō shuppansha), pp. 426–27.

[66] Kasaya Kazuhiko (1988), *Shukun oshikome no kōzō* (Tokyo: Heibonsha); Kasaya Kazuhiko (2005), *Bushidō to Nihon kei nōryoku shugi* (Tokyo: Shinchōsha sensho).

[67] Promotional pamphlet and schedule for the launch ceremony of the *Bushidō* Association, 31 January 2008. (Bushidō kyōkai (2008), *Hakkai kinen kōen kai* (PHP). p. 1).

[68] Gomi Fumihiko (1997), *Sasshō to shinkō: bushi wo saguru* (Tokyo: Kakugawa sensho), p. 1.

engage with *bushidō* is exacerbated by its high popular profile, and many scholars are wary of engaging with a subject with such questionable roots and problematic associations. Furthermore, many scholars active during the resurgence of *bushidō* in the 1980s and 1990s considered it to be a recent and, most likely, passing phenomenon with little connection to earlier history. The perceived vagueness of the origins of *bushidō* also contributes to historians' caution, as many scholars feel that its roots are to be found outside their own area of expertise. Just as Gomi directs readers in search of *bushidō* to the modern period, historians of modern Japan often point towards the pre-modern or early modern periods, resulting in a lack of critical treatments in the scholarship.

INTERNATIONALIST *BUSHIDŌ* AND THE REVIVAL OF NITOBE INAZŌ

While chauvinistic *bushidō* theories promoted by figures such as Hiraizumi and Mishima remained influential in certain quarters, the tremendous growth in popular interest in *bushidō* that occurred in the 1980s revived a different set of pre-war interpretations. Along with 1970, the most important year in the late Shōwa development of *bushidō* was 1984, when a portrait of the then-obscure Nitobe Inazō appeared on the new 5000-yen note in a move widely ascribed to the efforts of the former prime minister (and Christian) Ōhira Masayoshi (1910–80).[69] From 1985 on, the number of research works relating to Nitobe increased dramatically, with more than one hundred books published in the following decades. This trend corresponds to the publication patterns of *Bushido: The Soul of Japan*, with new editions of the Japanese translation appearing at a rate of more than one every year over the same period. The influence of Nitobe's book in recent decades is hard to overestimate, and his ideas are pervasive not only in popular culture, but in politics, business, and sport.

The recent popularity of *Bushido: The Soul of Japan* in Japan, as well as its related centrality in *bushidō* discourse, broke with existing patterns. Nitobe himself was not a major subject of research until the late twentieth century, in spite of his many writings and remarkable career as the principal of the Tokyo First Higher School, chair of Colonial Policy at Tokyo Imperial University, and Under-Secretary General of the League of Nations. As John Howes pointed out in the early 1990s, 'One would expect that the name of such a man would be memorialized in numerous institutions and studies, but this is not the case. Sixty years later almost no one remembers Nitobe. A student will seek in vain reference to him in standard sources'.[70] Ōta Yūzō relates that by the 1970s, many people did not know how to pronounce Nitobe's name.[71]

---

[69] Fruin, Mark W. (1995), 'Foreword', in John Howes (ed.), *Nitobe Inazō: Japan's Bridge Across the Pacific*, (Boulder: Westview Press), p. ix.

[70] Howes, John F. and Oshiro, George (1995), 'Who was Nitobe?', in John Howes (ed.), *Nitobe Inazō: Japan's Bridge Across the Pacific* (Boulder: Westview Press), p. 4.

[71] Ōta Yūzō (1986), *Taiheiyō no hashi toshite no Nitobe Inazō* (Tokyo: Misuzu shobō), p. 1.

The focus on Nitobe in recent evaluations of *bushidō* is not entirely new, however, and reflects early Shōwa views of the Meiji period. As early as 1930, the army's *Moral Training for Soldiers* portrayed Nitobe as the first formulator of modern *bushidō*, and many subsequent works followed this convention. According to historian Nishimura Shinji (1879–43), Meiji Japanese had been blinded by Western thought and were led to recognize their *bushidō* by Nitobe, whose own Westernized life conversely allowed him to appreciate the value of the warrior ethic.[72] One major factor in the emphasis on Nitobe was the timing of the publication of *Bushido: The Soul of Japan* in 1900, as *bushidō* was first entering mainstream discourse in Japan. In addition, earlier Meiji works on *bushidō* had been almost completely forgotten by the early twentieth century, as they were largely superseded by more nationalistic texts. Ultimately, the moderate success of Nitobe's book in Japan when the translation finally appeared in 1908 rode on the *bushidō* boom that had begun a decade earlier, as well as its high profile as a bestseller abroad. As a result, Nitobe's impact on the content of *bushidō* discourse in Japan was negligible, with the influence of *Bushido: The Soul of Japan* further limited by the cumbersome language of the first translation. It was only in 1938 that the more readable translation most commonly used today was completed by Yanaihara Tadao (1893–1961), a Christian who had been imprisoned a year earlier for his anti-war stance.[73]

Although the relatively pacifistic internationalism of Nitobe's *bushidō* deviated from mainstream *bushidō* discourse in his own time, it was well-suited to the mood of Japan in the late twentieth century, while providing foreigners with an explanation of the Japanese national character that successfully blended the familiar and exotic. In the 1970s and especially in the 1980s, *bushidō* was widely cited as a vital factor in Japan's rapid growth, resulting in a theoretical framework that became widely accepted in Japan and abroad. These ideas tended to disregard the view of historians that the ostensibly traditional Japanese management structure was essentially a product of the early post-war period.[74] Instead, as Andrew Barshay has pointed out, the concepts of *ie* (household) and '*bushidō* redux' were typically portrayed as the origins 'of today's corporate ethos of group competitiveness, individual self-sacrifice, and loyalty to firm'.[75] Nitobe Inazō's work was eagerly bought by businesspeople seeking to understand the secret of Japan's corporate culture, while new editions of samurai classics such as the *Hagakure* and Miyamoto Musashi's *Book of Five Rings* (*Gorin no sho*) filled bookshop shelves. CEOs described their thoughts on *bushidō* in corporate newsletters, with these essays often a pastiche of Nitobe's theories and a few quotes attributed to famous samurai. The market for Japanese corporate theories collapsed in the 1990s along with the economic

---

[72] Nishimura Shinji (1940), *Nihon to sono bunka* (Fuzanbō), pp. 227–28.

[73] Bushidō gakkai, Kokusho kankō kai (eds.) (2013), *Bushidō dokuhon* (Kokusho Kankō Kai), pp. 1–2.

[74] Yasumaru Yoshio (2006), *Gendai nihon shisō ron: rekishi ishiki to ideorogī*, (Tokyo: Iwanami Shoten), p. 8.

[75] Barshay, Andrew E. (2004), *The Social Sciences in Modern Japan: The Marxian and Modernist Traditions* (Berkeley: University of California Press), pp. 73–74.

'bubble', and *bushidō* came to be portrayed as the reason behind Japanese perseverance in difficult times. When it seemed as though the economy was beginning to improve in the early 2000s, *bushidō* was briefly brought to the fore as the 'very ancient system' that enables 'the Japanese to reinvent themselves with shocking vigour... and shocking success... They are the best model we can think of for renewal'.[76]

The pacifism and internationalism of Christian *bushidō* theorists, including Nitobe, Uemura Masahisa, and Uchimura Kanzō, made their works agreeable to the largely demilitarized Japan of the late twentieth century, while the Victorian moralism and patriotic optimism that permeate *Bushido: The Soul of Japan* continue to be attractive to those seeking to instill similar virtues in the 'lost' youth of post-bubble Japan.[77] Ishii Shirō credits the resurgence of Nitobe's *bushidō* in recent decades to his desire to create an ethical system that met 'international standards', an ideal that resonates in an age of increasing globalization.[78] In the autumn of 2006, *bushidō* found frequent mention in the debates regarding fundamental reforms to Japan's education legislation, including calls for *bushidō* to be reintroduced into schools for purposes of moral education, and lamentations that the current perceived educational malaise is caused by a lack of '*bushidō* spirit' among the nation's youth. The extent to which *bushidō* entered into deliberations in the Diet was registered by the *Asahi shimbun* newspaper, which discussed the great popularity of Nitobe's *Bushido: The Soul of Japan* among Diet members occupied with the project of education reform.[79]

Pressure to bring *bushidō*-based moral education into schools comes primarily from older conservatives who blame the post-war education system for eliminating *bushidō* from the curriculum.[80] *The Japan Times* describes the efforts of one concerned civic group: 'Sokichi Sugimura, 72, feels elements of Japanese society have lost their moral compass to the point of being downright rude and he and his associates want to put them back on course, and in the process embrace samurai values'. Sugimura's views are representative of much wider sentiment, and after forming a group in 2006 to read *Bushido: The Soul of Japan*, he spent the following years organizing popular field trips to examine how great warriors of Japan's past 'laid the foundation for Bushido and Japanese public morals'.[81] Grassroots efforts of this sort receive inspiration and support for their ideals from the many influential books dealing with *bushidō* and contemporary morality, such as Takushoku University professor Seki Hei's *The Heart of Japan I Want to Teach my Child: The*

---

[76] Fuller, Mark B. and John C. Beck (2006), *Japan's Business Renaissance: How the World's Greatest Economy Revived, Renewed, and Reinvented Itself* (McGraw-Hill), p. 14.

[77] Willcock, Hiroko, 'The Political Dissent of a Senior General: Tamogami Toshio's Nationalist Thought and a History Controversy', *Asian Politics & Policy* 3:1 (2011), p. 38.

[78] Ishii Shirō, 'Basil Hall Chamberlain and Inazo Nitobe: a Confrontation over Bushido', *University of Tokyo Journal of Law and Politics* 3 (2006), p. 25.

[79] 'Nitobe Inazō *Bushidō* ninki: kyōiku kihon hō kaisei/hantai ryōha no ronkyo', *Asahi Shimbun* (7 Dec. 2006).

[80] Ōkoda Yahiro (2010), *Bushidō dokuhon* (Kaya Shobō), pp. 232, 249.

[81] Kawabata, Tai, 'Bad Public Manners Irk Bushido Proponent', *The Japan Times* (3 June 2008).

Source of the Bushidō Spirit (2012), which is marketed as an explanation of 'how *bushidō* became the DNA of the Japanese people'.[82] Also in 2012, one of the most prolific contemporary writers on *bushidō*, Kitakage Yūkō, published *A Primer on Bushidō for Educators*, intended for teachers looking to instill samurai virtues in their charges. While recommending the *Hagakure* and other texts that found use in pre-war spiritual education, Kitakage suggests that instructors amend the most problematic death-focused passages to make them more acceptable. For example, the famous first line of the *Hagakure* is to be read '*Bushidō* is finding death (in the name of good for the world and other people)'.[83]

Perhaps the most influential work in this vein is mathematics professor Fujiwara Masahiko's nationalistic treatise *The Dignity of the Nation (Kokka no hinkaku)* (2005), which has sold over two million copies. Fujiwara attacks what he sees as the evils of Western-led globalization and the moral vacuum that has arisen from excessive emphasis on freedom and equality. The solution Fujiwara offers to these problems is the 'revival of the *bushidō* spirit' based on ancient traditions, although his interpretations rely most heavily on Nitobe Inazō's work.[84] The critique of globalization became a common theme in writings on *bushidō* from the 1990s onward as disillusionment with Japan's economic fortunes set in. These critical views have become considerably more widespread since the start of the global financial crisis in 2007–2008, and represent a significant break with earlier invocations of *bushidō* in the context of rapid economic growth. Instead, they are much closer to the anti-capitalist *bushidō* theories that were popularized in early Shōwa after a similar global economic collapse—the stock market crash of 1929.

Although internationalist *bushidō* lost much of its lustre with the decline in Japan's economy, one area in which the concept retained a high profile was in the world of sport. The intimate connection between *bushidō* and sport from the late nineteenth century onwards had a powerful influence on the post-war sporting landscape, especially under the Allied Occupation. As part of its programme to eradicate 'feudalistic' and militaristic culture, SCAP banned martial sports from schools along with military training, while at the same time encouraging baseball as a 'democratic' and 'progressive' alternative.[85] In an argument reminiscent of Meiji baseball promotions, the authorities reasoned that teamwork made baseball more suitable for rebuilding society than 'individualistic' martial arts.[86] People in Japan needed little encouragement to continue participating in the nation's most popular sport, but as baseball had been played throughout the wartime period, it also required a degree of ideological rehabilitation. In his 1949 *Baseball Guide for Boys*, Mihara Osamu addressed the work to be done in order to establish 'clean baseball' rather than that corrupted by a 'mistaken *bushidō* spirit'. According to Mihara, baseball had become extremely coarse from Taishō onward, with players

[82] Seki Hei (2012), *Wagako ni oshietai Nihon no kokoro: bushidō seishin no genryū* (PHP kenkyūjo).
[83] Kitakage Yūkō (2012), *Kyōshi no tame no bushidō nyūmon* (Bensei shuppan), p. 191.
[84] Fujiwara Masahiko (2005), *Kokka no hinkaku* (Tokyo: Shinchōsha), pp. 116–29.
[85] Kawai Kazuo (1979), *Japan's American Interlude* (Chicago: University of Chicago Press), p. 187.
[86] Blackwood, Thomas, 'Bushidō Baseball? Three "Fathers" and the Invention of a Tradition', *Social Science Japan Journal* 11:2 (2008), pp. 235–37.

often breaking rules and attempting to injure one another through charging, bean balls, aggressive sliding, and other measures. For Mihara, this degeneration occurred when the 'ancient Japanese *bushidō* spirit' entered the sport, imbuing it with a win-at-all-costs mentality that ran counter to the 'true spirit of sport'. Unfortunately, Mihara wrote, there were still many in Japan who had this under-handed approach to sport when they should be working diligently to improve their game and become skilled enough to win fairly.[87]

Mihara's rejection of *bushidō* and insistence on fair play reflects both the ambiva-lence towards *bushidō* in the immediate post-war period, as well as the general ambiguity of the concept. Owing largely to its close relationship with the English gentlemanship on which it was originally modelled, many in Japan believed that a spirit of fair play was an inherent characteristic of *bushidō*, and also *bushidō* baseball. As Thomas Blackwood points out with regard to baseball in Japanese schools, these differing interpretations of *bushidō* baseball coexisted from Meiji onward, with a version 'emphasizing fair play' becoming the 'dominant ideology of school baseball' in the post-war period.[88] Even among professional players, *bushidō* and samurai imagery have been invoked in the context of baseball throughout the post-war period, with these symbols used and understood in various ways. This is especially true of international matches, when the specific content of *bushidō* becomes even less important and its primary utility is to promote a team spirit by appealing to nationalistic ideals. In this way, the Japanese national baseball team has been known by the nickname 'Samurai Japan' since Hara Tatsunori became general manager in 2008, when he reinforced his long-standing view that 'the way of baseball is understood through *bushidō*'.[89] Addressing his team after Japan's second straight success in the World Baseball Classic in 2009, Hara praised them: 'you've become splendid samurai!'.

The situation is similar in football (soccer), where the official nickname of the Japanese national men's football team has been 'Samurai Blue', referring to the colour of their uniforms, since before the 2006 World Cup in Germany. In a press conference held after Japan's qualification for the 2010 World Cup in South Africa, head coach Okada Takeshi made the bold prediction that Japan would reach the semi-final, in spite of its poor results before the tournament and world ranking of 45th, because Japan 'has a strength called *bushidō*. It is just that our fighting instinct has not yet been switched on'.[90] The team lost to Paraguay in a penalty shootout two games short of Okada's stated goal, although this result was better than many outside observers had expected. Okada's focus on fighting spirit reveals that his understanding of *bushidō* goes beyond fair play, and his use of samurai imagery seems intended primarily to stoke national pride among players and supporters.

As was the case in the pre-war period, the extensive use of *bushidō* rhetoric in baseball after 1945 has been more than matched by its appearance in the martial arts. The often problematic connection between *bushidō* and *budō* carried on into

---

[87] Mihara Osamu (1949), *Shōnen yakyū dokuhon* (Yomiuri shinbunsha), pp. 19–21.

[88] Blackwood, Thomas, 'Bushidō Baseball?', p. 237.

[89] *Sponichi annex*, 25 March 2009.   [90] *Sponichi annex*, 18 December 2009.

the post-war, and was further complicated by SCAP's association of militarism with the martial arts. Not only were both the *bushidō* sportsmanship and fighting spirit found in baseball also present in the martial arts, but the concept was also used as a marketing device to appeal to a sense of tradition and improve their public image. This mobilization of *bushidō* was similar to that in late Meiji, and it is frequently invoked by promoters of newer martial arts and competitions, who use '*bushidō*' in the titles of competitions due to its high recognition factor.

As with baseball and football, *bushidō* frequently appears in the martial arts in an internationalist context, with an emphasis on supposedly Japanese characteristics of fair play and fighting spirit. The projection of *bushidō* on to Japanese athletes in international competition is encouraged by a reciprocal recognition of *bushidō* by foreigners. In the martial arts, the study of *bushidō* is often portrayed as essential to success, and the subject is one of the most popular themes for foreigners writing in Japanese. Similarly, Japanese martial arts practitioners will often comment with pride on foreign interest in *bushidō*, which acts as a validation for the ethic much as it did in late Meiji. Araya Takashi, the head of the martial arts hall at Meiji Shrine, discusses German and French students who attend international martial arts seminars, and he sees them as more in tune with *bushidō* virtues than the vast majority of Japanese. According to Araya, Europeans feel that they have lost their former spirit and connection with God and nature, and believe that Japan has retained these characteristics. These practitioners feel that it is possible to reconnect with this spirit through the martial arts, Araya argues, resulting in rapid growth in the martial arts in other countries even as they shrink in Japan, which is mired in its own crisis of *bushidō* decline.[91] Conservative attempts to arrest this process led to the introduction of mandatory martial arts classes in schools, but these have met with a considerable backlash from parents and educators concerned about the high number of fatalities and debilitating injuries suffered by children participating in judo, the most widely practised martial art.[92] In the last few decades, views of *bushidō* in sports and the martial arts, as in Japanese society in general, have been heavily influenced by Nitobe's gentlemanly ideals of internationalism, fair play, and diligence, although interpretations continue to be diverse and the concept certainly retains ample capacity for nationalistic mobilization.

BUSHIDŌ AND JAPAN'S POST-WAR MILITARY

The high profile that *bushidō* enjoys in Japan is not limited to civilian society and the concept has been experiencing a resurgence in military circles in recent decades. Spikes in interest in *bushidō* among politicians have coincided with political debates on issues concerning Japan's military and its heritage, including national defence, constitutional changes, educational reforms, and the deployment of

---

[91] Araya Takashi (2010), *Tatakau monotachi he: Nihon no taigi to bushido* (Tokyo: Namiki Shobō), pp. 50–53.
[92] Aspinall, Robert, 'Judo in Japanese Schools—Concerns about Safety', *Asia Pacific Memo 191* (20 Nov. 2012).

troops overseas. *Bushidō* has also entered Diet discussions regarding Japanese negotiations with North Korea, national budgets, transportation, and the disaster and
ongoing nuclear crisis in Fukushima. Post-war *bushidō* is largely a continuation of
many pre-war cultural trends, and the spectre of its potential reintroduction into
policy debates and education are especially controversial. On the other hand, the
very difficulties that the pre-war and wartime state had in defining and controlling
bushidō orthodoxy are even more pronounced in the much freer and more diverse
cultural environment of democratic post-war society.

The place of *bushidō* in the post-war military reflects both the potential and
challenges its use presents. Very few of the young men and women who join
the armed forces in Japan today are conscious of the legacy of wartime imperial
bushidō, which was attacked by many veterans after 1945. They are, however,
highly aware of the general idea of *bushidō* through socialization and exposure
to popular culture, presenting an opportunity for directed opinion-forming not
entirely dissimilar to that undertaken in the 1920s. *Bushidō* also finds use in
the marketing of the military to domestic and international audiences, including politicians and other policymakers. In support of the Japanese participation
in the US and UK-led occupation of Iraq, Assistant Director General of the
Defense Agency and Liberal Democratic Party member Imazu Hiroshi stated on
30 November 2006 in the plenary session of the Diet, 'as samurai of Japan, the
nation of *bushidō*, the efforts of the (Japan Self Defense Force) troops are highly
esteemed not only by the Iraqi people, but also by the international community'.
A year later, on 27 November 2007, in a meeting of the Diplomacy and Defence
Committee regarding the use of the Japan Air Self Defense Force in Iraq, member
of the House of Councillors and former SDF officer Satō Masahisa argued that
use of the military for humanitarian support was '...a human duty and a duty of
the nation of *bushidō*, Japan'. These statements assume a high level acceptance of
the identification of *bushidō* with the Japanese military, although the focus here
is very much on a humane and ethical reading of *bushidō* heavily influenced by
Nitobe's thought.

Bushidō is a significant marker of broader issues facing the Japan Self Defense
Forces in terms of their mission, identity, and desired values. After the surrender
of Japan in August 1945, the Allies demobilized the imperial military over the
course of the following months, although the repatriation of Japanese troops from
overseas took considerably longer. Along with democratization, demilitarization
was an important aim of the reconstruction process, and became a cornerstone of
the post-war constitution drafted initially by SCAP representatives and brought
into effect in 1947. The American origins of the constitution have since been a
common point of attack by conservative forces, especially, who argue that it was
forced on the Japanese people by a foreign occupying force. They especially question the validity of Article 9, which has proved most contentious in recent years:

> Article 9: Aspiring sincerely to an international peace based on justice and order, the
> Japanese people forever renounce war as a sovereign right of the nation and the threat
> or use of force as means of settling international disputes.

In order to accomplish the aim of the preceding paragraph, land, sea, and air forces, as well as other war potential, will never be maintained. The right of belligerency of the state will not be recognized.

The United States government soon realized that pacifistic readings of what came to be labelled as the 'peace constitution' severely restricted Japan's potential to contribute to American security interests in Asia.[93] Unable to lend active support abroad, Japan instead provided a prime location for US military bases and boosted its own economy by producing large amounts of matériel for use in the Korean War. As the Cold War intensified, Japan began to rearm under no small pressure from its American allies. The establishment of the Self Defense Force (SDF) in 1954 was a major turning point in this direction, and the new air, naval, and ground forces were staffed with thousands of former imperial military officers.

The highly disputed signing of the Treaty of Mutual Cooperation and Security in 1960 placed Japan firmly under the US umbrella, while making the SDF responsible for domestic security. Japan's military expenditure stayed relatively steady at around one per cent of GNP, but economic growth meant that the defence budget effectively tripled in the decade to 1970.[94] At the same time, increasingly hawkish statements by a series of prime ministers changed the perception of Japanese military capabilities and intentions. In 1969 Satō Eisaku and Richard Nixon described 'the security of Korea as indispensable to the security of Japan', a statement repeated in largely similar terms in 1975 by Miki Takeo and Gerald Ford.[95] On both these occasions, the link between Japan's security and that of other East Asian countries struck many as reminiscent of the early twentieth century, causing concern at home and abroad. Three years later, Fukuda Takeo became the first prime minister to visit Yasukuni Shrine following the inclusion of the fourteen Class A war criminals and promoted the idea that the SDF should be sent on overseas engagements.[96] The prime minister and former imperial naval officer Nakasone Yasuhiro had a strong influence on perceptions of the SDF, as he was able to push the defence budget beyond the symbolic limit of one per cent GNP in 1987. Nakasone also made what were, at the time, the most publicized visits to Yasukuni Shrine by a post-war prime minster in 1984 and 1985, while his statements regarding the nature of Japan's intentions in Second World War portrayed it as a struggle for Asian liberation.[97]

In contrast to controversial statements from politicians, the SDF itself has always strictly emphasized its subjugation to civilian control and consciously avoided the use of military terminology wherever possible, in order to assuage domestic and

---

[93] For an overview of the readings of Article 9, see Lummis, Douglas C. 'It Would Make No Sense for Article 9 to Mean What it Says, Therefore It Doesn't. The Transformation of Japan's Constitution', *The Asia-Pacific Journal*, 11:9:2 (Sept. 30, 2013).

[94] Schaller, Michael (1997), *Altered States: The United States and Japan since the Occupation* (Oxford: Oxford University Press), p. 229.

[95] Tsuzuki, Chishichi, *The Pursuit of Power in Modern Japan 1825–1995*, p. 426.

[96] Tsuzuki, Chishichi, p. 429.   [97] Tsuzuki, Chishichi, pp. 440–41.

foreign concerns regarding Japan's remilitarization.[98] At the same time, Japan has built up one of the most technically advanced military forces in the world, with total defence spending in 2012 similar to France and the UK, with this group exceeded only by the US, China, and Russia.[99] The conflicting purposes of justifying the great expenditure for the maintenance of a large armed force for national defence while simultaneously downplaying the military character of the same has resulted in serious identity issues for SDF personnel. As Sabine Frühstück demonstrates, there is a strong desire among SDF personnel to become a 'normal' military similar to those in other countries, rather than as what they themselves often perceive to be a poor imitation.[100] The demartialization of the SDF extends to its recruiting methods, with critics arguing that the advertising portrays the military as a non-governmental organization rather than a fighting force.[101] In an attempt to tap into the popularity of video games among the youth as the US army has done with the popular title *America's Army*, the Maritime Self Defense Force released a mobile phone game application in 2010 as a recruiting tool. Unlike its American counterpart—a tactical first-person shooter representative of the genre—the MSDF's *Salute Trainer* is designed for players to perfect their salutes, emphasizing form with no ostensibly martial content.[102]

The image of the SDF since the early 1990s has been defined primarily by its missions, which have mostly been for humanitarian purposes. Within Japan, one of the most important tasks of the SDF has been disaster relief, such as following the Great Hanshin (Kobe) Earthquake of 1995. The response was widely criticized for its slowness, although the SDF was able to deflect much of the blame towards the civilian bureaucrats who oversaw the operations.[103] A subsequent revision of policies gave the SDF authority to respond automatically after an earthquake of magnitude 5.0 or greater, enabling it to act far more quickly and effectively after the 2004 Chūetsu Earthquake in Niigata Prefecture. The greatest boost to the humanitarian image projected by the SDF has been its relief efforts following the Great Tōhoku Earthquake and Tsunami on 11 March 2011, especially in comparison with the widely derided responses from the civilian government and the executives of the Tokyo Electric Power Company. These incidents have had a tremendous positive impact on domestic perception of the SDF, with the prominent *bushidō* promoter Kitakage Yūkō optimistically speculating that the 2011 disaster response might restore public respect for the military to levels similar to those of the heyday of the Russo-Japanese War.[104]

---

[98] For an overview of these issues, see Frühstück, Sabine and Eyal Ben-Ari. ' "Now We Show It All!" Normalization and the Management of Violence in Japan's Armed Forces', *Journal of Japanese Studies* 28:1 (2002), pp. 2–4, 14–15.

[99] Information from Stockholm International Peace Research Institute, http://www.sipri.org/research/armaments/milex/milex_database (accessed 1 Oct. 2013).

[100] Frühstück, Sabine, *Uneasy Warriors: Gender, Memory, and Popular Culture in the Japanese Army*, p. 8.

[101] Fuse Yūjin (2012), *Saigai haken to 'guntai' no hazama de: tatakau jieitai no hitodzukuri* (Kamogawa Shuppan), pp. 141–42.

[102] Fuse Yūjin, pp. 135–36.

[103] Frühstück, Sabine and Eyal Ben-Ari, ' "Now We Show It All!" ', p. 33.

[104] Frühstück, Sabine and Eyal Ben-Ari, p. 5.

The most contentious overseas engagement, however, was the involvement of the Air SDF and the Ground SDF in the reconstruction process in Samawah, Iraq, between 2004 and 2006. While this mission, like all previous SDF actions abroad, did not directly involve any combat operations, by placing Japanese troops on the ground during a war for the first time since 1945, it attracted criticism from various shades of the political spectrum. Opponents of an expanded international role for the military denounced the operation for also making Japanese institutions and citizens into targets, and the killing of two Japanese diplomats near the Iraqi city of Tikrit in November 2003 was viewed as a direct result of Japan's support for the occupation. Criticism also came from conservatives otherwise supportive of the deployment, who felt that the SDF should take a more engaged role similar to that of other coalition forces. By being insulated from combat and focusing on humanitarian work, the SDF was seen to be neglecting its true calling as soldiers and bearers of the nation's *bushidō* legacy. As Kitakage writes in his *Introduction to Bushidō for Self Defense Force Personnel*, the ultimate purpose of the SDF is to win wars, and Japanese troops should always have death on their minds.[105] According to Kitakage, although 'SDF personnel are the samurai of today', they do not have a sufficient understanding of *bushidō*, something that should be rectified partly through the study of the *Hagakure, Budō shoshinshu*, Inoue Tetsujirō's writings on National Morality, and other texts that were widely used in early Shōwa spiritual education.[106]

Bushidō-based criticism of the SDF has been strongest from those closest to the force, with General Tamogami Toshio the most prominent figure. Sacked as Chief of Staff of the Air Self Defense Force in 2008 over a controversial article that questioned the aggressive nature of imperial Japan's military expansion, Tamogami has repeatedly called for the reintroduction of *bushidō* into the SDF. According to Tamogami, SDF officers are the spiritual heirs of the samurai of the past, and should look to *bushidō* for moral strength in the same way as their forebears.[107] In 2004, Tamogami outlined a ten-point programme for improving the spirit of the Air SDF in the journal *Hōyū*, published by the Air Staff College Staff Association. Based on over thirty years of personal experience, Tamogami described the role of the SDF as a crucial moral compass for a society that placed value only on the rights of the individual. In contrast, the SDF 'admirably maintains the ancient *bushidō* spirit of our country', and has become the great supporting pillar of the nation in the post-war period.[108] For Tamogami and his supporters, it is essential that the SDF be able to draw on the nation's previous military traditions, including the Imperial Japanese Army, and that the constitution be revised to remove restrictions that prevent the SDF from taking decisive action to protect the country.

Tamogami claims that his views are shared by many SDF personnel, even if they do not make them public. One prominent figure who echoes Tamogami's

---

[105] Frühstück, Sabine and Eyal Ben-Ari, pp. 136, 149.
[106] Frühstück, Sabine and Eyal Ben-Ari, pp. 1, 199–248.
[107] Willcock, Hiroko, 'The Political Dissent of a Senior General: Tamogami Toshio's Nationalist Thought and a History Controversy', pp. 38–39.
[108] Tamogami Tomio, 'Kōkū jieitai wo genki suru 10 no teigen (Part III)' *Hōyū* 30:2 (July 2004), 1–24.

criticisms is Araya Takashi, who describes Japan's 'constitutional pacifism' as a 'slave mentality' as it leaves the country exposed to foreign threats with no means of destroying the power bases of potential invading countries.[109] Araya is a former member of the Ground SDF, and was the first head of the Special Forces Group activated in 2004 as a counter-terrorist unit based on US models, especially the Green Berets. Following his retirement in 2008, Araya took up a post as an instructor at the Shiseikan martial arts hall at Meiji Shrine in Tokyo, becaming head of the Shiseikan the following year. In 2010, Araya published a guide directed at 'young samurai' entitled *To Those Who Fight: Japan's Great Duty and Bushidō*, which went through four printings in its first year. Recounting an incident during his time training with US Special Forces, Araya expressed his surprise on entering the administration office of the Green Berets' and seeing the word '*bushidō*' displayed prominently. Asking his hosts whether they knew the meaning of the term, Araya was convinced by their answers that the US special forces understood *bushidō*, but was simultaneously dismayed that its meaning had been largely forgotten in Japan.[110]

As a response, Araya himself developed a '*Bushidō* for Special Forces Group Members' consisting of four precepts: 1) having a definite spiritual standard (justice) and being decisive without regard to life or death; 2) having the courage to act without hesitation, and training the willpower that maintains this courage; 3) cultivating the real ability (wisdom, skill, physical strength) to accomplish one's tasks; 4) unifying speech and conduct and maintaining faith.[111] Araya considers these precepts especially important as the SDF has been contaminated by individualistic thought and weakened through Japan's unique habit of not teaching children to fight for the nation. According to Araya, even Russia has been consistent in instilling patriotism and a spirit of self-sacrifice in its people, even through periods of tremendous political upheaval and transition.[112] In contrast, Araya claims, although pre-war Japan was distinguished by a sense of responsibility, justice, and independence, this 'true heart of the Japanese people' has been diluted over 'the decades since the start of spiritual education under the Occupation Constitution'.[113]

Araya's theories draw heavily on the ideals of imperial *bushidō* in their content, invoking appeals to the *bushidō* spirit of the mythical Emperor Jimmu, emphasizing the virtues of filial piety and imperial loyalism (*chūkō*), and positing the medieval hero Kusunoki Masashige as a model for the Special Forces Group.[114] This idealization of the pre-war period is a most sensitive issue for the SDF, which has made a concerted effort to disassociate itself from the Imperial Japanese Army in particular, and instead emphasizes its post-war accomplishments.[115] It is common to most armed forces that their members do not publically express criticism of their employers, but former personnel have been most vocal after being discharged. In Tamogami's case, his comments while in active

---

[109] Araya Takashi, pp. 4, 86–87.   [110] Araya Takashi, pp. 7–8.
[111] Araya Takashi, p. 194.   [112] Araya Takashi, pp. 90–91.
[113] Araya Takashi, pp. 67–68.   [114] Araya Takashi, pp. 5, 47, 55, 93–94.
[115] Frühstück, Sabine and Eyal Ben-Ari. '"Now We Show It All!"', pp. 27–30.

service led to his dismissal, while Araya retired before publishing *To Those Who Fight*, reflecting the discomfort that the expression of pro-military views causes in the SDF. As a forum, Tamogami has founded and led the right-wing political party Ganbare Nippon! National Action Committee, while Araya has also featured in some of the many *bushidō*-themed programmes of its affiliated online TV station, Channel Sakura.

While their dedicated supporters are certainly a minority in Japan, a number of the arguments put forward by figures such as Tamogami and Araya resonate not only among older conservatives. One of these is a strong critique of 'global capitalism' and the waging of war for what is perceived as economic purposes—i.e. the financial benefit of a select few. Araya describes the US War on Terror in the early twenty-first century as 'a military tactic to ensure the safety of the globalization strategy', arguing that the number of terrorists will inevitably increase as more people are impoverished by the global financial crisis that began in 2007–2008.[116] Araya attributes this process primarily to the growth of self-centred individualism, which acts like a cancer on greater society. Echoing a concern of conservative *bushidō* theorists in Meiji, Araya laments that in an order dominated by individualism and capitalist globalization anything that is not explicitly prohibited by law is allowed, with no moral foundations to keep people from exploiting their fellow man by manoeuvring in the spaces between.[117] Tamogami is similarly critical of what he sees as Japan's subservience to the United States, as Hiroko Willcock points out, and he is primarily concerned with re-establishing Japan's strategic and military independence.[118]

When contemporary thinkers appeal to *bushidō* theories reminiscent of the imperial *bushidō* of early Shōwa—emphasizing death, loyalty, selflessness, etc.—aggressive and expansionist elements are typically lacking. Nostalgic idealism for the period among contemporary writers is primarily focused on the common soldiers, as in Kitakage Yūkō's praising of valiant death in battle as the 'fulfillment of *bushidō*'. Here, Kitakage invokes imagery intimately linked with the Imperial Japanese Army in his use of the euphemism 'shattering like a jewel' to describe dying soldiers.[119] Similarly, the security analyst and thirty-six-year veteran of the Ground SDF Ōkoda Yahiro contends that the Special Attack Forces were the 'manifestation of *bushidō*'.[120] In contrast, Japan's wartime leadership is subject to harsh criticism, as in Ōkoda's assertion that Tōjō Hideki had a warped understanding of *bushidō*, and that the ethic disappeared from the army under his rule.[121] Ōkoda supports this claim by stating that Tōjō became a prisoner of war in 1945, rather than taking his own life.[122]

---

[116] Araya Takashi, *Tatakau monotachi he: Nihon no taigi to bushidō*, pp. 32–33.

[117] Araya Takashi, pp. 35–37.

[118] Willcock, Hiroko, 'The Political Dissent of a Senior General: Tamogami Toshio's Nationalist Thought and a History Controversy', pp. 35–36.

[119] Kitakage Yūkō (2012), *Jieikan no tame no bushidō nyūmon* (Bensei shuppan), p. 194.

[120] Kitakage Yūkō, *Jieikan no tame no bushidō nyūmon*, p. 194; Ōkoda Yahiro, *Bushidō dokuhon*, p. 195.

[121] Ōkoda Yahiro, *Bushidō dokuhon*, p. 177.   [122] Ōkoda Yahiro, p. 206.

In spite of widespread disdain for the wartime leadership, Ōkoda echoes Hiraizumi Kiyoshi's criticism of the Tokyo war crimes trials, writing that 'Japanese civilization was unilaterally tried and convicted' without a chance to defend itself. 'This seriously injured the purity of the *bushidō* spirit, and robbed the Japanese people of their pride and confidence'.[123] Similarly, Araya portrays the conflict between the US and Japan as essentially a clash of values, arguing that the subsequent trials were a case of judging Japanese values by Western ones.[124] According to Ōkoda, the occupation authorities overlooked the fact that the core value of *bushidō* was compassion, leading them to abolish the Imperial Rescript on Education due to a mistaken belief that it was militaristic.[125] The result of this action was to eliminate compassion and morality from the post-war education system along with the *bushidō* ethic which epitomized these qualities.[126] The notion that foreigners are unable to understand *bushidō* has been a common theme among post-war apologists especially, and is often used in defence of Japan's wartime activities. Ōkoda and others invoke this argument to question the legitimacy of the Tokyo Trials, providing the further example that Westerners are not able to grasp the *bushidō* spirit of the Special Attack Forces.[127] This attempted escape into cultural exceptionalism can frustrate critics of imperial Japan, and is not conducive to building international trust with regard to Japan's military intentions—or absence thereof.

Writing in 1993, historian and activist Ienaga Saburō assessed the situation shortly after the end of the Cold War: 'Looking back over the past decade, I see scant possibility of a revival of the militarism that overwhelmed pre-war Japan. Yet we must be mindful of the constant strengthening of the Self-Defense Forces to the point where they now rank among the major military organizations in the world and have been dispatched overseas'. Ienaga did not see room for complacency regarding the current situation, continuing: 'Furthermore, there is an increasing promilitary slant in education . . . It is not surprising therefore that China and other Asian nations fear a resurgence of militarism in this country. Having paid the terrible price of imperialistic expansion in the past, many Japanese share those misgivings'.[128]

Taking a longer-term view along the lines of Ienaga's concerns, the relationship between *bushidō* and the military in early Shōwa is similar to that of the early twenty-first century in several significant ways. Given the events of the 1930s and early 1940s, the emphasis placed on death and self-sacrifice by certain writers, the reprinting of spiritual education materials such as the 1930 *Moral Training for Soldiers*, efforts to revise historical interpretations, and the push to reintroduce *bushidō* into military education are all seen as causes for concern. Other aspects of early Shōwa *bushidō* are also repeating themselves. The Tamogami controversy and the critical writings of former soldiers such as Araya demonstrate that, even if

[123] Ōkoda Yahiro, p. 255.

[124] Araya Takashi, *Tatakau monotachi he: Nihon no taigi to bushidō*, p. 40.

[125] Ōkoda Yahiro, *Bushidō dokuhon* (Kaya Shobō, 2010), pp. 7, 153, 253.

[126] Ōkoda Yahiro, p. 232.   [127] Ōkoda Yahiro, pp. 45, 193–98.

[128] Ienaga Saburō, 'The Glorification of War in Japanese Education', *International Security* 18:3 (Winter 1993/94), 113–33.

it desired to do so, the SDF would be similarly limited in its ability to control the content of *bushidō* discourse as was the imperial military. The widespread criticism of individualism, capitalism, and globalization among more nationalistic *bushidō* theorists is reminiscent of the anti-industrialist mood of many young officers following the stock market crash of 1929, at least in their choice of targets for blame. In contrast, in perhaps the most significant departure from the earlier period, the power relationships in contemporary Japan between the civilian government and the military mean that the influence of *bushidō* discourse in the former has considerably more weight in determining the strategic course of the country.

CONSIDERING POST-WAR *BUSHIDŌ*

In comparison with *kokutai* and other concepts associated with imperial ideology, *bushidō* recovered remarkably quickly after 1945 as a result of the diversity and flexibility integral to its resilience over the previous half-century. The idea that *bushidō* was an ancient tradition that had been corrupted by militarists in early Shōwa soon came to dominate popular understandings of the subject, and scholars embarked on the task of seeking 'true' *bushidō* in Japan's earlier history. The dismissal of imperial *bushidō* as an aberration was made possible in no small part by the continued existence of diverse streams of *bushidō* thought throughout the wartime period, some of which directly challenged the official orthodoxy. This also facilitated the invocation of *bushidō* for rebuilding the nation's morale, while the rediscovery of its Meiji heritage in the 1950s provided an avenue for saving aspects of Japan's troubled modernity. The potential of *bushidō* for positive reconstruction was further reflected in its continued use for integrating regions into the national whole, as localities throughout the country 'reconstructed' castles out of concrete and celebrated local samurai heroes in an attempt to lure tourism and investment.

From the 1960s, as the immediacy of the war dissipated and popular resentment towards the American legacy grew, more problematic *bushidō* interpretations from the first half of the century returned to prominence, even if they were denied official support. By relying on different readings of various historical incidents and documentary sources, post-war theorists created *bushidō* interpretations that, among other things, called for military strengthening, imperial 'restoration', and anti-foreign agendas. More recently, *bushidō* has found favour among critics of globalization and 'Western' capitalism, many of whom seek greater political and military independence from the United States. At the same time, Nitobe Inazō's internationalist ideals have been a significant factor behind the unprecedented levels of popularity reached by his relatively pacifistic *bushidō* from the 1980s onward. In another continuation from pre-war patterns, recognition of *bushidō* from abroad has been crucial to its legitimacy, as even nationalistic commentators cite foreign interest in the subject as evidence of its uniqueness and global significance. Although Nitobe's work assumed a dominant position in *bushidō* discourse in the late twentieth century, the variety of *bushidō* interpretations in the post-war period has been as broad as in the decades before 1945.

Conclusions and Considerations

DIVERSITY, LEGITIMACY, AND RESILIENCE

The revival of *bushidō* in the post-war era is consistent with its modern development, with much of recent *bushidō* discourse consciously or unconsciously drawing on Meiji, Taishō, and early Shōwa precedents. The *bushidō* of the decades before 1945 is often portrayed as functional ideology promoted by elites to induce certain behaviours, a description that best applies to institutional strands of imperial *bushidō*. In contrast, the reasons behind the adoption of *bushidō* by most people in Japan as a genetic ideology—an ideology that is adopted by a social group in spite of apparent conflict with their objective interests—are as varied as its definitions and applications.[1]

There are two important considerations in this context, especially during the late Meiji period. As some contemporary critics of *bushidō* pointed out, the concept was not widely known before 1900, and the majority of Japanese living during the *bushidō* boom that ended around 1914 would not have been exposed to it in their youth. The issue in this case is why *bushidō* would be accepted and adopted by certain social groups, such as soldiers and the growing industrial proletariat, when tenets of the ideology, especially loyalty, obedience, and self-sacrifice, seemed to be opposed to their own best interests. Later generations who were exposed to *bushidō* from their earliest school experiences would have less reason to question its legitimacy, but this was not yet the case in Meiji. The idea that an ideology could be suddenly and effectively imposed from the top down is too simplistic, and Maruyama Masao's 'elitist' view of ideology as affecting only the 'foolish people' in the lower classes and not the intelligentsia has come in for justifiable criticism.[2] Certainly, many people who accepted *bushidō* in the first decade of the twentieth century did so consciously, consuming *bushidō*-related culture while being aware of its questionable origins. In the case of the elite social groups who typically benefit from ruling ideologies, their acceptance of the same may be seen as more self-serving, but different models are needed to explain the adoption of *bushidō* across all sections of society.

In this sense, one important factor during the *bushidō* boom of late Meiji and early Taishō was the use of *bushidō* in various types of popular literature and performance. Writers supplied the market with compelling narratives hinging on

---

[1] Geuss, Raymond (1981), *The Idea of a Critical Theory: Habermas and the Frankfurt School* (Cambridge: Cambridge University Press).

[2] Hirota Teruyuki (1997), *Rikugun shōkō no kyōiku shakaishi: risshin shusse to tennōsei* (Tokyo: Seori shobō), pp. 8–13.

conflicts between characters' *bushidō* duty on the one hand, and their private obligations and desires on the other. These stories were bolstered by an apparent historical legitimacy that appealed to large numbers of people, including accounts of the Sino-Japanese and Russo-Japanese Wars, new dramatizations of the Akō vendetta, and tales of figures mythical and real. Popular works included a great deal of highly idealized historical fiction, and mass culture became a carrier of *bushidō* for much of the pre-war period, even if specific interpretations often diverged from 'official' views. This, combined with the institutional promotion of *bushidō* aimed at groups such as soldiers and students, and later the general populace, contributed significantly to the cumulative exposure to *bushidō* ideology in late Meiji and early Taishō, helping to further popularize the concept while taking advantage of its existing popularity in a reciprocal process.

Another primary force driving the establishment of *bushidō* as a genetic ideology was popular nationalism, the ebb and flow of which also caused interest in *bushidō* to fluctuate accordingly, a pattern that holds true today. The relationship between nationalism and other ideologies is invariably complex, and while nationalism drove the development of *bushidō*, *bushidō* was an important vehicle for promoting and disseminating the growing nationalistic ideals. Meiji *bushidō* grew together with modern nationalism in Japan, and was an integral part of the subsequent modernization and nation-building process from the forward-looking *bushidō* theories of Ozaki Yukio onward. The modern nationalism promoted by the Meiji government did not reach all areas of Japanese society, and was arguably not accepted by the majority of the population before the end of the period, but *bushidō*—as product and producer of nationalism—accelerated the dissemination of national ideals in modern Japan through the education system, the military, sports, and popular culture. At the same time, the traditional image of *bushidō* provided an anti-modern alternative for those dissatisfied with the rapidity and content of change. The strong anti-capitalist currents in much of early Shōwa *bushidō* discourse have their counterpart in the sentiments against globalization found in more recent works, giving their proponents a patriotically sound basis for their arguments that ostensibly does not rely on socialism, communism, anarchism, or other 'foreign' ideals that are considered to be more objectionable.

Perceived foreign threats have historically been a major driver of popular nationalism, but *bushidō* also benefitted from the related dynamic of popular narcissism, which Peter Nosco describes as 'characteristic of a significant corpus of later nineteenth- and twentieth-century thought in Japan'.[3] Already in the 1890s, foreign recognition and opinion were central concerns of *bushidō* promoters, and commentaries in the foreign press were often translated in Japan. Similarly, what popularity Nitobe's *Bushido: The Soul of Japan* had in Japan before the 1980s was largely due to its status as a foreign bestseller, and *bushidō* was a source of pride for Japanese interacting with foreigners throughout the pre-war era. This was also the case during the post-war economic boom, which many cultural theorists credited

---

[3] Nosco, Peter (1990), *Remembering Paradise: Nativism and Nostalgia in Eighteenth-Century Japan* (Cambridge, MA: Harvard University Press), p. 8.

to the samurai ethic. Even more nationalistic and chauvinistic *bushidō* discourses emphasize foreign recognition of *bushidō*, citing praise of the ethic from abroad.

While foreign recognition is highly valued, popular narcissism also manifests itself in the many arguments for the inability of foreigners to comprehend *bushidō*, with these two lines of reasoning often found in tandem. Before 1945, especially, this apparent deficiency on the part of non-Japanese was attributed to their lack of a 'Japanese spirit', a charge that was also levelled against domestic critics of *bushidō*. After the war, the incomprehensibility of Japanese culture was used to relativize Japan's wartime activities as the result of 'mutual misunderstanding'.[4] More recently, proponents of the incomprehensibility argument invoke scientific terms in addition to the 'Japanese spirit', stating that *bushidō* is part of a unique Japanese DNA.[5] Seeking refuge in these unverifiable claims gives *bushidō* a mystical air and apparent exclusivity that satisfies narcissistic desires. It is also an attractively simple approach, removing the burden of explanation from the explainer as any failure of the audience to understand or agree with the professed *bushidō* theories is ultimately due to their innate inability to comprehend the same.

While a 'national' ideology in its origins and core characteristics, *bushidō* was also inclusive of regionalism within its broader scope, an attribute that further contributed to its acceptance and resilience. Unlike national polity- or emperor-centred ideologies, *bushidō* was frequently appropriated for narrower regional purposes. By focusing on famous warriors or events in their own areas, promoters of *bushidō* could encourage local pride while tying into the national spirit. This was especially useful for those regions that had been on the wrong side of the Restoration conflict, such as the Tokugawa loyalist domain of Aizu in Fukushima prefecture. By celebrating the deaths of the 'White Tigers' as 'Aizu *bushidō*', it was possible to retain regional honour while entering the national fold.[6] Similarly, discussions of Mikawa *bushidō* brought other Tokugawa regions into the national ideology, while Satsuma *bushidō* contributed to the rehabilitation and veneration of Saigō Takamori as a symbol of both local and national ideals.[7] These regional *bushidō* discourses remained strong after the war, with imperial *bushidō* dismissed as a 'national' aberration removed from more authentic local manifestations. This was most pronounced in research on the *Hagakure*, an explicitly regional text often described as 'Saga *bushidō*'. The diverse regional *bushidō* discourses also contributed to the resilience of the ethic by providing scope for regionalism within the larger national order, a characteristic that was far less pronounced in other 'national' ideologies.

The diversity of the development process of *bushidō* as a response to modernizing trends in modern Japan endowed the concept with great flexibility and

---

[4] Ienaga Saburō, 'The Glorification of War in Japanese Education', *International Security* 18:3 (Winter 1993/94), p.130.

[5] Ōkoda Yahiro (2010), *Bushidō dokuhon* (Kaya Shobō), pp. 204, 312, 315.

[6] Recent examples include Nakamura Akihiko (2006), *Aizu bushidō: samurai tachi ha nan no tame ni ikita no ka* (PHP kenkyūjo); Hoshi Ryōichi (2006), *Aizu bushidō: 'naranu koto ha naranu' no oshie* (Seishun Shuppansha).

[7] Recent examples include Nangō Shigeru (1991), *Bushidō to Satsuma gishi* (Hito to bunka sha); Satsuma shikon no kai (eds.) (2011), *Satsuma bushidō (Satsuma Spirits)* (Nihon keizai shinbun shuppansha).

resilience. The roots of modern *bushidō* are found not in the historical samurai class, although *bushidō* theorists picked up pre-Meiji writings in the twentieth century to legitimize their ideas. Instead, the first discussions of *bushidō* in the late nineteenth century were a nativist response that sought to provide an indigenous alternative to Western ideals while distancing Japan from China. Furthermore, the theories of the first generation of Meiji *bushidō* theorists were strongly influenced by their respective foreign experiences, which were, in turn, coloured by views of their own nation and culture relative to foreign 'others'. In spite of its diversity, the *bushidō* that emerged from this organic process of development was very much a product of the period before the Sino-Japanese War. Characteristics of many early *bushidō* theories included the absence or marginalization of martial elements, as well as idealistic views of European chivalry, which greatly limited the longevity of these writings as nationalistic and militaristic trends increased. Nitobe's translation of *bushidō* as 'the way of the fighting knights' is symbolic of the inherent ambiguity of the term, which was understood as referring to knights, samurai, or warriors in various contexts.

By dismissing the writings of Ozaki Yukio and other early *bushidō* theorists, thinkers and activists after 1900 were able to select elements from mythology, history, sociology, or other fields to assemble new *bushidō* theories to suit their goals. From the beginning of modern discourse on *bushidō*, the concept served as a vessel for myriad philosophies, giving it the great resilience seen in its continued prominence. Conversely, *bushidō* lost significance or was even rejected when it became too closely identified with another ideology or specific period. The first of these slumps occurred after 1914, when *bushidō* came to be seen as a defining trait of traditional, 'feudal', 'pre-modern' Japan, especially as manifested in the person of General Nogi. As popular culture and the national mood moved further towards modernity, internationalism, and self-determination, most Japanese came to see *bushidō* as an anachronism with limited relevance to the new age.

An adapted *bushidō* survived in educational institutions and the military, and rapidly became a defining ideology of early Shōwa when emperor-centred militaristic nationalism came to dominate the national agenda. *Bushidō* reached the apex of its popularity in the decade before 1945, and through its imperial interpretation became more closely associated with the state than at any other time. The identification of *bushidō* with militaristic ideologies meant that the post-war backlash against *bushidō* was more severe than in early Taishō. Within a decade, however, other non-imperial currents of *bushidō* again began to attract interest from politicians, scholars, writers, and the public, which increased rapidly as national confidence grew along with the economy. The dramatic and anachronistic suicide of one of the most prominent promoters of *bushidō* in the post-war period, Mishima Yukio, generated similar unease as Nogi's death had over half a century before, but also inspired further research into 'true' *bushidō* as a counterpoint to Mishima's supposedly misguided interpretation.

With the exception of Nitobe's *Bushido: The Soul of Japan*, post-war *bushidō* discourse has tended to ignore most developments from the pre-war period, and instead sought the roots of *bushidō* in earlier Japanese history. In this context, most post-war

researchers reverted to a focus on *bushidō* as a 'way of the samurai' as it had been originally formulated in Meiji, rather than the more expansive 'way of the warrior' that
dominated early Shōwa discourse. Historical events or samurai texts were again used
to make various assertions regarding the nature of *bushidō*, with writers arguing for
precedents for nuclear disarmament, corporate structures, or moral education. This
post-war boom is similar to that of late Meiji in its diversity and reliance on carefully
selected historical texts and events to promote a wide variety of concepts and causes,
and *bushidō* regained any flexibility it had lost during the last years of the imperial
period. On the one hand, appeals to historical ties popularly legitimize *bushidō*, while
on the other hand, the lack of historical evidence regarding any commonly accepted
definition of *bushidō* before Meiji gives its modern interpreters considerable flexibility
and allows the concept to be adapted for various purposes. For this reason, *bushidō* has
been able to change and survive well over a century of political, social, technological,
and military transitions that saw many other ideological constructs arise and disappear. Significantly, post-war *bushidō* has not been tied to any specific ideology in the
popular mind, and while the surge in interest in *bushidō* in the 1980s was directly
related to the nation's economic strength and renewed geopolitical assertiveness, the
collapse of the bubble economy did not greatly affect the popularity of the subject.
Instead, *bushidō* moved into debates on social morality, educational reforms, and the
role of the Japanese military, with peaks in popular *bushidō* discourse observable during public debates relating to nationalism in Japan.

The resilience of *bushidō* is exceptional among the ideologies that developed in
imperial Japan. Most similar militaristic and nationalistic concepts from the pre-war
period were rejected or ignored after 1945, but in the case of *bushidō* this was only
temporary, and it was soon reintroduced into popular discourse. Today, no great
notice is taken in Japan when politicians mention *bushidō* in parliamentary debate,
and it is still widely discussed as a defining cultural characteristic. This causes greater
consternation abroad, however, especially in countries that suffered from Japanese
militarism in the early twentieth century. As long as territorial disputes and contro-
versies over interpretations of history continue, the notion that Japan is guided by
a martial ethic will cause problems. This is exacerbated by recent trends to reissue
imperial *bushidō* texts from early Shōwa, both in print and online, often without
any contextualization. A similar example is Mizuma Masanori's *Quick Guide to the
Bushidō Spirit of the 'Sino-Japanese War' Era* (2013), which brings together photo-
graphs from early Shōwa propaganda magazines in an attempt to argue that the
Imperial Japanese Army in occupied China had a positive influence.[8]

People in China are understandably among the most wary of *bushidō*, and hundreds of books and articles have been published on the subject since the 1980s,
reflecting the important role it continues to play in popular opinion towards Japan.
In his 2012 survey of the field of Chinese studies of Japanese culture from 1981 to
2011, Cui Shiguang of the Institute of Japanese Studies at the Chinese Academy
of Social Sciences argues that, in the practical interests of China, there is a need for

---

[8] Mizuma Masanori (2013), *Hitome de wakaru 'Nichū sensō' jidai no bushidō seishin* (PHP
Kenkyūjo).

more and deeper research on the fundamentals of Japanese culture, especially the emperor system, Shinto, and *bushidō*.[9] While the work of many Chinese academics aligns with trends in post-war Japanese scholarship on *bushidō*, examining the potential influence of *bushidō* on Japan's modernization, economic development, or social organization, others attempt to explain modern Japanese militarism and aggression as part of a national tradition.[10] In this vein, Lou Guishu, a historian at Guizhou Normal University who has published widely on *bushidō*, argues that Nitobe Inazō aestheticized *bushidō* in order to strengthen Japan militarily, while Nitobe's emphasis on loyalty and dedication was designed to conceal the 'murder and war' inherent in the ideology.[11]

As concerns among Chinese scholars and the public indicate, the recent revival of *bushidō*, especially by persons close to the military, has the potential for creating further misunderstandings as these serve to legitimize militarism as an ancient and uniquely Japanese tradition. As Mary Elizabeth Berry points out, '[j]ust because samurai and swords are obsolete, their imagery and their functions are not benign...'[12] This could be seen in the common practice among Japanese troops carrying samurai swords into China and Manchuria in the 1930s and 1940s as symbols of their supposed spiritual ancestry, and samurai and swords are no more obsolete in the twenty-first century than they were in early Shōwa. Even more than these concrete symbols, which are tied to specific historical situations and conditions, the amorphous concept of *bushidō* is as relevant today as ever before. The diversity and flexibility of the concept prevented the imperial state from exclusively defining *bushidō*, but by focusing on a timeless 'way of the warrior' rather than the more limiting historical samurai, this invented tradition can be mobilized for almost any contingency.

[9] Cui Shiguang (2012), 'Zhongguo de Riben wenhua yanjiu 30 nian zongshu', in Li Wei (ed.), *Dangdai Zhongguo de Riben yanjiu (1981–2011)* (Beijing: Zhongguo shehui kewue chuban she), p. 294.

[10] See, for example, Zhu Dongxu, Wang Xin, 'Riben wushidao yu Riben youyi shili guanxi lun (On the Relationship between *Bushidō* and Japanese Right-Wing Forces)', *Tangshan shifan xueyuan xuebao*, 31:4 (July, 2009), pp. 78–80; Zhu Lifeng, 'Wushidao yu Riben duiwai qinlüe kuozhang fangzhen de queli (*Bushidō* and Japan's Policy of Aggression and Expansion)', *Jilin shifan daxue xuebao* 1 (Feb. 2007), pp. 89–92; Huang Zhen and Cao Lü, 'Jindai Riben zhenlü xing wenhua de lishi yuanyuan ji jiexi (On The Historical Origins and Interpretations of Modern Japan's Aggressive Culture)', *Riben wenti yanjiu* 23:3 (Sept. 2009), pp. 58–64.

[11] Lou Guishu, 'Riben wushidao he junju zhuyi de bianhu ci: yipping Xinduhu Daozao de Wushidao', *Guizhou Shifan Daxue Xuebao (Shehui Kexue Ban)* 167 (Oct. 2010), pp. 120–28.

[12] Berry, Mary Elizabeth, 'Presidential Address: Samurai Trouble: Thoughts on War and Loyalty', *The Journal of Asian Studies* 64:4 (Nov. 2005), p. 841.

Select Bibliography

Abe Masato (ed.), *Joshidō: Tesshū fujin Eiko danwa* (Tokyo: Daigakukan, 1903).

Abe Masato (ed.), *Tesshū genkō roku* (Tokyo: Kōyūkan, 1907).

Adachi Ken'ichi, *Tachikawa bunko no eiyūtachi* (Tokyo: Chūō kōronsha, 1987).

Adachi Ritsuen, *Bushidō hattatsu shi* (Tokyo: Tsujimoto shugaku dō, 1901).

Adams, Michael C. C., *The Best War Ever: America and World War II* (Baltimore: Johns Hopkins University Press, 1994).

Aki Kiyoka, *Tosa no bushidō* (Kōchi: Aki Kiyoka, 1906).

Akiyama Goan and Inoue Tetsujirō (eds.), *Gendai taika bushidō sōron* (Tokyo: Hakubunkan, 1905).

Akiyama Goan and Inoue Tetsujirō (eds.), 'Jijo', in *Gendai taika bushidō sōron* (Tokyo: Hakubunkan, 1905), 1–4.

Akiyama Goan and Inoue Tetsujirō (eds.), *Zen to bushidō* (Tokyo: Kōyūkan, 1907).

Akutagawa Ryūnosuke, 'Hankechi', in *Meiji bungaku zenshū 26: Akutagawa Ryūnosuke shū* (Tokyo: Chikuma shobo, 1953), 27–31.

Akutagawa Ryūnosuke, 'Ryūzoku', in *Akutagawa Ryūnosuke zenshū 10* (Tokyo: Iwanami Shoten, 1955), 35–36.

Akutagawa Ryūnosuke, 'Saru kani gassen', in *Kumo no ito/toshi shun/torokko/hoka 17 hen* (Tokyo: Iwanami shoten, 1990), 259–62.

Akutagawa Ryūnosuke, 'Yasukichi no techō kara', in *Meiji bungaku zenshū 26: Akutagawa Ryūnosuke shū* (Tokyo: Chikuma shobo, 1953), 198–203.

Alexander, Michael, *Medievalism: The Middle Ages in Modern England* (New Haven: Yale University Press, 2007).

Allen, G. C., *A Short Economic History of Modern Japan, 1867–1937* (London: George Allen & Unwin Ltd., 1946).

Amemiya Eiichi, *Wakaki Uemura Masahisa* (Tokyo: Shinkyō shuppan sha, 2007).

Ames, Van Meter, *Zen and American Thought* (Honolulu: University of Hawaii Press, 1962).

Anderson, Benedict, *Imagined Communities: Reflections on the Origin and Spread of Nationalism* (London: Verso, 2006).

Anderson, Joseph L. and Donald Richie, *The Japanese Film: Art and Industry* (Princeton: Princeton University Press, 1982).

Ansart, Olivier, 'Loyalty in Seventeenth and Eighteenth Century Samurai Discourse', *Japanese Studies* 27:2 (Sept. 2007), 139–54.

Anshin, Anatoliy, 'Yamaoka Tesshū no zuihitsu to kōwakiroku ni tsuite', *Chiba daigaku Nihon bunka ronsō* 7 (June 2006), 104–92.

Aoyoshi Katsuhisa, *Dr. Masahisa Uemura: A Christian Leader* (Tokyo: Maruzen & Co., 1941).

Araki Ryūtarō, 'Nihon ni okeru Yōmeigaku no keifu', in Ōkada Takehiko (ed.), *Yōmeigaku no sekai* (Tokyo: Meitoku shuppan, 1986), 357–422.

Araki Sadao, 'Chūjin meishō wo kataru', in Bushidō Gakkai (ed.), *Bushidō nyūmon* (Futara Shobō, 1941), 232–48.

Araya Takashi, *Tatakau monotachi he: Nihon no taigi to bushido* (Namiki Shobō, 2010).

Arima Sukemasa and Akiyama Goan (eds.), *Bushidō kakun shū* (Tokyo: Hakubunkan, 1906).

Arima Sukemasa, 'Bushidō ni tsuite' *Gendai taika bushidō sōron* (Hakubunkan: 1905), 273–84.

Arima Sukemasa, 'Meiji bushidō', *Gendai taika bushidō sōron* (Hakubunkan: 1905), 285–88.

Ariyama Teruo, *Kōshien yakyū to Nihonjin: media no tsukutta ibento* (Tokyo: Yoshikawa kobunkan, 1997).

Asada Kyōji, *Nihon shokuminchi kenkyū shi ron* (Tokyo: Mirai sha, 1990).

Ashina Sadamichi, 'Uemura Masahisa no Nihonron (1): kindai Nihon to Kirisutokyō' *Ajia/ Kirisutokyō/tagensei* 6 (March 2008), 1–24.

Aspinall, Robert, 'Judo in Japanese Schools—Concerns about Safety', *Asia Pacific Memo 191* (20 Nov. 2012; http://www.asiapacificmemo.ca/judo-in-japanese-schools-concerns-about-safety).

The Athenaeum, 4060 (19 Aug. 1905), 229.

Atkins, E. Taylor, *Blue Nippon: Authenticating Jazz in Japan* (Duke University Press, 2001).

Azuma Eiichiro, *Between Two Empires: Race, History, and Transnationalism in Japanese America* (Oxford: Oxford University Press, 2005).

Babb, James, 'The Seirankai and the Fate of its Members: The Rise and Fall of the New Right Politicians in Japan', *Japan Forum* 24:1 (2012), 75–96.

Banks, Louis Albert, *20 seiki no bushidō* (Tokyo: Naigai shuppan kyōkai, 1907).

Banno, Junji, 'External and Internal Problems After the War', in Harry Wray and Hilary Conroy (ed.), *Japan Examined: Perspectives on Modern Japanese History* (Honolulu: University of Hawaii Press, 1983), 163–69.

Bargen, Doris G., *Suicidal Honor: General Nogi and the Writings of Mori Ōgai and Natsume Sōseki* (Honolulu: University of Hawai'i Press, 2006).

Barshay, Andrew E., *The Social Sciences in Modern Japan: The Marxian and Modernist Traditions* (Berkeley: University of California Press, 2004).

Beard, Charles Austin, *President Roosevelt and the Coming of the War, 1941: Appearances and Realities* (New Haven: Yale University Press, 1948).

Benesch, Oleg, *Bushido: The Creation of a Martial Ethic in Late Meiji Japan* (PhD dissertation at the University of British Columbia, 2011).

Benesch, Oleg, 'National Consciousness and the Evolution of the Civil/Martial Binary in East Asia', *Taiwan Journal of East Asian Studies* 8:1:15 (June 2011), 129–71.

Benesch, Oleg, 'Samurai Thought', in James Heisig et al. (ed.), *Japanese Philosophy: A Sourcebook* (Honolulu: University of Hawaii Press, 2011), 1103–112.

Benesch, Oleg, 'Wang Yangming and Bushidō: Japanese Nativization and its Influences in Modern China', *Journal of Chinese Philosophy* 36:3 (Fall 2009), 39–454.

Bennett, Lance, 'Myth, Ritual, and Political Control', *The Journal of Communication* 30:4 (December 1980), 166–79.

Berry, Mary Elizabeth, 'Presidential Address: Samurai Trouble: Thoughts on War and Loyalty', *The Journal of Asian Studies* 64:4 (Nov. 2005), 831–47.

Bialock, David T., 'Nation and Epic: *The Tale of the Heike* as a Modern Classic', in Haruo Shirane (ed.), *Inventing the Classics: Modernity, National Identity, and Japanese Literature* (Stanford: Stanford University Press, 2000), 151–79.

Bielefeldt, Carl, 'Koken Shiran and the Sectarian Uses of History' in Jeffrey P. Mass (ed.), *The Origins of Japan's Medieval World* (Stanford: Stanford University Press), 295–317.

Blackwood, Thomas, 'Bushidō Baseball? Three "Fathers" and the Invention of a Tradition', *Social Science Japan Journal* 11:2 (2008), 223–40.

Blomberg, Catharina, *Samurai Religion II: The Akō Affair, A Practical Example of Bushidō* (Uppsala: Universitet, 1977).

Bradley, Henry, *A New English Dictionary on Historical Principles: Founded Mainly on the Materials Collected by the Philological Society* 4 F and G (Oxford: Clarendon Press, 1901).

Brandon, James R., *Kabuki's Forgotten War: 1931–1945* (Honolulu: University of Hawaii Press, 2009).

Brink, Dean Anthony, 'At Wit's End: Satirical Verse Contra Formative Ideologies in Bakumatsu and Meiji Japan', *Early Modern Japan* (Spring 2001), 19–46.

Brinkley, Frank, *Japan, its History, Arts and Literature* 2 (Boston: J. B. Millet, 1901–1902).

Brownlee, John S., *Japanese Historians and the National Myths, 1600–1945* (Vancouver: UBC Press, 1997).

Burkman, Thomas W., *Japan and the League of Nations: Empire and World Order, 1914–1938* (University of Hawaii Press, 2008).

Burkman, Thomas W., 'Nationalist Actors in the Internationalist Theatre: Nitobe Inazō and Ishii Kikujirō and the League of Nations', in Dick Stegewerns (ed.), *Nationalism and Internationalism in Imperial Japan: Autonomy, Asian Brotherhood, or World Citizenship?* (New York: RoutledgeCurzon, 2003), 89–113.

Burns, Susan L., *Before the Nation: Kokugaku and the Imagining of Community in Early Modern Japan* (Durham, NC: Duke University Press, 2003).

Bushidō gakkai, Kokusho kankō kai (eds.), *Bushidō dokuhon* (Kokusho Kankō Kai, 2013).

Bushidō gakkai (eds.), *Bushidō nyūmon* (Futara Shobō, 1941).

Bushidō kyōkai, *Hakkai kinen kōen kai* (PHP, 2008).

Calman, Donald, *The Nature and Origins of Japanese Imperialism: A Reinterpretation of the Great Crisis of 1873* (London: Routledge, 1992).

Chae Soo Do, 'Kokuryūkai no seiritsu: Genyōsha to tairiku rōnin no katsudō wo chūshin ni', *Hōgaku shinpō* 109:1/2 (2002), 161–84.

Chakrabarty, Dipesh, 'Afterword: Revisiting the Tradition/Modernity Binary' in Stephen Vlastos (ed.), *Mirror of Modernity: Invented Traditions in Modern Japan* (Berkeley: University of California Press, 1998), 285–96.

Chamberlain, Basil Hall, *The Invention of a New Religion* (London: Rationalist Press, 1912).

Chen Jidong, 'Zai Zhongguo faxian wushidao—Liang Qichao de changshi', *Taiwan Journal of East Asian Studies* 7:2 (Dec. 2010), 219–54.

Chiba Chōsaku, *Nihon budō kyōhan* (Tokyo: Hakubunkan, 1908).

Chiba Chōsaku, *Kokumin kendō kyōhan* (Tomida Bun'yōdō, 1916).

Chien Shiaw-hua, 'Xi lun zhicun zhengjiu zhi jidujiao yu wushidao guanxi', *Dong hua renwen xuebao* 8 (Jan. 2006), 147–72.

Chihara Masatake (ed.), 'Bukkyō shōgaku, Bukkyō honron, Bukkyō kōroku, Shiginokugatachi', *Suikōsha kiji* 7: 3 (Sept. 1910).

Chūtō Kyōiku Danwa Kai (eds.), *Chūtō gakkō ni okeru kō no kyōiku* (Tokyo: Sanseidō, 1935).

Cleary, Thomas (trans.), *Code of the Samurai: A Modern Translation of the Bushido Shoshinshu of Taira Shigesuke* (Tokyo: Charles E. Tuttle, 1999).

Clement, Ernest W., 'Instructions of a Mito Prince to His Retainers', *Transactions of the Asiatic Society of Japan* 26 (Dec. 1898), 115–53.

Colcutt, Martin, *Five Mountains: The Rinzai Zen Monastic Institution in Medieval Japan* (Cambridge: Harvard University Press, 1981).

Colcutt, Martin, 'Musō Soseki', in Jeffrey P. Mass (ed.), *The Origins of Japan's Medieval World* (Stanford: Stanford University Press, 1997), 261–94.

Conlan, Thomas, *State of War: The Violent Order of Fourteenth-Century Japan* (Ann Arbor: University of Michigan Press, 2003).

Cook, Haruko Taya and Theodore F., *Japan at War: An Oral History* (London: Phoenix Press, 2000).

Coox, Alvin D., 'Chrysanthemum and Star: Army and Society in Modern Japan', in David MacIsaac (ed.), *The Military and Society: The Proceedings of the Fifth Military History Symposium* (Washington, DC: Office of Air Force History, 1975), 37–60.

Coox, Alvin D., *Nomonhan: Japan Against Russia, 1939* (Stanford: Stanford University Press, 1985).

Coox, Masayo Umezawa and Peter Duus (trans.), *Unlikely Liberators: The Men of the 100th and 442nd* (Honolulu: University of Hawai'i Press, 1987).

Corbett, P. Scott, 'In the Eye of a Hurricane: Americans in Japanese Custody during World War II', in Karl Hack and Kevin Blackburn (eds.), *Forgotten Captives in Japanese-Occupied Asia* (London: Routledge, 2008), 111–24.

Craig, Albert, *Choshu in the Meiji Restoration* (Cambridge: Harvard University Press, 1961).

Crowley, James B., *Japan's Quest for Autonomy: National Security and Foreign Policy 1930–1938* (New Jersey: Princeton University Press, 1966).

Cui Shiguang, 'Zhongguo de Riben wenhua yanjiu 30 nian zongshu', in Li Wei (ed.), *Dangdai Zhongguo de Riben yanjiu (1981–2011)* (Beijing: Zhongguo Shehui Kewue Chuban She, 2012), 276–94.

Daidōji Yūzan, 'Budō shoshinshū', in Saeki Ariyoshi (ed.) et al., *Bushidō zensho* 2 (Tokyo: Jidaisha, 1942), 297–367.

Dai Nihon bujutsu kōshū kai (ed.), *Bushidō* 1:1 (Feb. 1898).

Davis, Fred, *Yearning for Yesterday: A Sociology of Nostalgia* (New York: The Free Press, 1979).

Davis, Winston, 'The Civil Theology of Inoue Tetsujirō', *Japanese Journal of Religious Studies* 3:1 (March 1976), 5–40.

Davis, Winston, *The Moral and Political Naturalism of Baron Kato Hiroyuki* (Berkeley: Institute for East Asian Studies, 1996).

Dazai Shundai, 'Akō 46 shi ron', in Ishii Shirō (ed.), *Kinsei buke shisō (Nihon shisō taikei* 27)*, (Tokyo: Iwanami shoten, 1974), 404–11.

Desser, David, 'Toward a Structural Analysis of the Postwar Samurai Film', in Arthur Nolletti, Jr. and David Desser (eds.), *Reframing Japanese Cinema: Authorship, Genre, History* (Bloomington: Indiana University Press, 1992), 145–64.

Dickinson, Frederick R., *War and National Reinvention: Japan in the Great War, 1914–1919* (Cambridge, MA: Harvard University Press, 1999).

Doak, Kevin Michael, *A History of Nationalism in Modern Japan: Placing the People* (Leiden: Brill, 2007).

Doak, Kevin Michael, 'Liberal Nationalism in Imperial Japan', in Dick Stegewerns (ed.), *Nationalism and Internationalism in Imperial Japan: Autonomy, Asian Brotherhood, or World Citizenship?* (New York: RoutledgeCurzon, 2003), 17–41.

Dobson, Hugo and Kosuge Nobuko (eds.), *Japan and Britain in War and Peace* (London: Routledge, 2009).

Dorsey, James, 'Culture, Nationalism, and Sakaguchi Ango', *Journal of Japanese Studies* 27:2 (Summer, 2001), 347–79.

Dorsey, James, 'From an Ideological Literature to a Literary Ideology: "Conversion in Wartime Japan"', in Dennis Washburn and A. Kevin Reinhart (ed.), *Converting Cultures: Religion, Ideology and Transformations of Modernity* (Leiden & Boston: Brill, 2007), 465–83.

Dorsey, James, 'Literary Tropes, Rhetorical Looping, and the Nine Gods of War: "Fascist Proclivities" Made Real', in Alan Tansman (ed.), *The Culture of Japanese Fascism* (Durham: Duke University Press, 2009), 407–31.

Dower, John, *Embracing Defeat: Japan in the Aftermath of World War II* (London: Allen Lane/Penguin Press, 1999).

Dower, John, *War Without Mercy: Race and Power in the Pacific War* (New York: Pantheon, 1987).

Drea, Edward J., *In the Service of the Emperor: Essays on the Imperial Japanese Army* (Lincoln: University of Nebraska Press, 1998).

Drea, Edward J., *Japan's Imperial Army: Its Rise and Fall, 1853-1945* (Lawrence: University Press of Kansas, 2009).

Dudden, Alexis, *Japan's Colonization of Korea: Discourse and Power* (Honolulu: University of Hawaii Press, 2005).

Duus, Peter, 'The Takeoff Point of Japanese Imperialism', in Harry Wray and Hilary Conroy (ed.), *Japan Examined: Perspectives on Modern Japanese History* (Honolulu: University of Hawaii Press, 1983), 153–57.

Earhart, David C., *Certain Victory: Images of World War II in the Japanese Media* (London: M.E. Sharpe, 2008).

Ebara Soroku, 'Shukushi', *Bushidō* 1:1 (Feb. 1898), 9.

Ebina Danjō, 'Shin bushidō' *Shinjin* 2:10 (May 1902), 1–15.

Edgar, John G., *The Boyhood of Great Men: Intended as an Example to Youth* (New York: Harper & Brothers, 1854).

Edwards, Bernard, *Blood and Bushido: Japanese Atrocities at Sea, 1941–1945* (New York: Brick Tower Press, 1997).

Edwards, Simon, '*Bushido*: Romantic Nationalism in Japan', in Teruhiko Nagao (ed.), *Nitobe Inazo: From* Bushido *to the League of Nations* (Sapporo: Hokkaido University, 2006).

Eida Takahiro, 'Hankotsu no genron nin Ukita Kazutami: Waseda daigaku sōsōki no kyojin' Lecture held at Waseda University, 30 March 2003.

Eizenhofer-Halim, Hannelore, *Nishimura Shigeki (1828–1902) und seine Konzeption einer 'neuen' Moral im Japan der Meiji-Zeit* (Neuried: Ars Una, 2001).

Flower, Sibylla Jane, 'Memory and the Prisoner of War Experience: The United Kingdom', in Karl Hack and Kevin Blackburn (eds.), *Forgotten Captives in Japanese-Occupied Asia* (London: Routledge, 2008), 57–72.

Fogel, Joshua A., 'On Translating Shiba Ryōtarō', in James C. Baxter (ed.), *Historical Consciousness, Historiography, and Modern Japanese Values* (Kyoto: International Research Center for Japanese Studies, 2006), 153–55.

Foulk, T. Griffith, ' "Rules of Purity" in Japanese Zen', Heine, Steven and Dale S. Wright (eds.), *Zen Classics: Formative Texts in the History of Zen Buddhism* (Oxford: Oxford University Press, 2006), 137–69.

Friday, Karl F., 'Bushidō or Bull? A Medieval Historian's Perspective on the Imperial Army and the Japanese Warrior Tradition', *The History Teacher* 27:3 (May 1994), 339–49.

Friday, Karl F., *Samurai, Warfare, and the State in Early Medieval Japan* (New York: Routledge, 2004).

Fridell, Wilbur M., 'Government Ethics Textbooks in Late Meiji Japan', *The Journal of Asian Studies* 29:4 (Aug. 1970), 823–33.

Frühstück, Sabine, *Uneasy Warriors: Gender, Memory, and Popular Culture in the Japanese Army* (Berkeley: University of California Press, 2007).

Frühstück, Sabine and Eyal Ben-Ari, ' "Now We Show It All!" Normalization and the Management of Violence in Japan's Armed Forces', *Journal of Japanese Studies* 28:1 (2002), 1–39.

Fruin, Mark W., 'Foreword', in John Howes (ed.), *Nitobe Inazō: Japan's Bridge Across the Pacific*, (Boulder: Westview Press, 1995), ix–x.

Fuji Naotomo, 'Bushidō no tenkai to kōkoku seishin', *Chisei* 6:11 (Nov. 1943), 14–19.

Fuji Naotomo, *Nihon no bushidō* (Osaka: Sōgensha, 1956).

Fujii, James A., *Complicit Fictions: The Subject in the Modern Japanese Prose Narrative* (Berkeley: University of California Press, 1993).

Fujiwara Akira, *Gunjishi* (Tokyo: Tōyō keizai shinpōsha, 1961).

Fujiwara Gyōzō, *Nihon kinshū shi* (Tokyo: Nihon kokumin kinshū dōmei, 1941).

Fujiwara Masahiko, *Kokka no hinkaku* (Tokyo: Shinchōsha, 2005).

Fukasaku Yasubumi, *Rinri to kokumin dōtoku* (Tokyo: Kōdōkan, 1916).

Fukuchi Gen'ichirō, 'Bushidō', *Bushidō* 1:1 (Feb. 1898), 8–9.

Fukuda Yoshihiko, 'Shōwa senzenki ni okeru rekishi kyōiku jōhō no juyō to shōtō kyōin no shishitsu keisei: *Rekishi kyōiku kōza* no kōsei to sono tokushoku no kentō kara', *Ehime daigaku kyōiku gakubu kiyō 58* (2011), 191–208.

Fukuhara Kenshichi, *Nihon keizai risshihen* (Osaka: Sōeidō 1881).

Fukuzawa Yukichi, *Meiji jūnen teichū kōron, yasegaman no setsu* (Tokyo: Kōdansha gaku-jutsu bunko, 2004).

Fukuzawa Yukichi: Kiyooka Eichi (trans.), *The Autobiography of Yukichi Fukuzawa* (New York: Columbia University Press, 1966).

Fukuzawa Yukichi: Dilwoth, David A., Hurst III, G. Cameron (trans.), *An Outline of a Theory of Civilization* (New York: Columbia University Press, 2009).

Fuller, Mark B. and John C. Beck, *Japan's Business Renaissance: How the World's Greatest Economy Revived, Renewed, and Reinvented Itself* (New York: McGraw-Hill, 2006).

Funabiki Takeo, *Nihonjin ron saikō* (Tokyo: NHK Publishing, 2003).

Fuse Yūjin, *Saigai haken to 'guntai' no hazama de: tatakau jieitai no hitodzukuri* (Kamogawa Shuppan, 2012).

Gauntlett, John Owen (trans.), *Kokutai No Hongi: Cardinal Principles of the National Entity of Japan* (Cambridge, MA: Harvard University Press, 1949).

Gellner, Ernest, *Nations and Nationalism* (Oxford: Oxford University Press, 1983).

Gerow, Aaron, 'Narrating the Nation-ality of a Cinema: The Case of Japanese Prewar Film', in Alan Tansman (ed.), *The Culture of Japanese Fascism* (Durham: Duke University Press, 2009), 186–211.

Gerring, John, *Social Science Methodology: A Criterial Framework* (New York: Cambridge University Press, 2001).

Geuss, Raymond, *The Idea of a Critical Theory: Habermas and the Frankfurt School* (Cambridge: Cambridge University Press, 1981).

Gilmore, Allison B., *You Can't Fight Tanks with Bayonets: Psychological Warfare against the Japanese Army in the Southwest Pacific* (Lincoln, NE: University of Nebraska Press, 1998).

Girouard, Mark, *The Return to Camelot: Chivalry and the English Gentleman* (New Haven: Yale University Press, 1981).

Gluck, Carol, 'The Invention of Edo', in Stephen Vlastos (ed.), *Mirror of Modernity: Invented Traditions in Modern Japan* (Berkeley: University of California Press, 1998), 262–84.

Gluck, Carol, *Japan's Modern Myths* (Princeton: Princeton University Press, 1985).

Goi Ranshū, 'Baku Dazai Jun Akō 46 shi ron', in Ishii Shirō (ed.), *Kinsei buke shisō (Nihon shisō taikei 27)* (Tokyo: Iwanami shoten, 1974), 418–24.

Gomi Fumihiko, *Sasshō to shinkō: bushi wo saguru* (Tokyo: Kakugawa sensho, 1997).

Goodman, David G. and Miyazawa Masanori, *Jews in the Japanese Mind: The History and Uses of a Cultural Stereotype* (New York: The Free Press, 1995).

Gordon, Andrew, *The Evolution of Labor Relations in Japan: Heavy Industry, 1853–1955* (Cambridge, MA: Harvard University Press, 1985).

Griffis, William Elliot, *The Mikado's Empire* (New York: Harper, 1887).

Griffis, William Elliot, *Religions of Japan* (New York: Charles Scribner's & Sons, 1895).

Grossberg, Kenneth Alan, *Japan's Renaissance: The Politics of the Muromachi Age* (Ithaca: Cornell University Press, 2001).

Gunjingaku shishinsha, *Hohei no honryō* (Tokyo: Gunjigaku shishinsha, 1912).

Gunju Shōkai (ed.), *Gunjin seishin kyōiku to kōgeki seishin to no rensa* (Tokyo: Tōkyō Gunju shōkai, 1916).

Guttman, Allen and Lee Thompson, *Japanese Sports, A History* (Honolulu: University of Hawai'i Press, 2001).

Hada Takao, *Bushidō to shidō* (Tokyo: Baifūkan, 1940).

Hagiwara Sakutarō, 'Hihan seishin no nai shidan', *Nihon he no kaiki* (Tokyo: Hakusuisha, 1938), 195–99.

Hagiwara Sakutarō, 'Nihon bunka no tokushusei', *Kigōsha* (Tokyo: Hakusuisha, 1940), 3–22.

Hagiwara Sakutarō, 'Nihon no gunjin', *Nihon he no kaiki* (Tokyo: Hakusuisha, 1938), 1928.

Hagiwara Sakutarō, 'Nō to sengoku bushi', *Hagiwara Sakutarō zenshū 8* (Tokyo: Shōgaku Kan, 1944), 313–16.

Hagiwara Sakutarō, 'Rekishi no shashisen', *Hagiwara Sakutarō zenshū 10* (Tokyo: Shōgaku Kan, 1943), 41–60.

Hagiwara Sakutarō, 'Seiyō no urayamashisa', *Rōka to shitsubō* (Tokyo: Dai-ichi Shobō, 1936), 293–98.

Hagiwara Sakutarō, *Shi no genri* (Tokyo: Sōgensha, 1950).

Hagiwara Sakutarō, 'Yosano tekkan ron', *Kigōsha* (Tokyo: Hakusuisha, 1940), 188–231.

Hamilton, Malcolm B., 'The Elements of the Concept of Ideology', *Political Studies* 35:1 (March 1987), 18–38.

Hane, Mikiso, *Peasants, Rebels, Women, and Outcastes: The Underside of Modern Japan* (Lanham, MD: Rowman & Littlefield, 2003).

Harada Keiichi, *Kokumingun no shinwa: heishi ni naru to iu koto* (Tokyo: Yoshikawa kobunkan, 2001).

Hardacre, Helen, 'Asano Wasaburo and Japanese Spiritualism', in Sharon Minichiello (ed.), *Japan's Competing Modernities: Issues in Culture and Democracy 1900–1930* (Honolulu: University of Hawai'i Press, 1998), 133–53.

Hardacre, Helen, *Shinto and the State, 1868–1988* (Princeton: Princeton University Press, 1989).

Hasegawa Ryōichi, *15 nen sensō ki ni okeru Monbushō no shūshi jigyō to shisō tōsei seisaku: iwayuru 'kōkoku shikan' no mondai wo chūshin toshite* (Chiba: Chiba University Graduate School Institute of Social and Cultural Sciences, 2006).

Hashimoto Minoru, *Bushidō no shiteki kenkyū* (Tokyo: Yūzankaku, 1934).

Hashimoto Minoru, *Bushidō shiyō* (Tokyo: Dainihon kyōka tosho, 1943).

Hashimoto Minoru, *Shōnen bushidō shi* (Tōkyō: Ikubunsha, 1942).

Hata Ikuhiko, *Nihon no horyo: Hakusonkō kara Shiberia yokuryū made* (Hara shobō, 1998)

Hayashi Hōkō, 'Fukushū ron', in Ishii Shirō (ed.), *Kinsei buke shisō (Nihon shisō taikei 27)* (Tokyo: Iwanami shoten, 1974), 372–75.

Hiraizumi Kiyoshi, *Bushidō no fukkatsu* (Tokyo: Shibundo, 1933).

Hiraizumi Kiyoshi, *Nihon no higeki to risō* (Tokyo: Hara Shobō, 1977).

Hiraizumi Kiyoshi, *Nihon seishin 2* (Osaka: Ōsaka-fu Keisatsubu Keimuka, 1937).

Hiraizumi Kiyoshi, *Sensen daichokukin kai* (Tokyo: Asahi Shinbunsha, 1942).

Hiraizumi Kiyoshi, *Shōnen Nihon shi* (Ise: Kōgakkan Daigaku Shuppan, 2005).

Hirano, Kyoko, *Mr. Smith Goes to Tokyo: Japanese Cinema under the American Occupation, 1945–1952* (Washington: Smithsonian Institution Press, 1992).

Hiraoka Toshio, *Nichirō sengo bungaku no kenkyū* (Tokyo: Yuseido, 1985).

Hirose Yutaka (ed.), *Kō-Mō yowa* (Tokyo: Iwanami shoten, 1943).

Hirose Yutaka (ed.), *Gunjin dōtoku ron* (Tokyo: Bushidō kenkyūkai, 1928).

Hirose Yutaka (ed.), *Gunjin shōkun* (Tokyo: Bushidō kenkyūkai, 1927).

Hirose Yutaka (ed.), *Gunjin shōkun kaichō zōho* (Tokyo: Bushidō kenkyūkai, 1935).

Hirose Yutaka (ed.), *Yamaga Sokō heigaku zenshū* (Tokyo: Kyōzaisha, 1943).

Hirose Yutaka (ed.), *Yamaga Sokō zenshū* 1 (Tokyo: Iwanami shoten, 1942).

Hirose Yutaka, 'Yoshida Shōin no bushidō', in Bushidō gakkai eds. *Bushidō shinzui* (Tokyo: Teikoku shoseki kyōkai, 1941), 204–24.

Hirose Yutaka (ed.), *Yoshida Shōin zenshu* (Iwanami Shoten, 1935).

Hirota Teruyuki, *Rikugun shōkō no kyōiku shakaishi: risshin shusse to tennōsei* (Tokyo: Seori shobō, 1997).

Hishikawa Yoshio, 'Meiji sanjū nendai no bunmeiron: bunmei hihyō no seiritsu to tenkai 1' *Hokkaidō Gakuen Daigaku jinbun ronshū* 6 (31 March 1996), 43–54.

Hitchman, Francis, *The public life of the Right Honourable the Earl of Beaconsfield* (London: Chapman & Hall, 1879).

Hitomi Tecchō, *Bushidō no hana Nogi taishō* (Tokyo: Hiyoshidō shoten, 1912).

Hobsbawm, Eric J., *Nations and Nationalism since 1780: Programme, Myth, Reality* (Cambridge: Cambridge University Press, 1990).

Hobsbawm, Eric J. and Terence Ranger, *The Invention of Tradition* (Cambridge: Cambridge University Press, 1983).

Holmes, Colin and A. H. Ion, 'Bushido and the Samurai: Images in British Public Opinion, 1894–1914', *Modern Asian Studies* 14:2 (1980), 309–29.

Hoshi Ryōichi, *Aizu bushidō: 'naranu koto ha naranu' no oshie* (Tokyo: Seishun Shuppansha, 2006).

Howes, John F., *Japan's Modern Prophet: Uchimura Kanzo 1861–1930* (Vancouver: UBC Press, 2005).

Howes, John F. and George Oshiro, 'Who was Nitobe?' in John Howes (ed.), *Nitobe Inazō: Japan's Bridge Across the Pacific* (Boulder: Westview Press, 1995), 3–23.

Howland, Douglas R., 'Samurai Status, Class, and Bureaucracy: A Historiographical Essay', *The Journal of Asian Studies* 60:2 (May 2001), 353–80.

Huang Zhen and Cao Lü, 'Jindai Riben zhenlü xing wenhua de lishi yuanyuan ji jiexi', *Riben wenti yanjiu* 23:3 (Sept. 2009), 58–64.

Humphreys, Leonard A., *The Way of the Heavenly Sword: The Japanese Army in the 1920s* (Stanford: Stanford University Press, 1995).

Hur, Nam-lin, *Prayer and Play in Late Tokugawa Japan: Asakusa Sensōji and Edo Society* (Cambridge, MA: Harvard University Press, 2000).

Hurst III, G. Cameron, 'Death, Honor, and Loyality: The Bushidō Ideal', *Philosophy East and West* 40:4 (Oct. 1990), 511–27.

Hurst III, G. Cameron, 'The Warrior as Ideal for a New Age', in Jeffrey P. Mass (ed.), *The Origins of Japan's Medieval World* (Stanford: Stanford University Press, 1997), 209–33.

Hyōdō Hiromi and Henry D. Smith II, 'Singing Tales of the Gishi: Naniwabushi and the Forty-seven Rōnin in Late Meiji Japan', *Monumenta Nipponica* 61:4 (2006) 459–508.

Ichinose Toshiya, *Meiji, Taishō, Shōwa guntai manyuaru: hito ha naze senjō he itta no ka* (Tokyo: Kōbunsha, 2004).

Ienaga Saburō, 'The Glorification of War in Japanese Education', *International Security* 18:3 (Winter 1993/94), 113–33.

Iida Kanae, 'Fukuzawa Yukichi to bushidō: Katsu Kaishū, Uchimura Kanzō oyobi Nitobe Inazō to no kanren ni oite', *Mita gakkai zasshi* 83:1 (April 1990), 16–33.

Iida Kanae, '*Yasegaman no setsu* to *Hikawa seiwa*: Katsu Kaishū to Fukuzawa Yukichi no aida', *Mita gakkai zasshi* 90:1 (April 1990): 1–18.

Ikegami, Eiko, *The Taming of the Samurai: Honorific Individualism and the Making of Modern Japan* (Cambridge, MA: Harvard University Press, 1995).

Ikushima Hajime, *Seidan tōron hyakudai* (Tokyo: Matsui Chūbei, 1882).

Imai, John Toshimichi, 'Bushido', *South Tokyo Diocesan Magazine* 9:28 (Dec. 1905), 78–84.

Imai, John Toshimichi, *Bushido in the Past and Present* (Tokyo: Kanazashi, 1906).

Inoue Isao, 'Tokugawa no ishin: sono kōdō to rinri', in Inoue Isao (ed.), *Kaikoku to bakumatsu no dōran (Nihon no jidai shi* 20) (Tokyo: Furukawa Kōbunkan, 2004), 231–70.

Inoue Jukichi, *A Concise History of the War between Japan and China* (Tokyo: Y. Okura, 1895).

Inoue Shun, *Budō no tanjō* (Tokyo: Yoshikawa kōbunkan, 2004).

Inoue Shun, 'The Invention of the Martial Arts: Kanō Jigorō and Kōdōkan Judo', in Stephen Vlastos (ed.), *Mirror of Modernity: Invented Traditions in Modern Japan* (Berkeley: University of California Press, 1998), 163–73.

Inoue Tetsujirō, *Bushidō* (Tokyo: Heiji zasshi sha, 1901).

Inoue Tetsujirō (ed.), *Bushidō sōsho* (Tokyo: Hakubunkan, 1905).

Inoue Tetsujirō, 'Bushidō wo ronjiawasete *Yasegaman no setsu* ni oyobu', *Senken ronbun 2 shū* (Tokyo: Fuzanbō, 1901), 85–100.

Inoue Tetsujirō, 'Bushidō to shōrai no dōtoku', in Akiyama Goan and Inoue Tetsujirō (eds.), *Gendai taika bushidō sōron* (Tokyo: Hakubunkan, 1905), 116–40.

Inoue Tetsujirō, *Chokugo engi* (Tokyo: Inoue Sokichi, 1891).

Inoue Tetsujirō, 'Josetsu', in Saeki Ariyoshi (ed.), *Bushidō hōten* (Tokyo: Jitsugyō no Nihonsha, 1939).

Inoue Tetsujirō, *Kokumin dōtoku gairon* (Tokyo: Sanseidō, 1912).

Inoue Tetsujirō, 'Miyamoto Musashi to bushidō', *Tōyō tetsugaku* 21:1 (1914), 1–22.

Inoue Tetsujirō, *Nihon kogakuha no tetsugaku* (Tokyo: Fuzanbō, 1915).

Inoue Tetsujirō, *Nihon yōmeigakuha no tetsugaku* (Tokyo: Fuzanbō, 1900).

Inoue Tetsujirō, *Rinri to kyōiku* (Tokyo: Kōdōkan, 1908).

Inoue Tetsujirō, 'Kōron: <Shi no kenkyū> bushidō gakuha no shiseikan', *Chūō kōron 28* (Oct. 1913), 78.

Inoue Tetsujirō, 'Ukita Satō ryōshi no ronsō ni tsuite', in Akiyama Goan and Inoue Tetsujirō (eds.), *Gendai taika bushidō sōron* (Tokyo: Hakubunkan, 1905), 235–41.

Inoue Tetsujirō, 'Ukita shi no kōben wo yomu', in Akiyama Goan and Inoue Tetsujirō (eds.), *Gendai taika bushidō sōron* (Tokyo: Hakubunkan, 1905), 256–64.

Inoue Tetsujirō, 'Yamaga Sokō sensei to Nogi taishō' *Nihon kogakuha no tetsugaku* (Tokyo: Fuzanbō, 1915), 794–829.

Inoue Tetsujirō, and Saeki Ariyoshi (ed.), *Bushidō zensho* (Tokyo: Jidaisha, 1942).

Inoue Tetsujirō, and Saeki Ariyoshi (ed.), *Bushidō hoten* (Tokyo: Jitsugyō no Nihonsha, 1940).

Ion, A. Hamish, *The Cross and the Rising Sun: The Canadian Protestant Missionary Movement in the Japanese Empire, 1872–1931* (Waterloo: Wilfrid Laurier University Press, 1990).

Ion, A. Hamish, 'Japan Watchers: 1903–31', in John Howes (ed.), *Nitobe Inazō: Japan's Bridge Across the Pacific* (Boulder: Westview Press, 1995), 79–106.

Irie Katsumi, *Nihon fashizumu shita no taiiku shisō* (Tokyo: Fumaido shuppan, 1986).

Iriye, Akira, *Power and Culture: The Japanese-American War 1941–1945* (Cambridge: Harvard University Press, 1981).

Irokawa Daikichi: Marius Jansen (trans.), *The Culture of the Meiji Period* (Princeton: Princeton University Press, 1988).

Ishida Hideto, 'Fukuzawa Yukichi to Ozaki Yukio', *Jikyoku 144* (Jan. 1949), 24–28.

Ishii Shirō, 'Bushidō ni miru Nihonjin no shikō patān—teigi naki gainen no ran'yō', *Kagaku gijutsu to chi no seishin bunka: kōen roku 3* (June 2007), 1-23.

Ishii Shirō, 'Basil Hall Chamberlain and Inazo Nitobe: a Confrontation over Bushido', *University of Tokyo Journal of Law and Politics 3* (2006), 1–26.

Ishikawa Takuboku, *Meiji bungaku zenshū 52: Ishikawa Takuboku shū* (Tokyo: Chikuma shobo, 1970).

Ishiwara Kanji, *Sensō shi taikan* (Tokyo: Chūō kōron sha, 1941).

Ishizu Masao, 'Seinen kunrenjo ni kansuru taiiku shiteki kenkyū', *Taiiku gaku kenkyū* 20:1 (Aug. 1975), 5–13.

Isono Kiyoshi, *Nihon bushidō shōron* (Tokyo: Meguro shoten, 1934).

Ives, Christopher, 'Ethical Pitfalls in Imperial Zen and Nishida Philosophy: Ichikawa Hakugen's Critique', in James Heisig and John Maraldo (eds.), *Rude Awakenings: Zen, the Kyoto School, & the Question of Nationalism* (Honolulu: University of Hawai'i Press, 1994), 16–39.

Ives, Christopher, *Imperial-Way Zen: Ichikawa Hakugen's Critique and Lingering Questions for Buddhist Ethics* (Honolulu: University of Hawaii Press, 2009).

Iwano Hōmei, *Meiji bungaku zenshū 71: Iwano Hōmei shū* (Tokyo: Chikuma shobo, 1965).

Iwasa Shigekazu, *Gunjin seishin no shūyō* (Tokyo: Kōbundō shoten, 1913).

Iwashi Junsei and Toyoshima Yōzaburō (eds.), *Tōyō rinri: shūyō hōkan* (Tokyo: Hakubunkan, 1909).

Iyenaga Toyokichi, *The Constitutional Development of Japan 1863–1881* (Baltimore: Johns Hopkins University Press, 1891).

Izawa Nagahide (Banryū), 'Bushi kun', in *Bushidō zensho 4*, Saeki Ariyoshi et al. (eds.), (Tokyo: Jidaisha, 1942), 253–93.

Izumi Kyōka, 'Indo sarasa', *Kyōka zenshū 9* (Tokyo: Shun'yōdō, 1926), 311–26.

Izumi Kyōka, 'Yasha ga ike', *Kyōka zenshū 14* (Tokyo: Shun'yōdō, 1926), 413–60.

Jansen, Marius, 'Japan Looks Back', *Foreign Affairs*, 47:1 (Oct., 1968), 36–50.

Jansen, Marius, *The Making of Modern Japan* (Cambridge, MA: Belknap Press of Harvard University, 2000).

Jansen, Marius, 'Ōi Kentarō: Radicalism and Chauvinism', *The Far Eastern Quarterly* 11:3 (May 1952), 305–16.

Kaigo Tokiomi (ed.), *Kindai Nihon kyōkasho sōsetsu kaisetsu hen* (Tokyo: Kōdansha, 1969).

Kaigun kyōiku honbu, *Kaigun dokuhon* (Tokyo: Kaigun kyōiku honbu, 1905).

Kaiten Nukariya, *Religion of the Samurai: A Study of Zen Philosophy and Discipline in China and Japan* (London: Luzac & Co, 1913).

Kaneko Kūken and Kitamura Daisui, *Bujin hyakuwa seishin shūyō* (Tokyo: Teikoku gunji kyōkai shuppanbu, 1912).

Kang Ching-Il, 'Tenyūkyō to "Chōsen mondai": "Chōsen rōnin" no tōgaku nōmin sensō he no taiō to kanren shite', *Shigaku Zasshi* 97:8 (1988), 1321–57.

Kanno Kakumyō, *Bushidō no gyakushū* (Tokyo: Kōdansha gendai shinsho, 2004).

Kanō Jiguro and Watari Shōzaburō, *Shinsen shihan shūshin sho 4* (Tokyo: Kinkodō, 1918).

Kasaya Kazuhiko, *Bushidō to Nihon kei nōryoku shugi* (Tokyo: Shinchōsha sensho, 2005).

Kasaya Kazuhiko, *Shukun oshikome no kōzō* (Tokyo: Heibonsha, 1988).

Kasza, Gregory J., *The State and the Mass Media in Japan, 1918–1945* (Berkeley: University of California Press, 1988).

Kataoka Kenkichi, 'Hōken bushi to Kirisuto shinsha', *Bushidō* 1:2 (March 1898), 6.

Katō Hiroyuki, 'Satō tai Ukita ron nit suite', in Akiyama Goan and Inoue Tetsujirō (eds.), *Gendai taika bushidō sōron* (Tokyo: Hakubunkan, 1905), 265–72.

Katō Hiroyuki, *Tokuiku hōan* (Tokyo: Tōkyō yūeisha, 1887).

Katō Hiroyuki, 'Wanryoku ha toku ni kokka no shuken ni takusubeshi', *Tensoku* 1:9 (1889), 212–17.

Katō Totsudō, *Zen kanroku* (Tokyo: Ireido, 1905).

Katō Yōko, *Chōheisei to kindai Nihon* (Tokyo: Yoshikawa kōbunkan, 1996).

Katsube Mitake, *Yamaoka Tesshū no bushidō* (Tokyo: Kakegawa sofia bunko, 2003).

Kawabata, Tai, 'Bad Public Manners Irk Bushido Proponent', *The Japan Times* (3 June 2008).

Kawai Kazuo, *Japan's American Interlude* (Chicago: University of Chicago Press, 1979).

Kawakami Tasuke, 'Bushidō no genryū', *Hitotsubashi ronsō* 1:6 (1938), 763–83.

Kawakami Tasuke, 'Bushido in its Formative Period', *The Annals of the Hitotsubashi Academy* 3:1 (1952), 65–83.

Keene, Donald, *Dawn to the West: Japanese Literature of the Modern Era (Vol. 1, Fiction)* (New York: Holt, Rinehart, and Winston, 1984).

Keene, Donald, *Yoshimasa and the Silver Pavillion: The Creation of the Soul of Japan* (New York: Columbia University Press, 2003).

Keirstead, Thomas, 'Inventing Medieval Japan: The History and Politics of National Identity', *The Medieval History Journal* 1:47 (1998), 47–71.

Keisatsu kōshū jo (ed.), *Keisatsu kōwa roku* (Tokyo: Shōkadō shoten, 1943).

Kenseikai (ed.), *Bushidō yōi* (Tokyo: Kenseikai, 1933).

Ketelaar, James Edward, *Of Heretics and Martyrs in Meiji Japan: Buddhism and its Persecution* (Princeton: Princeton University Press, 1993).

Kihira Tadayoshi, 'Waga kokutai ni okeru wa', in Monbushō Kyōgaku Kyoku (eds.), *Kokutai no hongi kaisetsu sōsho* (Monbushō Kyōgaku Kyoku, 1944), 243–303.

Kikuchi Kan, 'Bushidō no hanashi', in Bushidō gakkai eds. *Bushidō shinzui* (Tokyo: Teikoku shoseki kyōkai, 1941), 130–49.

Kinmonth, Earl H., *The Self-Made Man in Meiji Japanese Thought: From Samurai to Salary Man* (Berkeley: University of California Press, 1981).

Kirita Kiyohide, 'D. T. Suzuki on Society and the State', in James Heisig and John Maraldo (eds.), *Rude Awakenings: Zen, the Kyoto School, & the Question of Nationalism* (Honolulu: University of Hawai'i Press, 1994), 52–74.

Kita Terujirō, *Kokutairon oyobi junsei shakai shugi* (Tokyo: Kita Terujirō, 1906).

Kita Terujirō, *Nihon kaizō hōan taikō* (Tokyo: Nishida Mitsugi, 1928).

Kita Terujirō, *Shina kakumei gaishi* (Osaka: Daitōkaku, 1921).

Kitagawa Hakuai, *Sumō to bushidō* (Tokyo: Asakusa kokugi kan, 1911).

Kitakage Yūkō, *Kyōshi no tame no bushidō nyūmon* (Tokyo: Bensei shuppan, 2012).

Kitakage Yūkō, *Jieikan no tame no bushidō nyūmon* (Tokyo: Bensei shuppan, 2012).

Klöpper, Clemens; Suzuki Chikara (trans.), *Kyōiku tetsugaku shi* (Tokyo: Hakubundō, 1889).

Knapp, Arthur May, *Feudal and Modern Japan* (Boston: Joseph Knight Company, 1898).

Kobayashi Ichirō, 'Bushidō no hihan (I)', *Tetsugaku zasshi* 17:187 (10 Sept. 1902), 48–74.

Kobayashi Ichirō, 'Bushidō no hihan (II)', *Tetsugaku zasshi* 17:187 (10 Oct. 1902), 25–45.

Kobayashi Ichirō, 'Hābāto, Spensā', *Tetsugaku zasshi* 19:206 (10 May 1904), 1–11.

Kōfūkan Hensanjo (eds.), *Shihan kokubun: dai ichibu yō kyōjū bikō 7* (Tokyo: Kōfūkan shoten, 1938).

Kōfūkan Hensanjo (eds.), *Chūgaku kokubun kyōkasho kyōjū bikō 5 (23rd Edition)* (Tokyo: Kōfūkan shoten, 1935).

Koga Hideo and Stacy Day (eds.), *Hagakure: Spirit of Bushido (Proceedings of the International Symposium on Hagakure, November 1992, Saga, Japan)* (Fukuoka: Kyushu University Press, 1993).

Koike Yoshiaki, *Hagakure: bushi to 'hōkō'* (Tokyo: Kōdansha gakujutsu bunko, 1999).

Kojima Tsuyoshi, *Kindai Nihon no Yōmeigaku* (Tokyo: Kōdansha sensho metier, 2006).

Kokugo Kenkyūkai (ed.), *Chūgaku kokubun kyōkasho sankōsho: dai 2 gakunen yō* (Tokyo: Seibidō shoten, 1913).

Kokumin reihō chōsakai (ed.), *Kokumin dōtoku wo chūshin to shitaru reigi sahō no riron to jissai* (Tokyo: Meiseikai, 1912).

Kokumin seishin bunka kenkyūjo (ed.), *Kokumin seishin bunka kenkyū* (Tokyo: Kokumin seishin bunka kenkyūjo, 1938).

Kokushi daijiten henshū iinkai (ed.), *Kokushi dai jiten* (Tokyo: Yoshikawa kobunkan, 1983).

Kōno Masayoshi, *Bushidō no tenkei Nogi taishō* (Tokyo: Tōkyō kokumin shoin, 1913).

Kōno Tsukasa (ed.), *Ni ni roku jiken* (Tokyo: Nihon shūhōsha, 1957).

Konoe Fumimaro, 'Kokutai to bushidō', in *Bushidō nyūmon* (Tokyo: Futara shobō, 1941), 20–27.

Kornicki, P. F., 'The Survival of Tokugawa Fiction in The Meiji Period', *Harvard Journal of Asiatic Studies* 41:2 (Dec. 1981), 461–82.

Kōsaka Jirō, *Genroku bushigaku: 'Budō shoshinshū' wo yomu* (Tokyo: Chūōkōron, 1987).

Kosuge Ren, *Kyōiku jihei* (Denpō Mura: Kosuge Ren, 1894).

Koyasu Nobukuni, *Nihon kindai shisō hihan: ikkokuchi no seiritsu* (Tokyo: Iwanami gendai bunko, 2003).

Kuki Shūzō, 'Jikyoku no kansō', *Bungei shunshū* 15:12 (Oct. 1937), 36–37.

Kumata Ijō (Shūjirō), *Onna bushidō* (Tokyo: Tenchidō, 1908).

Kumazawa Banzan, 'Shūgi washo (shōroku)', in Saeki Ariyoshi et al. (eds.), *Bushidō zensho* 4 (Tokyo: Jidaisha, 1942).

Kuroiwa Ruikō, *Bushidō ichimei himitsubukuro* (Tokyo: Fusōdō, 1897).

Kurozumi Makoto, 'The Nature of Early Tokugawa Confucianism', *Journal of Japanese Studies* 20:2 (summer 1994), 337–75.

Kurozumi Makoto, '*Kangaku*: Writing and Institutional Authority', in Haruo Shirane (ed.), *Inventing the Classics: Modernity, National Identity, and Japanese Literature* (Stanford: Stanford University Press, 2000), 201–19.

Kushner, Barak, *The Thought War: Japanese Imperial Propaganda* (Honolulu: University of Hawaii Press, 2006).

Kutsumi Sokuchū, 'Kyōiku to bushidō', *Bushidō* 1:4 (May 1898), 6–8.

Kyōiku gakujutsu kenkyūkai, *Rekishika kyōjūryō kaitei kokutei kyōkasho* (Tokyo: Dōbunkan, 1910).

Kyōiku kenkyūkai, *Chūtō kyōka meiji dokuhon teisei jikai* (Tokyo: Tōundō shoten, 1909).

Kyōiku kenkyūkai, *Shintei chūtō kokugo tokuhon jikai* (Tokyo: Tōundō, 1909).

Kyōiku sōkan bu (ed.), *Bujin no tokusō* (Tokyo: Kaikōsha, 1930).

Liang Qichao, *Zhongguo zhi wushidao* (Shanghai: Liang Qichao, 1904).

Liang Qichao, 'Zhongguohun Anzaihu', *Yinbing shi wenji lei* 2 (Shimokobe Hangorō, 1904), 693–94.

Lincicome, Mark E., 'Nationalism, Imperialism, and the International Education Movement in Early Twentieth-Century Japan', *The Journal of Asian Studies* 58:2 (May, 1999), 338–60.

Lone, Stewart, *Provincial Life and the Military in Imperial Japan: the Phantom Samurai* (Abingdon: Routledge, 2010).

Lou Guishu, 'Riben wushidao he junju zhuyi de bianhu ci: yipping Xinduhu Daozao de Wushidao', *Guizhou Shifan Daxue Xuebao (Shehui Kexue Ban) 167* (Oct. 2010), 120–28.

Lummis, Douglas C., 'It Would Make No Sense for Article 9 to Mean What it Says, Therefore It Doesn't. The Transformation of Japan's Constitution', *The Asia-Pacific Journal*, 11:9:2 (30 Sept. 2013).

Lupack, Alan and Barbara, *King Arthur in America* (Cambridge, MA: D. S. Brewer, 1999).

MacKenzie, S. P., 'Willpower or Firepower? The Unlearned Lessons of the Russo-Japanese War', in David Wells and Sandra Wilson (eds.), *The Russo-Japanese War in Cultural Perspective, 1904–05* (London: MacMillan Press, 1999), 30–40.

Maeda Chōta (trans.), *Seiyō bushidō [Leon Gautier* La Chevalerie *no yakuhon]* (Tokyo: Hakubunkan, 1909).

Maguire, Joseph and Masayoshi Nakayama (eds.), *Japan, Sport, and Society: Tradition and Change in a Globalizing World* (London: Routledge, 2006).

Mainichi shinbun 'Yasukuni' shuzai han, *Yasukuni sengo hishi: A kyū senhan wo gōshi shita otoko* (Tokyo: Mainichi shinbun sha, 2007).

Maruyama Masao, *Chūsei to hangyaku: tenkei ki Nihon no seishin shiteki isō* (Tokyo: Chikuma gakugei bunko, 1998).

Maruyama Masao, *Studies in the Intellectual History of Tokugawa Japan* (Princeton: Princeton University Press, 1974).

Mason, Philip, *The English Gentleman: The Rise and Fall of an Ideal* (London: Andre Deutsch, 1982).

Mass, Jeffrey P., *Antiquity and Anachronism in Japanese History* (Stanford: Stanford University Press, 1992).

Matsumae Shigeyoshi, *Budō shisō no tankyū* (Tokyo: Tōkai daigaku shuppankai, 1987).

Matsumoto Aijū, 'Bushidō', *Tōyō tetsugaku* 4:2 (15 April 1897), 90–94.

Matsumoto Aijū, 'Bushidō', in Akiyama Goan and Inoue Tetsujirō (eds.), *Bushidō sōron* (Tokyo: Hakubunkan, 1905), 1–19.

Matsunami, Jirō, *Aikoku no netsujō to bushidō* (Tokyo: Hakuseisha, 1942).

Matsunami, Jirō, *Hagakure bushidō* (Tokyo: Ichiro shoen, 1938).

Matsunami, Jirō, *Hagakure bushidō seishin* (Tokyo: Ichiro Shoen, 1940).

Matsusaka, Yoshihisa Tak, 'Human Bullets, Nogi, and the Myth of Port Arthur', in Steinberg, John W., Bruce W. Menning, David Schimmelpenninck van der Oye, David Wolff, and Shinji Yokote (eds.), *The Russo-Japanese War in Global Perspective: World War Zero* (Leiden: Brill, 2005), 179–201.

Matsushima Tsuyoshi, *Heieki kakushinron okudzuke* (Tokyo: Yamato shōten, 1927).

Matsuzawa Hiroaiki, *Kindai Nihon no keisei to seiyō keiken* (Tokyo: Iwanami shoten, 1993).

McClellan, Edwin, 'Tōson and the Autobiographical Novel', in Donald Shively (ed.), *Tradition and Modernization in Japanese Culture* (Princeton: Princeton University Press, 1971), 347–78.

McCrae, R. R. 'Cross-Cultural Research on the Five-Factor Model of Personality (Version 2)', *Online Readings in Psychology and Culture* (Unit 6, Chapter 1/V2) June, 2009.

McDonald, Lachie, 'MacA Puts Back the Glamour', *Daily Mail*, (19 Oct. 1945), 3.

Mehl, Margaret, *Eine Vergangenheit für die japanische Nation* (Frankfurt: Peter Lang, 1992).

Meiji kyōikusha (ed.), *Bunken juken yō kokumin dōtoku yōryō* (Tokyo: Meiji kyōikusha, 1916).

Mie-Ken seishōnendan honbu (eds.), *Seishōnen senji kyōyō dokuhon* (Mie: Mie-ken seishōnendan honbu, 1945).

Mihara Osamu, *Shōnen yakyū dokuhon* (Tokyo: Yomiuri shinbunsha, 1949).

Mikami Reiji, *Nihon bushidō* (Tokyo: Kokubunsha, 1899).

Minami Hiroshi, *Sōsho Nihonjinron 2: kokumin no shin seishin* (Tokyo: Ozorasha, 1996).

Minami Hiroshi, *Nihonjin ron: Meiji kara kyō made* (Tokyo: Iwanami gendai bunko, 2006).

Minami Hiroshi, *Shōwa bunka 1925–1945* (Tokyo: Keisō shobō, 1987).
Minami Hiroshi, *Taishō bunka, 1905–1927* (Tokyo: Keisō shobō, 1988).
Minamoto Ryōen, 'Yokoi Shōnan ni okeru jōi ron kara kaikoku ron he no tenkai', *Ajia bunka kenkyū 26* (March 2000): 224–97.
Mishima Yukio, *Hagakure nyūmon* (Tokyo: Kōbunsha, 1967).
Mishima Yukio: Kathryn Sparling (trans.), *Yukio Mishima on* Hagakure: *The Samurai Ethic and Modern Japan* (London: Souvenir Press, 1977).
Mitani Hiroshi, 'Foreword', in Makito Saya: David Noble (trans.), *The Sino-Japanese War and the Birth of Japanese Nationalism* (Tokyo: International House of Japan, 2011), ix–xvii.
Mitsukuri Genpachi, *Rekishi sōwa* (Tokyo: Hakubunkan, 1907).
Miyaoka Naoki, *Kimi ni sasagete* (Tokyo: Gunji Kyōikukai, 1922).
Miyazawa Seiichi, *Meiji ishin no saisōzō: kindai Nihon no 'kigenshinwa'* (Tokyo: Aoki shoten, 2005).
Mizuho Tarō, 'Bushidō wo goji kankō suru mono ha dare zo', *Bushidō* 1:3 (April 1898), 1–4.
Mizuho Tarō, 'Hatsujin no koe', *Bushidō* 1:1 (Feb. 1898): 1–5.
Mizuma Masanori, *Hitome de wakaru 'Nichū sensō' jidai no bushidō seishin* (Kyoto: PHP kenkyūjo, 2013).
Mori Ōgai, *Gojiin ga hara no katakiuchi* (Tokyo: Iwanami shoten, 1955).
Morikawa Tetsurō, *Hagakure nyūmon* (Tokyo: Nihon bungeisha, 1975).
Morikawa Tetsurō, *Nihon bushidō shi* (Tokyo: Nihon bungeisha, 1972).
Morioka Iwao and Kasahara Yoshimitsu, *Kirisuto kyō no sensō sekinin* (Tokyo: Kyobunkan, 1974).
Morris, Lea, *Bushido: Krijgsmanseer, de erfenis der godenzonen* (Amsterdam: Nieuwe Wieken, 1947).
Mullins, Mark, *Christianity Made in Japan: A Study of Indigenous Movements* (Honolulu: University of Hawai'i Press, 1998).
Muramatsu Seiin, *Nogi taishō shōka bushidō no hana* (Tokyo: Sanmeisha shoten, 1912).
Muro Kyūsō, 'Akō gijin roku', in Ishii Shirō (ed.), *Kinsei buke shisō (Nihon shisō taikei 27)*, (Tokyo: Iwanami shoten, 1974), 272–73.
Nagahori Hitoshi, *Seishin kyōiku teikoku gunjin sōsho dai-ippen: Akō gishi* (Tokyo: Tsūzoku gunji kyōiku kai, 1919).
Nagatani Togetsu, *Bushidō to bukkyō* (Tokyo: Kendō shoin, 1913).
Naimushō Keihokyoku (eds.), *Keisatsu kanbu yokuonkan kōwa roku* (Tokyo: Keisatsu kyōkai, 1939).
Najita, Tetsuo, *Visions of Virtue in Tokugawa Japan: The Kaitokudō Merchant Academy of Ōsaka* (Chicago: University of Chicago Press, 1987).
Nakae Tōju, 'Bunbu mondō', in Saeki Ariyoshi et al. (eds.), *Bushidō zensho* 2 (Tokyo: Jidaisha, 1942), 245–62.
Nakahara Nobuo, 'Ozaki Yukio ni okeru nashonarizumu: Meiji 21–23 nen Ōbei manyūki wo chūshin ni', *Rekishigaku kenkyū 265* (June 1962), 45–52.
Nakamura Akihiko, *Aizu bushidō: samurai tachi ha nan no tame ni ikita no ka* (Kyoto: PHP kenkyūjo, 2006).
Nakamura Mototsune, 'Shōbu ron', in Saeki Ariyoshi et al. (eds.), *Bushidō zensho* 6 (Tokyo: Jidaisha, 1942).
Nakamura Tamio (ed.), *Kendō jiten: gijutsu to bunka no rekishi* (Tokyo: Shimadzu shobō, 1994).
Nakamura Tamio (ed.), *Shiryō kindai kendō shi* (Tokyo: Shimadzu shobō, 1985).

Nakamura Yoko, *Bushidō—Diskurs. Die Analyse der Diskrepanz zwischen Ideal und Realität im Bushidō-Diskurs aus dem Jahr 1904* (PhD thesis at the University of Vienna, 2008).

Nakano Hajimu, 'Kita Ikki and *The Structure of Iki*', in Thomas Rimer (ed.), *Culture and Identity: Japanese Intellectuals During the Interwar Years* (Princeton, NJ: Princeton University Press, 1990), 261–72.

Nakaoke Takeo, *Gunshin Sugimoto Gorō chūsa: shō kokumin no Nihon bunko* (Tokyo: Kōdansha, 1942).

Nakatani Togetsu, *Bushidō to bukkyō* (Tokyo: Kendō shoin, 1913).

Namekawa Michio, 'Taishūteki jidō bungaku zenshi toshite no "tachikawa bunko"', in Nihon bungaku kenkyū shiryō kankōkai (ed.), *Jidō bungaku* (Tokyo: Yuseido, 1977).

Nangō Shigeru, *Bushidō to Satsuma gishi* (Tokyo: Hito to bunka sha, 1991).

Nanjō Bun'yū, 'Bushidō to bukkyō no kankei ni tsuite', in Akiyama Goan and Inoue Tetsujirō (eds.), *Gendai taika bushidō sōron* (Tokyo: Hakubunkan, 1905), 416–19.

Narasaki, Toshio, 'Kūsen hōki hattatsu shi joron', *Hōgaku shinpō*, 36:4 (1926), 40–61.

Narasaki, Toshio, 'Kūsen naishi kūsen hōki to bushidō', *Hōgaku shinpō*, 36:9 (1926), 58–75.

Naruse Kanji, *Shizoku* (Tokyo: Seibunsha, 1923).

Naruse Kanji, *Tatakau Nihontō* (Tokyo: Jitsugyō no Nihonsha, 1940).

Natsume Sōseki, *Rondon tō/Maboroshi no tate* (Tokyo: Iwanami shoten, 1951).

Nihon toshokan kyōkai (eds.), *Ryōsho hyakusen 2* (Tokyo: Nihon toshokan kyōkai, 1935).

Niki Shōha, *Nihon seishin to bushidō* (Tokyo: Kōbunsha, 1934).

Ninagawa Tatsuo, *Nihon bushidō shi* (Tokyo: Hakubunkan, 1907).

Nishimura Shinji (1940), *Nihon to sono bunka* (Fuzanbō).

Nitobe, Inazō, *Bushido: The Soul of Japan* (Tokyo: Kenkyusha, 1939).

Nitobe, Inazō, *Bushido: The Soul of Japan* (Tokyo: Tuttle & Co., 2001).

Nitobe, Inazō, 'Heimindō', *Jitsugyō no Nihon* 22:10 (1 May 1919), 17–20.

Nitobe, Inazō, *The Intercourse between the United States and Japan: A Historical Sketch* (Baltimore: Johns Hopkins University Press, 1890).

Nitobe, Inazō, *Lectures on Japan* (Tokyo: Kenkyusha, 1936).

Nitobe, Inazō, 'Our Recent Chauvinism', *The Far East: An English Edition of Kokumin-no-tomo* 2:7 (Feb. 1896), 17–24.

Nitobe, Inazō, *Thoughts and Essays* (Tokyo: Teibi Publishing Company: 1909).

Nitobe, Inazō: Sakurai Ōson (trans.), *Bushidō* (Tokyo: Teibi shuppansha, 1908).

'Nitobe Inazō *Bushidō* ninki: kyōiku kihon hō kaiseī/hantai ryōha no ronkyo', *Asahi Shimbun* (7 Dec. 2006).

Nogi Maresuke, 'Bushidō mondō', *Shiyū* (Tokyo: Gunji kyōiku kai, 1907).

Nogi Maresuke, 'Nogi taishō yuigonsho', *Shimin* 7:8 (7 Oct. 1912).

Nosco, Peter, *Remembering Paradise: Nativism and Nostalgia in Eighteenth-Century Japan* (Cambridge, MA: Harvard University Press, 1990).

Nose Hiroaki, *Shōnen aikoku dokuhon: sensō no hanashi* (Tokyo: Kōseikaku shoten, 1934).

Nunneley, John and Kazuo Tamayama, *Tales by Japanese Soldiers of the Burma Campaign 1942–1945* (London: Cassell & Co, 2000).

Nygren, Scott, *Time Frames: Japanese Cinema and the Unfolding of History* (Minneapolis: University of Minnesota Press, 2007).

Oates, Leslie Russell, *Populist Nationalism in Prewar Japan: A Biography of Nakano Seigō* (Sydney: George Allen, 1985).

Ōbuchi Rō, *Nogi shōgun genkō roku* (Kyoto: Shinshindō shoten, 1912).

Ochiai Naobumi (ed.), *Chūtō kokugaku dokuhon 9* (Tokyo: Meiji shoin, 1913).

O'Conroy, Taid, *The Menace of Japan* (London: Hurst & Blackett, 1933).

Ogasawara Naganari, 'Nichiren shugi to bushidō', *Miho kōen shū* 1 (Tokyo: Shishiō bunko, 1911).

Ōgawa Yoshiyuki, *Kendō taikan: seinen kyōiku* (Tokyo: Bunbukan, 1918).

Ogyū Shigehiro, 'Bakumatsu—Meiji no Yōmeigaku to Min Qin shisō shi', in Minamoto Ryōen, (ed.), *Nihon bunka kōryū shi sōsho 3: shisō* (Taishūkan shoten, 1995), 404–44.

Ogyū Shigehiro and Barry Steben, 'The Construction of "Modern Yōmeigaku" in Meiji Japan and its Impact in China', *East Asian History 20* (Dec. 2000), 95–96.

Ogyū Sorai, '47 shi ron', in Ishii Shirō (ed.), *Kinsei buke shisō (Nihon shisō taikei* 27), (Tokyo: Iwanami shoten, 1974), 400–401.

Ōhama Tetsuya, *Nogi Maresuke* (Tokyo: Kawade shobō, 1988).

Ōhashi Yukio, *Aogeba sonshi sokoku Nihon yo: Nihon he no kenpaku isho* (Tokyo: Bungeisha, 2006).

Ōhata Hiroshi, *Bushidō to katei* (Tokyo: Seirindō, 1910).

Ohnuki-Tierney, Emiko, *Kamikaze, Cherry Blossoms, and Nationalisms: The Militarization of Aesthetics in Japanese History* (Chicago: University of Chicago Press, 2002).

Ōi Kentarō, 'Bushidō ni tsuite', *Bushidō*, 1:3 (April 1898), 7–8.

Oka Yoshitake, 'Generational Conflict after the Russo-Japanese War', in Tetsuo Najita (ed.), *Conflict in Modern Japanese History* (Princeton, NJ: Princeton University Press, 1982), 197–225.

Okada, Meitarō, 'Bushidō rinri no shiteki kenkyū (part 1)', *Kaikōsha kiji 640* (1927), 3–28.

Okada, Meitarō, 'Bushidō rinri no shiteki kenkyū (part 2)', *Kaikōsha kiji 641* (1927), 1–23.

Okada Ryōhei, 'Nogi taishō no bushidō jitsugen', in Horiuchi Ryō (ed.), *Okada Ryōhei hōtoku ronshū* (Tokyo: Dai Nihon hōtokusha, 2005), 147–51.

Okakura, Kakuzō, *The Awakening of Japan* (New York: The Century Co, 1905).

Okakura, Kakuzō, *The Book of Tea* (New York: Fox Duffield & Company, 1906).

Okamoto Shumpei, 'The Emperor and the Crowd: The Historical Significance of the Hibiya Riot', in Tetsuo Najita (ed.), *Conflict in Modern Japanese History* (Princeton, NJ: Princeton University Press, 1982), 258–75.

Okano Ryōgan (ed.), *Senji Bukkyō* (Toyama: Kobayashi Shinchūdō, 1905).

Okazaki Masamichi, 'Yokoi Shōnan no seiji shisō: bakusei kaikaku to kyōwa seiji ron', *Artes Liberales 64* (1999): 96–116.

Ōkoda Yahiro, *Bushidō dokuhon* (Tokyo: Kaya Shobō, 2010).

Ōkubo Kaoru, *Kokushi kyōju no konpon mondai* (Tōkyō: Hōbunkan, 1922).

Ōkuma Shigenobu, *Fifty Years of New Japan* (II) (London: Smith, Elder & Co., 1909).

Ōkuma Shigenobu, *Ōzei wo takkan seyo* (Tokyo: Hōbundō, 1922).

Ōmachi Keigetsu, *Gunkoku kun* (Tokyo: Hakubunkan, 1904).

Ōnishi Hajime, 'Bushidō tai kairakushugi', *Ōnishi hakushi zenshū* (6) (Tokyo: Keiseisha, 1904), 268–73.

Ōnishi Hajime, 'Stoa no seishin to bushi no kifū to wo hikaku shite waga kokumin no kishitsu ni ronjioyobu', *Ōnishi hakushi zenshū* (6) (Tokyo: Keiseisha, 1904), 599–615.

Oshiro, George, 'The End: 1929–1933', in John Howes (ed.), *Nitobe Inazō: Japan's Bridge Across the Pacific* (Boulder: Westview Press, 1995), 253–78.

Ōsuga Shūgō, *Senji dendō taikan* (Kyoto: Hōzōkan, 1905).

Ōsugi Sakae, *Ōsugi Sakae jijoden* (Tokyo: Chūō bunko biblio 20 seiki, 2001), 119.

Ōta Yūzō, *Taiheiyō no hashi toshite no Nitobe Inazō* (Tokyo: Misuzu shobō, 1986).

Ōta Yūzō, 'Mediation between Cultures', in John Howes (ed.), *Nitobe Inazō: Japan's Bridge Across the Pacific* (Boulder: Westview Press, 1995), 237–52.

Otomo Ryoko, '"The Way of the Samurai": Ghost Dog, Mishima, and Modernity's Other' *Japanese Studies* 21:1 (2001), 31–43.

Ozaki Yukio, *Gunbi seigen* (Tokyo: Nihon hyōronsha, 1929).

Ozaki Yukio, *Naichi gaikō* (Tokyo: Hakubundō, 1893).

Ozaki Yukio, 'Ōbei man'yū ki', *Ozaki Gakudō zenshū* 3 (Tokyo: Kōronsha, 1955), 323–755.

Ozaki Yukio, *Ozaki Gakudō zenshū* 3 (Tokyo: Kōronsha, 1955).

Ozaki Yukio, *Seiji kyōiku ron* (Tokyo: Tōkadō, 1913).

Ozaki Yukio, *Shōbu ron* (Tokyo: Hakubundō, 1893).

Ozaki Yukio, 'Shōgyō to bushidō', *Bushidō* 1:1 (Feb. 1898): 10–11.

Ozaki Yukio, 'Tai Shin tai Kan ronsaku', *Ozaki Gakudō zenshū* 2 (Tokyo: Kōronsha, 1955), 78-187.

Ozaki Yukio, 'Yū Shin ki (Records of a Journey to Qing)', *Ozaki Gakudō zenshū* 4 (Tokyo: Kōronsha, 1955), 239–300.

Ozaki Yukio: Hara Fujiko (trans.), *The Autobiography of Ozaki Yukio: The Struggle for Constitutional Government in Japan* (Princeton, NJ: Princeton University Press, 2001).

Paine, S. C. M., *The Sino-Japanese War of 1894–1895: Perceptions, Power, and Primacy* (Cambridge: Cambridge University Press, 2003).

Peattie, Mark, *Ishiwara Kanji and Japan's Confrontation with the West* (Princeton, NJ: Princeton University Press, 1975).

Pincus, Leslie, *Authenticating Culture in Japan: Kuki Shūzō and the Rise of National Aesthetics* (Berkeley: University of California Press, 1996).

Pincus, Leslie, 'In a Labyrinth of Western Desire: Kuki Shuzo and the Discovery of Japanese Being', *boundary 2* 18:3 (Autumn, 1991), 142–56.

Pinnington, Adrian, 'Introduction', in Peter O'Connor (ed.), *Critical Readings on Japan, 1906–1948: Countering Japan's Agenda in East Asia* 1 (Tokyo: Edition Synapse, 2008).

Powles, Cyril H., '*Bushido*: Its Admirers and Critics', in John Howes (ed.), *Nitobe Inazō: Japan's Bridge Across the Pacific* (Boulder: Westview Press, 1995), 107–18.

Prang, Margaret, *A Heart at Leisure from Itself: Caroline MacDonald of Japan* (Vancouver: UBC Press, 1997).

Pyle, Kenneth B., *The New Generation in Meiji Japan: Problems of Cultural Identity, 1885–1895* (Stanford: Stanford University Press, 1969).

Raku Yōsei, *Seishinteki kakko kyōren* (Tokyo: Gunji kyōiku kai, 1912).

Rankin, Andrew, *Seppuku: A History of Samurai Suicide* (Tokyo: Kodansha International, 2011).

Reicher, Stephen and Nick Hopkins, *Self and nation: categorization, contestation and mobilization* (London: SAGE, 2001).

Reiss, Stefan, *Fichtes „Reden an die deutsche Nation," oder, Vom Ich zum Wir* (Berlin: Akademie Verlag, 2006).

Reitan, Richard M., *Making a Moral Society: Ethics and the State in Meiji Japan* (Honolulu: University of Hawaii Press, 2010).

Reitan, Richard M., 'National Morality, the State, and "Dangerous Thought": Approaching the Moral Ideal in Late Meiji Japan', *Japan Studies Review* 5 (2001), 23–58.

Richter, Giles, 'Entrepreneurship and Culture: The Hakubunkan Publishing Empire in Meiji Japan', in Helen Hardacre (ed.), *New Directions in the Study of Meiji Japan* (Leiden: Brill, 1997), 590–602.

Rikugunshō, Kaigunshō (eds.), *Chokuyu kasha 50 nen shukuga kōen shū* (Tokyo: Rikugunshō, 1932).

Roberts, Luke S., *Performing the Great Peace: Political Space and Open Secrets in Tokugawa Japan* (Honolulu: University of Hawai'i Press, 2012).

Russell, Edward F. L., *The Knights of Bushido* (London: Cassell, 1958).

Saeki Ariyoshi (ed.), *Bushidō hōten* (Tokyo: Kangyō no Nihonsha, 1939).

Saeki Ariyoshi, 'Bushidō hoten no sue ni daisu', *Bushidō hōten* (Tokyo: Jitsugyō no Nihonsha, 1939).

Saeki Ariyoshi, et al. (eds.), *Bushidō zensho* (Tokyo: Jidaisha, 1942).

Saeki Ariyoshi, et al. (eds.), *Bushidō zensho* (Tokyo: Kokusho kankō kai, 1998).

Saeki Ariyoshi, 'Jijo', *Bushidō hōten* (Tokyo: Jitsugyō no Nihonsha, 1939).

Saeki Shin'ichi, *Senjō no seishinshi* (Tokyo: NHK Books, 2004).

Saeki Yoshirō, *Keikyō hibun kenkyū* (Tokyo: Tairō shoin, 1911).

Sagara Tōru (ed.), *Kōyōgunkan, gorinsho, hagakure-shū (Nihon no shisō 9)* (Tokyo: Chikuma shobō, 1968).

Saiki Kazuma et al. (eds.), *Mikawa monogatari, hagakure (Nihon shisō taikei 26)* (Tokyo: Iwanami shoten, 1974).

Saitō Kaname, *Nihon bushidō no saiginmi* (Tokyo: Daitō shuppansha, 1937).

Saitō Ryū, *Seinen shōkō no shūyō* (Tokyo: Heiji zasshi sha, 1915).

Saitō Setsudō, 'Shidō yōron', in Saeki Ariyoshi et al. (eds.), *Bushidō zensho* 6 (Tokyo: Jidaisha, 1942), 293–318.

Saitō Shōji, *Yamato damashii no bunkashi* (Tokyo: Kōdansha gendai shinsho, 1972).

Sakaguchi Ango, 'Daraku ron', *Shinchō* 43:4 (1 April 1946), 39–44.

Sakaguchi Ango, 'Interi no kanshō', *Bungei shunjū* 27:3 (1 March 1949), 27–30.

Sakaue Yasuhiro, *Nippon yakyū no keifu gaku* (Tokyo: Seikyusha, 2001).

Sakurai, S., *Old and new Japan: Samurais and their descendants* (San Francisco: Chrysanthemum Press, 1897).

Sakurai Tadayoshi, *Human Bullets: A Soldier's Story of Port Arthur* (London: Archibald Constable, 1908).

San'yūtei Enchō, *San'yūtei Enchō zenshū 2* (Tokyo: Kakugawa shoten, 1975).

Sargent, Lyman Tower, *Contemporary Political Ideologies: A Comparative Analysis* (St Louis: University of Missouri Press, 1999).

Satō Kōjirō, *Kokubō jō no shakai mondai zusho (Gendai shakai mondai kenkyū 18)* (Utsunomiya: Tōkasha, 1920).

Satō Naokata, 'Satō Naokata 47 nin no hikki', in Ishii Shirō (ed.), *Kinsei buke shisō (Nihon shisō taikei 27)* (Tokyo: Iwanami shoten, 1974), 378–84.

Satō Tadashi, 'Futatabi Ukita shi no benron ni tsuite', in Akiyama Goan and Inoue Tetsujirō (eds.), *Gendai taika bushidō sōron* (Tokyo: Hakubunkan, 1905), 248–55.

Satō Tadashi, 'Gakusha no jasetsu wo yabusu', in Akiyama Goan and Inoue Tetsujirō (eds.), *Gendai taika bushidō sōron* (Tokyo: Hakubunkan, 1905), 228–34.

Satō Tadashi, 'Ōi ni shiki wo shinsaku seyo', Akiyama Goan and Inoue Tetsujirō (eds.), *Gendai taika bushidō sōron* (Tokyo: Hakubunkan, 1905), 224–27.

Satō Takumi, *'Kingu' no jidai: kokumin taishū zasshi no kōkyōsei* (Tokyo: Iwanami shoten, 2005).

Satsuma shikon no kai (eds.), *Satsuma bushidō (Satsuma Spirits)* (Nihon keizai shinbun shuppansha, 2011).

Sawada Ken, *Gendai Nihonron okudzuke* (Tokyo: Dai Nihon yūbenkai kōdansha, 1927).

Saya Makito: David Noble (trans.), *The Sino-Japanese War and the Birth of Japanese Nationalism* (Tokyo: International House of Japan, 2011).

Schad-Seifert, Annette, 'Constructing National Identities: Asia, Japan, and Europe in Fukuzawa Yukichi's Theory of Civilization', in Dick Stegewerns (ed.), *Nationalism and Internationalism in Imperial Japan: Autonomy, Asian Brotherhood, or World Citizenship?* (New York: RoutledgeCurzon, 2003), 45–67.

Schaller, Michael, *Altered States: The United States and Japan since the Occupation* (Oxford: Oxford University Press, 1997).

Schiffer, Wilhelm, 'Bushido Hoten (Handbuch des Bushido)', *Monumenta Nipponica*, 3:1 (Jan. 1940), 331.

Schivelbusch, Wolfgang, *Die Kultur der Niederlage- Der amerikanische Süden 1856, Frankreich 1871, Deutschland 1918* (Frankfurt: Fischer, 2003).

Seki Hei, *Wagako ni oshietai Nihon no kokoro: bushidō seishin no genryū* (Kyoto: PHP kenkyūjo, 2012).

Sekiyama Naotarō, *Kinsei Nihon no jinkō kōzō: Tokugawa jidai no jinkō chōsa to jinkō jōtai ni kansuru kenkyū* (Tokyo: Yoshikawa kōbunkan, 1958).

Shaku Sōen, *Sentei roku* (Tokyo: Kōdōkan, 1909).

Shigeno Saburō, *Han bushidō ron* (Tokyo: Bungeisha, 2014)

Shigeno Yasutsugu, 'Bushidō ha ōtomo-mononobe futauji no okiri hōritsu seiji ha fujiwara uji ni naru', *Shigaku fukyū zasshi 8* (1 April 1893): 7–9.

Shigeno Yasutsugu, *Nihon bushidō* (Tokyo: Daishūdō, 1909).

Shimaji Mokurai, 'Bushidō no shōrai', in Akiyama Goan and Inoue Tetsujirō (eds.), *Gendai taika bushidō sōron* (Tokyo: Hakubunkan, 1905), 411–15.

Shimano Sōsuke, *Kokyū seizajutsu bushidō shin eisei* (Hokkaido: Teikoku zaigō gunjin kai osamunai bunkai, 1912).

Shimoda Jirō, *Undō kyōgi to kokuminsei* (Tokyo: Yūbunkan, 1923).

Shimokawa Ushio, *Kendō no hattatsu* (Kyoto: Dai Nihon butokukai, 1925).

Shimonaka Kunihiko, *Nihon jinmei dai jiten 3* (Tokyo: Heibonsha, 1979).

Shingyōji Ryōsei, *Gakkō kagai taiiku yōgi* (Tokyo: Bunkyō shoin, 1926).

Shirakawa Jirō, *Jidai no bushi meishō itsuwa* (Tokyo: Hakubunkan, 1912).

Shiraki Yutaka, 'Bunbu kakusho', *Jissen joshi daigaku kiyō 7* (March 1962): 56–68.

Shirane Haruo, 'Curriculum and Competing Canons', in Haruo Shirane (ed.), *Inventing the Classics: Modernity, National Identity, and Japanese Literature* (Stanford: Stanford University Press, 2000), 220–50.

Shirayanagi Shūko, *Oyabun kobun: eiyū hen* (Tokyo: Tōādō shobō, 1912).

Shively, Donald H., 'The Japanization of the Middle Meiji', in Donald Shively (ed.), *Tradition and Modernization in Japanese Culture* (Princeton, NJ: Princeton University Press, 1971), 77–119.

Siniawer, Eiko Maruko, 'Liberalism Undone: Discourses on Political Violence in Interwar Japan', *Modern Asian Studies*, 45:4 (2011), 973–1002.

Smethurst, Richard J., *A Social Basis for Prewar Japanese Militarism: The Army and the Rural Community* (Berkeley: University of California Press, 1974).

Smiles, Samuel, *Self-help: with Illustrations of Character and Conduct* (Boston: Ticknor and Fields, 1866).

Smith II, Henry D., 'The Capacity of Chūshingura', *Monumenta Nipponica* 58:1 (Spring 2003), 1–42.

Smith II, Henry D., 'The Media and Politics of Japanese Popular History: The Case of the Akō Gishi', in James C. Baxter (ed.), *Historical Consciousness, Historiography, and Modern Japanese Values 75–97* (Kyoto: International Research Center for Japanese Studies, 2006).

Smith II, Henry D., 'The Trouble with Terasaka: The Forty-Seventh Rōnin and the *Chūshingura* Imagination', *Japan Review 16* (2004), 3–65.

Smythe-Palmer, Abram, *The Ideal of a Gentleman, or A Mirror for Gentlefolks* (London: George Routledge & Sons Limited, 1908).

Sonoda Hidehiro, 'The Decline of the Japanese Warrior Class, 1840–1880', *Japan Review 1* (1990), 73–111.

Spang, Christian W. and Rolf-Harald Wippich, 'Introduction—from "German Measles" to "Honorary Aryans": An overview of Japanese-German relations until 1945', in Christian

W. Spang and Rolf-Harald Wippich (eds.), *Japanese-German Relations 1895–1945: War, Diplomacy, and Public Opinion* (New York: Routledge, 2006), 1–18.

Sponichi annex (25 March 2009).

Sponichi annex (18 Dec. 2009).

Standish, Isolde, *A New History of Japanese Cinema: A Century of Narrative Film* (New York: Continuum, 2006).

Stanley, Arthur Penrhyn, *The Life and Correspondence: Thomas Arnold, D. D., Late Head-Master of Rugby School, and Regius Professor of Modern History in the University of Oxford in Two Volumes* II (London: B. Fellowes of Ludgate Street, 1845).

Starrs, Roy, 'Writing the National Narrative: Changing Attitudes towards Nation-Building among Japanese Writers, 1900–1930', in Sharon Minichiello (ed.), *Japan's Competing Modernities: Issues in Culture and Democracy 1900–1930* (Honolulu: University of Hawai'i Press, 1998), 206–27.

Steele, M. William, '*Yasegaman no setsu*: On Fighting to the Bitter End', *Asian Cultural Studies Special Issue 11* (30 Sept. 2002), 139–52.

Stern, Fritz, *The Politics of Cultural Despair: A Study in the Rise of the Germanic Ideology* (Berkeley: University of California Press, 1974).

Sugawara Katsuya, '20 seiki no bushidō: Nogi Maresuke jijin no hamon', *Hikaku bungaku kenkyū 45* (April 1984), 90–116.

Sugimoto Gorō, *Taigi* (Tokyo: Heibonsha, 1938).

Sumiya Mikio, *Nihon Purotesutanto shi ron* (Tokyo: Shinkyō shuppansha, 1983).

Suzuki Chikara, *Gokoku no teppeki* (Tokyo: Hakubundō, 1888).

Suzuki Chikara, *Katsu seinen* (Tokyo: Hakubundō, 1891).

Suzuki Chikara, *Kokumin no shin seishin* (Tokyo: Hakubuntō, 1893).

Suzuki Chikara, *Masurao no honryō—ichimei tōzai risshihen* (Tokyo: Gakuenkai, 1892).

Suzuki Chikara, *Nagasaki miyage: shin shin* (Nagasaki: Suzuki Chikara, 1890).

Suzuki Chikara, Minami Hiroshi (ed.), *Sōsho Nihonjinron 2: kokumin no shin seishin* (Tokyo: Ozorasha, 1996).

Suzuki Daisetz T., 'Zen to bushidō', in Bushidō gakkai (eds.), *Bushidō nyūmon* (Tokyo: Futara shobō, 1941), 64–77.

Swale, Alistair, 'Tokutomi Sohō and the Problem of the Nation-State in an Imperialist World', in Dick Stegewerns (ed.), *Nationalism and Internationalism in Imperial Japan: Autonomy, Asian Brotherhood, or World Citizenship?* (New York: RoutledgeCurzon, 2003), 68–88.

Swale, Alistair, *The Political Thought of Mori Arinori: A Study in Meiji Conservatism* (Richmond: Routledge, 2000).

Takahashi Seiko, *Bushidō kagami* (Tokyo: Gunji kyōiku kai, 1910).

Takahashi Seiko, *Nogi taishō bushidō mondō* (Tokyo: Gunji kyōiku kai, 1913).

Takahashi Tomio, 'Bushi no kokoro, Nihon no kokoro', in Matsumae Shigeyoshi (ed.), *Budō shisō no tankyū* (Tokyo: Tōkai Daigaku Shuppankai, 1987), 249–307.

Takahashi Tomio, *Bushi no kokoro, Nihon no kokoro* (Tokyo: Kondō shuppansha, 1991).

Takahashi Tomio, *Bushidō no rekishi* (Tokyo: Shinjinbutsu ōaisha, 1986).

Takayanagi Mitsutoshi, *Bushidō: Nihon bunka kenkyū 8* (Tokyo: Shinchōsha, 1960).

Takeda Izumo and Namiki Sōsuke; Miyazaki Sanmai (ed.), *Kanadehon Chūshingura* (Tokyo: Fuzanbō, 1906).

Takeda Yasuji, *Nihon sensha no tamashii* (Kyōyōsha, 1944).

Takenobu Yūtarō, 'Bushidō', *Taiyō* 2:16 (5 Aug. 1896), 39–40.

Takenobu Yūtarō, 'Bushidō', *Taiyō* 2:17 (20 Aug. 1896), 35–37.

Takenobu Yūtarō, 'The Bushido or 'Ways of Samurai'', *Taiyō* 2:16 (5 Aug. 1896), 34–38.

Takenobu Yūtarō, 'The Bushido or 'Ways of Samurai (Continued)', *Taiyō* 2:17 (20 Aug. 1896), 30–34.

Tamogami Tomio, 'Kōkū jieitai wo genki suru 10 no teigen III', *Hōyū* 30:2 (July 2004), 1–24.

Tanaka Hidemitsu, 'Sayōnara', *Sayōnara hoka sanpen* (Tokyo: Kadokawa shoten, 1956), 35–66.

Tanaka, Stefan, *Japan's Orient: Rendering Pasts into History* (Berkeley: University of California Press, 1993).

Teikoku haihei isha kai (ed.), *Nihon sekijūjisha hattatsu shi* (Tokyo: Teikoku haihei isha kai, 1906).

Thelle, Notto R., *Buddhism and Christianity in Japan* (Honolulu: University of Hawaii Press, 1987).

'The Man Japan Wants to Forget', *The Economist* (Saturday, 11 November 1995), 143–44.

Thompson, Lee A., 'The Invention of the *Yokozuna*', in Stephen Vlastos (ed.), *Mirror of Modernity: Invented Traditions in Modern Japan* (Berkeley: University of California Press, 1998).

The Times, 'Japan Deeply Moved By War Film', *The Times* (Wed. 29 May 1957), 3.

Timperley, H. J., *Japan: A World Problem* (New York: The John Day Company, 1942).

Tipton, Elise K., *Modern Japan: A Social and Political History* (London: Routledge, 2002).

Titus, David A., 'Political Parties and Nonissues in Taishō Democracy', in Harry Wray and Hilary Conroy (eds.) *Japan Examined: Perspectives on Modern Japanese History*, (Honolulu: University of Hawaii Press, 1983), 181–90.

Togawa Shūkotsu, *Bonjin sūhai* (Tokyo: Arusu, 1926).

Togawa Shūkotsu, 'Hi bushidō ron', *Jidai shikan* (Tokyo: Hidaka yūrindō, 1908), 132–33.

Tōgō Kichitarō, *Gunjin bushidō ron* (Tokyo: Gunji kyōiku kai, 1909).

Tokugawa Nariaki, 'Kokushi hen', in Saeki Ariyoshi et al (eds.), *Bushidō zensho* 7 (Tokyo: Jidaisha, 1942), 19–40.

Tokutomi Iichirō (Sohō), *The Future Japan* (Edmonton: University of Alberta Press, 1989).

Tomobayashi Mitsuhira, 'Omoide gusa', in Saeki Ariyoshi et al. (eds.), *Bushidō zensho* 7 (Tokyo: Jidaisha, 1942), 194–215.

Tomoda Yoshikata, *Bushidō kun* (Tokyo: Ōno shoten, 1908).

Tomizu, Hirondo, 'Bushidō to kongo no kyōiku', in Akiyama Goan and Inoue Tetsujirō (eds.), *Gendai taika bushidō sōron* (Tokyo: Hakubunkan, 1905) 219–23.

Tosu Tamaki, 'Jo', in Hirose Yutaka, *Gunjin dōtoku ron* (Tokyo: Bushidō kenkyūkai, 1928).

Toyamabō hensanbu (eds.), *Kokugoka Kyōju no jissai: teikoku jitsugyō dokuhon teiyō 5* (Toyama: Toyamabō, 1938).

Trefalt, Beatrice, *Japanese Army Stragglers and Memories of the War in Japan, 1950–1975* (London: RoutlegeCurzon, 2003).

Troiano, Ileana, *Hungarian Bushido: Atrocities Committed During the Occupation of Northern Transylvania in September 1940* (Oxford: I. Troiano, 1943).

Tsuda Sōkichi, *Bungaku ni arawaretaru waga kokumin shisō no kenkyū* (Tokyo: Rakuyōdō, 1917).

Tsuda Sōkichi, 'Bushidō no engen ni tsuite', in Shigeno Yasutsugu (ed.), *Meiji shi roshū* 2 (Tokyo: Chikuma shobō, 1976), 316–18.

Tsuda Sōkichi, *Inquiry into the Japanese Mind as Mirrored in Literature* (Tokyo: JSPS, 1970).

Tsūzoku Kyōiku Kenkyūkai (ed.), *Tsūzoku kyōiku kokumin jōshiki kōwa* (Tokyo: Meiseikan shobō, 1912).

Tsuzuki, Chishichi, *The Pursuit of Power in Modern Japan 1825–1995* (Oxford: Oxford University Press, 2000).

Tucker, John Allen, 'Tokugawa Intellectual History and Prewar Ideology: The Case of Inoue Tetsujirō, Yamaga Sokō, and the Forty-Seven Rōnin', *Sino-Japanese Studies 14* (2002), 35–70.

Uchida, Roan, 'Nijūgonenkan no bunjin no shakaiteki chii no shinpo', *Tsuzuki shimi hanjōki* (Tokyo: Shomotsu tenbōsha, 1934), 133–51.

Uchida, Roan, *Tsuzuki shimi hanjōki* (Tokyo: Shomotsu tenbōsha, 1934).

Uchida Ryōhei, *Jūdō* (Tokyo: Kokuryūkai shuppanbu, 1903).

Uchimura, Kanzō, 'Untitled', *Seisho no kenkyū 186* (10 Jan. 1916), reproduced in Matsumae Shigeyoshi, *Budō shisō no tankyū* (Tokyo: Tōkai daigaku shuppankai, 1987), 91.

Uchimura, Kanzō, 'Untitled', *Seisho no kenkyū* 210 (1916), reproduced in Matsumae Shigeyoshi, *Budō shisō no tankyū* (Tokyo: Tōkai daigaku shuppankai, 1987), 92.

Uchimura, Kanzō, 'Lack of Japanese Morality', in *Uchimura Kanzō zenshū* 4 (Iwanami shoten, 1980–1984), 68.

Uchimura, Kanzō, 'Moral Traits of the Yamato Damashii', in *Uchimura Kanzō zenshū* 1 (Iwanami shoten, 1980–1984), 113–35.

Ueda Kazutoshi, *Kokugogaku sōwa* (Tokyo: Hakubunkan, 1908).

Uemura Masahisa, 'Kirisutoyō to bushidō', *Bushidō* 1:2 (March 1898), 13–22; also in *Uemura Masahisa chosakushū* 1 (Tokyo: Shinkyō shuppansha, 1966), 391–97.

Uemura Masahisa, 'Nani wo motte bushidō no sui wo hozon sen to suru ka', *Uemura Masahisa chosakushū* 1 (Tokyo: Shinkyō shuppansha, 1966), 398.

Uenaka Shuzo trans., 'Last Testament in Exile: Yamaga Sokō's Haisho Zampitsu', *Monumenta Nipponica* 32:2 (Summer 1977), 125-52.

Ukita Kazutami, 'Bungaku hakase Inoue Tetsujirō kun no hihyō ni tou', in Akiyama Goan and Inoue Tetsujirō (eds.), *Gendai taika bushidō sōron* (Tokyo: Hakubunkan, 1905), 242–47.

Ukita Kazutami, *Bunmei no yo* (Tokyo: Hakubunkan, 1915).

Ukita Kazutami, 'Bushidō ni kansuru sanshu no kenkai', *Taiyō* 16:10 (July 1910), 1–6.

Ukita Kazutami,, 'Nichiro sensō to kyōiku', *Nihon* 5482 (31 Oct. 1904), 4.

Uno Chūjin, *Nihon kokumin to demokurashii* (Tokyo: Funasaka Yonetarō, 1919).

Unoda Shōya, 'Bushidō ron no seiritsu: seiyō to tōyō no aida', *Edo no shisō 7 (shisō shi no 19 seiki)* (Tokyo: Perikan sha, 1997).

Uwa Shichō Gakumuka (ed.), *Bushidō kyōhon* (Uwa: Uwa Shichō Gakumuka, 1935).

Victoria, Brian Daizen, 'A Buddhological Critique of "Soldier-Zen" in Wartime Japan', in Mark Jurgensmeyer and Michael Jerryson (eds.), *Buddhist Warfare* (Oxford: Oxford University Press, 2010), 105–30.

Victoria, Brian Daizen, 'The "Negative Side" of D. T. Suzuki's Relationship to War', *The Eastern Buddhist* 41:2 (2010) 97–138.

Victoria, Brian Daizen, *Zen at War* (Oxford: Rowman & Littlefield, 2006).

Vinh, Sinh, 'Shiba Ryōtarō and the Revival of Meiji Values', in James C. Baxter (ed.), *Historical Consciousness, Historiography, and Modern Japanese Values*, (Kyoto: International Research Center for Japanese Studies, 2006) 143–51.

Vlastos, Stephen, 'Tradition: Past/Present Culture and Modern Japanese History', in Stephen Vlastos (ed.), *Mirror of Modernity: Invented Traditions in Modern Japan* (Berkeley: University of California Press, 1998), 1–16.

Volpicelli, Zenone (1856- Vladimir), *The China-Japan War. Compiled from Japanese, Chinese and foreign sources* (London: Sampson Low, 1896).

Wakai Toshiaki, *Hiraizumi Kiyoshi: mikuni no tame ni ware tsukusanamu* (Kyoto: Mineruva shobō, 2006).

Wakatsuki Shiran, *Shūgyō sōsho 2* (Tokyo: Shingetsu Sha, 1920).

Watanabe Noboru, 'Bushidō', *Bushidō* 1:2 (March 1898), 6.

Watanabe Yosuke, *Musashi bushi* (Tokyo: Hakubunkan, 1913).

Watsuji Tetsurō (ed.), *Nihon no shindō, Amerika no kokuminsei* (Tokyo: Chikuma shobō, 1944).

Westney, D. Eleanor, *Imitation and Innovation: The Transfer of Western Organizational Patterns to Meiji Japan* (Cambridge, MA: Harvard University Press, 1987).

Willcock, Hiroko, 'The Political Dissent of a Senior General: Tamogami Toshio's Nationalist Thought and a History Controversy', *Asian Politics & Policy* 3:1 (2011), 29–47.

Wilson, Sandra, 'The Russo-Japanese War and Japan: Politics, Nationalism, and Historical Memory', in David Wells and Sandra Wilson (eds.), *The Russo-Japanese War in Cultural Perspective, 1904-05* (London: MacMillan Press, 1999), 160–93.

Wilson, Sandra, *The Manchurian crisis and Japanese society, 1931–33* (London: Routledge, 2002).

Wilson, Sandra, and David Wells, 'Introduction', in David Wells and Sandra Wilson (ed.), *The Russo-Japanese War in Cultural Perspective, 1904–05* (London: MacMillan Press, 1999), 30–40.

Wray, Harold J., 'A Study in Contrasts: Japanese School Textbooks of 1903 and 1941–5', *Monumenta Nipponica* 28:1 (spring 1973), 69–86.

Yamaga Sokō, *Yamaga Sokō (Nihon shisō taikei 32)* (Tokyo: Iwanami shoten, 1970).

Yamagami Sōgen, *Hagakure bushi no seishin* (Tokyo: San'yūsha, 1942).

Yamagata Kōhō, *Shin bushidō* (Tokyo: Jitsugyō no Nihonsha, 1908).

Yamamoto Hirofumi, *Nihonjin no kokoro: bushidō nyūmon* (Tokyo: Chūkei shuppan, 2006).

Yamamoto Hirofumi, *Otoko no shitto: bushidō no ronri to shinri* (Tokyo: Chikuma shobo, 2005).

Yamamoto Tsunetomo, *Hagakure zenshū* (Tokyo: Gogatsu shobō, 1978).

Yamamoto Tsunetomo, Nakamura Ikuichi (ed.), *Hagakure* (Tokyo: Teiyūsha, 1906).

Yamamoto Tsunetomo, Ōkuma Miyoshi (ed.), *Hagakure: gendaiyaku* (Tokyo: Shinjinbutsu ōraisha, 1975).

Yamamuro Kentoku, *Gunshin: kindai Nihon ga unda 'eiyū' tachi no kiseki* (Tokyo: Chuōkōron shinsha, 2007).

Yamaoka Tesshū, Kuzū Yoshihisa (ed.), *Kōshi Yamaoka Tesshū: denki sōsho 242* (Tokyo: Ozorasha, 1997).

Yamashita Shigekazu, 'Herbert Spencer and Meiji Japan', in Hilary Conroy et al. (eds.), *Japan in Transition: Thought and Action in the Meiji Era, 1868–1912* (Rutherford: Farleigh Dickinson University Press, 1984), 77–95.

Yasumaru Yoshio, *Gendai nihon shisō ron: rekishi ishiki to ideorogī*, (Tokyo: Iwanami Shoten, 2006)

Yates, Charles L., "Saigō Takamori in the Emergence of Meiji Japan" in Peter Kornicki (ed.) *Meiji Japan: Political, Economic and Social History 1868-1912* (New York: Routledge, 1998), 182–202.

Yates, Charles L., *Saigō Takamori: The Man behind the Myth* (New York: Kegan Paul International, 1995).

Yokoi Shōnan, 'Kokuze sanron', in *Watanabe Kazan, Takano Chōei, Sakuma Shōzan, Yokoi Shōnan, Hashimoto Sanai (Nihon shisō taikei 55)* (Tokyo: Iwanami shoten, 1971), 438–65.

Yoshida Kenryū, 'Sutoa tetsugaku to *bushidō*', Akiyama Goan and Inoue Tetsujirō (eds.), *Gendai taika bushidō sōron* (Tokyo: Hakubunkan, 1905), 475–95.

Yoshida Sei'chi, *Kokumin dōtoku yōryō* (Tokyo: Tokyo hinbunkan, 1916).

Yoshida Shōin, *Yoshida Shōin zenshū* (Tokyo: Iwanami shoten, 1940).

Yoshida Yutaka, 'Ajia-taiheiyō sensō no senjō to heishi', in *Senjō no shosō (Ajia-Taiheiyō sensō 5)* (Tokyo: Iwanami shoten, 2006), 59–88.

Yoshida Yutaka, *Nihon no guntai: heishi tachi no kindai shi* (Tokyo: Iwanami shinsho 816, 2002).

Yoshimoto Mitsuhiro, *Kurosawa: Film Studies and Japanese Cinema* (Durham, NC: Duke University Press, 2000).

Yuhara Motoichi, 'Bushidō no shumi 1', *Ryūnankai zasshi 37* (7 June 1895), 4–8.

Yuhara Motoichi, 'Bushidō no shumi 2', *Ryūnankai zasshi 38* (30 June 1895), 4–8.

Zachman, Urs Matthias, *China and Japan in the Late Meiji Period: China Policy and the Japanese Discourse on National Identity, 1852–1904* (London: Routledge, 2009).

Zhu Dongxu, Wang Xin, 'Riben wushidao yu Riben youyi shili guanxi lun', *Tangshan shifan xueyuan xuebao*, 31:4 (July, 2009), 78–80.

Zhu Lifeng, 'Wushidao yu Riben duiwai qinlüe kuozhang fangzhen de queli', *Jilin shifan daxue xuebao 1* (Feb. 2007), 89–92.

Index

Printed and bound by CPI Group (UK) Ltd, Croydon, CR0 4YY